Evolution and Growth of IIM Calcutta *and* ME

A BRIEF HISTORY OF IIMC FROM **1960** TO **2013**

(UPTO 50TH BATCH)

AKSHOY KUMAR SINGHA

Ex-Research Staff

Indian Institute of Management Calcutta

INDIA • SINGAPORE • MALAYSIA

ISBN 979-8-89133-777-0

"The Institute existed only in a File but started as a small institution in the late 1961. It has blossomed today into one of the leading management schools in South Asia and the Asia-Pacific region. A great story of the evolution of the IIM Calcutta, which I have witnessed closely and participated enthusiastically have germinated in my mind is being described in this book"

Dedicated to:

Professor Nirmal Kumar Chandra,

Who changed my life.

CONTENTS

SECTION – II

CONFLICTS, CHAOS, COURT CASES AND GOVERNMENT INTERVENTIONS IN RECENT TIMES

SECTION – III

MY LONG ASSOCIATION WITH THE INSTITUTE

LIST OF TABLES, EXHIBITS AND FIGURES

THE INSTITUTE

India celebrated her 75 years of independence when some institutes of national importance have shaped India globally. These Institutes (IITs and IIMs) are regarded as jewels in India's crown. The Planning Commission in collaboration with MIT's Sloan School of Management and the Ford Foundation established the Indian Institute of Management at Calcutta in 1961 under the Union Ministry of education. It was the first public, autonomous institute of management education in India. The Institute earned reputation of Indian managers across the globe and their Alumni occupying top slots in MNCs globally. The world wide stature of the Institute owes their quality of students, teaching and research in management education. The IIM brand is regarded as at per with the world's best. This Institute became an Indian brand that we are proud of.

The institute is fully residential and have accommodated more than five thousand students. This Joka campus is designed around seven lakes on 135 acres of land. The Institute can boast of state-of-the-art classrooms, research labs, hostels, guest houses and other facilities. The Institute offers several management programs, training, consultancy and research in different fields of management. The Fellowship Program is meant for research and teaching in different areas of management. The alumni members are a proud lot who constantly interact with their alma mater. They help with donations, placements, workshops and industry interactions.

The Institute became a member of CEMS, an elite club of 28 management institutes in the world and is the only member from India. The CEMS-

MIM is taken up simultaneously with PGP. As part of internationalization, the Institute offers a dual degree program with ESCP in Europe. In the student exchange program (STEP), the students have opportunity to study in foreign institutes. The institute won triple accreditations from all three accreditations agencies in the globe. The FT and QS has ranked our institute in the Global Business School Ranking. I feel proud for being associated with the Institute for long thirty six years, a half of my life.

ABOUT THE BOOK

The book is based on my own experiences and observations for long thirty six years of association with the Institute. The idea of writing the book came in after reading Dr. Sancheti's Ph D Thesis on IIM Calcutta from the University of London. Her Thesis has elaborated three phases of development till 1984. But, I have studied the evolution and growth of the Institute till 2013 covering fifty batches. The corona epidemic helped a lot, as I was forced to confine at home and study room.

The book contains three sections - the first section is on evolution and growth of the Institute till 50th batch. The relevant topics during its incubation stage to Internationalisation stage have been discussed. The decadal growth in terms of student enrolment, faculty strength and participation of women in PGP has been discussed. I analysed the changes in total fees for PGP both at current and constant prices. The study contains the increase in student intake, representation of women students, faculty members and tuition fees in last fifty years. The enrolment at Fellowship Program and representation of women students has also been discussed. The introduction of new programs in different periods and the impact of reduction of Central Grants have also been discussed.

The second section delves on present crisis, chaos, conflicts, Court Cases and Government interventions. The crisis was on view of reservation of OBC students in PGP. The Alumni Network demanded reservation of SC, ST and OBC among faculty members and students in Fellowship Program. They moved to Supreme Court and the Government accepted their demand. The third section delves with my activities and academic achievements during my long association. I have assisted a dozen of eminent faculty members in different groups. I have also academic interests in research and the Institute published a dozen of my Working Papers. I have published articles in daily Newspapers and presented Papers in the National and International Seminars. I performed invigilation duty in PGP, PGPEX and PGPEX-VLM Examinations. As administrative duty; I also assistedthe Chief Administrative Officer (CAO) regarding Board meetings. I paid my heartfelt tribute to Prof Chandra and fifty old and eminent Professors of the Institute.

ABOUT THE AUTHOR

The author was born and brought up in a remote village, close to the abandoned TATA's Nano Car factory in Singur. After passing B. Sc, he joined the Institute as Junior Project Assistant. Thereafter, he joined two Certificate Courses in Indian Statistical Institute (ISI). He passed both the courses with Certificate of Merit from ISI. Later, he passed M A in Economics from Rabindra Bharati University. He joined the Institute in Emerald Bower Campus in 1974. In 1977, he moved to Joka Campus along with other staffs. He worked in both the Emerald Bower and Joka Campuses He retired in 2010 and he provided research assistance to a dozen of eminent Professors, including present and past Directors. He also assisted eminent Professors - Dr. Ashok Mitra, Deepak Nayyar, Prof. Saibal Chattopadhayay (Ex-Director) and Prof. Uttam Kumar Sarkar the present Director.

He published features in English and Bengali dailies. A dozen of his Working Papers have been published by the Institute and an article was published in Institute's house journal DECISION. He presented Papers in National and International Seminars in Calcutta, Bhubaneswar and New Delhi. He retired from the Institute after thirty six years of service and passed half of his life at this Institute. Being attached with this Institute, he had elaborated facts with free mind without any restriction. The value of the academia is realized as much in critical thinking, debate, dissent and analyzed problems to arrive at alternative solutions to make decisions.

PREFACE

In this book, I have tried to describe and analyse the evolution and growth of the institute in last fifty years. All the aspects like - student's enrolment, faculty strength, fellowship scholars, participation of women students and general staffs have been discussed. This book is based mostly on Neelu Sancheti's PhD Thesis on IIMC from the University of London in 1986. She joined our Institute as Faculty Member in 1990 and demised shortly. My book is based on memories of faculty members of early stage, students of initial years and the available Annual Reports of the Institute. The recent crisis is based on Reports, Newspapers and articles in different periodicals. My contribution to the institute is my own experience during thirty six years of service in the institute. At the end, I have provided reference and statistical table for authenticity. I hope, readers will be satisfied by accumulating information for last fifty years.

I have cited writings of eminent management Gurus. I have consulted Annual Reports of the Institute, Sandesh –a biannual of the Institute. I have cited fromThe Mint, The Wires, The Print, MBA Universe, The Success etc. I have cited from wide circulated dailies – The Economic Times, The Indian Express, The BusinessToday, Financial Express, The Deccan Herald etc. My daughter insisted me to write a book, instead of numerous writing in daily Newspapers. The idea came in three years ago, when Corona Epidemic forced us to stay confined at home. My wife was eager to complete the book as early as possible. My grandson Riddhiman became three to six by sitting on my lap, while I was working on the computer. I am thankful to Saurav, Khokan and Sonai for their help in typing of the materials. Special thanks to my colleague Sabon for the Photos.

Serampore, Hooghly
9th September, 2023
akshoy@email.com

Akshoy Kumar Singha
Ex-Research Staff
Indian Institute of Management Calcutta

SECTION – I

EVOLUTION AND GROWTH OF IIM CALCUTTA

CHAPTER 1.1

PLANNING FOR A MANAGEMENT INSTITUTE IN INDIA: INCUBATION STAGE AT BARACKPORE CAMPUS, 1960-1964

1. FELT NEEDED FOR MANAGEMENT EDUCATION IN INDIA

Based on the recommendation of the Indian Planning Commission, Pundit Jawaharlal Nehru, the first Prime Minister of India initiated the establishment of an Institute of Management. The Central Government provided financial grants and other infrastructural facilities. It was established as a result of technical assistance projects of MIT and funded by the Ford Foundation. "When our nation's leaders founded IIM Calcutta, India was a very poor country that had problems in even feeding its population. Through those difficult early years, government funded us in the hope that such public investments would trigger a qualitative change in the whole of management education in this country (Balkrishna, 2012). At that time, the crisis for food grains was so acute that, India has to import food grains from USA under the PL480, as the main crisis in India was "Feeding India's Growing Millions."

After India became independent in 1947, the Planning Commission was entrusted to oversee and direct the development of the nation. India grew rapidly in the 1950s and the Planning Commission started facing difficulties in finding suitable managers for the large number of just established public sector enterprises, as a part of its new industrial policies. The political independence in India was a normative commitment to rapid socio-economic development through greater economic growth and greater economic equity. The new intellectual climate in India felt the urgent need for re-organising higher education. The emphasis was to reduce the dependency on foreign personnel to train our professional manpower. The Plan body recommended establishment of management Institute, which are equivalent in quality and standards to their counterparts in advanced industrialised societies.

In 1949, the University Education Commission also identified the need of management education in India. The first Five Year Plan saw the shortage of manpower as a bottleneck to India's plan for economic development. "Prime Minister Nehru and Sir Shanti Swarup Bhatnagr visualised the needs to develop management education as a con-commitment requisite for development" (Dogra, 2010). The seeds were sown in mid-1950s,when the Second Five Year Plan set up a committee under the Chairmanship of industrialist Sir Ramaswamy Mudaliar. It was appointed "to estimate the managerial requirement of future expansions of industrial and commercial sectors. The committee recommended the setting up of special training facilities outside the Universities for greater flexibility and autonomy and for quickening the pace of management training and education in India" (MBAuniverse 2016).

In 1953, the All India Council of Technical Education recommended the setting up of a Permanent Board of Management Studies and establishment of management studies programme. The second Five Year Plan suggested the setting up of Post Graduate Institutions for the professional training of managers. A permanent Board of Management Studies was created in 1953 and acted as an Advisor to the Central Ministry of Education.In May 1956, the New Industrial Policy Statement was presented to '*Lok Sabha*' by Prime Minister Nehru. The policy statement emphasised the importance of competent industrial and technical management. Securing highly trained management professionals was a matter of the greatest urgency both for government and private business.

2. ESTABLISHMENT OF MANAGEMENT INSTITUTES IN INDIA

In 1956, the Ford Foundation entered the scene as catalyst and broker for the idea of professionalised managerial expertise at the top and middle level. The first step was to initiate the discussions to convince Indian leadership of the importance of this project for the sake of India's development (Hill & Ensminger, 1957). The staffs of annual Advanced Management Programme of MIT discussed with Indian Prime Minister for establishment of an IIM. This project has been formulated in cooperation of the Planning Commission and the unqualified support of Prime Minister. The Ford Foundation organised the visit to American Business School by a selected group of influential Indians. Moreover, to ensure the support of the Industrialist, the Ford Foundation sponsored "Advanced Management" seminar at a picturesque resort of Srinagar in Kashmir. Initially staffed by MIT, the seminar helped further towards American style professional management to Indian industrialists.

Till 1958, the purpose of management education in the beginning was to develop professional management ethosin business and industrial organisations, as well as in the Government through education and training of working executives and officers. The main aim of management education then became to develop a cadre of young professional managers who would transform the Indian business and industry through high quality knowledgeable professional mangers. In 1959, the planning Commission invited Professor George Robbins, Associate Dean of the University of California, Los Angeles (UCLA), and a consultant to the Ford Foundation, to formulate a scheme for establishment of an All India Institute of Management (Nangia, 2014).

In 1959, the Ford Foundation released grant for MIT's seminars for higher management in India. In 1957, the participation of Ford Foundation and the Sloan School of Management was most direct in planning and establishment of IIM Calcutta. The Meriam-Thurlby Report suggested the establishment of National Institute of Management Studies within the

University of Bombay. Based on the recommendations of Prof. Robbins, the Government of India decided to set up two elite management institutes. The first one was named India Institute of ManagementCalcutta established on 13 November 1961 in collaboration with the Sloan School of Managementat MIT, the government of West Bengal, the Ford Foundation and the Indian industry. On the other hand, the second one was named as Indian Institute of Management Ahmadabad, established on 11th December 1961 in collaboration with the Harvard Business School.

For establishment of the Management Institute in Calcutta, the Core Team consisted of renowned academicians like - Paul Samuelson, Jagdish Seth, Jati Kumar Sengupta, Peter S King and Thomas Hill. In early 1961, Prof. Hill of MIT was invited to spend three months in Calcutta for examining the viability of the Institute in Calcutta. On his recommendation, the Ford Foundation approved the first grant of $4.34 Lakhto push the project and to secure the agreement of the Central Government for bearing the recurring expenses and the State Government for providing land and building in establishing the Institute. The Central Government agreed to bear the recurring expense and the State government agreed to meet the cost of land and building at a sum of Rs. 30 Lakh.

The State Government acquired 135 acres of land at Joka village, more than 20 kilometres away from the city. The Ford Foundation sanctioned further Grants of $6.1 Lakh in 1962, $3.0 Lakh in 1963, $6.65 Lakh in 1965, $2.78 Lakh in 1968 and $1.05 Lakh in 1971. Thus, during the first ten years (1961 to 1971), the Ford Foundation sanctioned a total Grant of $23.92 Lakh. So, the financial support of Ford Foundation was crucial for establishment of a management institute in Calcutta. The first meeting of Planning Commission for the "Establishment of a Central Institute of Management Studies" was held at Calcutta on 18thFebruary 1961 (Sancheti, 1986). The decision was that the Central Government will bear the recurring expense and the State will provide land and building. In 1961, the State government meet the cost of land and building amounting to Rs. 30 Lakh. At this meeting the members present were representatives of Ford Foundation and MIT along with the Officials from the Central and State Government and a representative from Industry (Metal Box) in presence of Prof. Humayun Kabir, a Central Minister and Dr. B C Roy, the then Chief Minister of West Bengal (Sancheti, 1986).

3. INCUBATION AT BARACKPUR CAMPUS

a) Campus

Till October 1961, the IIM Calcutta had no physical existence. It was existed only in Files and Folders on the table of Dr. B C Roy, the then Chief Minister of West Bengal. The Institute was initially started in the Flag-Staff House, the Governor's river side summer retreat at Barrackpur, 20 kilometres north of Calcutta along river Ganges. The left out colonial Governor General's House was handed over to the State after independence. The vast garden having many large trees was locally known as '*latbagan*' or the Garden of '*latsahibs*'. Martyr Mangal Pandey of *Sepoy Mutiny* was hanged here by the British. In this campus, the IIM Calcutta started in November 1961 by offering four AMPs annually. There were only a few Faculties and the Staffs were mostly Hindi speaking ex-servicemen and especially from Gorkha Regiment. The Institute operated from this campus for about first three years i.e. 1961 to 1964.

Both the Ford Foundation and MIT played an institutional role in negotiating the location arrangement for the Institute. In 1960, the Institute acquired an impressive stretch of 135 acres of land at Joka village. But, the State had offeredan alternative location in the extensive ground owned by the Nizams of Hyderabad at central Calcutta. The Ford Foundation aggressively favoured the idea of an exclusive campus as a self-sufficient unit. The Ford Foundation insisted on an American University Style campus with ample space, residential facilities and also a site far from the congested surrounding of the city. In this time, a Case was pending before the Calcutta High Court for acquisition of vast agricultural land in Joka. The landowners pleaded against the acquisition of huge paddy land, when the State was facing acute food crisis. Finally, the Institute won the Case and Dr. Roy was informed before his death on July, 1962 (Chandy,

2007). The Hill Report was also critical of geographical locations chosen to set up IIMs: The locations of both the IIMs were politically influenced and unrelated to the objectives. The delay in location arrangement had hampered the development of the Institute.

b) Library

In 1962, the Ford Foundation specified that the $ 1, 25,000 allocated for books, materials and equipments not available in India, should be spent according to the purchase list of Ford Foundation's office in India (Sancheti, 1986). Our Library was named as Dr. B. C. Roy Memorial Libraryafter the death of Dr. Roy, the then CM and the first Chairman who died in July 1962. The library is primarily envisioned to meet the requirements of the Institute's academic programmes and gets financial support from the government.

4. FORMULATION AND ADOPTION OF POLICIES

a) Administration

The Robbins Report envisaged a form of organisation, where there be freedom and flexibility. The administrative structure consists of a Board of Governance, Executive Council, Director, Faculty Members, Administrative Officers and Staffs. In the Board of Governance, Executive Council should consistof 9 members. The Director should be an Indian by nationality and have exposed to foreign universities. The Director should be assisted by a Librarian and Director of Research, Chairman of Educational Programs, Placement Officer and Provost.

b) Autonomy

In 1959, The Indian Management Education Study Team visited USA universities along with the representatives of Ministry of Scientific Research and Cultural Affairs. The team was headed by the Minister, Prof. Humayun Kabir along with Kamala Chowdhry, a Ford Foundation Officer in Delhi. The Study team also consists of members of existing management department of leading Universities in India. The Team,after visiting the

Business Schools in USArecommended the establishment of Management Institute within existing University system. It was clearly not their intent to advocate an "Autonomous Institute". A member of the study team, Prof. Sanyal, the first Director of ISWBM recommended upgrading the university based courses rather than the setting up of separate institute. The decision to keep IIMs out of the conventional university system was to ensure freedom to the Institute in all academic and administrative matters. The Universities were not willing to create institutional structure that provided more autonomy, flexibility and delegation of academic, financial and administrative authority. The Indian Universities were very slow in accepting management education and their MBA course was like a commerce course. The insistence of Ford Foundation to ensure Autonomy arose from their perceptions of Indian University structures. They felt that the proposed transform of American Business School could not take place adequately within the existing framework of Indian Universities.

The Ford Foundation representative, Prof. Ensminger wrote that "The decision was taken by me and supported by the Planning Commission, to develop the IIM Calcutta, outside universities" (Sancheti, 1986). The favour for the Institutional Autonomy was the approval of four influential Indian Cabinet Ministers -Prof. Humayun Kabir, Sir V T Krishnamachari, T. T. Krishnamachari and C D Deshmukh. The actual process of policy adoption was however undertaken by Indian Planning Commission. The Commission also directed that the proposed Institute was to be registered under the "Indian Society Act." In 1960, a Ford Foundation instigated decision was made to constitute the Management Institute as an "Autonomous Society", independent of existing University structure inherited from the British. The Ford Foundation, with the help of a section of the Indian political leadership pushed through a decision to establish IIM Calcutta in a particular structural mode (Sancheti, 1986).

Professor G W Robbins was invited to formulate a scheme for establishment of an All India Institute of Management Studies Outside Indian University system. In February 1960, Ford Foundation recommended that establishing new Institute where new building, faculty, library etc. must be established and completely detached from the existing universities. The Constitution of the Society as set out in the "Memorandum of Association and Rules of the new IIMC" was based on the prescription of Robbins with four important goals. Those were - a) To select and prepare outstanding and talented mature young people for careers leading to management responsibility, b) To provide opportunities for practising executives in middle and top management to obtain training and education in management, c) To develop an Indian literature in management through research and publications of studies concentrated about the nature and role of the enterprise units in India and d) To provide suitable physical facilities for resident students, classes, laboratories, administrative and teaching staffs and a thoroughly equipped librarycontaining a good collection of foreign publications as well as superior collection of Indian materials (Sancheti, 1986).

Prof. Robbins recommendations were accepted by the Planning Commission and the decision was to keep IIM out of the university system. It was to ensure freedom to providemore autonomy, flexibility and delegation of academic, financial and administrative authority. In March 16, 1961, the guiding principles were agreed up in the first meeting of the Planning Commission held at Chief Ministers' Office at Calcutta. The strong persuasion of the Ford Foundation and the enthusiasm of Dr. B C Roy, Chief Minister of the State made the establishment of an "Autonomous" Institute in Calcutta (Sancheti, 1986). Finally, IIM Calcutta became an Autonomous Institute registered under the SocietyRegistration Act 1961.

c) Plan of Development

In 1960, a letter was written to Dr. B. C. Royby Prof. Humayun Kabir, the Central Minister. The letter pointed out that "The Ford Foundation offered that they will be willing to help in the following three ways. i) Finding for at least the first five years top-ranking experts from abroad who would come as whole-timer in the Institution, ii) Providing Fellowship to enable Indian teachers of theInstitutionto go abroad for further studies and iii) Finding the necessary funds for building up the Libraries of the Institution.

Since almost all books will have to be from abroad, these amounts will be entirely in foreign exchange." (IIMC, 2012)

The first effort toward policy adoption of prescribed aims at the Institute was the preparation of a "Proposed Plan of Development" by the MIT advisors with the help of Indian Directorof the Institute. The Proposed Plan was placed before the Governing Board and it was approved and accepted. It became the guiding documents of the new Institute for the initial period of five years. The Plan suggested that the Institute should aspire towards its Post-Graduate Programme for about 300 students of two years duration and will lead to an internationally recognised Master degree. The MIT's technical collaborators and the Ford Foundations, both played important role in formulation and adoption of our policies in the Institute. Both of Ford Foundation and MIT played their strategic role in defining the institutional status, organisation relation, teaching, research and consultancy. The IIM Calcutta's collaboration with MIT was short-lived and ended in 1963. The Hill Report on this matter stated that "It seems clear to me that the SSM's role in Calcutta has degenerated from that of a partner in institution-building to that of recruiting agent. Our present position is that of giving MIT endorsement to activities over which we have no effective control".

5. SELECTION PROCESS

a) Chairman

Initially, Prof. Humayun Kabir, the Central Minister was the Chairman of IIM Calcutta. Thereafter, Dr, Bidhan Chandra Roy, the Chief Minister (1948-1962) of West Bengal became the Chairman of the Institute in January 1962 and continued till his death on July 1962.

b) Director

First Search Committee for Director in 1960 consisted of: V Isvan, N Shodha, Prof. Hanen, Dr. Vikram Sarabhai and P L Tandon as Convenor. The Ford Foundation officers and MIT team played active role in the selection of Director and faculty members. The faculties trained in USA ensuring loyalty to them were preferred. In 1960, Dr, B C Roy, the then CM invited Mr. K T Chandy to help in setting up of IIM Calcutta. In 1961, Mr. K T Chandy, former Director of Hindustan Lever, was selected as the first Director. The Ford Foundation appointed Mr. Chandydespite "being told by India's former Ambassador in USA that Mr. Chandy was a Card Carrying Communist" (Study Team 1959). In 1961, Prof. Hill in his letter to Ford Foundation described the Director Mr. Chandy as an "Exceptionally promising business leader". In 1962, Mr. Chandy became grantee of supplementary Funds from the Ford Foundation by replacing the previous grantee Prof. Kabir, the Central Minister. Finally, Mr. Chandy's appointment was welcome by both the Ford Foundation and MIT. Mr. Chandy served the Institute as Director for five years from 1961 to 1966.

c) Faculty Members

Prof. Meriam-Thurlby, the Ford Foundation Consultants elaborated the process of faculty recruitment. It was explained in the Minutes of the Planning Commission meeting held at March 16, 1961 at Calcutta. In the initial years, different criterion was imposed by Ford Foundation and MIT. The faculties were selected from three different sources. Firstly, the talented, high calibre candidates were selected from Indian Universities. Secondly, the Executives of British dominated Industry in India and lastly Indian students or teachers in management department of any American University. So, initial policy on faculty recruitment was emphasised more on matured faculty from USA and India. Director Mr. Chandy set up a strong and highly talented faculty base by selecting the prospective faculty from India. He purposefully recruited people with highly Leftist tendencies and were Communists. In initial period, the Institute had several renowned academics and visionaries. They formed the core team who helped much in the development of the Institute at the initial stage.

Among the team, the foreign faculty members were Douglas McGregor, Paul Samuelson, Warren Bennis, Peter S King, and Thomas Hill. While, the eminent Indian academicians were Jagdish Seth, Jati K. Sengupta,

Ravi Mathai, Ashok Mitra, Barun De, Kamini Adhikary, Ishwar Dayal and Kamala Chowdhry. Later, Ravi Mathai, Ishwar Dayal and Kamala Chowdhry left to set up the IIMA. Prof. Surajit Sinha left to head Anthropological Survey of India and later Viswa Bharati. During 1965-66, the number of faculty members dropped from 24 to 14, as serving members left to take more prestigious appointments. It created sudden shortage of faculty in the Institute and the Director appointed new faculty members to fill the gaps.

The first Director in his five-year tenure assembled a motley group of bright and heterogeneous scholars at the Institute. Almost all were distinguished themselves as scholars and institution builders. It was marked of Chandy's vision as an institution builder and his persuasive powers that he was able to recruit such a stellar bunch of individuals. He recruited several highly talented Marxist scholars - Paresh Chattopadhayay, Nirmal Kumar Chandra, N Krishnaji, Anjan Mukherji, Yoginder Alagh, Ranjit Sau, Sabyasachi Bhattacharya, Amalendu Guha etc.Mr. Krishna Mohan became the next Director by succeeding Mr. Chandy.

d) Admission of PGP Students

The policies relating to admission in IIM Calcutta were formulated by MIT technical assistants. The Meriam-Thurlby Report stressed more on careful consideration for selection of students, who will be ambitious, sensitive and practical and like to work with others. Selection of students should be promise of eventually becoming important business executives. The Indian Study Team made no recommendations. But, Robbins stressed on students who are ambitions, realistic as well as of sound mental health. He also stressed on academic records, interview and work experience. Thus, students should be from a variety of disciplines like - Engineering, Mathematics, Natural Science, Social Science etc. Broad guiding principles for admission were agreed upon atthe first meeting of the Planning Commission on March 1961. The Constitution of the Society in the "Memorandum of Association and Rules of the new IIMC" was based on the prescription of Robbins, who recommended selecting and preparing outstanding and talented mature young people for careers in management. Thus, the Institute continued to be highly selective in student admission and premium job offers. The elite status and high social prestige was attached to the students who got admission. The important mechanism forcultural penetration was made by prescribed procedures for selection of students.

6. ACADEMIC ACTIVITIES

The Institute planned to offer Post-Graduate and Doctoral programmes in management, as well as, bouquets of executive education programmes. The Institute also planned to engagein research, consultancy, seminars, academic conferences and publications. The management education aimed at educating bright young students, both fresher's and with some industry experience, selected through a rigorous test and interviews. The aims were to develop a cadre of young professional managers. The academic activities prescribed by the MIT were - a) Post-Graduate Programme (PGP), b) Executive Development Programme (EDP), c) Doctoral (Fellowship) Programme, d) Research and e) Consultancy.

a) Post-Graduate Programme (PGP)

In 1962, the Post-Graduate Programme in management was accepted as a Core Programme of the Institute. Robbins Report suggested the teaching programme should cover the following four major areas - i) Management Concept and Practice, (ii) Major Operational areas of enterprises - Marketing, Production, Finance and Personnel. iii) Tools for Management Analysis and (iv) Environmental influence in Social, Culture and Governmental Change. The MIT's technical assistance transferred its own curriculum biases to the Institute. Traditional lecture base methods were prescribed for classroom teaching. They prescribed the evaluation system vastly different from Indian University system. Performance of students should not be determined by marks in final examination but on the basis of all examinations. Evaluation should use the reports, term papers, class performance etc. Instead of marks, grades of 9 points were suggested to be awarded.

b) Fellowship Programme (FPM)

The Meriam-Thurlby Report placed the priority for teachers training in management education. The Fellowship Programme aimed at fulfilling the shortage of management teachers in India and to help Universities in India as well as in Asian countries. So, training of teachers of business administration would lead to a Ph. D. degree. Not the Thesis, but the research training in a broad basis on realistic materials on Indian managementproblems.

c) Executive Development Programme

In 1959, Robbins emphasised on the Executive Development Programme (EDP) for executives at the top and middle level. These EDPs will lead to: i) Important service to present managers, ii) Spread the Institute's values, iii) Enhance the acceptance of Institute's graduates and iv) Encouragethe faculty members for both money contribution and opportunities. Thus, the stress on EDP was a direct outcome of MIT's influence. In the first year, the Institute planned for four EDPs, as it lacked the physical facilities for starting the MBA. So, EDPs started at Barrackpore Campus and these EDPs were a renowned feature of MIT, as it had already involved in the annual "Advanced Management Programme".

d) Research

The importance of research was clearly underlined by MIT's technical assistants. All three Reports suggested for research activities and research became an integral part of the Institute. The research grounded in the Indian environment and has an important role in our industrialization. It was aimed at Indian management practices and problems. It was to encourage creative activities among facultymembers and to furnish appropriate teaching materials. Research was mostly faculty based but not through a Research wing. In the initial years, a number of research projects started mostly sponsored by external agencies. The Ford Foundation favoured three Research Centres: a) Prof. Kamini Adhikari was granted $25,000 for her Centre for Entrepreneurship Studies, b) Prof. Dharni P Sinha was granted $13,800 for his Centre for Management Education System and Prof. Satyesh Chakraborti was granted $100,000 for his Centre for Urban Studies.

e) Consultancy

Three major preparatory documents on the establishment of the Institute suggested Consultancy as a supplementary activity. It adopted to attract more talented teachers, who may not be available due to restricted pay scale. Consultancy was aimed to attract more talented faculty for additional income, keeping in touch with current problems in business. Each faculty was allowed one day in a week or 54 days in a year on consultancy work. Such efforts were for keeping faculty members in touch with the real business world.

7. POLITICAL ENVIRONMENT IN CALCUTTA DURING 1960S

In 1953-1954, the movement by Anti Fare Enhancement Resistance Committee led by Left Parties have resulted burning of Trams, as the fare of second class tram journey increased by '*one paisa*'. In 1959, the food movement started due to scarcity of food and step rise in prices of essential goods including kerosene. "Food crisis and sky-rocketing food price are nothing new in West Bengal. In September 1959, there was an outburst of mass-agitation against the State Government for supply of food at reasonable prices.... the agitation this year may take a more aggressive form, as people's discontent has been mounting with shooting food prices" (Mitra, 1960). "The backdrop of historic food movement was due to collapse of Public Distribution System and artificial scarcity of rice created by State Government, Landlords, Rich Peasants, Trades/Hoarders and Rice mill owners. With price of rice sky-rocketing, there were loud protests on the streets (Das and Bandopadhay, 1999). The city of Calcutta in the 1960s was a city of political upheavals, mass agitation, labour strike and students' unions protest. De-industrialisation of the state began to take place, leaving the youths high and dry. The European business was shrinking and the *Marwaris* were rising. due to labour unrest, many private companies shifted to other Cities.

A massive flow of refugees from East Pakistan added to Calcutta's socio-political stagnation (Indian Eagle). Moreover, 'severe power shortage, strife in labour relations including strikes by workers and layoffs by employers and a militant Marxist-Maoist movements leads to economic stagnation in the State. (Samaddar, 2018). In 1964, the Hindu-Muslim Riot in Calcutta has aggravated the political situations. The riot was followed by loot, arson, attack, burning, stabbing and bomb throwing in some pockets of Calcutta. Busses and trams have been taken off and shops and markets were completely closed (BBC 2005). In this time, the Institute suffered from lack of strong and independent Chairman during this political environment. After the demise of Dr. B C Roy, the next CM, P. C. Sen. became our next Chairman, who paid less attention, because of political instability. So, the "Institute followed a "Bengali' course of development. If only IIMC had a Vikram Sarabhai or a Kasturbhai perhaps the leadership problem would not have been such a serious one" (Sancheti, 1986)

CONCLUSION

The IIM Calcutta was established as a public business school with full autonomy to offer management education. The Institute aims to engagein research, consultancy, seminars, academic conferences and publications. Three major preparatory documents had heralded the establishment of the Institute. The proposed institute was firstly named as Central Institute of Management Studies, then All India Institute of Management, then National Institute of Management Studies and finally Indian Institute of Management. The Institute was based on foreign model and has been established with assistance from MIT and Ford Foundation. The first meeting of Planning Commission for the "Establishment of a Central Institute of Management Studies" was held at Calcutta on 18th February 1961, which may be regarded as the birth day of IIMC, even though it was officially established in 13 November 1961. When our nation's leaders founded the Institute in early 1960s, India was a very poor country and was suffering severe problems, even in feeding its growing population. The government funded the Institute in the hope that such public investments would trigger a qualitative change in the management education and work as a catalyst for national development.

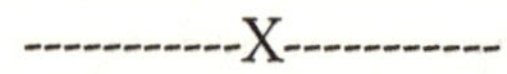

NOTE:

This chapter is based mostly on Neelu Sancheti's PhD Thesis on IIMC from the University of London in 1986. She joined our Institute as Faculty Member in 1990 and demised shortly.

CHAPTER 1.2

THE JOURNEY BEGINS AT EMERALD BOWER CAMPUS: 1964-1975

INTRODUCTION

In the early1960s, the Institute was in incubation stage, while it started in mid-1960s. It was at infantry stage in mid-1960s to mid-1970s..The Institute started its root in Barrackpur Campus but began to bloom in Emerald Bower (EB) Campus. In 1964, the Institute moved from Governor's House at Barrackpur '*Lat Bagan*' to E.B. Campus on Barrackpur Trunk Road in North Calcutta and about ten kilometres north from the City Centre. The EB Campus was about three kilometres close to the Indian Statistical Institute. In E.B. campus, the Post -Graduate Programme in management started in 1964 and so was the Executive Development Programs. But, the Fellowship Programme in started here in 1971. I was appointed in 1974 in EB campus, an old and unimpressive mansion of Tagore family

1. THE EMERALD BOWER: AN ICONIC MANSION

One of the most iconic and oldest addresses in Calcutta was the Emerald Bower, the palace of Pathuriaghata Tagore family. The Emerald Bower, known as '*Marakat Kunja*'and was a two-storied mansion, built by the Tagore families. In the past, eminent Bengalese like - Sadhak Bamakhyapa, Bankim Chandra Chattopadhya visited this place and Rabindra Nath came here in 1873 at the age of only 12. The Emerald Bower was built by Hara Kumar Tagore uncle of Rabindra Nath. In 1884, the Emerald

Bower became the garden house of Maharajah Sir Jatindra M Tagore. Later, Pradoot C Tagore beautified the splendid interiors and outsides of the Emerald Bower. The huge hall in the ground floor was used for musical performance and known as *'Jalsa ghar'*. The nostalgias of the Emerald Bower were the cast Iron gate, dry fountains, ponds full of grass and pathways flanked by hedges and shrubs.

But, that was not so 150 years ago. A Sinhalese poetess visited this place in 1883, as a guest of Tagore family. She was amassed by its ambience and splendid beauty. She wrote "Emerald Bower is a palatial building...paved with fine caravan marble.... replete with oil paintings of contemporary Italian masters...the costly furniture...the floors covered with lovely carpets.... the spacious compound......palm trees.... two splendid working fountains with marble figures. The fountains, tall trees, on the boarders of garden, the building and its costly furniture, the ponds, streams, one of them spanned by a cast iron bridge, were so artistically laid out that we can safely pronounce it a treat to spare neither a little expense a time to pay avisit to the country seat of Rajah Tagore: THE EMERALD BOWER" (Goonaratne 2009).

The mansion and huge parklands around Emerald Bower stand for pleasant retreats under the shades of green wood trees or climbing plants in the garden or wood. Now, the Emerald Bower has been declared as a 'Heritage Building'. "To maintain the heritage buildings, experts were brought from London to protect the building from the humid climate. A special fluid was injected into the walls to make it damp-proof...Conservation architects have been appointed to preserve them. The State Government issues Rs. 65 Lakh annually and a Committee was formed for make sure proper maintenance work" (Times of India, 2018). In the EB Campus, there was a private run Polytechnic in southern side and the Economics Department of Calcutta University was in northern side.

a) Recalling Old Days:

i) Views of Students of First Batch

Prof. Sudas Roy student of the first batch stated that "At the initial years in mid-1960s, management education was an unknown breed. There was no guarantee of getting well paid jobs.... even in the corporate sector. Early students have makeshift classrooms, old borrowed building and hostels. The infrastructure was basic and the building was infected with mosquitoes and no proven reading materials. We were attracted because of its association with US - B schools. Since that first day, the next two years were a blur of hectic activities, late-night preparations, unending tests and quizzes, classes........my student days is tinged with admiration for faculty, pride for the alma mater and an overall sense of pioneering adventure" (Connection, 2011)..

Mr. Raju Swamy, Governor of Mizoram and student of the first batch recalled that "There was no CAT type examination for entrance into IIMC. There were multiple choice questions. When we joined IIMC, the enthusiasm of the faculty and staffs were in welcoming us. They help us to adjust in a relatively revolutionary change in the ambience of the institute, compared to a typical Indian College/University. Most Professors were accessible and inter acted with us. Teaching quality was high and they motivated us to learn and the pressure was extra-ordinary. The EB campus was an old and unimpressive mansion won by Tagore families. It housed the Library and Administrative office. There were two hostels - Tagore Hall and Ramanujam Hall. The campus was in a traditional Calcutta neighbourhood. For coffee, drinks, tea, we have to go '*Sinthee More*'or Shyambazar. There were occasional trip to Chowrnghee for vegetarian and non-vegetarian Thalis or Tandors (Connection, 2012).

b) Views of Eminent Alumni and Professors

Mr. Ajit Balkrishna a student of sixth batch, who became Chairman of the Institute for two consecutive terms of ten years, recalled that "the makeshift campus at Emerald Bower was awfully short in amenities but long in history". Prof. Barun De, the Marxist historian served the Institute for ten years, from 1963 to 1973. He recalled the old days in EB Campus with his old colleague Prof Ashok Mitra. He recalled Prof. Mitra as "He introduced me into the Indian Institute of Management and I had the privilege of working in the same room as his in our old Emerald Bower Campus" (De, 2005). Prof. Iswar Dayal joined the Institute in 1963 and left in 1967 for joining in IIMA. He wrote his experience of IIMC at EB Campus, where he stayed for more than four years (Nangia, 2014). Prof. D P Sinha in his autobiography "Learning From Life" wrote that "I joined IIMC in 1966 and decided to leave on 1975. I was upset.... I joined ASCI under pressure from other faculties" (Sinha 2007).

2. LAND ACQUISIION FOR OWN CAMPUS AT JOKA

In 1960, a vast track of low laying agricultural land measuring 135 acres was acquired by the State Government for construction of our own campus at Joka village in undivided 24-Parganas district. The Joka village was 20 kilometres away from the city centre toward south. Next year, a group of landholders, whose land was acquired, filed a Case at Calcutta High Court against IIM Calcutta. Their objection was why the Government wasting this huge agricultural land, when the State was under famine? The Case was dissolved just before the demise of the then Chairman and State Chief Minister, Dr. Bidhan Chandra Roy in July 1962. After a few years in 1965, construction works started in Joka Campus. The area was a very low and submerged by adjacent canal water in most of the time. So, before construction, the Lakes were dug to prepare high lands for construction of buildings and peripheral roads. The Hindustan Building Construction Corporation had built the Buildings and Campus.

In 1965, the then Deputy Prime Minister of India, Mr. Morarji Desai laid down the foundation stone. After partial completion, the Institute moved to its own Campus at Joka after ten years of foundation. In 1975, the Campus was inaugurated by the then Governor of West Bengal, Prof. Nurul Hassan. Our main office moved partially from our old Emerald Bower Campus in July 1975 to Joka Campus. But, the Institute moved fully from EB campus in 1977, when I was also shifted to new Office at Joka. Because of shifting, the students of eleventh batch (1974-1976) have to complete first year of study in EB campus while the second year in Joka Campus.

3. INFRASTRUCTURES

a) The Offices

The State acquired the Zamindary property, Emerald Bower (EB) in 1950s and handed over to IIM Calcutta in early-1960s for running the Indian Institute of Management Calcutta. The EB housed the Library and the Director's Office. The library was set up in the ground floor of beloved *'jalsa ghar'* (dance floor)) and the first floor was used as Director Office. Students and Classrooms used to be in two hostels - Ramanujam Hall and Tagore Hall, where two students have to share a room. In the first batch, there were only two women, who have no hostel. So, they were housed in Girls Hostel at ISI. At the junction of the two hostels, there was a Telephone Exchange. The Professors and other Staffs used to sit in a series of make shift single floor Asbestos shaded rooms. The floor of the rooms was very low, and in 1976 flood, there was knee deep water in our rooms that resulted to soak our files kept in Almirah. The old servants' quarters were used for residential purpose of our Group D staffs. Someone used to prepare Tea and some Professors used to go there in lunch break.

The EB Campus has a long history but short in amenities like Post Office, Bank, Tea shops etc. The Canteen was very small and opened for half an hour and was supervised by Rathin Pal (No. 2). In the canteen, only Tea, Coffee, Toast, Stew, Boiled Vegetables, Alur Doom, Ghugni etc. were available but no Rice, Dal, Vegetables and Fish. There was no rush in the Canteen, as most staffs were local residents and used to go home for lunch. In the EB campus, there was a State Central Library, apex body of the library system in West Bengal. It was established in 1956 but it has shifted now near Air Port. I used to visit this library for reading different Newspapers stacked on the table and covered by iron bars, so nobody can displace from proper place. I became member of this library and used to borrow story books.

b) The Office Space

The faculty members and general staffs worked in the Asbestos shaded series of rooms. The office was a rectangular in shape and each side had a series of rooms with a common Veranda. The middle space was vacant but full of grasses that have never been mended. Each room was divided into two compartments, the front one was used by subordinate staffs and the rear one by faculty members. In the middle of a row, there was a hall called "Typist Pool" occupied by some typists. The total area of the building was around 6000 square foot, of which the vacant area in the middle was about 1000 square foot. So, roughly 5000 square foot of office space was used by faculty members and staffs. The allotted office space for a faculty was about 40 square foot while for general staff it was 30 square foot. The project assistants have to share one table by two of us.

c) The Library

The library was first set up in 1964, in the ground floor (*Jalsa ghar*) of Emerald Bower, with huge stock of foreign books and Journals. In late 1962, the Library was named as Dr. B C Roy Memorial Library after the demise of Dr. B. C. Roy, the then State Chief Minister and our first Chairman. The library is primarily envisioned to meet the requirements of the Institute's academic programmes. It houses over 160,000 volumes and also subscribes to hundreds of management journals. The library got huge financial aids from the Ford Foundation and other support from the government. In 1962, the Ford Foundation specified that the $ 1,25,000 allocated for books, materials and equipments which are not available in India, should be spent according to the purchase list of Ford Foundation officials in India. Till 1974, the Ford Foundation has granted $ 2,26,930 for Imports of Books and Equipments for the Library (Sancheti, 1986).

In February 1975, when my first appointment for three months expired, I have to submit a "No Objection Certificate" (NOC) from the library. The certificate should mention that I have borrowed no books from the library. I went to this library and met both Mr. Ashoke Mukhopadhay, and Mr. Ranajit Mukherjee, who were present in front of the library. After receiving the NOC from the Library, I submitted it to Director's Office in upstairs. First, I meet the Librarian Mr. Ashoke Mukhopadhay and Assistant Librarian Mr. Ranajit Mukherjee. Mr Mukhopadhay had education in library science from a British Institute and his rank was equivalent to a Professor. But, Ranajit'da was appointed for putting accession number to the huge number of books procured from foreign countries. The library assistants were arranging those books accordingly and some were in reader's desk to supply the requisitioned books to students and faculties. Till 1976, I was not a member of this library and have no access in the library. After 1976, I became a member our library with one reading room card and five borrower cards.

4. ADMINISTRATION

a) Board of Governance

The role of Board of Governance in the administration of the Institute was mostly a Policy Formulation Body. The Board members were mostly from Government and Business; and a few members could not address adequately the problems of the Institute. The tradition of having the Chief Minister as Chairman of the Board, the members lent an air of formality to Board meetings. The weakness of the Board in the Institute existed till 1975.In this period, the State was under President's Rule for four times and had three different Chief Ministers. Because of unstable Chief Ministers as well as the Chairman of the Institute, it hampered the development in the Institute. Finally, the Chairmanship was entrusted to the Governor of the State. In 1976, Mr. A L Dias, the Governor of the State became the Chairman of the Institute.

b) General Administration

During 1974, in discharging administrative functions of the Director, who was assisted by a Chief Administrative Officer, Assistant Administrative

Officers, Accounts Officer and Executive Engineer. The Engineer was looking after the work of Campus development in Joka. In 1975, the CAO was Mr. D. C. Bhattacharya, who hailed from Howrah and was a very strict person. The Senior Administrative Officer was Mr. S C Dasgupta, who resided in close proximity to EB Campus. He was very kind hearted and absorbed some poor youths known to him. Mr. P N Chakraborty was the Accounts Officer. The office hour was 9-30 a.m. to 4-30 p. m. and second and fourth Saturdays were holidays.

c) Number and Salaries of Staff

When I joined the Institute in late 1974, there were no Computers, Xerox machines nor Electronic Calculators. There were about 30 type machines, 20 Facit Calculators for calculations and a 'Gestatner' machine for cyclostyling. The Office orders, Course Materials, Projects Reports were first typed in stencil papers then it was cyclostyled for more copies. During this time, there were 38 Faculty members, 5 Officers, 10 Accounts staff, 5 Stenos, 10 Typist, 3 Telephone operator, 5 Library staff, 2 Drivers and 20 Group D staffs including Mali (gardener) and Sweepers.So a total of 60 general staffs were permanent employees. Moreover, there were about 10 Research Fellows/Research Assistants and 10 Project assistants as contractual staffs.

Among the employees, there was widespread gender inequality. Among all faculty members, only one was female and among 60 general staffs only 9 were females. Moreover, there were two female Research Fellows/Research Assistants and one female Project Assistant. So, among all employees, only 10 were females. Thus, the representation of female among all staffs was only 10 percent. In 1961, the Director was placed in the pay scale of Rs 2000 -100 – 2500 and a maximum of Rs 3500. During 1975, the average monthly salary for Professors was Rs. 1700, Officers Rs. 1500, Steno Rs. 900, Typist Rs. 500 and Group D staff Rs. 250 The consolidated monthly salary of Research Fellows was Rs. 900, Senior ProjectAssistants Rs. 600 and Junior Project Assistant Rs. 400 with a nominal annual increment. The permanent employees received DA (Dearness Allowances), Medical expenses etc. but Research Staffs and Project Staffs were debarred from those facilities. I was placed in the pay scale 400=30-900 pay scale with annual increment of Rs. 30 only.

5. FUNCTIONING OF THE INSTITUTE

a) Admission in PGP

In 1962, the Post-Graduate Programme (PGP) in management was accepted as a core activity of the Institute. The PGP was a two year full time compulsory residential programme. The MIT transferred their own curriculum to IIM Calcutta. Robbins suggested the teaching should cover the four major areas of - i) Management Concept and Practice (ii) Major operational areas of enterprises - Marketing, Production, Finance and Personnel. iii) Tools for Management Analysis and iv) The Environmental Influence in Social, Culture and Governmental change. The PGP course was designed to train students as excellent managers and decision makers. The PGP was to develop a global perspective while responding effectively to changes in the economic, political, cultural and technological environments. A set of specific skills be taught to students in the sphere of finance, accounting, marketing, operations etc. Traditional lecture base methods were prescribed for classroom teaching. Performance of students should not be judged by marks in final examination but on the basis of all examinations. Evaluations to be based on reports, term papers and class performance. Instead of marks, grades of 9 points were to be awarded.

In the admission process, MIT prescribed, at least 21 years of age, holds a university degree and meet approved standards in English and Mathematics. The common admission test (CAT) for IIMCand IIMA, was to test the candidate's ability in Verbal and Quantitative reasoning, Data interpretation, Mathematical capacity and English knowledge. The weight-age of the Test was 60%, Academic records 15%, Interview and Group Discussion 20% and Work experience 5%. Candidates must be a graduate with 60% marks for General category and 50% marks for Scheduled Castes and 45% marks for Scheduled Tribes. Due to the shortage of Girls' hostel, only three girls were admitted per year in the EB Campus. The basic disciplines taught were Mathematics, Statistics, Behavioural Science and Economics, while the functional areas were Marketing, Personnel, Finance and Accounting.

b) Number of Students

In the first batch (1964-1966) at EB Campus, a batch of 39 students was admitted, against the sanctioned capacity of 40. Gradually it varied from 70 to 100 in successive batches in the first decade. In the EB Campus, till the twelfth batch in 12 years, a total of 1009 students were admitted (Table 1.2.1). So, on an average, 85 students were admitted annually. In this period, a total of 30 females have enrolledand on an average, less than 3 females enrolled annually. The representation of female was only 3%. The female students were housed in the Hostel of ISI, about 3 kilometres away from the Institute.

The number of female students was stagnant at 3 for the scarcity of women hostel. It is also to be mentioned that, the students of twelfth batch has completed first year in EB Campus and moved to Joka Campus for second year. The representation of students from home state (West Bengal) was a few and some of the *Bengalese* students belonged to other states. Initially, students were mostly from Science, Humanities and Commerce streams and a few from engineering stream, but it was reversed later. In first batch, composition of students was 38% from Humanities, 31% from Science, 23% from Engineering and 8% from Commerce, Law etc. In tenth batch, composition was 9% from Humanities, 9% from Science, 77% from Engineering and rest 5% from others. Thus, the representation of students from engineering stream increased sharply. Till 1975, the Institute at EB Campus has produced one thousand Mangers, who were employed in Private and Public sectors. (Chowdury K, 1986)

c) Total fees and Placements

In the EB Campus, the total fees for two years in first an second batches were only Rs. 1,090. It increased to Rs. 1,290 for next two years, Rs. 1,550 for next two years, and increased to 2,305 in twelfth batch at EB Campus (Table 1.2.2). In the first batch, the total fees for two years was Rs. 1,090 while the Placement was at Rs. 600 per month i.e. Rs.7, 200 per annum. After a decade in 1975-77, the total fees increased to Rs. 9,000 while the Placement was at Rs. 1,500 per month i.e. Rs 18, 000 per annum. Regarding placement of our PGP students, Prof. D P Sinha observed "I recall, for the first two years (1966-68) in IIM Calcutta placed all its resources and energy to bring business leaders to participate in MDPs --- - - -the first task of B-Schools (IIMA & C) in India was to educate business leaders and create market for post-graduate programme in management" (Sinha 2004). In mid 1960s, our Professors had to indulge considerable hard sell to convince companies to recruit our MBAs. But, by mid-1970s, there was a sea change in the situation. Now MBA degrees become a magic password to corporate sectors (India Today, 1990).

d) The Faculty Strength

The faculty strength varied widely as high calibre intellectuals who joined at early stage left within three to four years for more prestigious positions. Moreover, MIT team returned home as the initial contract for three years ended. The Institute showed a very impressive faculty base till 1965. After that, the faculty strength dropped from 24 to 14. The shortage of faculty was largely in functional areas. The second Director, Dr. Mohan tackled the problem of faculty shortage by recruiting some adequately qualified faculty members from Indian States. As a result, faculty strength rose from 14 to 24. In 1975, a new era was ushered in the Institute with phasing out of a major Grant from the Ford Foundation. A significant shift in faculty recruitment taken place and resulted an increase in faculty strength from 24 to 38. So, in EB Campus, the number of faculty member fluctuated from 24 in 1963 to 14 in 1965 again increased to 24 in 1968 and lastly jumped to 38 in 1975(Sancheti, 1986).

e) Name of the Faculty Members

i) Initial Years

In 1964-1968, the foreign faculty members were – Douglas McGregor, Miles Kennedy, Warren Bennis, Paul Samuelson, Prof. Camp, Prof. Smith Alfred, Bill Thomas, Prof. John Wynmeretc. The Indian faculty members were Ravi Mathai, Ashok Mitra, Barun De, Kamini Adhikari, Iswar Dayal, Jati K Sengupta, Gouranga Chattopadhyay, Dharni P Sinha, and Jagdish Seth. Prof. John Wynmer was the first PGP Program Director. The faculties in Quantitative Methods were–Prof. Camp, Shiv Gupta, Krishna Murthy, Smith, and Nikhil Barat. Profs. Ashok Mitra, Jati K Sengupta, T N Krishnan, Ranjit Sau were in Economics. In Organizational Theory, the faculties were Waren Bennis, Iswar Dayal, Alfred, Kamini Adhikari, Thomas and Nitish De. In Behavioral Science were - Suresh Srivastava, Kanungo, Gouranga Chattopadhyay, Balkrishnan and D P Sinha. Profs. Kennedy, Rabadi and Sheshagiri Rao were in Financewhile Ravai Mathai, Laxmi Venkatraman and Krishna Mohan were in Marketing. Moreover, Bani P Sinha was in Operations Research, Barun De in History, Sengupta in Law and K T Chandi as Director (Connection, 2011).

ii) In mid-1970s.

In 1975, I saw 38 faculty members in EB Campus. Those were – Prof. JK Sengupta (Director), A K Biswas, R Sau, N K Chandra, A Ray and A Bose in Economics. Prof. D P Sinha, J Ezikel, G Chattopadhyay, K C Shah, B Kumar and A Ghosh in PMIR. Prof. RP Aiyer, A Agarwal, P Srimani and A Bagchi in MIS. Prof. K K Bhattacharya, BDe, N K Rao and S K Chakraborty in Finance. Prof. A K Chowdhuri, B K Sinha, B R K Kashyap in Operations Research. Prof. C Mitra, A Arora, K C Bothra and M Das in Marketing, Prof. DK Lahiri, K Swaminathan and A Ram in Behavioural Science. Profs. M Bhattacharya, K Datta, B Sarkar and C Mustafiin Statistics. Prof. K Adhikari in Sociology, Prof. ABose in Law and Prof. S Chkraborty in Regional Development, So, there were 6 Professors each in Economics and PMIR, 4 each in MIS, Finance, Operations Research, Statistics and Marketing while one to three in other groups. The Economics group was strong in numbers and a powerful lobby.

f) Fellowship Programme

The Meriam-Thurlby Report placed the priority for teachers training in management education. The Fellowship Programme in Management (FPM) was aimed at fulfilling the shortage of management teachers. The training of teachers would lead to a Ph. D. degree. In the initial years, the FP was not started because of shortage of faculty and resources. After the Institute moved from Barrackpur to EB Campus, the FPwas planned to start in 1968, but it started late in 1971. In the EB Campus, the Fellowship was awarded only to Mr. M N Pal in Operations Research in 1975. Other who awarded Fellowship in EB Campus was - Mr. S CRay inEconomics, Mr. K J Pillai in Organisation Management, S K Basu in Finance & Control, Mrs. Purba Datta and Mr. S K Gupta both in Operation Research. These students were awarded Fellow later in 1977 in Joka Campus. I was invited in their Thesis Defence.

g) Executive Development Programme (EDP)

One of the proposed academic activities in the Institute was a program of training for already employed executive at the middle and top level. All three documents suggestedongoing occasional conferences of short duration. The Executive Development Programme aimed to spread the value of the Institute and to enhance the acceptance of our Graduates. Over the years, EDPs were continuing as originalplanedtheInstitute took over the staffing of annual AMPs offered by MIT in 1964. In the first decade (1964-74), the EDPs remained extremely popular and exceeded the Robbins anticipation of 80 participants annually. In mid-1970s, the scope of EDPs broadened but failed to evoke the anticipated response.

Recalling old days, Prof Sinha (2004) said "I recall, for the first two years (1966-68), IIMC placed all its resources and energy to bring business leaders to participate in Management Development Programme designed to re-educate them. In mid 1960s, IIMC collected the views of Business Leaders on the future of management education. This study indicated that the first task of B-Schools (IIM - A & C) was to educate business leaders and create market for post graduate programme in management." The EDPs were designed with the objective of providing practicing managers the insight into managerial concepts and implementing strategies in functional areas. The candidates for EDP must have Graduate degree from any university without no age limit. Duration of these EDPs varied from two to five days and a programme fee varies from Rs. 500 to Rs. 1500. In 1975, the EDPs were mostly for three to five days duration and it cost Rs. 900 to Rs. 1200 depending the venues. Some EDPs were held at Hotel Annapurna in Kathmandu and others in hotels in Darjeeling.

h) Research

In the EB Campus, the research became an integral part of the Institute to encourage creative activities among faculty members. Till 1970s, the research activities were more experimental to the testing of Western hypothesis in Indian situation. During 1971-1975, the Institute witnessed the establishment of five Research Canters, headed by chosen faculty members. The Ford Foundation supported Indian faculty members to set up three Research Centers within the Institute. Dr. Kamini Adhikary was given $25,000 to set up her Center for Entrepreneurship Studies. Dr. D P Sinha was given $13,800 for his Center for Management of Education System and Prof. Satyesh Chakraborti was given $100,000 for his Center for Urban Studies. Besides these Ford Foundation funded Centers, Prof. Nirmal Chandra headed the centre of 'Agrarian Change and Peasant Organisation might be financed by FAO (Food and Agricultural Organisation) and ILO (International Labour Organisation). Prof. Arun K Choudhriwas headedanother Centre on "Second West Bengal Project".

Prof. Kamini Adhikari headed the Centre for Entrepreneurship Studies along with Dr. K K Choudhury, a Research Fellow, Miss. Vaijayanti and Mr. Natarajan as Project Assistants. Prof. Sinha headed the Centre for Management Education System with Prof, B Kumar and other three Research Fellows-S Bandopadhaya, S Bhattacharya and A P Sinha. Prof. S

Chakraborty headed the Centre for Management of Urban System with a research team headed by Mr. Abdul Halim. Prof. Chandra headed the Centre of Agrarian Change and Peasant Organization and his team consists of Mr. A Manna, A Misra and Me. The "Second West Bengal Project" headed by Prof. Choudhury along with Mr. MNPal. The Research in EB Camps was mostly faculty based but not through a Director of a Research wing. Till 1975, only ten projects were completed and six projects were on-going. The last Ford Foundation grant allocated in 1975 was extended up to December, 1983(Sancheti, 1986).

6. ROLE OF FORD FOUNDATION AND MIT

a) Active Collaboration of FF and MIT

Through out the phase (1961-1967) of active collaboration with MIT, the broad goals set by Robbins remain uncontested. After 1965, Indian faculties attempted to take an increasingly independent stance towards the priorities set by Ford Foundation and MIT. The disagreement between American and Indian side centered around two issues. Firstly, the selective admission policies were restraining the Institute from meeting the growing national demands. Thus, efforts should be made to increase the intake of students. Secondly, the orientation of the Institute felt heavily biased towards private sector, which should be more relevant towards reality of Indian situation. In late 1966, when new Director Dr. Mohan was appointed, a need was expressed for new sense of purpose and direction. In February 1967, in a letter from MIT to the Director said 'during the first three years of collaboration, IIMC performed well but during last two years, resources in IIMC has been grossly over extendedand output correspondingly debased' (Sancheti, 1986).

The active collaboration of MIT ended in 1967, and after that the re-negotiation of IIM Calcutta's relationship with Ford Foundation was rewritten. The Director informed the Ford Foundation that he intended to make more independent stand. This became an important phase in the development process of IIM Calcutta. The Ford Foundation Grant was biased towards MIT and heavily concentrated during 1961 to 1967 but it reduced later. The principal item of expenditure from the Ford Foundation grant was the technical services provided by MIT. The excessive concentration of MIT personnel was also not helping to develop Indian faculties. In 1967, Prof. Hill proposed- 'the welcome opportunity to assist in rebuilding IIM Calcutta. So, Ford Foundation would not contribute towards MIT, but to support the land and building programmer of the Institute' (Sancheti, 1986).

The Ford Foundation sanctioned an initial grant of $ 4.34 Lakh in 1961 and subsequently granted $ 6.1 Lakh in 1962, $ 3.0 Lakh in 1963, $ 6.65 Lakh in 1965, $ 2.78 Lakh in 1968, $ 1.05 Lakh in 1971 and $ 3.00 in 1975. So, IIM Calcutta received a total of about $ 27 Lakh from Ford Foundation during 1961 to 1975. From the total grant of $ 27 Lakh, $ 14 Lakh i.e. more than half was paid to MIT for their technical services and others. The total expenditure was on import of books and equipments $ 2.3 Lakh, for physical development of plant $ 4.4 Lakh, for architectural services $ 0.3 Lakh, the others expenditure of $ 5.8 Lakh. So, out of the total grant provided by Ford Foundation, 53% was paid to MIT, 16% on physical development of plant, 8% on import of books and equipments, 1% on architectural services and rest 22% on other services (Sancheti, 1986).

The publication of our Annual Report for 1967-68 was delayed due to its administrative problems. As a result, the Ford Foundation was annoyed and advised no more payments could be made unless the Annual Reports were provided. Finally, it was completed and submitted with the help of Ford Foundation staff. In late 1960s, the Ford Foundation grants declined sharply. The Foundation regret the decision of locating IIM in Calcutta, as volatile leadership combined with hostile political environment in Calcutta. In the 1970s, Ford Foundation reduced the institutional building grants. But, liberal grants were made available to specific research projects. In 1975, MIT has no formal association with IIMC, but most faculties felt MIT association enhanced our prestige (Sancheti, 1986).

b) Leadership Crisis: 1967-1974

Since 1957, both The Ford Foundation and MIT recognized the importance of faculty developments, as the faculty members could be socialized in theory, practice and underlying values of American Management. After having achieved limited success in realizing the goals of Ford Foundation and MIT, during the first Director, they assumed a more vigilante stance in selecting the second Director. In 1966, the Ford Foundation wrote to the Chairman Mr. P C Sen, the then CM of West Bengal that until the new Director has been appointed, they cannot recommend for a supplementary grant. In 1967, Dr. Krishna Mohan was selected as second Director, who has no bias against foreigners and MIT. He recognized the need for a continuous and effective relationship with MIT.

The Ford Foundation and MIT played a more assertive role in selecting Dr. Mohan as Director, as he performed well to cling to MIT for support in the face of hostility of faculty members and the volatile political situation in Calcutta. However, his pro-American orientation did not popularize him within faculty groups. As other problems also arose, he was forced to resign within two years of Directorship. The hope of Ford Foundation and MIT for assuring a stable and compliant leadership at IIM Calcutta could not be realised, as it has been going through a period of crisis. In 1974, after Dr. Mohan, the faculty members selected first Dr. Krishna Murthy, then Dr. Krishna Mohan, then Mr. Nitish De and finally Dr. Jati K Sengupta as Directors. The Ford Foundation found their suitable Director, who continued till 1977. My first appointment was issued by Prof. JK Sengupta as Director in December 1974.

c) Factionalism Among Faculty Members

In 1965, the reduced leadership of Mr. Chandy, departure of MIT Professors and uncertain political environment in Calcutta, the Institute witnessed an increased factionalism among faculty members. An influential faction of faculty members exhibited Anti-American orientation. The leadership vacuum enhanced the active faculty participation in decision making process. The Institute continued to enjoy a heterogeneous mix of faculty members, who were displaying a diversity of outlook and interests. As a result of myopic faculty development policies, a major factionalism was created among the faculty members. The situation was fully exacerbated, when Mr. Chandy recruited several Marxist scholars, who soon assumed a position of power at the Institute.

The rift between faculty membersbelonging to the Basic disciplines, Quantitative areas and Functional areas has widened. Seeing such factionalism, someone has remarked that "if IIMC has n faculties, then 2n is their opinions, n square is their unions and n to the power n is their views". The role of the Director reduced merely to a mediator between rival faculty groups. The ad-hoc recruitment in 1965 aggravated the growing factionalism among faculties. When Dr. Mohan was appointed as Director, the Institute needs to install senses and direction for its development. He placed the priority on research development but the faculty community strongly opposed the priorities of MIT. In 1974, to stabilize the tussles between faculty members and Director, new position for academic administration was created. The newly created posts of Chairman in different functional areas had settledthe situation for the time being. The crisis stabilized as internal situation changed soon.

7. MYSELF AT THE EB CAMPUS

a) Office Work

In November 1974, I was appointed as Junior Project Assistant with Prof. Chandra, for his Project on "Agrarian Change and Peasant Organization". During 1972-73, the field survey has been completed in three villages of Burdwan. Before my joining, Mr. Kanchan Mukherjee was working as a Research Assistant to Prof. Chandra. He left for joining at the Centre for Development Studies in Trivandrum. I was appointed to analyse the survey data. I spent a lot of time at work hammering away at the hand operated FACIT calculating machine. The objective of the Project was to calculate the inequality in land holding and annual income among of all the households in those villages. Then, we estimated the extent of hunger among landless agricultural labourer households. We estimated the amount of "Levy" that can be imposed on rich peasants. The levy system was in practice by the State for procuring excess paddy from the landlords. We also measured the extent of exploitation among varies types of agricultural labourers. The children of the landless labourers were engaged by rich peasants as '*Bagal*', cowboy to herd the folk of cows. They were paid a meagre amount in cash and kind; their plight has been written by Prof. Chandra. The "Bagals of Bengal", was chapterised in the book: 'Subaltern Studies' edited by Mrs. Nirmala Banerjee, mother of Nobel Laureate Avijit B Banerjee. She acknowledged me in her book.

When my first appointment expired in March 1975 at EB Campus, Prof. Chandra engaged me on daily wage basis @ Rs. 18 per day on no-work-no-pay. It was a monthly exercise that, after each month Prof. Chandra had to issue an IOM (Inter Office Memo) to the Director for payment of my salary and it took another week to receive it. After completion of the project, Prof. Chandra left for a foreign trip for presentation of the Report on Burdwan. The main office has shifted partially to Joka in mid-1975, but some staffs were still working in EB Campus till 1977. I used to go for village survey for a week and next week to my office at EB. By this time, my room was demolished and I lifted to the first floor of the Hostel.

In this time, a person used to come in my room and enquire about Prof. Chandra. Later, I recognized him as Mr. Sushil Khanna, our alumni, whojoined later as Research Fellowand completing our FPM became faculty member in Economics group. In the same way, Mr. Ramanuj Majumder, ISI alumnialso used to meet Prof. Chitta Mitra, with whom I shared the room at EB Campus. Here I met a true gentleman Dr. K K Chaudhuri, sitting in my next room. He was Research Fellow attached to Mrs. Kamini Adhikariof Sociology group. My professor Nirmal Chandra and Mrs. Adhikari were good friends.

I completed the Certificate course in ISI on December 1975. After that, all four Project Assistants of Prof. Chandra were engaged in the survey on ten villages around Kheyadah in Sonarpur Block. The objective of the survey was enquiring land tenancy system prevailing in that area. The vast track of Vidyadhari Char has been occupied by the local landed gentry. Among them, Mr. Naskar of Kheyadah village was a sitting MLA in Dr. BC Roy Ministry. To reach Kheyadah from my village was a long journey. Generally, I went to Kheyadah on Monday and returned at Friday. We lived in a poor Bargadar's *kutchbha*house in Kheyadah and Atul babu cooked our food. While we were at Kheyadah village, Atul babu listened from his Radio on April 1977 that 'President's Rule' has been imposed in the State. He was much disappointed but I know nothing about 'President's Rule'

b) My Academic Activities

As I have joined the Institute in November 1974 for two months only, I decided to continue my studies after leaving the job. The salary for 12 days in the month of November 1974 was Rs.216. Taking the entire amount, I went to the Institute of Cost and Works Accounts and took admission there. They provided the Study Materials for the first Term. In December 1974, I was selected at Indian Statistical Institute (ISI) for a "One Year Evening Course in Statistical Methods and Applications" with a course fee of Rs. 400. I have applied for that course before joining this Institute. I decided to jointhe ISI and left studying of Cost Accountancy. In January 1975, I took admission at ISIin the evening programme where classes held from 6 p.m. to 8-30 p.m. In ISI, I have attended classes of Prof. Hanurav, Kanan and Rao etc. along with Nikhilesh Bhattacharya, Deepak Condoo, Taresh Moitra, I S Roy and B P Adhikari, husband of our Prof. Kamini Adhikari etc.

After office hour at EB campus, we Rohitaswas, Nagi, Sridharan and M N Pal walked for two minutes to reach '*Sinthee More*' for Tea. Mr. Reddy used to write Inland letters to his wife at Guntur. He showed the letter written in Telegu, that we could not read. Hehanded over the letter to me to drop at ISI post office. I took a local bus to reach ISI, a ten minutes journey by 10 Paisa fare. After the classes, I walked to Baranagar station to catch the Dankuni bound train then to catch Burdwan bound train and get down at my home station Madhusudanpur. Sometimes, I failed to catch the connecting Burdwantrain and I have to wait another one hour at Dankuni, where I revised my class notes. I returned home at mid night and my father come to the station with a hurricane lamp. Later, my friend asked me to stay in their Mess and I stayed. So, I started living with my friends in a Mess just opposite to ISI Campus. I started reading daily notes till 6 p.m. and then moved to ISI for my classes.

In December 1975, I appeared for the entrance examination of our PGP. I followed the book "Aptitude Test" authored by Professors of ISI. The admission test was on paper and pencil based and my seat for admission test was in a Cossipur Multi-Purpose High School, just opposite to our EB campus. A heavy booklet consisting more than 50 pages was the question paper with questions on multiple choicetypes. I was puzzled by seeing the questions in English test, but I did fairly well in Mathematical and Quantitative reasoning. Later, I received a regret letter, which I shown to Mr. Reddy, who told me it could have a few Cinema shows. The Admission Booklet cost of Rs. 100, one fourth of my monthly salary.

8. THE TURBULENT CALCUTTA IN THE SEVENTIES

a) The Cossipore-Baranagar Massacre

In the 1970s, the city of Calcutta was a City of political upheavals because of mass agitation, widespread labour unrest; famine and poverty, student unrests and severe power shortage. In this time, Calcutta saw a wave of protest and student's radicalism and youth unrest (Samaddar, 2017). A massive flow of starved, penniless refuge from East Pakistan (now Bangladesh) during the onset of Liberation War of 1971 added to Calcutta's socio-political stagnation. The city of Calcutta saw the rise of middle class intellectuals like film makers - Satyajit Ray, Mrinal Sen, and Ritwik Ghatak. During 1967 to 1977, the President's Rule was imposed in the State for four times and had three different Chief Ministers made the State politically unstable. During the Chief Ministership of Mr. S S Ray, the Cossipore-Baranagar Massacre on Naxalite activists happened in the adjacent areas of our E B Campus. In 1965, the Institute was a finest

Marxist School of Economics with French trained Marxist Economist Dr. PareshChattopadhya (Alagh, 2018). He was a Professor during 1964 to 1972 and reported formerly a Maoist and was arrested by Police.

When the State was under President's Rule, the Cossipore-Baranagar Massacre on Naxalite activists happened in 1971. At the helm of affair, the Union Minster Mr. S. S. Ray, was going to be the Chief Minister of the State. The Police and Congress backed ruffians to take on the Naxalite when Prime Minister told the armed rebelled would be fought to finish. The police cordoned the locality, enter the house, dragged the supporters out and kill them in full view of family and public (Bhattacharya, 2018). In the bloody history of police repression in 1970-1976, the common practice was arrest them and shoot them dead. Sometimes, they were taken to police custody, tortured to death and announced them as Naxalite or extremists. Two policemen Ranjit Gupta and Runu Guha Neogi gained notoriety for fake encounters in that period.

In the Cossipore-Baranagar Massacre, about 100 people were killed on August 1971, because they subscribed to a particular ideology. Corpses lay strewn on those fateful days. The victims were canned, singed the parts of the bodies with lit cigarettes and finally pumped bullets on their bodies (TOI, 2002). The Congress led government has restored to planned and systematic liquidation of opposite political workers between 1971 and 1976. Dead bodies were found everywhere in Calcutta, bodies with head cut-off, limbs lost, eyes gauged out, entail ripped open. These bodies were laid in streets and carried by rickshaw and handcarts to through away into the river Hooghly and the tidal bore washed them away (EPW, 1977).

In 2011, Mrs. Mamata Banerjee becoming first CMof the State constituted the Commission of enquiry on the infamous Cossipore-Baranagar Massacre. The Commission was initially headed by Justice A K Bishi, but transferred to Justice D P Sengupta, who submitted the Report in 2017. Human activist, Mr. SujataBhadra also submitted the APDR conducted report. Even though, the Government received the Report in 2017, it was not yet tabled in the Assembly. Thus, Mamata's promise ended with the constitution of the Commission and spending of Rs. 2.58 Crores during 2014-2017. (WIRE, 2020)

b) The Turbulent 1970s and Me

During college days in 1968-1971, mass agitation of student unions, famine and poverty affected my study. There were no regular classes, no examinations in time and late publication of results. Most of the days, classes were withheld for agitation by students' unions. So, I wasted four hours of to and fro journey. The final examination in our college was cancelled for mass copying. So, for re-examination, I had to go to a College in Calcutta. In 1975, after my evening classes at ISI, I was waiting at the end of Barahnagar Station platform around 9 p.m. A group of youths forcefully handed over a bunch of Newspapers and instructed not to open here. After reaching home at mid-night, I saw those papers printed in Red Ink and titled "LAL JHANDA". Next day, at the same time and same place I was enjoying cool breeze on the platform, a group of CRPF asked me why I was there. I replied that I was waiting for my train, butthey ordered to sit under the platform shed.

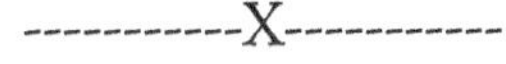

CHAPTER 1.3

THE FIRST DECADE IN JOKA: NEW CONSTRUCTIONS AND RE-ORIENTATION: 1975-1985

1. CONSTRUCTION OF BUILDINGS AND PERIPHERAL ROADS

In the middle of 1975, the Institute moved partially from Emerald Bower Campus to Joka, a southern outskirt of Calcutta. The foundation stone was laid down by Mr. Morarji Desai, the then Deputy Prime Minister of India in December 1968. The opening ceremony was inaugurated by Prof. Nurul Hassan, Governor of West Bengal in 1975. It took seven years to move the Institute to its own Campus, still unfinished. The Decade (1975-1984) of Construction dealt with the construction of '*Pucca*' Roads and Drains, Pipe Water Supply, Main Gate, Administrative Building, CAM (Computer Aided Management) Centre, New Classrooms (L3 & L4), Library Building, Power and Generator House etc. The construction works were in full swing till 1983, even after eight years of shifting from EB Campus. Accommodation of women students was still limited to nine, because of shortage of women's hostel. Due to shortage infrastructures, other programs were also affected.

During the initial years, there was more rush of construction labourers than the staffs of the Institute. The main gate was narrow just to cross the 'nullah' (reverie) for Lorries carrying construction materials. Initially, there was no official signboard, a big signboard was placed by the HBCC (Hindustan

Building Construction Corporation), engaged in construction work in the campus. Under this large signboard, 'Indian Institute of Management Calcutta" was written in a small signboard supported by two bamboos. The structure of our existing main gate was re-built in 1978, when the President of India, Mr. Fakuruddin Ali came to deliver our Convocation address. In the 1980s, the service canters like a Branch of State Bank of India, a Post Office and a Telephone Exchange were opened in our Joka Campus.

In 1985, all the construction of Administrative Building, Computer Aided Management (CAM) Centre, New Classrooms (L3 & L4) and Library Buildings were over. By this time, all roads have been covered with asphalt, all drains made *pucca* and supply of Piped Water began. The Main Gate has been broadened and a large signboard indicating the name of the Institute was set at the top. The Power and GeneratorHouse was set up for uninterrupted supplying power in classrooms and Office rooms during load shedding time. In this period, there were no air conditioners (AC) in any rooms except the CAM Canter. The library was shifted from asbestos shade godown to newly constructed three stored building.

2. THE VAST CAMPUS

a) Scenic Beauty

The Registered office of the Institute is in Harington Mansion at central Calcutta. But, the academic campus spread over an area of 135 acres in Joka village in 24 Parganas district. Joka is 20 kilometres away south of the City canter and connected by Diamond Harbour Road. This road was very narrow and congested and it was widened in 1976, as military movements suffered during Emergency Period. This campus consists of academic buildings, classrooms, conference rooms, hostels for students, library, executive training complex and staff quarters. The campus is spread with an area of. 55 hectares covering a half a square kilometre of area and its boundary length is about five kilometres. It is situated at 22°36.49' N and 88°23.02' E. The campus has natural beauty with verdant greenery and gorgeous lakes.

The compound and adjoining area has many wetlandsand covered a vast area of vegetation. There are densely planted areas with good ground cover and lots of open rice fields around it. Some of the wetlands are leased out for fishery.Still the unique Typhusbed that remains helps several birds and mammals to take shelter. In the marshy land, migratory ducks, strokesforage and roost and the birds of preyalso congregate there for hunting, at least in winter. The ongoing construction works inside the campus are interfering with the wild flora and fauna and these are depletingday by day (Ghosh, 2007). Bengal marsh Mongoose (Neul) is plenty in Typha reeds or grass beds in the semi natural wetland in the campus. It is essentially a bird sanctuary and provides budding opportunity to Photographers, Ornithologists and admirers of natural beauty. The campus as a bird sanctuary provides home of incredible number of rare species and exotic birds. The bird watchers can spot rare and migratory birds; the more common are Woodpecker, King Fisher, Cuckoos, Jungle babbler, Indian pond Heron, Greater Causal and folks of Crows and spotted Monitor Lizard.

Nature is at its picturesque best here with Lakes and lush green environs. The campus of seven lakes was envisaged to symbolise "Cauldrons of Knowledge" and named after seven most legendary Professors of the Institute. Myth has it, whenever these lakes overflow, the placement skyrocket for that year. The campus boasts of scenic locales and a miniature Howrah Bridge. There are fish flopping in the lake under Howrah Bridge, evening mint creeping in for the horizon. The campus is free from pollutions and stars can be easily seen in the night. Walk from the library at night is incomplete without accompanying fireflies glowing in the dark and endless birds chatters from the trees (Nagar, 2017). Though it is a peaceful place but turned out to be scarce for Snakes, Monitor Lizards, Wild Gigantic Spider, Snails, and Earth Worms in rainy seasons.

In early 1980s, the Central government provided huge fund for "Campus Beautification". Several thousands of plants were planted for five consecutive years. For this plantation drive, despite the existing Malis more of casual labours were deployed. To supervise the beautification drive, Mr. Kabiraj, a Horticulturist was deputed from Raj Bhavan and was controlled by

Cornel Nag, the Security officer. The plants were mostly Sal, Palash, Sirish, Coconuts, Mangos and Pears etc. As, both Mr. Nag and me sat in the same room, at ground floor of B-Block, I have overheard the daily progress of the plantation drive.

b) Campus Life of Students

The scenic beauty of the campus and its greenery is omnipresent. The day begins with early morning chirping of various species of birds and end reflecting at the lakes. The campus is not just a home to bunch of geeks but a melting pot of intellectuals well surrounded with culture, academia and technology. It is a hectic day as the classes starts at 7 a.m. and continue till 9 p.m. on most days. The amount of assignment, project works, presentations and case studies, keep them busy. They hardly had a few days with low activity. They enjoy an unsupervised student life, free movements of girls in the hostel and allowance for Drinks. There were plenty of opportunities in the hostel for recreation of them.According to IMRB survey, the campus life at IIM Calcutta ranked top. Heaven showed the pleasant places, serene, peaceful life with no regulation and no drinks. But, the hell showed the party places, vibrating music, drinks, celebration of social life in festivity (Srikant, 2000).

c) Communication Hurdles to Reach Joka

Due to the insistence of Ford Foundation, the campus was located in a remote village named Joka. The campus is 20 kilometres away from the city centre, 30 kilometres from Howrah, 25 kilometres from Sealdah stations and 45 kilometres away from the city Airport. In the initial years, there were no general Taxi (Black and Yellow), only Yellow Taxis were allowed to go to Joka, a rural area beyond City border. From Howrah, only buses of rout number 12C ply between Howrah and Pailan. It took more than two hours, as it followed the congested areas of Khidirpur, Hyde Road, Brace Bridge, Taratala, Behala and Thakurpukur. From Sealdah station, buses of only rout number 235 can be availed to reach Joka. Initially, there was no bus stoppage in front of our gate. We have to request the conductor to stop at the gate, but they slowed down the bus and pushed us to get down. After a few years, the buses started stopping by shouting "management school". When, the Government run State bus of route number L3E started plying from Howrah to Amtala, our Institute requested the Transport Authority to stop the bus in front of our Gate. Thereafter, all buses started stopping in front of our main Gate and we were easily stepped down from the buses.

Most of the faculty members and office staffs availed the Institute's buses to reach Joka. We the Projects Assistants were not entitled to avail the official transport service. When our Ex-Prime Minister Mrs. Indira Gandhi was assassinated in October 31, 1984, all public transports were stopped. So, all faculty members and employees have to walk for two to three hours to reach home. Post office is another mode of communication. The official mail (Letters and Parcels) were collected from Alipore Post Office in the City, as our postal address was Post Box No. 16757, P.O. Alipore, Calcutta – 700027. Some of my interview letters and Telegrams reached me late, as it was via Bishnupur Post Office. At that time, the Institute was under Bishnupur Block of 24 Parganas district.

d) Isolation of Joka Campus

Faculty members including Director and staffs have to commute everyday a long journey from their official residence. The lengthy journey across congested areas of the City has dampened their enthusiasm. So, coming to Joka everyday has hampered the progress. The locational disadvantage has limited the contact with other City Institutes including ISI (Indian Statistical Institute), Jadavpur University, and Calcutta University. Moreover, shuttling between Joka office and City office by Professor to attend the evening classes at Harington Mansion became troublesome. For Consultancy work, faculty members have to travel a lot and spend the entire day in the City. As the Joka Campus was in an isolated place, having no shops and markets, the Institute provided bus service once in week for purchasing the daily household needs of the faculty member and staffs residing in our Staff Quarters.

3. THE LIBRARY: ASBESTOS SHED GODOWN TO NEW BUILDING

In the Joka Campus, the Library was in a series of Asbestos shaded rooms with low floor height. Most books were stacked in '*Bundles*', it was opened only when necessity arises. Now, the Library seems to be a *godown* supervised by Ashok'da and Ranajit babu with five assistants. In 1983, the Library shifted to its own three floor air-conditioned building. As the Library was opened in its own building, some library assistants were also recruited at that time. Now, books and periodicals were being arranged in different stacks in different rooms. The Library assistants were recruited for the massive task of arranging huge number of books and periodicals. Now, among the total library assistants, a half of them were women. The first Xerox Machine in the Institute was gifted by the Government of Japan and it was installed in the ground floor of the Library in 1985. When, the Ashok babu left the Institute and Ranajit'da became Acting Librarian along with some Assistant Librarians. The 'vast Reading Room was a pleasant place to read the current Journals and Periodicals.

4. THE SCATTERED OFFICE SPACES

When we moved from EB Campus to unfinished Joka Campus in 1975, the office consists of the areas around the academic blocks - A, B and C. A common veranda connected all three Blocks and in between Block A and B, there were two Lecture Halls L1 and L2. In A-Block ground floor, there was a Telephone Exchange and Reception Counter on the right side and a series of small classrooms on the left. The other two floors were occupied by faculties and supporting staffs. In B-Block ground floor, there was a Data Processing Centre on the right and a few small rooms for PGP office on the left. The Director's office was on the top floor of B Block with a large Conference Room. The other floors were occupied by faculties and supporting staffs. In C- Block ground floor, the Fellowship office on the right side and some small rooms on the left side. The other two floors were occupied by faculties and supporting staffs.

A series of Staff quarters was in a faraway place opposite to a Lake.The Accounts office, Publications Office and the Branch of State Bank of India were in some Staff quarters. I was firstly placed in first floor of a Staff quarter in opposite side. The Library was placed in a series of Asbestos shaded rooms in a distant place. When the Library shifted to its own building in 1983, those rooms were being used by Kendriya Vidyalay. Opposite to the Lake, the EDP canter, named Tata Hall was completed and all EDPs were being held there. The new Administrative Building was being used by the Director Office, Accounts office, Admission office. I was moved from Staff quarter to this building. A few Hostels were completed before we moved here. So, male students were accommodated in their own Hostels. Due to shortage of Women's Hostels, women students were allocated a portion of Men Hostels. The newly constructed single floor CAM Canter was with Main Frame Computers, a few Desktop Computers and some small rooms for the Professors and supporting staffs.

During 1980s, in the initial years at Joka campus, about twenty Professors, a dozen of Typist and Stenos supporting the increased teaching staffs. Seven Library assistants, mostly females were recruited in the library, five in engineering division and some *Malis* and Security staffs were also recruited. About half a dozen of casual workers were recruited for cooking in the students hostels. About thirty Project Assistants were also recruited for the ongoing World Bank sponsored projects on Agricultural Marketing under the supervision of Prof. Chitta Mitra. As the Institute had no sufficient place, the Institute hired some rented rooms just opposite to the Institute. Thus, there was jump in number of both teaching and non-teaching staffs. The recruitments in this time were mostly through the Employment Exchanges and the Newspaper advertisement in few cases.

5. FUNCTIONING OF THE INSTITUTE

a) Admission in PGP

The Post-Graduate Programme (PGP) in management was continuing as usual in new Campus. This is two year full time compulsory residential programme. The eligibility for admission was judged by CAT (Common Admission Test) score, academic records, interview, group discussion and work experience. Candidates belonging to Scheduled Castes (SC) and Scheduled Tribes (ST) were enjoying their reservations. Due to the shortage of Women's hostel, only six women students were admitted per year. The Institute provided a number of Scholarship and Stipends for needy students. The SC and ST students were enjoying other benefits. Traditional lecture base methods were followed in classroom teaching performance of students was judged by all examinationsalong with reports, term papers etc. and Grades of 9 points were awarded as usual.

In the 1981-1983 batch, there were 5742 applicants, of which 561 was selected for interview and 123 got admission Thus, only 2% applicants were selected for admission in our PGP. Among those who have qualified the test, 85% were from only four large Cities – Delhi, Bombay, Madras and Calcutta. Among the qualified candidates, 512 were male and 49 were female. Among qualified candidates, only 9% were female. Against the reservation of 20%, only 32 SC and 7 ST candidates were qualified in the admission test (Sancheti, 1986). At the all India level, the aspirants for PGP in all IIMs sat for CAT were 5,000 in 1975, 15,000 in 1985 and 30,000 in 1990. It is to be noted that, there were only two IIMs in 1972, 3 in 1985 and 4 in 1990. Now, for the twenty IIMs, the aspirants reached to three laths.

b) Number of Students

During the first decade (1976-1985) at Joka campus, students enrolled in PGP varied from 90 to 128 per year and female students enrolled varied from 6 to 9, because of shortage of women's hostel. During first decade at Joka campus, a total of 1063 students were admitted, of which only 65 were women. On an average 106 students, of which 6 were women were admitted annually. In this period, the intake in PGP has not increased much because of shortage of teachers, classrooms and other infrastructures. The representation of students from home state was also a few and among the Bengalese, some were from other cities. The predominance of students from engineering background continued as usual.

c) Total fees and Placements

In the Joka Campus, the total feesfor two years in 1976-78 were Rs.2,700and it increased to Rs. 3,910in 1985-1987 (Table 1.2.2). During a period of ten years, the total fees increased marginallyonly by 5%.But, there was a sea change in the Placement of our students. Now, our PGDM diploma became a magic password to corporate sectors. The placement of our one hundred students was completed in just two days. In mid 1980s, there were unseeingly squabble among recruiting companies each wanting to become first to offer posts. While, in mid 1970s, the problem of our students lays not so much in finding job but in gaining acceptance. The Average salary on Placements of our students in mid-1970 was Rs.3,500 per month while it increased to Rs. 42, 000 per month in mid 1980s.

By analysing our placement data from our Annual Reports for successive five years (1979 - 1983), Sancheti found that only 7% to 22% of our students were placed in Public sector, while 78% to 93% joined Private sector. She found that our students were overwhelmingly preferred Large and Medium Foreign Companies. Their second choice was Public Sector Enterprise and a few was in family owned Large and Medium Indian Companies. Thus, our students ignored the demand for Agriculture and Rural Industries, Small Scale Business in urban areas, Government and Semi-Government Organizations. So, the Institute's placement lacked the grater relevance to Indian economy (Sancheti, 1986).

d) The Faculty Members

The strength of faculty members increased sharply, as some new faculty members joined in the first decade of Joka Campus. The number of faculty member increased from 38 in 1975-1976 to 50 in 1985-1986. Among these 50 faculty members, 10 were in Operation Research including Statistics, 9 in Behavioural Science 8 in Finance and Control, 6 each in Economics and PPM (including Sociology, Regional Development and Law), 4 each in

MIS and Marketing and 3 in PMIR. So, Operation Research, Behavioural Science and Finance & Control groups combined hold half of the total faculty members. But, faculty members in Economics were les but it was a powerful lobby. The newly recruited Faculty members were - B N Srivastava, S Bose, V N Reddy, S Khanna, D Nayyar, M S Mishra, S N Munshi, S Roy, S K Ghosh, A J Sen, B Chakraborty, A Sengupta and R Ghosh. The newly recruited women Professors were- Mrs. Leena Chatterjee, Jainab Ahmed and Ruby Roy Dholakia. By this time, some faculty members who joined early in EB Campus were either super annulated or left.Those were - Prof. Ajit K Biswas, ChittaMitra, Ranjit Sau, Deepak Nayyar, Nikhilesh Dholakia, Ruby Roy Dholakia and Manish Bhattacharya.

e) Fellowship Programme

The Fellowship Programme was aimed at fulfilling the shortage of management teachers. It started in 1971 at EB Campus. Till 1984, in the Joka Campus, the Institute awarded Fellowship to 24 students, of which only one was women. In the first decade, on an average, only two students have completed their Fellowship annually. Among these 24 Fellows, 6 were in 1983, 5 in 1976, 4 in 1977 and a few in most of the years (Table 1.2.3). Out of 24 Fellows - 8 were in Operations Research, 7 in Finance& Control, 4 in Economics, 3 in Marketing, one each in Organisational Behaviour and Regional Development.So, most of the Fellows were in Operations Research and Finance. & Control (Table 1.7.4).

During this time, those who completed Fellowship in Economics were Mr. R Vaidyanathan, Dilip Dutt and Sushil Khanna, with whom I have rapport and friendship.Other Fellows known to me were Mr S CRoy who joined at a University in USA with our ex-Director J K Sengupta. Mr. Mahadeb Nandi joined Tel Bhavan of ONGC at Dehradun. Mr. Dilip Roy appeared at the Indian Statistical Service Examination and stood second at All India level. He joined as Director of CSO in Calcutta and left this job and later joined as Head of a Management Institute under Burdwan University. Other Fellows known to me were - N Ramchandran, Sushil Khanna and Ramanuj Majumder, who became our faculty.

During first fifteen years since the inception of the FP, it had a limited success. It failed to attract more students. In 1979, only ten students were admitted, of whom two students dropped out. Nanda (1981) Committee reported that "1/3 of those who joined had discontinued". The FP was plagued by certain structural limitations, as the FP without a formal Ph.D. degree, have not attracted brilliant students. In 1983, it has been proposed that FP be modified to 'allow for specialisation in all branches of management'. Thus, it make possible to follow Fellowship Program in Economic. Prof. Chandra asked me to complete a MA degree, so that I can be absorbed in FP. But, I could not fulfil his dream.

f) Executive Development Programme and In-Company Training

One of the proposed academic activities in the Institute was a program of training for already employed executive at the middle and top level. The Executive Development Programme (EDP), aimed to spread the value of the Institute. Over the years, EDPs has remained extremely popular and the scope of EDPs has also broadened. The EDPs are designed with the objective of providing practicing managers the insight into managerial concepts and implementing strategies in functional areas. In mid-1980s, when EDPs failed the anticipated response, it began to supplement by a variety of Extension Programmes for junior and middle level managers. During the first decade at Joka, the duration of EDPs varied from 2 to 5 days and the fees varied from Rs. 500 to Rs. 1500. After 1980, EDPs were being held in our own EDP Centre at Tata Hall, which provide all facilities. The Institute initiated another training programme called -In-Company Training", where our faculty members will go to the Company's office and train their managers. The Companies will fix the number of participants and our faculties took classes by rotation.

g) Research and Centre for Management and Development Studies (CMDS

The research became an integral part of the Institute to encourage creative activities among faculty members. In 1976 all five research centres were amalgamated under the Centre for Management and Development Studies

(CMDS), the Research Wing of the Institute. Now, all research projects were sponsored through the CMDS under the Chairpersonship of Prof. Kamini Adhikari and Dr. K K Chaudhuri as Secretary. The establishment of CMDS has also created a problematic situation. Some faculty members were by-passing the CMDS and carrying out research with separate budgetary provisions and hiring their own research staffs. It had created tensions among faculty members who were with CMDS and who were beyond CMDS. A few years later, a further review was carried out on functioning of CMDS in 1979. In the research front, more new projects came in and it resulted an increase in number of projects staffs.

Till 1975, the IIM Calcutta witnessed the establishment of eight Research Canters in EB Campus. Two more research centres were added in 1980, thus the number of research increased to ten. The newly formed canters were - Agricultural Marketing Centre headed by Prof. Chitta Mitra and Rural Development Management Canter (RDMC) headed by Prof. Madhu S Misra. During 1977 to 1984, the Institute completed 45 research projects and 30 projects were in hand. Many of the research projects in 1983-1984 have transcended disciplinary boundaries. The focus is now on analysis of development problems. The emphasis was on research in Public Sector, Small Scale Industries and traditional Indian business. Now, research in Agriculture, Health Care and Education became an increased concern. Out of 33 projects, 11 started more than five years ago (Sancheti, 1986).

Dr. Kamini Adhikari was continuing with her Center for Entrepreneurship Studies with Mr. K. K.Choudhury, a Research Fellow and six Project Assistants.When Prof D P Sinha left, Prof. Binod Kumar was supervising the Center for Management of Education System, with three Research Fellows –S Bandopadhayay, S Bhattacharya and A P Sinha. All of them left the Institute and found their job elsewhere. Later, Miss. Nilanjana Kundu joined as a Post-Doctoral Research Fellow and she left for joining in Calcutta University. Prof. Satyesh Chakraborty headed the Centre for Management of Urban System with some Research Fellows and a team of project assistants headed by Mr. Abdul Halim. Prof. Arun K Choudhry completed his "Second West Bengal Project"with his associate M N Pal. Prof. Nirmal Chandra was continuing his centre of 'Agrarian Change and Peasant Organization'. His research team Atulbabu, Asit babu and me, were conducting field Survey in different villages. I used to visit those villages for a week and returned to assistProf. Chandra.

Prof. Chiatta Mitra undertook a World Bank Funded project to study the existing Agricultural Marketing Practices in West Bengal. His team leader was Mr. Suniti Manna along with five project Assistants and a dozen of field investigators. They were accommodated in a rented house outside the Campus. Moreover, the Rural Development Management Center was headed by Prof. Madhu S Misra with eight Project Assistants. The Center was continuously publishing 'The Directory of Voluntary Organisations" and "Bibliography on Rural Development". The Center was also conducted EDPs for Health Services Personnel in Tata Hall.Mrs. Shyamali Adhikaribeing a Project Assistant did Secretarial jobs.

6. THE DECADE OF RE-ORIENTATION

a) Attempts to Reorientation and Indigenisation

In 1977, Mr. Hiten Bhaya,Ex-Chairman of Hindustan Steel, was appointed as Director, who initiated a re-examination of Institute's priorities and direction to orient more specifically towards India's need. He felt that a significant change has taken place in Indian economy during last fifteen years (1962-1977). But, the management education in the Institute had not responded sufficiently. Despite a large industrial expansion in Public sector, our students are mostly joining MNCs (Multi-National Corporations). Thus, the needs of new industries were not met. Nearly 75% of our students came from IITs, but most of them took job in Marketing. Thus, we are wasting our engineering skills (Sancheti, 1986).

In this situation, the Director along with some faculty members felt for re-formulation of our priorities. They felt the need of the development of new areas like - Transport, Rural Development, Small Scale Industries and Agriculture.On the academic side, the need arose for replenishment of indigenous materials of fundamental, functional and applied nature. There were also needs for research in Behavioural areas, which are culture specific. All these efforts have been preceded in the official publication "Official Report" in 1981. Thus, the direction for development of the Institute began to change under the leadership of our Director, Mr. Hiten Bhaya. In 1980s, the emphasis was placed on the goal of Indigenization and relevance. It stressed the recognition of the need for India and making management education more culture specific. A formal re-statement of our goals has been initiated in 1978. In 1985, a shift had occurred in Institute's priorities and interests, Director Prof. Aiyar said "we are working towards appropriate directions and we have been operating successfully for last two decades. Now we may think of Training Programmes, Certificate Courses and EDPs. In view of the above, the Institute undertook several measures.

In 1981, the Institute offered specialties packages in three areas. Those were - General Management, Development Management and Management of Systems and Operations. The number of courses increased substantially as new courses were introduced on Trans-National Corporations, International Economics, Politics of Development, Management of Regional and Urban Development. Prof. S K Chakraborty defined a unique 'Indian Approach to Management' based on the wisdom of ancient Hindu Texts and Scriptures and stressed on the 'Ethos' in the Management. In 1992, he established Management Center for Human Values (MCHV) in the Campus with the help of Japanese Government. Prof. Jacob Mankidy also stressed on the Indian Cultural Heritage in management. All these efforts were towards 'Indigenization" of our management education.

During 1980s, the Institute has undertaken independent stance on admission procedures for PGP. The admission policies have been modified substantially and the number and content of courses have also been modified. In 1981, the Review Committee suggested the modification of the "Autonomous" status of the Institute. As the Institute is playing a vital role in national development, the Central Government should declare the Institute as "Institute of National Importance". Regarding autonomous statues, Director Prof. Aiyar said 'Flexibility in an environment of high intellectual calibre provides the setting for innovative behaviour. We have been constantly working on this direction'.

Over a period of time, a system has developed where the faculties reigns supreme in the decision making process. Prof. Aiyar remarked that the participative decision making process have delayed in arriving at a consensus. A significant shift occurred in the attitudes towards recruitment of new faculty members. The Institute started recruiting young and bright people who have potentials. In 1985, faculty recruitment was supplemented by the recruitment of Fellowship holders from IIMA and IITs. In the Institute, some of our Research Fellows were also recruited as faculty members. In 1985, Sushil Khanna, N Ramchandran and Ramanuj Maumder were recruited as Professor after completion of their Fellowship.

b) Introduction of a New Programme at City Office

A two-year evening course- "Certificate Programme in General Management" (CPGM) was introduced in 1981 in the City office. This programme was meant for working persons who could join classes after office hours. The classes were held at our City Office at Harrington Mansion in central Calcutta. The classes held at 6 p.m. to 9 p.m. with 30 to 40 students. Our faculty members were provided transport from Joka to City Office for taking classes. This city office had a library and other facilities like Fax, Xerox and Typing.About ten staffs were deputed there by rotation from the existing employees at Joka campus. Some employees were eager to join there, as the office starts at 12 noon and close at 9 p.m. As the Joka campus had no Fax Machines, I went to our City office first time in 1981 to Tele-Fax a Research Paper of Prof. Chandra for a seminar going to be held at Mexico. Because of rough weather, a forty page paper took about two hours to send it, even though the concerned staff helped me a lot. I went there again in 1990 onthe inaugural ceremony of an EDP hosted by my colleagues - Dr. Santwan Choudhuri and Dr. Tridib Chakraborty.

7. INSTABILITY IN THE INSTITUTE

a) Fragmentation Among Faculty Members

The most explicit form of fragmentation was manifested in the sharp division between faculty members of Basic disciplines, Quantitative areas and Functional areas. There were conflict among the faculty members in Economics, Statistics, Finance and Marketing. Mr. Bhaya, the then Director acknowledged that division. The dichotomy between the faculty members in the basic disciplines and in functional areas remained, which resulted some departmentalization. The diversity in outlook and orientation among faculty members had aggravated the problem of fragmentation and each group was competing for powers. The concrete decisions are seldom taken, which generates lots of dissatisfaction. The present Director, Prof. Aiyar thought that 'the polarization into Basic disciplines and Management is not the right way to look at. There is a need for both the basic disciplines and applied disciplines to co-exist within the Institute and to help each other grow'(Sancheti, 1986).

b) Changes in Leadership and Stabilisation

In the first decade at Joka, Prof. Jati K Ssengupta was Director till 1977. Later, Mr Hiten Bhaya, the Chairman of Hindustan Steel joined as Director for five years (1977-1982). After that, Prof. Ramswamy P Aiyer, a faculty member of MIS group was selected as Director and continued for two consecutive terms. During the time of Mr. Bhaya, there was no crisis. So was the situation during the first term (1982-1987) of Prof. Aiyer. But it worsened during second term of Prof. Aiyer (1987-92). Since 1977, with the appointment of Mr. Bhaya as Director and the continuous effort of next Director Prof. Aiyer, the leadership has been more stable. At that time, the administrative structures have changed substantially. The distinction between academic and general administration holds good today as before. According to Nanda Committee, the role of Director was 'all paper work should be removed from the table of Director whose work is of creative leadership'. The Committee recommended that the functional Chairman should spend a minimum time on non-academic activities.

c) The Left Out Research Fellows

Initially, the Research Fellows (RFs) were absorbed in the Institute as Assistant Professors. In 1980, the number of Research Fellows increased much and there was no scope to absorb them. Hence, Miss Sipra Mukherjee joined as a faculty in IIMA, Dr. KKChaudhuri joined at the Institute of Port Management in Calcutta. Mr. Anjan Ghosh joined as a Professor at the Centre for Studies in Social Science in Calcutta. Four Research Fellows -Bappaditya Chakraborty, N Ramchandran, Sushil Khanna and Ramanuj Majumder became Professor after completing FPM. Mr. Subhendu Dasgupta, Bhubanesh Mishra, Swaraj Bando-padhya, Swapan Bhattachary, Arun Sinha, Sweta Majumdar left out for new jobs elsewhere.

d) Movements of Research Staff and Land Losers

All Project assistants were placed in consolidated pay scales without allowances. When Ms. Krishna Chatterjee, a Project Assistant was terminated, she prayed to the Labour Tribunal for re-appointment. The then CAO, Mr. D C Bhattacharya was very stiff person and do not consider her case sympathetically. In this situation, the Project assistants formed 'Research Staff Association', a registered bodyunder the Societies Act, demanded permanent status. Later, a section of General Staff also joined with us and formed the "Research and General Staff Association." Our previous Director Mr. Bhaya while leaving the Institute wrote a 'note' to consider our case to the next Director Prof. Aiyar. At last, the Project assistants were in the process of regularization since 1982 and became permanent in 1987.

When my daughter was born in May 1985, I applied for reimbursement of Nursing Home charges, as we were not entitled any medical allowances. Prof. Chandra recommended to our Director Prof. Aiyer, who gave clearances for the payment. It was our first move for demanding medical allowance. There were frequent movements in the Campusin lunch time during the Directorship of Prof. Aiyar. These movements were for regularization of Project Assistant, Canteen staffs and Land losers etc. were the main issues.

The agitated employees pasted Posters and Placards and shouted slogans during lunch break. There was blockades in main gate by the wards of land losers who lost their land while building our Campus. There were two Employees Unions - one dominated by Congress and other by CPIM

e) Political Stabilityand the Institute

When the Institute moved to Joka, Mr. S S Roy was the Chief Minister of the State till 1977. After that, the President's Rule was imposed. During these turbulent days, Mr. A L Dias was the Governor of the State. During the period of political instability, the practice of Chief Minister becoming our Chairman has changed. So, the Governor Mr. Dias became our Chairman in 1976. He visited our Joka Campus first time in 1976 to attend a Board Meeting held in the Campus. He visited this Campus again in 1977 to attend 12th Annual Convocation of the Institute (Raj Bhaban, 2006). At that time, I was a Project Assistant and met Mr. Dias to hand over our memorandum for regularisation of our services.

In June 1977, Mr. Jyoti Basu became the Chief Minister and Mr. T N Sing became Governor of the State. The first Left Front Government was sworn in by Mr. Dias. Mr. Jyoti Basu hosted a farewell dinner for Mr. and Mrs. Dias. In the farewell Broadcast, Mr. Dais was very much concerned about the burning problems of the State. He discussed the problems of influx of refugees, promotion of intensive agriculture, effective PDS etc. He pleaded for an atmosphere in educational Institutes conductive to study and research (Raj Bhvan, 2006). After that, the Chairman of the Institute was being nominated by the Central Ministry. The next nominated Chairman by Central Ministry was Mrs. Sheila Kaul. I also met her in the Campus in 1980 with the same plea. The rampant political instability that was existed in the State became stable after mid-1977. The political unstable situation that culminated in the victory of Left Front in the State, It was viewed with great appreciation by some of our faculty members in IIM Calcutta (Sancheti, 1986).

8. MY FIRST DECADE IN JOKA

a) My First Day in Joka

In 1977, Prof. Chandra came to my Hostel room at EB and asked me to be ready in the next mooring around 7 a.m. I reached the EB Campus around 7 a.m. and saw a Truck is waiting for me. All the filled upvillage schedules, computation sheets, files and folders along with Almirah, Chair, Table and Facit machine were loaded in the truck. The Truck followed the Strand Road on the bank of river Ganges and crossed, the Cossipore railway yard, passed under the Hooghly Bridge, Princep Ghat to reach Khidirpore then followed the Diamond Harbour road and finally reached Joka at 11 a.m. So, my first journey to Joka campus was on Truck by sitting in driver's cabin. I can remember a travelogue titled 'Truck Bahane McMohane' by Nabanita Debsen, wife of Amartya Sen.So, for the first time, I came to Joka by sitting in Driver's cabin of a Truck from EB campus.

I reached an unknown place full of trees, grass and lakes. By passing a lake, I reached near a building built for residential purpose. I was allotted a room there and I stored there the goods I carried from EB Camus. After a few months, opposite to my room, a Branch of State Bank of India was opened. In the first floor of that building, there was our Accounts Office. When I reached Joka for the first time, the new office was under full fledge construction. There were no '*pucca*' roads and drains with rough roads full of brickbats. Arranging all items in my room, I went to meet Prof. Chandra, in B Block first floor (B-203). After a few months, I was again evicted to third floor of the newly constructed Administrative Building in 1978. Here I met Miss Nalanjana Sanyal, a Research Fellow attached to Prof. B Kumar. Within a year, she left for joining the Calcutta University as Professor. In 1980, I was again evicted from Administrative Building to B Block ground floor room no B-102. I have to share this room with eight people, including three Research Fellows, one typist, three persons Chandra's team and the Security Officer Cornel Nag. Around 1982, I was again evicted to ground floor of C Blok room no.C-103. In this room,

I have to share my room with six Project Assistants. In the first decade at Joka, I moved to different rooms in different buildings.

b) Official Work

During 1977-1982, I was engaged in surveying eighteen villages in ten districts of West Bengal from Digha to Darjeeling. Generally, I spent one week in the field survey and next week in Joka Campus to assist Prof. Chandra in his research and academic activities. The academic activities were reviewing the student's answer scripts, to put total marks, checking if he has missed to put marks, final tabulation of marks and submit to PGP office. In 1978, he was studying the existing monopoly practices followed by Indian Large Business Houses like - Tata, Birla, JK, Mafatlal etc. He gave me a book 'The Corporate Private Sector: Concentration, Ownership and Control" by R K Hazari. The Report on MRTP by Subimal Dutt (1966), has estimated that, 48 Large Industrial House having assets above 21 crores each, collectively own Rs. 4000 crores. The Birla family owns 280 companies, Tata family owns 84 companies and so were others (Forum 2007).

The Dutt Committee report consists of business statistics like value of fixed assets, working capital, number of employees etc. of those companies for few years. He asked me to up to date the relevant data from the National Library, Commercial Library and our Library. After collection of relevant data, he asked me to compute some statistic. Finally, it was resulted as an article, "Monopoly Capital, Private Corporate Sector and the IndianEconomy: A Study in Relative Growth 1931-76".It was published in EPW in 1979, where he observed that "under Indian conditions, it is quite possible that the companies are not 'legally' inter-connected, but are in fact controlled by one business family. The widespread practice of '*benami* shareholders, where by the de facto owner for a variety of reasons has the shares recorded in the member of a relative or a protégé helps to underscore this above lacuna."

In 1980, Prof. Chandra took me to the National Library to compile various data on Indian economy. I have also visited CSO library and Commercial library. After one year of frequent visit to these Libraries, I have collected a huge data, as Prof. Chandra directed me to do some calculations. By this time, he also directed me to evaluate the cost of maintenance and new buildings in my own village. After completing this task, he was delighted by seeing the extent of value addition in rural housing sector. It was quite different from the Central Government's estimates in calculating National Income. Lastly, it gave birth the article "Long Term Stagnation in the Indian Economy, 1900-1975, published in EPW in April 1982.

Since 1980, Prof Chandra's office was in B Blok first floor Room number 203. I have a separate table in his room. In 1980, another table was added as Mr. Sudip Choudhuri joined as a Teaching Assistant to help Prof. Chandra's teaching in PGP. Sudip was doing his Ph. D. at JNU in New Delhi. After receiving Doctorate Degree, he was absorbed in the Institute as Assistant Professor in 1984. Me and Sudip were in the same age group and became friend. Around 1980, a young man frequently visited Prof. Chandra's office. He was Mr. Bernard De'Mello a Fellowship student under his supervision. He used to come regularly at the end of the day to discuss his academic matters with Prof. Chandra. He completed his Fellowship in 1988 and left. After a few years, he joined the EPW in Bombay as Assistant Editor. Once he came to the Institute and I showed him that I have completed a Bibliography on Agriculture on the basis of articles published in EPW. He encouraged me to do so for other issues, but I failed.

c) Personal Work

i) Research and Publications

During 1977-1983, I published nineteen Features written in Bengali. Among these Features, eight were in *Bhumilaxmi*, a bi-weekly of Ananda Bazar Patrika group and five in *DainikBasumati* a Bengali daily both published from Calcutta. The rest four were published in *Curtain,* a fortnightly magazine published from Hooghly. Moreover, I published two Features in English in 'PTI Feature' published from Bombay.In *Bhumilaxmi* (1977-1980), I have discussed the topics - Economic miseries in rural life, Agricultural labour and minimum wages, Pesticides in agriculture, Villages in West Bengal, Increasingtrend of poverty, Economics of jute cultivationand Mud house and *pucca*house in villages of West Bengal. In CURTAIN, a Fortnightly Little Magazine from Hooghly, a lengthy article has been published in four parts in 1981 on 'Peasantry of West Bengal' (Banglar Krishak). In *Dainik Basumait* (1982 -1983), I have discussed the topics –Agriculturalprice, Income inequality, Consumer expenditure, Indebtedness and Savings of rural households in West Bengal. Two Articles written in English in "PTI Features" in 1982-1983 were on the Importance of Invalid Votes and Role of Panchayat Leaders in Rural Development.

In 1977-78, the Left front came to power in West Bengal. On the basis of our village survey data, I have collected socio - economic data of the elected Panchayat Members in just completed Panchayat election in the State. I completed a write up on the class character of the newly elected Panchayat members in different villages in different districts. To collect the names of elected members, I went to Government Press at Alipore to purchase the Gazettes, mentioning the names of newly elected Panchayat members in all the districts of West Bengal. On the basis of our field survey data, I found that the Panchayat representatives were mostly from poor and middle class, who may serve the Panchayat well.

By that time, our Institute was going to organize a National Seminar on Research Gaps in Management. The Chairman of the Seminar was Prof. Arun K Choudhuri who asked me to explain the relevance of my paper in the seminar. Dr. K K Choudhuri, a Research Fellow was the Secretary of the seminar helped me to explain. My paper was selected for the seminar. This article was chapterised in the Seminar proceeding "Research Gaps in Management" Edited by Prof. A K Choudhuri et el, and published by our Publication Department. I have also presented another paper 'Management of Rural Credit Towards the Upliftment of Rural Poor' in the Seminar organised by the Comprehensive Area Development Corporation (CADC), a Govt. of West Bengal Undertaking.

ii) Academic Activities

During this time, our Director Prof. Aiyer insisted me for a Masters Degree. So, I met Prof. D K Sinha, VC of Jadavpur University to allow me in their evening course - M. Sc in Mathematics. As the course was solely for working school teachers, he cannot help. Then, I took admission in the Correspondence Course in M. A. in Economics at the Rajasthan University. The University provided me the Study Material but, within a month they send the Admit Card and asked to appear at the first Term examination to be held at Jaipur. I could not go there. So, studying of my M. A, in Economic at Rajasthan University ended. In 1978, I appeared in an admission test for the Post Graduate Diploma in the Institute of Rural Management, Anand (IRMA) in Gujarat. The venue of the examination was the Presidency College in Calcutta. After a month, I received no letter from the Institute. One of our Professors, Vidyanada Jha have qualified and completed the same course from IRMA.

In 1978-1979, I appeared two times for the 'Statistician Diploma' examination in Indian Statistical Institute. As I could not succeed, I requested Prof. Ambuj Mohanty, but he could not find time, I approached Prof. Sujit Basu, who advised me to attend his PGP classes and have done so. By that time, my friend accompanied me to Prof. Rahul Mukherjee of Calcutta University. I was attending his tuition in his residence in Netaji Nagar in Calcutta. It took more than four hours to and fro journey from my village home. After two months, he joined ISI and could not continue my tuition. So, studying of Statistician Diploma ended.

At last in 1981, I joined a six week full time Training program in Indian Statistical Institute. The course was 'Programming and Applications of Electronic Computers'. The Computer at that time was only Mini Frame Computer of IBM, but no Desk Top Computers. In Mini Frame Computers, a user can put command not by pressing a key but through Punch Cards. I have learnt Punch Card operating and data processing techniques. I also learnt Mathematical Analysis, Interpolation, and Extrapolation etc. I have attended classes of Prof. B P Adhikari, husband of Prof. Kamini Adhikari and classes of Prof. J Roy, an eminent Professor. I received the 'Certificate of Merit' after completing the course. During this time, I could not go to Joka as the course was a full time one and have taken permission from our Director and the course fee of Rs. 200 was disbursed by my office.

iii) Finding a Permanent Job

When the CMDS was formed in 1976, I was offered second appointment by the then Director, Prof. Aiyar. Then, I was placed in the consolidated pay scale of Rs. 400 – 30 – 700, without any allowances. Because of my two years of experience, I was placed with two increments at Rs. 460 per month. In 1980, the Business Standard Research Bureau (BSRB) of ABP group advertised for a post of Statistical Assistant. I applied for the post and they send me a call letter for an interview. As the letter reached via Bishnupur Post Office, it reached after a few days. Even the date of interview was over; I went to BSRB and met Mr. Kuruvilla, who gave me some calculations. After an hour, he asked me to meet Mr. Tushar K Mohanti, head of BSRB. I met him and discussed about my publications in '*Bhumalaxmi*'. After a few months, my colleague Miss. Krishna Chatterjee joined there. She left the job and as she was re-insisted in the Institute after a Court Order.

In 1981, the State Government advertised for recruitment of 17 District Evaluation Officers in Panchayat Department. I appeared for the examination conducted by the State Public Service Commission. I was very much exited as I have stood first in the written examination. A few days later, I appeared for an interview in front of the Government officials and showed them my paper "Panchayat and Management of Rural Economic Growth'that I presented a few days ago in our seminar. Within few days, I received the Appointment letter and sowed it to Prof. Chandra. I was eager to leave the Institute for a permanent job. But, he insisted me not to join there as our case is being considered. Finally, in 1982 our case was being considered for permanent positions. The process for absorbing us was being considered by the Board of Governors. In 1987, I was absorbed as Research Assistant in permanent scale of pay with all admissible allowances.

9. UPSURGE OF LEFT POLITICS IN WEST BENGAL

During 1967-1972, the Left politics in West Bengal significantly enlarged the power base by strengthening the labour militancy in urban areas and land-grab movements in rural areas. During 1967, our Professors Nitish R De and Suresh Srivastava have written a series of articles in EPW about the "Gheraosin West Bengal" (De and Srivastava, 1967). Mr S S Ray became CM, by undemocratically rigging the elections in 1972 resorted to a reign of semi-fascist terror. Throughout his term as CM, he could do little to curb the continuing political violence and industrial dispute backed by Left politics.Mr. Kohli (Kohli 1991) described this climate of violence as '*goonda* – politicians - police' nexus in Calcutta politics.

The formation of the Left Front Government in West Bengal was under the leadership of Comrade Jyoti Basu. The culmination of decade long struggles by various sections of the people have resulted the formation of LF government. The Left Front came to power by gaining peoples verdict in June, 1977. In 1978, the Left Front government introduced "*Operation Barga*" and set security of tenancy rights to farmers. Next year, the Left Front government established a decentralised model of local self-government through a three-tier Panchayati Raj. The major initiatives of the first Left Front government (1977-1982) were to carry out thoroughland reforms and establishing a vibrant Panchayati Raj. On the formation of Left Front Government in West Bengal, some of our Professors were delighted and some were offered top positions in different State organisations as Chairman.

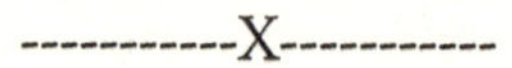

-----------X----------

CHAPTER 1.4

DECADE OF EXPANSIONS AND REDUCTION OF CENTRAL GRANTS: 1986-1995

1. INTRODUCTION

This decade has witnessed the expansion of Infrastructures, Crisis in Leadership, Reduction of Central Government Grants, regularization of a batch of staffs and celebration of the Silver Jubilee of the Institute. The Institute completed a successful journey of twenty five years in 1987. In this decade, the expansion of infrastructures were - the construction of Administrative Building, CAM (Computer Aided Management) Centre Building, the conical shaped '*stupa*' of the MCHV (Management of Human Values) building and two large sized classroom (L3 & L4). Now, the newly constructed Library Building stared functioning. The Director, Prof. Aiyar continued his second term and Mr. Subir Chowdhury became the next Director in 1992 and continued till 1997. In view of the New Economic Policy started in India during 1990s, the Central Government started curtailment of Institute's grant since 1992. So, the Institute had to be self reliant by earning from various sources. During last term of Prof. Aiyar, he had to recruit about fifty staffs and regularized them in Institute pay roll. This resulted a huge jump inthe monthly salary bill of the Institute.

2. CAMPUS LIFE

The student wing OIKOS, the "IIMC- Club" that take care of the Campus greenery. In the Campus, construction completed for five Hostels buildings well equipped with common room, study room and games room. Four Hostels are for men only while old one is Co-educational having separate wing for women students. There were several recreational facilities for Sports, Drama and Photography etc. The Campus has a number of concrete blocks but not designed for surrounded lakes and rice fields. The unsupervised free hostel life, playingof Bridge and drinking a lot of Rums and discover students as an adult.

3. LIBRARY

The Library has 16000 volumes of Management Journals. Our library is the largest management library in Asia. About half a dozen of women Library Assistants were recruited around 1987. In 1990. Mr. Ranajt Mukherjee retired and Ms. Swati Bhattachary was appointed as Librarian in 1992. So, the library was headed by a woman and most Assistants were also women. The library was serving the needs of faculties, students and research staffs.

4. ESTABLISHMENT OF NEW CENTERS

a) CAM Canter

The fully air conditioned single floored building equipped with about fifty personal computers, an inkjet printer and a set of servers were installed with the help of Central Government in 1985. All the faculty members of MIS (Management Information Service) group were accommodated in this building. One room was reserved for the Computer Servicing Agency to look after the computers of the Faculty members and the students. Another room was used as a store room for supplying CDs (Compact Discs) for data storage, Ribbons and paper roll for printing. There was only a small class room.

b) Management Center for Human Values (MCHV)

The Management Centre for Human Values (MCHV) embodies the striving towards evolving the `Vedantic Ethic' from the Indian deep structure. It aims at bridging a vital gap between the `Protestant Ethic' of West and the `Confucian Ethic' of the East. A large segment of managers and professionals in India has for long been awaiting filling up of this end. The MCHV is the contemporary adaptations of the perennial corpus of Indian psycho-philosophical wisdom. It is to integrate the dimension of human values with the mainstream of skill-dominated management education. The lives and writings of many great modern Indians thinkers like - Rabindranath, Vivekananda, Gandhi and Aurobindo, were outstandingly in both purity and practicality. So, the MCHV, consecrated as it is to them, represents a commitment to discharge our '*rishi rin*' - debts to these sages.

The Institute had mandated a very special responsibility upon MCHV while blessing its birth in 1992. The Financial support from sources outside the government and the Institute budget were the Tata, UTI, HDFC, SBI, ACC etc, who come forward with donations. Now, the MCHV is financially self-sufficient in capital cost and recurring expenses. With such generous support from the donors, the MCHV became a reality and was consecrated on 1995, through a dignified inaugural ceremony. Prof. S. K Chakraborty of Finance & Accounting group has set up this MCHV Center. It is recognized as one of the first to use the "*shastras*' in management education. He introduced the Human Values and Indian Ethics in management education. The MCHV is entirely non-denominational center built among lush green environment in a '*stupa*'- shaped building. The MCHV center is located in a serene part of the campus and surrounded by beautiful gardens. Its striking conical buildings are architectural masterpieces on the outside and quite sanctums of learning and contemplation on the inside. The MCHV center offers unique experience to students and faculty members.

The large statue of Gautama Buddha erected in front of the MCHV was donated by the government of Japan. Our Ex-Director, Mr. Subir

Chowdhuri has attended the inauguration ceremony in 1994. Prof. Chakraborty was awarded as the "Best Management Teacher" in 1994 by the Association of Management Schools in India. But, some faculty colleagues of his own group asked him how is your 'Mandir' (Temple) going on? How pranimis are pouring in. I personally visited the MCHV in 1998 to attend the seminar by the eminent Economist Dr. Ankileswar Aiyer. After that, I visited the MCHV for several times to conduct PGP examinations as an Invigilator.

5. INTRODUCTION OF NEW COURSES

a) PGDCM

A two years residential full time Post Graduate Diploma in Computer Aided Management was introduced in 1992 to cater the needs of the Information age. This course was given additional emphasis on use of Information Technology in Management. The fifty seated PGDCM was in addition to existing PGP. In this year, the number of total student increased by fifty percent. The students of PGDCM will sit with PGDM students in first year, but they will sit in CAM center in second year classes and practice in computers.

b) PGDBM

The two years evening Certificate Programme in General Management (PGCGM) started in 1981 was upgraded to a three years diploma program called PGDBM in 1994, with an intake capacity of fifty students. The classes be held in our City Office at Harington Mansion in Central Calcutta and the timing will be same 6 p.m. to 9 p.m. as before.

c) LONG DURATION PROGRAMME

Around 1995, the Institute realized to develop a programme of longer duration. It intended to develop a six month to one year tailor-made program called –LDP.

6. FUNCTIONING OF THE INSTITUTE

a) Admission in PGP

The Post-Graduate Programme in management was continuing as usual. This is a two year full time compulsory residential programme.The eligibility for admission was judged by CAT (Common Admission Test) score, academic records, interview, group discussion and work experience. Candidates belonging to Scheduled Castes (SC) and Scheduled Tribes (ST) were enjoying their reservations. Now, there is no shortage of Women's hostel, so the Institute accommodated more than six women per year.

As two large classrooms L3 and L4 were ready, so the crisis of classroom has solved.The newly built CAMCanter is ready to use. Thus, the Institute Introduced a two years PGDCMin 1992. It became urgent to cater the growing needs of the Information Technology. The Common Admission Test (CAT) was introduced in 1983 and Prof. Binod Kumar was founding father of CAT examination in India. It was paper pencils base objective type questions for three IIMs (A, B & C). In 1990, against the total seat of 500, the number of aspirants was 2500 in three IIMs. Now, the number of IIMs increased and other private Management Schools were using our CAT score for their admission.

b) Number of Students

In second decade (1986-1995) in Joka, the intake in PGDM was 105 per year till 1991. But it increased to 150 for 50 additional intakes since 1992, when PGDCM was introduced (Table 1.2.1). In this time, a total of 1333 students were enrolled and 133 students enrolled annually at that time. The enrolment of women students increased from 9 to 15. In this decade, a total of 112 women students have enrolled. Annually, 11 women studentswere enrolled at that time.In this period, the representation of women was still below 10%.

c) Total fees and Placements

In the period 1986-1995, the total fees for two years were Rs.3,910 which increased to Rs. 82,000 in 1995-1996. So, tuition fees increased by twenty times in this decade, because of curtailment of Central Government grants. But, there was a sea change in the Placement of our students, as PGDM diploma became a magic password to corporate sectors. The placement of one hundred students have completed in just two days. Now, there were unseeingly squabble among recruiting companies each wanting to become first to offer posts. The Average annual salary on Placements of our students was Rs.30,000 in 1986-1987, but it increased to Rs.42,000 in three years i.e. in 1989-1990.

d) The Faculty Strength

The faculty strength increased sharply, as some new faculty members were recruited in this decade. The number of faculty member increased from 38 in 1975-1976 to 50 in 1985-1986 and now 60 in 1995-96. In 1995-1996, among the total sixty faculty members, eight were in MIS, seven each in Economics and Finance & Control and six in Operation Research. There were four faculty members in each of Marketing, Statistics and PMIR, while three each in OM and Sociology, two each in BS, RD, History and MCHV. The rest groups have only one each faculty. So, MIS, Economics, Finance & Control and Operation Research groups combined had majority of the faculty members. But, faculty members in Economics group were a powerful lobby. Among total 60 faculty members, 6 were women - Mrs. Kamini Adhikari, Zainab Ahmed, Mousumi Ghosh, Leena Chatterjee, Sunita Sing Sengupta and Annapurna Shaw. By this time, some faculty members have either super annulated or left.

e) Fellowship Programme

The Fellowship Programme was continuing as before. During this decade (1986-1995) in Joka, 23 students have been awarded Fellowship. Only two students have completed their Fellowship annually. Among them, 4 were in 1986, 1987, 1989, 3 in 1988, 2 in 1990, 1994 and one each in the rest of the years. So, most of them have been awarded Fellowship in first four years, 1986 to 1989. Among these Fellows, 7 were in Operations Management, 5 in Finance & Control, 3 in Economics, 2 each in Marketing and Management Information System and one each in Organisation

Behaviour, Regional Development, Social Studies and Human Resource Management. So, most of the Fellows were in Operations Management and Finance & Control. The Fellowship Thesis was supervised mostly by Profs. S K Chakraborty, A K Chaudhuri, N K Chandra, B K Sinha. Prof. K K Bhattacharya and Prof. N K Rao, In1986, Mrs. Usri Sengupta became the second women Fellow and I was invited to attend her Thesis defence. I knew personally the Fellows in Economics - Mr. C Samba Murty, Bernard D'Mellow and S L Morris. Among other Fellows, Mr. Purosottam Sen, P K Sett and S D Vaidy became the faculty members in our Institute.

f) Executive Development Programme and In-Company Training

One of the academic activities in our Institute was a program of training for already employed executive at the middle and top level. The Executive Development Programme (EDP), aimed to spread the value of the Institute and to enhance the acceptance of our Graduates. Over the years, EDPs has remained extremely popular and the scope of EDPs has also broadened. The EDPs are designed with the objective of providing practicing managers the insight into managerial concepts and implementing strategies in functional areas. In 1980s, when our EDPs failed the anticipated response, the EDPs began to supplement by a variety of Extension Programmes for junior and middle level managers.In Joka campus, duration of EDPs varied from two to five days. The fees charged for the programme varied from Rs. 500 to Rs. 1500, depending upon the venues. After 1980, EDPs were mostly held in our own EDP Center at Tata Hall, which consists of classrooms, residential rooms, suits, Conference rooms and Dining Hall. The Institute initiated another type of training programme - "In-Company Training". In this type of training, our faculty members will go to the Company's office and train the managers of the Company. In this training, number of participants will be fixed by the Company and a few faculty members will take classes by rotation.

7. MANPOWER IN THE INSTITUTE

During 1995-1996, the manpower strength in the Institute reached to its peak at 472. Among them, 60 were faculty members, of which 53 were regular and 7 were visiting full timer. Among 400 administrative staffs, 20 were Senior Administrative Officers, 20 Administrative Officers, 30 Executive Assistants, 30 Stenos and 50 Typists. Moreover, there were 100 clerical staffs and 100 Group D staffs. The top officers were Chief Administrative Officer, Finance & Accounts Officer, Executive Engineer and Librarian. The Administrative Officers were attached to different sections like Accounts, Admission, Placement, PGP, FP, Publications, Engineering, Purchase and Transport. To assist these Officers, there were Executive Assistants. The Chairmen, of different functional areas were assisted by Administrative Officer, Executive Assistants, Clerical staffs and Group D staffs. The Administrative Officers - Asoke Sengupta, Animesh Basu, T N Naskar, Joydeb De, and N. Mascharak were de facto the administrators. The twelve Research staffs were assisting their concerned faculty members in teaching and research activities.

8. A. REDUCTION OF CENTRAL GRANTS

In early 1990s, the IMF and World Bank prescribed economic reforms in India. The neo-liberal economic policies have been introduced since then. This policy included Stabilization and Structural Adjustments, which required a drastic cut in public expenditure in higher education. 'Allocation for 8th and 9th Five Year Plans (FYP) combined during 1992 to 2002, touched all time low at 7% to 8%, while it was 25% in 4th FYP (1969-1974). The drastic cut in public expenditure was recorded most in technical and professional education (Tilak 2012). In 1992, a second Review Committee headed by Dr. V Kurien, taking note of the national fiscal crisis, proposed that IIMs stop depending on the Government.

It suggested that Corpus funds to be created at each IIM that the Government put to next five years. The Report proposed that IIMs stop depending on Government grant and the IIMs must be given more autonomy and must develop financial independence. 'The government thought to freeze the non-plan maintenance grants of the IIMs at the level of 1991-1992. It has brought home the urgency for the IIMs to augment their own resources... the Committee believed that, there is good scope for taking up a variety of measures by the IIMs for raising their internal revenues such measures include upward revision of the fee structure, charging recruitment fees during placements...Steps should be taken to build Corpus Fund in the Institute' (Kurien, 1992).

The Committee estimated that an IIM with 800 students can generate Rs. 40 to 50 Cores by tuition fees and Consultancy. They measured the staffing index as the ratio of administrative staff to academic staff. They observed that IIMs are over staffed, so they should reduce the work force. Subsequently three IIMs (A, B & C) decided not to avail any Government grant and create their own Corpus funds. According to Ministry of Human Resource and Development (MHRD), 3.35% of total central budget for higher education goes to IIMs having 0.12% of total students. Till now, IIMs have received a lot of attention as a favourite child. They are autonomous, free to hike fees, hire faculty and manage themselves, without any Government interference. Thus, the IIMs should be persuaded to take step to generate additional resources, so that they became self-reliant. So, IIMs have taken steps as fee hike, increase in intake and introduction of new courses.

The MHRD recommended that IIMs Professors should spent 45% time on classroom teaching of PGP, 25% on executive education, 15% on research and 15% in administration. The non-plan expenditure of IIM Calcutta increased much during five years, from Rs. 130 Lakh in 1985-86 to Rs. 272 Lakh in 1990-91. The major reason was implementation of Pay Commission. The Institute could meet about one-third of the expenditure from its own resources in 1990-91 (Kurien 1992). After the cut in Government subsidy, the Institute has been largely funding its activities through internal accruals. The Institute increasedits earning by increasing student intake, tuition fees, other charges etc. The large share of funding came from tuition fees and though Research, Consultancy and MDPs.

8. b. IMPACT ON REDUCTION OF GRANT

When the order of the central government reached the Institute in 1992, there was newly appointed Director Mr. Subir Chaudhuri. In the history of the Institute, a corporate executive headed the Institute first time for 1992 to 1997. He was an Ex-Director of ISWBM (Institute of Social Welfare and Business Management) in Calcutta. Earlier he was an executive in ICI (Imperial Chemical Industries). It was a bolt from the blue to him, as well as the Institute community. The Director called for general meeting to discuss the problems to all of us. Only a few faculty members attended, but the meeting was crowded with general staff specially group-D, as there was distribution of food packets. The Director began to elaborate the government Order and asked for suggestions. The general staff suggested intensive fishery in our seven lakes, some suggested cultivation of medicinal plants and others suggested planting of large valuable trees Seguin, Sal etc. in the campus. The Director also elaborated some steps to reduce Institute's expenditure.

As the Kurien Committee remarked that the Institute is over staffed. So, the first step will be reduction of employees by retrenchment of some over-aged Group D staffs. Among the clerical staff, he suggested one family one job, among the working couples, one of them be sacked. Some employees have brothers and sisters working here, so one of them be sacked. Finally, none of these materialized and continued as before. In order to reduce cost, he intended to purchase daily News Papers in the evening, when it is cheap. To reduce electricity bill, he engaged some employees to put off the fan and light, when no one is in the room. He engaged one person who resides in the campus, to put off the unnecessary street lights after 9 p.m. The dispatch section was endorsed to open the foreign mails of faculty members, to check whether it is personal or official. These were the silly attempts to reducing the office expenditure. In day to day need, he encashed the Institute's saving in NSC in Post office. All payments to vendors like supplier of Books, Printers etc to pay once in a fortnight.

But, he never thought of increasing intake in PGP, increasing the tuition fees, increasing the participation fees in EDPs; more research Projects and Consultancy etc. He called for a meeting with us, the Research Assistant to help in augment Institute income. Two of us offered EDP on their subjects, where they will take classes with the Institute's faculty members. After few EDP, some faculty made objection to Director that these EDPs are tarnishing the quality of Institute's EDPs. The EDPs run by the Research Assistants have more participants, as they make better liaison with the Corporate Houses.

9. MY ACTIVITIES: OFFICIAL AND PERSONAL

A. Official Work

a) Assistance to Dr. Ashok Mitra

In 1990, Prof. Chandra accompanied me to meet Dr. Ashok Mitra in his Sonali Apartment in Alipore. Dr. Mitra had some data analysis job relating to the Reserve Bank of India sponsored project on agricultural financing in different States of India. It was my regular job to attend Dr. Mitra in the morning around 9 a. m. in his Apartment before coming to Joka. After showing him the result of calculations that I have done, I returned to office around noon. As the main data was in a Tape Disc supplied by RBI, our CAM centre personnel have to be involved to run the data by Main Frame Computer in our office. They charged excusably, so Dr. Mitra could not pay any honorarium to me. After this job, in 1991 he asked me to meet at Rainy Park for another job. I was engaged in analysing data on Primary Education, in connection with the Education Commission headed by Dr. Mitra.This job continued for about two years and the Report on Education Commission was published

b) Assistance to Prof. Nirmal Chandra

In 1988, Prof. Chandra published his first book the "Retarded Economics", a collection of his articles published earlier in EPW during 1980s. The book has been published by Oxford University Press. I have done the "Index" pages at the end of this book with the help of Mr. Sushanta Ghosh, Librarian of CSSSR. I have put the corresponding page number in the index. For this job, I have been paid by the EPW.In 1986, Prof. Chandra was working on "Export-Oriented Growth" and "North and South Hemisphere" of the globe. In 1990, he was engaged in "Cost of German Unity". In 1984, he was working on "Peasantry as a Single Class: A Critique of Chayancy. This article has been published in EPW and adapted in Ashok Mitra edited book "The Truth Unites" in 1985.

Next year he was also engaged in the studies "Notes on Bukharin, Peasants and Soviet Industrialisation" and "Bukharin's Alternative to Industrialisation 'Without Forced Collectivisation'. In 1991, he worked on the problems of foreign investment in India in his article "Planning and Foreign Investment in Indian Manufacturing". In 1992, his interest was on the collapse of Soviet Union and he wrote "Was the Collapse of the CPSU Inevitable? A Political Essay. In 1993, his interest was on Russia's Sinking Economy: External Dimensions and India's Rouble Debt and the Depreciating Rouble. After Russia, he started studying China, and wrote "China's Tryst with Globalisation" in 1994. In the same year, he wrote "The Political Economy of Consumer Subsidies" in view of World Bank and IMF prescribed New Economic Policy in India. He also wrote "Trade, Technologyand Development" in EPW

c) Assistance to Profs. Hrishikesh Bhattacharya and Mousumi Ghosh

The day I was shifting from the rented house to my own house, that day both of them visited my new home. They went to me for data analysis job on Small Scale Industries in the State. The project was sponsored by the Government of West Bengal. I have to analyse the performance and prospects of small Industrial units spread all the districts of the State.

B. Personal Work

a) Education

In 1987, I have attended the Central Government Sponsored ten weeks MDP held at the Institute. The course was organized by Prof. Ambuja Mohanty of CAM centre and was meant for the Professors who will teach MCA (Master of Computer Applications) in their own Institutes. The participants were from the Bengal Engineering College and National Institutes of Technology in different States. It was full time course from 10 a. m. to 5 p.m. and the classes were taken by our Professors as well as

Professors from Jadavpur University and Indian Statistical Institute. In this Course, I have developed a railway reservation system with my partner Prof. Pal, who teaches at B E College at Shibpur in Howrah. Moreover, I have passed B A (Special Honours) in Economics in 1987 and M A in Economics from Rabindra Bharati University in 1989. Finally, I obtained a Masters degree in Economics.

b) Research and Publications

During 1990 to 1995, I published five Working Papers, of which, two were with Mr. Atul Manna, my colleague. Those papers delve with the development of Indian economy as well as development of the society. The first one was on the problem of Butter or Gun?The Central government was increasing Defence expenditure by reducing budget on food production. The second one was on social justice in the light of Mandal Commission Report. By analyzing our village survey data, we found that implementation of the Mandal Committee's Report was most urgent need in reducing the social inequality. The last three papers were on the impact of New Economic Policy introduced in India since 1991. These papers were on Agricultural Reforms, Structural Deterioration in Indian Agriculture and the impact of Globalisation on Indian Agriculture. The last paper was presented in the seminar organized by Indian School of Social Science in Calcutta and this was inaugurated by the then Finance Minister, Prof. Asim Dasgupta. The article "Winds of Change in Indian Agriculture" was published in two parts on August 26 and 27, 1993 in the Business Standard.

c) Regularisation of Project Staffs

The process of regularization started in 1982. The Project staffs were regularized as Research Assistant in 1987 and were entitled for Dearness Allowances, House Rent and Medical facilities. and also entitled to avail office transport. The office arranged a small bus to pick and drop for Howrah bound staffs. There were about sixteen staffs including - Engineer, Librarian, Accounts Officers, Executive, Stenos etc. The bus picked up us at 8:30 a. m. from Howrah station and reached office at 9:15 a. m. The bus leaves the Campus after office hour and reached Howrah at 7 p. m. The sufferings of public transport for last ten years reduced.

d) Uprooted From Village to Town

In 1986, I was uprooted from my village in Singur and settled in Serampore town, both in Hooghly district. The first reason was smoothening of wife's journey to her school. Earlier, she has to board four trains now she have to travel by one up and returned in down train. Earlier, she had to wait for about an hour in Saktigarh, famous for *Langcha, a variety of sweets.* Secondly, I shifted for my daughter's better education in town. From my village to Calcutta, I have to travel one hour journey with limited number of trains. But, in Serampore, the travel time has halved and with very frequent train services. There was no electricity in my village but it is available in Town. No piped water in my village, so one has to pump out from tube well for drinking, bathing, washing etc. No light in my village roads, so one has to walk in the dark. As there was no power supply, so no amusement in TV except Radio set.

There was no motor able road, so no Rickshaw, Toto, Autos were available in my village. Walking was the only mode of transportation and no Landline Telephone. But, rice, vegetables were grown in our own field. So, we have plenty of fresh vegetables from our fields. Only for groceries and stationery items, one has to go to market five kilometres away. The main problem was scarcity of helping hand especially women for doing household choir. Despite, one fourth of our villagers have no square meal a day, but they cannot do these jobs for social taboos. The most important problem was medical facilities. No MBBS doctor was available within five kilometres, only a few homeopaths. The health centre is about ten kilometres away, but no communicating road. The village life was cool, calm and lazy while urban life is fast, chaotic, without any social bandings. In 1986, I was uprooted from my village home to a rented house in Serampore town. In 1990, I have applied for the house building loan from the Institute and received the first instalment in 1990. I started my house building but not completed. Still I stated living in my own incomplete house since 1991 to save the house rent that I was paying.I built my own house in the "*Amulya Kanan*", a garden of ex-Zamindar of Goswami family.

In this time, Prof. Hrishikesh Bhattacharya and Mosoumi Ghosh were amazed by viewing the greenery around my plot. Prof. Sudip Choudhuri also came when my house was under construction in connection to his visit to relative's house here.There was no water supply no electricity only a wide kutcha road. For water, I bore a hand pump tube well for drinking water and cooking and a kutcha well for washing, gardening etc. The electricity connection was delayed for the dispute between the Calcutta Electricity Supply Corporation and West Bengal State Electricity Board. Finally, WBSEB supplied electricity at my home.

10. CALCUTTA IN THE DECADE: 1986 TO 1995

The "Economic Reforms" introduced in 1900s and the Central Government embarked upon economic liberalization in 1991. In this decade (1986-1995), overwhelming electoral victory of Left Front Government in the State continued. The intelligentsia and the civil society had traditionally supported them. "By the mid-1980s, disillusionment with socialism and with China had set in, and in 1989, there was the collapse of Berlin Wall. The CPIM had hegemony over the State and the urban middle class" (Ramaswamy, 2011). At that time, the economic liberalisation policies begun to change the aspirations of the middle class in Calcutta. There was also new aspiration, students did not want to study in Calcutta and there was an exodus to Bangalore and Delhi. The middle class wanted to send their children abroad. The technology induced restructuring and transformation in 1990, have not changed the city of Calcutta, as the IT sector beginning to come in very slowly. The city of Hyderabad has transformed to Cyberabad and representing a new entity in Global economy. This decade was the decade of transformation, but Calcutta lagged in. The incidence of poverty reduced drastically, both in rural and urban West Bengal. In 1987, the tram line of Calcutta Tramways was extended to Joka from Behala in presence of the then Chief Minister, Com. Jyoti Basu.

The notable Bengalese cultural icon, filmmaker Mr. Satyajit Ray passed away in 1992. In that year, he was awarded the honorary "Oscar: by the Academy of Motion Picture Arts and Science. He was also awarded "Bharat Ratna", a highest civilian award by Government of India. Following his death on April 1992, the city of Calcutta came to a virtual standstill, as people gathered around his house to pay their last respects. I was also suffered on that day, as there were no traffic movements; I have to walk from Rainy Park to reach Esplanade. .Another important event in Calcutta was opening of the Second Hooghly Bridge (Vidyasagar Setu) for traffic in 1992. The existing only bridge over the river Hooghly was Howrah Bridge (Rabindra Setu), which was subject to much traffic congestion. The second bridge will help to smooth movements of traffics from other cities. Following the protest led by Mamata Banerjee of the Congress Party in 1993, thirteen supporters were killed by police firing in Calcutta. In 1995, the underground Metro rail service was introduced from Esplanade to Tollygunge.

CHAPTER 1.5

DECADE OF INFRASTRUCTURE AUGMENTATION: 1995-2004

1. INTRODUCTION

This decade witnessed the expansion of Infrastructures like - the Auditorium and the New Teaching Block (NTB) with two new classrooms C1 and C2. During this time, Prof. Amitava Bose became Director in 1997 by replacing Mr. Subir Chaudhuri. After that, Prof. Sekhar Chaudhuri, Ex-Faculty member of IIM Ahmadabad became our Director in 2002 by replacing Prof. Bose. During this period, about twenty faculty members were superannuated or left. On the contrary, about twenty new faculty members were recruited mostly in 1996 to 1998. There was no recruitment of general staffs. During this period, I have presented papers in the three seminars, two in New Delhi and one in Bhubaneswar. The Institute published a dozen of my Working Papers, some of which were published in daily English newspapers. Since 1997, the research assistants were engaged as Invigilators in the PGPexaminations.

2. CAMPUS

In the Campus, construction completed for the New Teaching block and the Auditorium. The well manicured gardens around these buildings have enhanced the greenway and beauty of the campus. Two more classrooms have been added along with several rooms for faculty members and supporting staffs. Till now, the Campus was full of some concrete blocks but now the new constructions have added well designed architectural beauty.

3. LIBRARY

The Library has 16000 volumes of Management Journals. Our library is the largest management library in Asia. Ms. Swati Bhattachary was continuing as Librarian since 1992 with five Senior Assistants. During this time, a few library staffs have superannuated and left. The application of computer was rigorously followed in finding a book in the library. The use of computer had been introduced for all other purposes in the library.

4. NEW CONSTRUCTIONS:

a) Auditorium

This sophisticated Auditorium was founded in 2002 and became a part of the campus. The750 seated world-class new Auditorium is ultra-modern in design, lighting and sound system. The greenery and gardens around the well maintainedAuditorium and very spacious Our Auditorium is very nice in ambience and the best among those on any academic campus in the country. The world-class facility was built at a cost of over Rs. 9 crore. In addition to air-conditioning, it is equipped with ultra-modern, professional level light and sound system.

It hosts all the mega events on the campus. It is the venue for all major events like Convocation, Intaglio and visits of important personalities. My first visit was on the day of inauguration of the auditorium. I visited next at the farewell ceremony of our colleagues. In all earlier occasions, I have to sit with audience, but now I was invited by the Director on the Dais in 2007 to receive the "Memento" presented for my twenty five years of service in the Institute. Even though, I was serving the Institute without break since 1974, my service was recorded since 1982, the day when the then Director Mr. Bhaya issued a note for our regularization. I was offered a permanent post of Research Assistant in 1987, by ignoring the earlier eight years placed in consolidated pay scale.

b) The New Teaching Block

Around the year 1996-1998, some faculty members have been recruited. The old four classrooms (L1, L2, L3 and L4) became insufficient, as the student intake has been doubled in 1997. To meet the demand for teacher's rooms and classrooms, the New Teaching Block (NTB) was constructed in 2000 and it very close to the Auditorium. I first went to the NTB to meet Prof. Saibal Chattopadhyay in connection to his project sponsored by the Central Ministry of Food Processing. The NTB has well equipped Air-conditioned and medium size two classrooms (C1 and C2), whereI performed invigilation duty in PGP examinations.

5. CHANGE IN ADMINISTRATION

Earlier Director, Mr. Subir Chaudhuri, used to meet employees to solve their problems. He called upon the Research Assistance to earn money for the Institute or render service to the Institute in Administration. I was entrusted to study the Minutes of the Board Meetings and write a note on the "Governance of IIM Calcutta" in last few years. Prof. Bose became the Director in 1997 and created two posts of Deans – one for Planning &Administration and the other for Programme Initiative. Incidentally, both the Deans were form the same group of Economics and both were his close associates. The creation of the post of Deans was to ease Directors task in the internal affairs like daily administration other jobs. He never meets any employees for any purpose, as the Deans were entrusted to solve the internal problems. This system continued when Prof. Sekhar Chaudhuri became Director in 2002. In 1999, the Research Assistants were engaged as Invigilators in the PGP examinations. Instead of Director, the Dean (Planning & Administration) called for a meeting to entrust us the job of Invigilators.So, the PGP Chairman started issuing roaster of our Invigilation duty by date and venue. Later, not the Chairman, but the Clerks started issuing the roaster of invigilation duty.

6. FUNCTIONING OF THE INSTITUTE

a) Admission in PGP

The Post-Graduate Programme in management was continuing as usual. The eligibility for admission was judged by CAT (Common Admission Test) score, academic records, interview, group discussion and work experience. Candidates belonging to Scheduled Castes (SC) and Scheduled Tribes (ST) were enjoying their reservations. Now, there is no shortage of Women's hostel, so the Institute accommodated more women students. The CAT was introduced in 1983 and Prof. Binod Kumar was its founding father. It was paper pencils base objective type questions for all IIMs. The number of aspirants increased exponentially to about two Lakh. Now, the number of IIMs also increased and other private Management Schools were also using our CAT Score for admission there.

b) Number of Students

In this decade (1996 to 2005), the intake in PGDM doubled from 105 in 1996-1998 to 210 in next batch, as a precondition to release Block Grant from the Central Government. But, intake in PGDCM remained as usual around 50. The total students varied from 148 to 272, PGDM students from 105 to 220 and PGDCM students from 43 to 53 (Table 1.7.1). During this decade a total of 2510 students were admitted, of which 2012 in PGDM and 498 in PGDCM. On an average, 251 students were admitted annually, of which 201 in PGDM and 50 in PGDCM. In this time, the number of women students varied from 15 to25, mostly in PGDM. A total of 210 women students hadenrolled in this period. Annually, only 21 female students have enrolled in PGP, both the PGDM and PGDCM combined.

c) Total fees and Placements

In the period 1996-2005, the total fees for two years were Rs.0.92Lakhto Rs. 3.02Lakh. So, total fees increased by around four times in this decade. Initially, total fees increased from Rs. 0.92 Lakh to Rs. 1.05 Lakh to Rs. 1.56 Lakhand to 1.67 Lakh. Next year it increased to Rs. 2.07 Lakh to

Rs. 2.25 Lakh. It remained static at Rs. 2.54 Lakh for next three years but increased to Rs. 3.02 Lakhin last year (Table 1.7.7). But, there was a sea change in the placements. The Average annual salary on placements of our students varied from 6 Lakh to 12 Lakh with the average around Rs.9. Lakh.

d) The Faculty Members

The faculty strength increased sharply, as some new faculty members were recruited in this decade. The number of faculty member increased from 38 in 1975 to 50 in 1985, 60 in 1995 and became stagnant at 60 in 2004. As intake double in 1997-1999, a batch of ten faculty members were appointed in three years 1996 to 1998. In this period, about 20 early recruited faculty members have super annulated or left the Institute.To fill up the gaps, the Institute recruited another 20 new faculty members. Thus, the number of faculty members remained same at 60.

Among 60 faculty members in 1995-96, 12 were in Operation Research, 9 in Finance & Control, 8 each in MIS and PPM, 7 in Economics and 4 each in Marketing, OB and PMIR. Moreover, two faculty members were in each of B S and Strategic Management. So, majority of the faculty members were concentrated in Operation Research including Statistics, Finance & Control, MIS and Economics. In 2004-05, among 60 faculty members 14 were in Operation Research,10 in MIS, 7each in Economics and PPM, 6 in Finance & Control, 5 in Marketing and 4 in PMIR. Moreover, there were two faculty members in each of BS, OB, Strategic Management and one in MCHV. So, majority of the faculty members were concentrated in five groups - Operation Research MIS, Economics, Finance & Control and PPM. Now, the faculty members in Operation Research and MIS groups combined formed the powerful lobby by replacing the old Economics group.

The newly recruited Faculty members were – Profs. Shekhar Chaudhuri (Director), Uttam Sarkar, Debashish Saha, Mritunjoy Mohanty, Anindya Sen, B B Chakraborty, Saibal Chattopadhaya, Sahadeb Sarkar, Vidyananda Jha, Biju P Abraham, Avittahur Balaram, Sanjoy Mukherjee, Jayanta

Bandopadhyay,Debashis Bhattacharjee and Annapurna Shaw. At present, there were four women faculty members - Mousumi Ghosh, Leena Chatterjee, Sunita Sing Sengupta and Annapurna Shaw. By this time, among women faculty members - Kamini Adhikari and Zainab Ahmed retired. By this time, some faculty members have either super annulated or left. Among sixteen faculty member who retired or left, were - Sitangshu K. Chakraborti, N K Rao, K. K Bhattacharya, Ranjit Sau, V N Reddy, Bani K Sinha, Sujit Basu, Shyamal K. Ghosh,N Ramchandran, Nilotpal Chakraborty, Ajeet N Mathur, Ashok P Arora, Binod Kumar, Nalinaksha Bhattacharya, Sailo Ghosh and B K Chatterjee.

e) Fellowship Programme

The Fellowship Programme was continuing as before. During this decade (1996-2005), 34 students have been awarded Fellowship. So, the Fellowship awardees have increased from 23 in preceding decade to 34 in this decade. On an average, a little over three students have completed their Fellowship annually. Among them, a maximum of six were awarded Fellowship in 2002, four each in 1998, 2003, 2005, three each in 1996, 1999, 2000, 2001, 2004 and only one in 1997. So, most of them have been awarded Fellowship in last four years (2002 to 2005), while a few in first six years.

Among these Fellows, 11 were in MIS, 10 in Operations Management and Systems, 5 in Organisation Behaviour and 2 each in Economics, Finance & Control, Human Resource Management and Marketing. So, most of the Fellows were in Management Information System, Operations Management and Systems and Organisation Behaviour. Among these Fellows, there were only 7 women, of which 2 each were in HRM, MIS, OB and only one in Marketing. So, the representation of women in Fellowship Programme was 7 out of 34, i.e. 20. Among these Fellows - Mr. Bodhibrata Nag and Ms. Kaushiki Chaudhuri joined our Institute after completing their Fellowship. Prof. Amitava Bagchi and B N Srivastava supervised the Fellowship Thesis of three students each. Other six Professors - A K Chatterjee, M N Pal, B K Sinha, N Ramachandran, Leena Chatterjee and

S D Vaidya had supervised two students each. The rest students have been supervised by other Professors. So, one third of the Fellowship Thesis was supervised by Prof. Bagchi and Prof. Srivastava.

f) Executive Development Programme and In-Company Training Programme

One of the academic activities in the Institute was a program of training for already employed executive at the middle and top level. The Executive Development Programme (EDP), aimed to spread the value of the Institute and to enhance the acceptance of our Graduates. Over the years, EDPs has remained extremely popular and the scope of EDPs has also broadened. The EDPs are designed with the objective of providing practicing managers the insight into managerial concepts and implementing strategies in functional areas. The candidates for EDP must have Graduate degree but no age limits. In 1980s, when our EDPs failed the anticipated response, the EDPs began to supplement by a variety of Extension Programmes for junior and middle level managers.

The duration of EDPs varied from two to five days. The fees charged for the programme varied from Rs. 500 to Rs. 1500, depending upon the venues. In Bombay it cost higher while low in Calcutta. In the past, EDPs were held at Hotel Annapurna in Kathmandu in Nepal and some in hotels at Darjeeling. But now, after 1980, EDPs were mostly held in our own EDP Center at Tata Hall. The Tata Hall has a few small and medium size classrooms and fifty six residential rooms, four suits and three Conference rooms and a long Dining Hall. The Institute initiated another type of training programme - "In-Company Training". In this type of training, our faculty members will go to the Company's office and train the managers of the Company. In this training, number of participants will be fixed by the Company and faculty members will take classes by rotation. The Institute developed a programme of longer duration and started six month to one year tailor-made Long Duration Program.

7. MANPOWER IN THE INSTITUTE

During 2004-05, the manpower reduced from 472 to 357. But, the number of faculty members remained unchanged at 60. Earlier, there were 400 administrative staffs, now it has reduced to 287. Number of research staff also reduced from 12 to 10. Thus, during last decade, the number of faculty members remained unchanged, while Research staff reduced by 17 per cent and General staff reduced by 28%. As a whole, the manpower was reduced by 24%, as envisaged by Central Government to reduce the over staffed in the Institute. Most of the Senior Administrative Officers and Administrative Officers have super annulated and left. Some new Officers have been recruited at the top positions having past experience. They were mostly in contractual terms and likely to be renewed for next years.

Among twelve Research assistants Ms. Shyamali Adhikari expired and Mr. Amal Saha retired. So, the number of research assistants reduced to ten. They were assisting their concerned faculty members in teaching and research activities along with Invigilation duty. Among them, three were with Prof. Mishra and rests with other professors. By this time, about a hundred of Group D staffs have been retired. Most of their jobs are being done by Manpower Agency who supplied their personals as and when required. The house keeping in Hostels and MDP Centres were being done completely by Agency staffs. The clerical staffs in PGP, FP and Deans Office, Telephone Exchange etc. are being managed by Agency personnel, who were ill paid and have no job guarantee and job security.

8. MY ACTIVITIES: 1996-2005

A: Official Work:

i) Assistance to Different Professors

After Prof. Chandra's retirement, Prof. Reddy wrote to the Director that he will engage me in his research activities. Since then, I was assisting Prof. Reddy in his project "Socio-Economic and Educational Survey" in four districts of West Bengal. I surveyed a dozen of villages in Hooghly district in 1977-78. I was supervising the field survey of the Project "Status of Primary Education in West Bengal", sponsored by the UNICEF and the Government of West Bengal. Prof. Chattopadhayay was the team leader. I was entrusted for supervising the survey in seven districts in and around Calcutta. For this, I have temporary offices in Board (WBBPE) office, Women Studies department of Jadavpur University, room shared by Prof. Jasodhara Bagchi and in my residence. I have to go to Board office frequently to make liaison with the then Chairman Prof. Bhabesh Moitra. In 1999, the project was complete and I personally carried two sets of final Reports for submission to Board office.

In 2000, Prof. Chattopadhayay asked me to collect ASI (Annual Survey of Industries) Data on Factory Sector in West Bengal and India for the period 1979 to1997. This project was jointly with Prof. A B Bandopadhaya of MIT. As our library had no current volumes of ASI publications, I went to CSO office for about a month.The librarian was on leave and there was no desk assistant. So, I have to use wooden ladder to bring down the publications stacked up in racks. I completed the collection and analysis and submitted in 2001. In 2002, the MHRD sponsored a project on evaluation of Literacy Programme in some States of East and North-East Region in India. I prepared two reports – "Financing of Universal Elementary Education in the State of Assam" and "Evaluation of District Primary Education Programme in Assam". In continuance to the same project, I have analysed the literacy data on the state of Orissa. As, the data was available in Oriya language, I need the help of my collegegue Jaganaath Patra, who hailed from Orissa. I wrote the report "Evaluation of Post-Literacy in Khurdah district of Orissa" in 2005.

In 2004, the Central Ministry of Food Processing Industry sponsored a project on the scope of food processing industry in India as well as in our State. The team leader was Prof. R Chattopadhayay with other faculty members – Prof. Saibal Chattopadhayay and Prof. Uttam Sarkar. Prof, S Chattopadhya provided me the data on Agriculture in different States of Eastern and North Eastern regions in India.I have analysed the data and wrote the Report on "Agricultural Development in the States of East and North-East Region". He sent my write up directly to the Ministry. In this project, I have to visit those food processing units which were given Central assistance, for physical verification of the progress. After visiting those units, I prepared the report "Modernisation of Indian Food Chain: The Status of Food Processing Industry in India" and submitted to Prof. R Chattopadhaya and Prof. U Sarkar. In 2000, I have also assisted Prof. Hrishikesh Bhattachary in analyzing financial data of about five hundred companies engaged in catching fish in south Indian Sea. This was in connection to the project "Financing of Fishery Companies in India", sponsored by the Central Ministry.

ii) The Invigilation Duty in PGP I and II Examinations

In 1997-98, when Prof. Misra was Chairman of PGP, he asked the Ashoke Sengupta, AO (PGP) to call his team members from his Rural Development Centre (RDC), close to the examination halls. In addition to RDC staffs, Mr. Sengupta also requested us working in next room for invigilation. Next years, Prof. Anup K Sinha became Chairman of PGP and he called us in a meeting to co-operate with the Institute by providing invigilation duty. He issued a circular endorsed by the Director on this issue. In the roaster of invigilation duty, names of Research Assistant were included along with faculty members.

Some faculty members became furious, by seeing our names with them. The next roaster came in two sets - one for faculty members and other for Research Assistants. One faculty member, have not permitted one of us in examination hall as her name was not mentioned in his roaster. He became angry asked her to show if any other was allotted invigilation duty in this room. With the help of AO (PGP), the problem was solved. Initially, the circular of invigilation duty were issued by the Chairman PGP. But, now the circular was being issued by AO (PGP) instead of Chairman.PGP. We have not paid a penny except a cup of Tea/Coffee in examination hall. Alas, we became assistants to academic administration.

By PGP, we have meant students of both PGDM and PGDCM, and PGP I meant students of first year and PGP II means that of second year. For

PGP I, there were three terms (I, II and III), and for PGP II, the terms were IV, V and VI. Each term have two examinations - Mid-Term and End –Term. Generally examinations were held in a week and for a consecutive five days. Thus, in an academic year, the examinations hold for (3X2X2) 12 weeks i.e. 60 days. As, both the Mid-Terms of III and VI were held jointly. So, the total number of days for examinations in an academic year was 55. In a total of 240 working days in a year, 55 days were spent on examinations. So, about one-fourth of the annual workings days were spent in invigilation duty.

Moreover, in a day, the examinations were held in two shifts – Morning (10 a.m. to 12 a.m.) and Evening (2 p.m. to 5 p.m.). Thus, we have to perform invigilation duty in total 110 shifts of two to three hours duration. In the initial years, we have to perform three to four shifts in a week, but gradually it increased to ten. The examinations were not hold uniformly by months. In the Academic year 2004-05, as much as ten days were spent on August, nine days in March and eight days in December for invigilation duty while 5 days in other months. So, the months of August, December and March have more invigilation duty. While performing invigilation duty along with professors, I have met some arrogant Professors. But, invigilation duty with Prof. Amitava Bose, the then Director, was pleasant, as we met mostly in examination hall L2.

B: Personal Activities

i) Working Papers

During 1996 to 2005, about a dozen of my Working Papers have been published by the Institute. Initially, my research interest was on the Floricultural Industry, a highly Biotechnology based cultivation with modern technique of drip irrigation and use of Green Houses. This was sunrise industry having potential in earning more foreign exchanges by export of floricultural products. Within few years, the floriculture industry flourished in South India and many Corporate Sector companies have invested there. In West Bengal, traditional floricultural products were being produced in Midnapore and Nadia. For small land holding owners, I have suggested production of different plants in Nursery for creating rural employment, especially for women. The bio-technology based plants are very small and need great care that can be easily done by women. I have presented the paper "Floriculture and Rural Development" in a seminar organized by Jadavpur University.

In 1998, the NCERT called for papers relating to Common School System. My paper, "Economic Reforms and Education Through Common School System" was accepted for presentation in New Delhi. For this seminar, the NCERT, New Delhi provided the train fare for to and fro journey by Rajdhani Express and accommodation in their hostel. In this year, the NCERT was arranging another seminar on Community Participation in Management of Primary Education. Because of shortage of time, I could not attend the seminar. After completion the paper, it was published as a Working Paper. A part of this paper was published in the Statesman, a daily Newspaper from Calcutta in 1999 with the caption "Role of Panchayat Leaders in Primary Education".

In 1999, the West Bengal Primary Board was thinking about different measures through ANADAPATH to attract small kids in primary education. They have introduced certain measures. I have physically investigated how the schools were implementing these schemes in some schools in Hooghly district. This paper has been presented to the seminar organized by the NCERT Bhubaneswar. They provided me second class AC train fare of Jagannath Express and accommodation in their hostel.In this year, I have presented two papers on Primary Education in the seminar organized by the University of Delhi at Delhi. The provided me Air Fare for me to and fro journey and provided accommodation in infamous Ashoka Hotel. I have met Prof. Anil Sadgopal, the Convener of the seminar along with a dozen of Nobel Prize winners including Dalai Lama and Amartya Sen. I meet Andre Bettie, J B G Tilak, Tapas Majumdar, Manabi Majumdar and many educationists.

In 2001, Prof. Reddy observed that primary education was neglected in villages having low female literacy. I have investigated that axiom in different villages of Dhaniakhali Block of Hooghly district. I have identified villages with low female literacy and its impact on primary education. In 2002, the State initiated computing of Human Development Index in all districts. Prof. R. Chattopadhaya was entrusted for studying the status of Engineering and Technical Education in different districts. I investigated physically the Institutes offering those educations in five districts in and around Calcutta. I surveyed the Engineering Colleges, Polytechnics etc run by Public and Private. I published three Working Papers on this subject.

ii) Paper Presented in Seminars

In 1997, I have presented my paper "Biotechnology in Indian Agriculture" in the seminar organized by Agri-Horticultural Society of India, Calcutta Chapter. In the same year, I presented my paper "Floriculture and Rural Development" in the seminar organized by Jadavpur University with an NGO -Eastern India Agriculture and Biotechnology Society. Next year, I presented the paper "The Common School System: Elitist Education for Privileged Class?" organized by NCERT in New Delhi. In 1999, I have presented two papers in the seminars. The "ANANDA PATH in West Bengal – A Resume" was presented in NCERT, Bhubaneswar in Orissa. The next paper "Policy Level Constraints in Universalising Primary Education in West Bengal" was presented in South Asian Seminar on PrimaryEducation organized by the Delhi University, Delhi.

iii) Newspaper Publications

In 1997, I was very much involved in studying the status of Primary Education in West Bengal. I was supervising the survey of Primary Schools in different villages of the State. I wrote about the problems of Primary Education in the State. I was also studying the problems of Child Labour in different districts of the State. I published two features on those subjects in The Economic Times, a daily newspaper. In 1998, another feature the "Primary Education: Role of PanchayatLeaders" in *The Statesman*, a daily newspaper published from Calcutta. In 2001, I wrote another feature in Bengali –"Biswayan O Prathamik Shiksha", i.e.Globalisation and Its Impact on Primary Education, in Ajakal, a Bengali daily published from

Calcutta. In 2000, the article "Economic Reforms and Education Through Common School System" presented the Seminar organized by the NCERT was chapterised in the book- "Common School System in India", published by NCERT, New Delhi, 2000.

9. CALCUTTA IN THE DECADE: 1996 TO 2005

The State Government has changed the name of the city from Calcutta to Kolkata in 2001. The de-colonisation of name of the city was announced to reflect the original Bengali pronunciation of the city's name. The city's economic recovery gathered momentum after the "Economic Reforms in India" was introduced by the Central Government. Since 2000, the IT sector revitalized the city's stagnant economy and the manufacturing sector also experienced high growth.In 1998, Prof. Amartya Sen won Nobel Prize for Economics.

CHAPTER 1.6

DECADE OF INTERNATIONALISATION (2005-2014)

INTRODUCTION

The Indian Institute of Management Calcutta is the oldest among all IIMs in India. It completed 50 years since inception in 1961. In these 50 years, the Institute became a model of educational excellence. The Institute believed that this is a good time to take stock of what it has achieved during 50thyears of journey. The Institute celebrated its Golden Jubilee over two years, from 2010 to 2012. The Institute is focusing on excellence in teaching and heavily focusing on research as well. The Institute has collaborated with International Institutes as well as other IIMs (Chaudhury 2011). The primary goal of the Institute is excellence in teaching by inclusion of topics that address management issues in the global environment. Excellence in research also needed to make the Institute as a global Centre of Excellence.

1. INTERNATIONALISATION OF THE INSTITUTE

The Institute has been featuring in International Business School Ranking since 2013. The Institute Ranked No 1 in India, No 2 in Asia and No 17 Globally in Financial Times 2019. The Institute was also awarded coveted AACSB (Association to Advance Collegiate Schools of Business) accreditation, which is the hallmark of excellence in business education. The Accreditation with the AACSB is a global organization of educational institutions, businesses and other entities devoted to the advancement of management education. The Institute has already been accredited by

Association of MBAs (AMBA). This Institute is the only member in India of Community of European Management Schools (CEMS), an elite club of premier business schools across the world. So, IIM Calcutta is the only Institute in India to have dual accreditation by AACSB and AMBA and a member of CEMS.

The Institute is the first IIM and third Institute in India to gain AACSB Accreditation. Overall, AACSB found very high quality in a significant number of areas in the Institute. The AACSB and AMBA accreditation help further the Institute to get into many more partner-ships with other esteemed institutions. It would open up opportunity to collaborate with foreign faculty members, to teach our students and to be acquainted with global practices in business. Faculty members are committed to continuous improvement and supportive of any strategic changes for the betterment of quality. The Institute showed an overall ability to achieve desired outcomes and committed to excellence. The process encompasses the quality of students, faculty quality, research output, infrastructural facilities etc.

This quality assurance process will help the Institute to achieve its mission and vision. The Institute has been awarded the EFMD Quality Improvement System (EQUIS) Accreditation, which is the globally recognized international organization for management development. The EQUIS Accreditation Board conferred the EQUIS Accreditation in 2016. The Institute has also been accredited by the AACSB and the AMBA in 2014. Now, the Institute becomes the first Indian business school to achieve the "Triple Crown' in Accreditation". Continued Internationalisation is a thrust area for the Institute, to build our global reputations.An International Advisory Council (IAC) was formed with six luminaries across different countries - Japan, Spain, USA, Singapore and Switzerland. The Institute tied up with KAIST in South Korea and a Business School in China in 2005.

The success in Internationalization of the Institute was not achieved within a day. The Institute started it in 2004 with continuous effort to achieve it. During this time, the Institute introduced two steps for globalization of the Institute. The first one was STEP (Student Exchange Programme) with International Business Schools in - USA, Europe and South-East Asia, to improve quality of our programme. As a part of STEP, a batch of our students goes abroad for a term. Concurrently, we host a batch of foreign students from Foreign Centres for a term. The STEP has been quite beneficial to our students, in the era of globalization, as our students get exposure to foreign culture, education system and business scenario.

In 2015-16, a total of 92 students of our Institute went abroad. Concurrently, we host a batch of 72 students from Foreign Centres. Now, we have 68 partner schools, of which 43 were in Europe, 13 in Asia Pacific and 12 in USA.Lastly, the Institute introduced a Foreign Language Course to enable our students to perform effectively as managers in different parts of the world. In 2015-16, as much as 165 students have registered for foreign language course. Of them, 47 enrolled for French, 33 for Germany and 85 for Spanish languages (AR - 2015-16). Once, I have to help a foreign student from Portugal, in examination hall. She carried a Dictionary in her own language to English to understand the question paper.

In my Report on "Changes in the Governance of IIM Calcutta" for the years 2004 and 2005, I observed some important steps going to be taken by the Institute very soon. The first one was "Establishment of IIM Calcutta as a World Class Institute in Management Education". The Central Education Secretary stated that fund should not be a constrain to establish our institute as World Class Institute. Moreover, all IIMs were brought under the accreditation system of National Board of Accreditation under AICTE in 2005. To provide greater autonomy to IIMs, the Central Ministry introduced Block Grant Scheme to increase intake capacity. The Board (BoG) was advised for a strategic plan.

The Board advised to chalk out a strategic plan with tangible action plan keeping in view our Vision, Mission, Core Values and Beliefs. The Director rewrote the Vision and a strategic plan for next ten years for the Institute (Singha 2006). The second change was "Reforming the PGP curriculum", according to changes in global management. The Revenue

Maximising Committee" suggested introduction of some academic programmes. They suggested the introduction of a one year full time programme on International Management. Accordingly, the PGPEX (Post Graduate Program for Executives) was started in 2007, with the aim of developing experienced and ambitious executives for leadership positions. Concurrently, the PGPEX-VLM was started in collaboration with the Government of Japan, IIT Kanpur and IIT Madras.

The Governing Board in 2004 planned for setting up an International Management Center (IMC) near Science City. The Institute has applied for the land for its expansion. It was decided to acquire 20 acres of land near Rajarhat for this purpose. After waiting for more than a decade, the State Government handed over only 5 acres, instead of 20 acres of land in New Town in 2019 for the second campus of IIM Calcutta(Economic Times 2019). The Board suggested establishment of a Center for Corporate Governance. The Institute appointed a batch of Academic Assistants - Trainee Teaching Assistants (TTAs) in PGP office to assist the Faculty members in teaching and examinations. Those TTAs assisted the PGP office in invigilation duty with us. Those TTA were recruited on contractual basis for two years. The Director advised the Faculty members and Research Assistants (Invigilators) not to seek permission for leave during examination week.

2. CAMPUS DEVELOPMENT PROJECT

The Institute is blessed with large water pools, green foliage cover and diverse ecology. This oldest business school inherited a collection of mundane unrelated structures. Aware of the constraints in oldest campus, the Board (BoG) engaged a renowned architecture to conceptualise a comprehensive master plan, which focuses on sustainability and creating harmonious themes through a new building language, emplacing eco-friendly sewerage, waste and water management. A new entrance gate, roads around the periphery, an iconic foot-bridge and pedestrian pathways added to an academic milieu of international excellence. The enhanced campus has two focal areas – Academic Quadrangle and Residential Village

(Christopher Charles, 2014). In academic quadrangle, two large teaching wings use multi-level arcade, protected from rain to interconnect five levels of syndicate rooms, conference rooms, and class room with Amphitheatres, computer labs, support utilities and amenities.

The Residential Village consists of a major dining cum recreational facility, two hostel quadrangle and an Executive Training Center. Each hostel quadrangle houses common study room at the ground floor, 173 private rooms and a total 346 rooms at top floors. The Executive Training Center has 24 suits, 164 single rooms and a variety of dinning lounge and training facilities. These facilities allow 500 programme participants to live within the campus. The Residential Village opens through landscaped terrace and gardens to placid lotus ponds. This Village connects the Academic quadrangle by an iconic tubular steel pedestrian bridge on 150 feet wide lake.Our Campus Development Project started in 2007 to build a cover area of 5 Lakh square feet with a budget of Rs. 194 crore. The Central government provided Rs. 42 crore and the rest to be arranged from the Institute's Corpus Fund. A quarter-million square feet of our classrooms and hostel infrastructure, consisting of 11 classrooms, 11 syndicate rooms, faculty lounges, Computer Labs for hundreds of students. The built-up area of this project was 55,000 square meters in 110 acre of site area with existing structures (Balkrishnan 2007). The Project was completed in 2011, but I have never entered in the building, as I retired on 2010. I saw the construction work was in full swing.

3. LIBRARY

The B C Roy Memorial Library aims to meet the needs of its academic programmes. It has a huge collection of over 1.6 Lakh volumes of books and bound journals. The library also provides access to over 40,000 online journals. Our Library is one of the Asia's finest management libraries. In the financial year 2015-16, the Library procured Books, e-Books, Journals, e-Journals, Audio-Visuals and e-Data Base worth Rs. 450 Lakh. Our Library is making continuous efforts to ensure that users learn how to use the electronic resources. Several programs were held for students of

PGP, PGPEX and PGPEX-VLM. The Library continued to be members of different international organizations like CARNA, NASSCOM, International Video Library, British Council Library and American Center Library at Calcutta. The Library has successfully completed the Library Security Project. Now, the entire collection is under RFID tags. So, users can borrow or return books by themselves through the self check kiosk. Our Library has been recognized as one of the beneficiaries of the consortium – E-SODH-SINDHU, sponsored by MHRD.

4. COMPUTER CENTER

The Computer Aided Management Center (CAM) was established in early 1980s with the help of UNDP and Government of India. It was a single floor building. In 1990, the second floor of CAM center was built. Around 2000, the CAM center became defunct and renamed as Computer Center (CC). The Institute has enhanced the IT infrastructures in the campus. Many PCs of high configuration has been purchased and the Internet band width also increased to 370 Mbps. The institute is using unified means to access internet on educational campuses worldwide under the aegis of ERNET. The Computer Center is conducting regular training programme for administrative staffs. The Internet Solution Group (ISG), a students' initiative is running successfully for last 15 years. This platform maintained our link to external and internal stake holder of the Institute.

5. INTORDUCTION OF NEW PROGRAMS

In this period, the Institute introduced four new courses – PGPEX, PGPEX-VLM, PGDBA and LDP. First two courses were of one year full time residential programme. The third one was a two year residential full time programme while the last was an Online and classroom based programme of one year. Both the PGPEX and PGPEX-VLM were for working executives having more than five years of professional experiences. Both the courses started in academic year 2007-08 with intake capacity of 40 and 30 students respectively.

a) Post Graduate Programme for Executive (PGPEX)

The PGPEX started to provide mid-career professionals the platform to augment their existing skills. The one year residential programme for executives was to endeavour for senior and top management roles. Under the guidance of the country's leading management faculty, a passion for continuous learning synergizes with experiences from diverse backgrounds is to enrich learning environment. Learning beyond the classroom is an equally important, while case discussions enrich the practical experience of unravelling real life business puzzles. The PGPEX is a "One-Year Miracle" and many executives are using this as stepping stones to life-changing mid-life career switches. "The shorter duration is an attraction as most people with over five years of work experience don't want to spend two years in college again. We do not sacrifice content simply because it is a one-year course. The students learn everything that is needed; what are left out are things which they do not need because of experience. Students of executive MBAs are usually much more mature. They understand management principles and apply them better. They also better prepared and ready to handle middle and senior-level responsibilities" (Business Today.2008). During first ten years of PGPEX, the student intake increased from 39 to 68 and that of women increased to 10. The tuition fees increased much more. But,the Institute had cent percent placements.

b) Post Graduate Programme for Executive for Visionary Leadership in Manufacturing

The programme PGPEX-VLM was started in 2007 with the mission to develop future visionary leaders for the manufacturing sector in India, so as to enhance the global competitivenessin manufacturing sector. This program that fulfils the current industry's growing demand for techno-managerial leaders who shape the neo-industrial revolution. Laden with latest management skills and cutting-edge technology knowledge, these vanguards are being readied for meeting the challenges offered by the new wave of business enterprises. This is one year full time residential program with the focus on manufacturing focus that helps to appreciate an industry's metamorphosis in competitive times. The course is conducted jointly by three premier institutes - IIMC, IIT Kanpur and IIT Madras and it is designed by these Institutes in consultation with industry and M HRD.

But with an increasingly competitive environment, a need was felt to create a critical mass of visionary leaders to steer the manufacturing sector. Hence, the programme was developed by the National Manufacturing Competitiveness Council in collaboration with MHRD, IITs, IIM and CII. This program was to develop Leaders in Manufacturing under the Indo-Japan Cooperation. The Government of Japan extended cooperation to facilitate transfer of Japanese expertise, to expose the budding leaders to the pioneers of manufacturing technology. Since inception, the program has produced an array of visionary leaders who have marked their presence in industry. Three partnering Institutes teach their specialty in management education, guest lectures from Japanese faculty, industry experts and business leaders and an industry visit in Japan. During first ten years of inception, the number of total students varied from 29 to 40, while that of women students varied from 3 to 5. During this time, the tuition fees were Rs. 11.25 Lakh for IIM Calcutta, but that for IITs were not mentioned. On an average year, there were 33 students, of which only three were women.

c) Post Graduate Diploma in Business Analytic (PGDBA)

In 2015, a new two years full time course PGDBA (Post Graduate Diploma in Business Analytic) was introduced in lieu of old PGDCM. In the first batch, intake was only 51 students and the course fee for two years was Rs. 27 Lakh.

6. THE STUDENTS INTAKE

a) Students Intake in PGP, Tuition Fees and Placements

During this decade (2004-2013), there were heavy fluctuations in number of students 'intakein PGP. It varied from 259 to 462. This increase in number of student intake was due to MHRD direction to increase intake for reservations of OBC students. For implementation of OBC quota the batch size increased by 60 in 2012. Moreover, merger of PGDCM with PGDM in 2015 also increased the batch size by 50. To empower the women, the Institute also enrolled more women recently. Thus, the number of women increased from 25 in 2008 to 107 in 2013. Since 2008, the MHRD directed the Institute to increase the class capacity in PGDM by 54%, after 27% reservations of OBC. In 2009, the intake was increased due to inclusion of OBC students, directed by MHRD to increase from 278 in 2008 to 383 in 2009 (Table 1.2.1).

Of late, in 2015, the PGDCM was discontinued and its 50 seats have been merged with PGDM. So, it increased further from 404 in 2012 to 462 in 2013. The number of women was 20 to 30 in most years, but it crossed hundred and reached to 107 in last year. The percentage of women increased from 10% in earlier years to nearly 25%, a record in the history of the Institute. This was due to HRD's initiative to empower women and direction to enrol more women. In 2014-16, the social composition of all students in PGDM and PGDCM combined, out of 442 students, 218 were from Open Category, 62 from SC, 27 from ST, 14 Disabled and 121 from Non CreamyOBC. So, 49% students were from Open Category, 15% from SC, 6% from ST, 3% from Disabled and 28% from NC – OBC groups.

During this decade (2006-15), the total fees increased five times. Initially, it increased from Rs. 3.5 Lakh to Rs. 4 Lakh to Rs. 6Lakh, then to Rs. 9 Lakh in 2009 and finally to Rs. 13.5 Lakhin 2010 and remained static for four years and jumped Rs. 16.2 Lakh in 2015 (Table 1.2.2). The total fees of Rs. 16.20 Lakh, was payable in six instalments at the beginning of each of the six terms in two years. A student had to pay Rs. 7.80 Lakh in first year and Rs. 8.40 Lakh in second year. Out of total fees of Rs. 16.20 Lakh, Rs. 10.22 Lakh for tuition fees, Rs. 4.08 Lakh for academic charges and rest for other fees. In addition, a student has to pay monthly meal charges in Hostel and had to bear personal expenses like washing, barber etc.

b) Students, Tuition Fees and Placements in PGPEX

The PGPEX started in 2007 and it compared complete ten batches in 2016. During this decade (2007-16), there were little fluctuations in number of students in PGPEX. It was only 39 in first batch while it increased to 68 in tenth batches. In most of the years, the intake was around 50. Number of women student remained stagnant at 5 in first seven years, and then increased to 10 in last year. In PGPEX, on an average, there were 48 students including only 6 women. So, the representation of women was only 12%. During this period, the totalfees increased by three times. Initially, this fees was Rs. 8 Lakh which jumped to Rs. 14 Lakh, then to Rs. 18 Lakh and finally Rs. 22 Lakh in 2016-17.

c) Students and Tuition Fees in PGPEX-VLM

The PGPEX-VLM started also in 2007 and it it completed ten batches in 2016. During this decade, there were little fluctuations in number of students in PGPEX-VLM. It was only 30 in first batch while it increased to 40 in last batch. In most of the years, the intake was around 30. Number of women student was nil to five. In PGPEX-VLM, on an average, there were 33 students including 3 women. So, the representation of women was only 10%. In 2016-17, the tuition fees were Rs. 11.25 Lakh. The course is being conducted jointly by three institutes- IIM Calcutta, IIT Kanpur and IIT Madras.The tuition fees payable to IIT Kanpur and IIT Madras was not mentioned.

d) Students Intake and Tuition Fees in PGDBA

In 2015, a new two years full time course PGDBA was introduced. In the first batch intake consists only 51 students and the course fees for two years was Rs. 27 Lakh.

7. THE FACULTY STRENGTH

During this decade, the number of faculty members increased sharply from 60 to 92 in 2014-15. Among the faculty members, 14 were in OM. 12 each in MIS and Economics, 11 in Marketing, 9 in PPM, 8 each in Finance &

Control, BS and Strategic Management, 5 each in HRM and Business Ethics. Some Groups - Sociology, Regional Development, Environments were merged to Public Policy Management Group. Among the faculties, most of them were in OM, MIS, Economics and Marketing groups having more than ten faculty members. While, HRM and Business Ethics groups have less faculty members. In this period, a total of 50 faculty members were newly recruited. Among them, most were recruited in 2006 to 2010. Among total 92 faculty members, 17 were women. So, the representation of women faculty was about 20%. The number of women faculty doubled in this period, as a part of Central Government policy of empowering women. Most of them are young, as they were appointed currently. Prof. Amitava Bose, Aloke Ray, Amitava Bagchi, M N Pal, Raghbendra Chattopadhayay, Madhu S Misra, Suren Munshi, Sudas Roy, Hrishikesh Bhattacharya, Ms Mousumi Ghosh, Ms. Sunita Sing Sengupta, B B Chakraborty, Pulak Das, K S Mondal retired while Partha S Dasgupta (Died in Harness).

8. FELLOWSHIP PROGRAMME

The Fellowship Programme of the Institute is a full-time doctoral program in different fields of Management. This program focuses on training outstanding scholars for advance management education. These institutes look at FPM students as a pool for potential faculty. The specializations in FPMwere available in different specialised groups.In 2008, thc Board decided for 100% increase in the stipend for FPM students. The new stipend policy provides Rs. 20,000 to Rs. 24,000 per month and a Rs. 20,000 annual contingency grant. Students are also provided a one-time grant for field study. Students are also provided a one-time grant for field study, laptop grant and a fully supported international conference attendance anywhere in the world.The institute has also revised various rules and policies related to the FPM in order to ensure a more enriching academic experience. The Teaching Assistantships with exposure to designing courses and taking classes, which will fetch up to Rs. 11,000 per month for students in addition to the monthly stipend.The increase in stipend was supposed to attract more students, especially those with industry experience to get into an academic career. This move comes, when leading institutes are grappling with a faculty crunch coupled with a serious problem in attracting quality faculty. Presently, the FPM students were entitled Rs 11,000 per month and Rs 10,000 annual contingency grant.

During last ten years, 2005-14, 80 students were awarded Fellowship. Among them, 11 were in 2007, 10 each in 2006, 2008, 2012, 9 in 2013 and 5 to 7 in rest years. On an average, 8 students were awarded Fellowship annually. Among total 80, 26 were in MIS, 11 in Fiancé& Control, 8 each in Operations Research & System Analysis and Strategic Management, 7 in Organizational Behaviour, 5 in Regional Development and 4each in Economicsand Marketing, 3 each in HRMand Sociology, while only on in Mathematics (Table 1.8.4). Group-wise, half of the total Fellows were in MIS and Finance & Control groups. Among these 80 fellows, the dissertation of 66 fellows had been supervised by individual professors while the rest 15 were done jointly by two Professors. Prof. Sougata Ray of Strategic Management group supervised 6 Fellows, 5 each by Profs. Ambujasha Mohanti and Prof. Asim K Pal both of MIS group, 4 each by Prof. Ashis Chatterjee and Prof. M N Pal, both of OM group, 3 each by Prof. Ashis Bhattacharya of Finance & Control and Prof Subir Bhattacharya of MIS group. Eleven Professors have supervised two Fellows each while 14 Professors have supervised one Fellow each.

9. MANAGEMNET DEVELOPMENT PROGRAMMES (MDP)

As organizations become flatter and more agile or global and more complex, they create new opportunities for talented leaders. To capitalize on these opportunities, practicing managers need cross-functional skills, strategic vision and superior management expertise. Managers and Executives need to continuously hone their skills and upgrade their business acumen, to stay abreast of industry trends and leverage upon emerging opportunities. The MDPs of the Institute have been designed to effectively spread quality management education among practicing managers, across all levels. These programmes equip experienced professionals with powerful knowledge, tools and resources to tackle the most complex business challenges. The

Institute offers the Executive Education through three programmes - MDP, In-Company Training and Long Duration Programme.

a) Management Development Programme (MDP)

The MDPs are comprehensively structured classroom sessions and designed to address specific corporate training objectives. The Institute offers a calendarized set of MDPs, spreading across the functional areas in Management. In the year 2009-10, the Institute has conducted 75 MDPs, of which 6 were held outside Calcutta, of which four in Mumbai and one each in Bangalore and Chennai. The rest 69 MDPs were held in Calcutta, of which 63 were in our Tata Hall, 4 in Hotel Hindustan International and 2 in Hotel Taj Bengal.Among 75 MDPs, 5 were of two days duration, 31 of 3 days, 14 of 4 days, 22 of 5 days, 2 of 6 days and one of one month duration. Most MDPs were of three to five days.

The average fees for MDPs of 2 days duration was Rs. 20,000, 3 days was Rs. 25,000, 4 days was Rs. 30, 000, 5 days was Rs. 35, 000 and 6 days was Rs. 48, 000. A maximum of Rs, 2,33,000 was charged for a MDP of one month duration with a foreign trip. Among 75 MDPs, 48 were conducted by one Professor and 27 jointly by two or more. Among MDPs conducted by individual Professor, 10 were by Prof. P Bhatta, 9 by Prof. R Majumdar, 8 by Prof. B N Srivastava and 6 by Prof. P Agnihotri. These four Professors have conducted most of the MDPs. Nine Professors have conducted one to three MDPs. Prof. Leena Chatterjee had conducted more MDPs jointly with some other Professors (Success, 2019). In 2015-16, a total of 28 MDPs was conducted with 529 participants and the Institute earned Rs. 331 Lakh.

b) In–Company Training

The customized Training Programme known as In-Company Training. These are tailor-made modules created around specific mandates from discerning corporate clients. During 2015-16, the Institute conducted 70 In-Company training programs with 1950 participants and earned the revenue of Rs. 660 Lakh. In addition to these, the Institute also undertook 9 Consultancy projects and earned revenue of Rs. 103 Lakh.

c) **Long Duration Programme (LDP)**

In 2008, a one year Long Duration Programme (LDP) was introduced in the Institute. The LDPs was conducted on the distance learning format and was disseminated through satellite-based learning platforms, interspersed with brief in-campus sessions. In 2015-16, a total of 14 LDPs were conducted by the Institute. Among these, 5 LDPs were for six to eleven months while nine for one year duration. In these LDPs, the number of registered participants varied from 21 to 204. Among all LDPs, 3 LDPs have participants below 50, 5 have 50 to 100, another 5 have 100 to 200 while one has more than 200 participants. Most LDPs have 50 to 150 participants but on an average, a LDP had 133 participants.

10. MANPOWER IN THE INSTITUTE

During 2015-16, the total manpower reduced from 357 to 233. But, the number of faculty members increased from 60 to 87. The number of administrative staffs reduced to a half at 144 from 287 and the number of research staff reduced to 2 from 10. During this decade (2006-15), the number of faculty members increased by 50 %, while research staff decreased by 80% and general staff decreased by 50%. So, all non-teaching staffs reduced by 60%. This decade observed exponential growth in number of students and faculty members, despite reduction of general staff. To cope up with the shortage, the Institute out-sourced 90 staffs, mostly women on contractual terms.

11. INVIGILATION DUTY IN EXAMINATIONS

By PGP, we have meant students of both PGDM and PGDCM. By PGP I meant students of first year and PGP II meant that of second year. For PGP I, there were three terms (I, II and III), and for PGP II, the terms were IV, V and VI. Each term have two examinations - Mid-Term and

End–Term. Generally examinations were held throughout a week and continued for consecutive five or six days. Thus, in an academic year, the examinations hold for 12 weeks i.e. 60 to 65 days. As, both the Mid-Terms of III and VI were held jointly. So, the total number of days for examinations became 60. In a total of 240 working days in a year, 60 days were spent on examination duty. So, about one-fourth of the annual workings days were spent in invigilation duty. In a day, the examinations were held in two shifts – Morning (10 a.m. to 12 a.m.) and Evening (2 p.m. to 5 p.m.). Thus, we have to perform invigilation duty in total 120 shifts of two to three hours duration for PGP examinations.

Our invigilation duty was initiated only for PGP in 1997, but extended to PGPEX and VLMP also since 2007. During examination week, we have to attend five to six slots of one to three hours and in different Halls spread over the Campus. Not only in L1 to L4, A101 to A105 in A Block, C1 and C2 in New Teaching Block, MCHV Hall and Conference room in Library Building, Seminar room and Computer Hall in CAM center and also in Finance Lab at the top of State Bank Building. So, we have to travel from Finance Lab. in the west to MCHV on the east covering half a kilometre. In the rainy seasons, PGP does not arrange for transport. The PGP office allotted the nearest venues to some of us, while I and others were allotted far away examination centres. Initially, we have to perform three to four shifts in a week. Now we have invigilation duty of eight to nine shifts in a week. In 2009-10, I spent as much as 55 days out of 220 working days for invigilation duty. I spent 8 to 10 days in invigilation duty during the months of August, March and December.

12. MY ACTIVITES

Activities during last five years of service (2006-10) were –a) Assistance to different Professors b) Invigilation duty in PGP, PGPEX and PGPEX-VLM examinations and c) Assistance to the Secretary to the Board of Governance. During this time, I have also assisted different Professors in connection to different projects listed below.

A: Assistance to Different Professors

a) Evaluation of Post Literacy Programme

Profs. R Chattopadhayay and S Bhattacharya undertook a MHRD sponsored project on evaluation of Post Literacy Program (PLP) in 2006. The Total Literacy Campaign was organized by the Central Government across all the States in India. The PLP started in 2005 for new literates to achieve functional literacy. The Institute was entrusted to evaluate the PLP in two North Eastern States – Assam and Arunachal Pradesh. The team selected one district from each state. The Cacher district of Assam and Kurung Kumey district of Arunachal Pradesh were selected for evaluation. The team studied whether a significant difference exists among new learners belonging to different gender, caste and religions. To evaluate the success of TLP in Cachar District, an evaluation test was conducted to judge the Reading, Writing and Mathematical skills. The performance of learning centers has also been judged. The evaluation of PLP was also conducted the same test in Kurung Kumey district. I completed the Reports of both the districts in 2007.

b) Study of Effectiveness of BRCs & CRCs in Assam and Mizoram:

The Central Government initiated many programmes to attain the goal of Universalisation of Elementary Education. The Sarva Shiksha Abhiyan (SSA) launched in 2001 was a most significant step in achieving it. To bring about qualitative change in education under SSA, the Block Resource Centres (BRC) and Cluster Resource Centres (CRCs) were formed in each Block in every district. The BRCs and CRCs were established to improve the quality of education through regular in-service training for teachers. The academic support was provided to them through BRCs and CRCs. An important role of BRCCs and CRCCs was to visit schools and on the spot academic support and guidance to teachers. The MHRD entrusted our Institute to evaluate the 'Effectiveness of BRCs and CRCs in Elementary Schools' in Assam and Mizoram in 2007. The study was to assess the performance of BRCs and CRCs in those states. Prof. Chattopadhayay studied the Mizoram while Prof. Bhattacharya studied Assam. We completed the study and made suggestions for more effective functioning of BRCs and CRCs and wrote the Reports for both the States.

c) **Status of Elementary Education in Andaman Nicobar and West Bengal**

Prof. R. Chattopadhayay and S. Bhattacharya undertook another Study on Elementary Education in Andaman and Nicobar Islands and West Bengal during 2008. The study was based on DISE (District Information System for Education) data, receiving from schools from time to time. Based on that, we delved into the status of elementary education in those states. Prof. Bhattacharya was engaged in studying the Status of Elementary Education in Andaman and Nicobar Islands. Prof. Chattopadhayay was engaged in Studying the Status of Elementary Education in West Bengal. We explored the status of Primary, upper Primary and elementary education in both the States. The Primary education was imparted almost entirely by government schools in both the States. We have also assessed the impact of the recent initiatives like - distribution of School Development Grants to schools, TLM grants to teachers and the distribution of free textbooks, uniforms and scholarship to students. We have completed the Reports on Elementary Education in both the States in 2008.

d) Mentoring and Evaluation of SARVA SIKSHA AVIYAN

Monitoring under the SSA programme was envisaged at three levels - at the local community level, State level and the National level. At the local level, the Community based monitoring was done by Village Education Committees (VEC) in rural areas and Ward Education Committee (WEC) in urban areas. They were entrusted of ensuring that the schools are functioning effectively. The community-based monitoring will ensure the properly functioning of the system. For State level monitoring, the MHRD identified two Academic Institutions for each States – IIM Calcutta and Viswa Bharati for West Bengal. Our Institute was entrusted for monitoring and evaluation of SSA in ten districts of West Bengal. Our team consists of

Prof. R Chattopadhayay and U Sarkar. I was supposed to analyse data and writing the Report. We have to cover ten districts, but failed to complete it in Darjeeling district for political disturbances. Finally, we completed monitoring and evaluation of SSA in nine districts. The Viswa Bharati conducted the monitoring and evaluation of SSA in rest districts. We evaluated the impact of SSA in selected sample schools in nine districts. The Evaluation Reports for each district were submitted to MHRD.

e) Half-Yearly Monitoring Reports on SSA in West Bengal

During 2009-2010, Prof. R. Chattopadhayay was engaged in studying the Half-Yearly Monitoring Reports on SSA in four districts. The Reports were based on data submitted by concerned District Project Director, who provided data on the recent SSA activities in sample schools. After receiving the data, we analysed them and the Report was written.

f) Evaluation of Mid Day Meal in West Bengal

We have discussed the Mid Day Meal (MDM) programme in those sample schools as discussed above. We found that 98% schools were serving hot cooked food and 2% schools were serving dry food or ration. The most common items were - rice, pulses, vegetables, soya beans and eggs. Instead of cooked food, fruits were served in a few schools. The cooked MDM Programme started in 2003. During 2006-07, 92 Lakh children in 70 thousand schools participated in MDM in West Bengal. In this year, Rs. 299 Cr. of Central Assistance was utilized, of which, Rs. 223 Cr. for cooking costs, Rs. 59 Cr. for kitchen shed, Rs. 10 Cr. for kitchen devices, Rs. 6 Cr. for management etc. and Rs. 3 Cr. for transport subsidy. Moreover, the State also contributed Rs. 299 Cr. So, the total expenditure for MDM was Rs. 598 Cr. Thus, cost of midday meal was rupees five per child per day.

g) Assistance to Prof. Rahul Roy

In 2007, another project was to "Study on the Central Sector Schemes on the Development and Strengthening of Infrastructural Facilities for Production and Distribution of Quality Seeds". Prof. Roy was the Project

Coordinator along with other Professors. I prepared the Questionnaire for the field survey on different stakeholders and agencies in seed industry. Those were producers, distributors and transporters of quality seeds and the state government departments dealing with different seeds.I sent the Questionnaires to them and after receiving the filled up questionnaire, I have entered the data but no honourium was paid.

h) MIT Collaboration Project

In 2006, IIM Calcutta had housed two prestigious research projects in collaboration with MIT and Yale University. Profs. R. Chattopadhayay and Prof. A V Bandopadhayay of MIT were involved. The first project dealt with the impact of women's leadership in Panchayats and the second one was on good governance. Total project cost had been paid by MIT, Yale and UNICEF (The Economic Times, July 24, 2006). The first part of the first project had started with Prof. Dufflo of MIT along with Prof. Chattopadhayay. They looked into the distribution of public goods in villages with women Pradhans in Birbhum district. The second was on Rajasthan police for good governance.

B. Activities in Administration

To fulfil the Institute's Administrative requirements and giving adequate exposures, I was given a posting in Administrative duty, along with other academic activities. I was posted in Board Office and had to report the Secretary to Board (CAO) and Dean (P & A). I was entrusted to write a Report on "Changes in IIMC Governance During 2004-2005". I have read the Agenda and Minutes of all the Board meetings held in last two years. I observed some noteworthy changes in the administration. Those were – Establishing IIMC as a World Class Institute, Reforming the PGP curriculum, Maximisation of Institute's Revenue, Implementation of CMP, RTA, Government Directives and e-Governance, Joint Ventures of BSNL & TTSL etc (Singha 2006). I have assimilated the relevant information and submitted my report to the CAO and Dean (P&A), but none of them discussed me about my report. In this time, Prof. Sudip Chowdhuri,

Chairman FPR called all the Research Assistants, for a meeting with other Committee members. The academic council felt that the services of RAs are being grossly underutilized. So, the Committee will look after the matter and have to come up with a concrete proposal for better utilization of them. Alas, this initiative came in, when all RAs were on the verge of retirement!

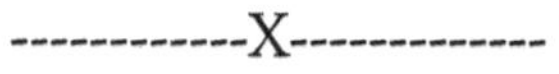

CHAPTER 1.7

GLOBAL EXPANSION, ACCREDITATIONS AND WORLD RANKING (2005-2014)

1. MOVING TOWARDS INTERNATIONALISATION

Continued internationalisation is a thrust area for our Institute, which aspires to further build our global reputation and become a global destination for quality management education.The Institute formed an International Advisory Council comprising six luminaries across different geographies and with extensive academic and corporate expertise, along with a Pan American Board. The two initiatives were taken for internationalisation. One is the Student Exchange Program (STEP), and the other is a Double Degree Program - Master in International Management (CEMS-MIM) with Global Alliance in Management Education

a) The Student Exchange Program (STEP)

For the Student Exchange Program (STEP),the Institutecurrently has a list of 100 partner schools spread over USA, Europe and South-East Asia. In STEP, our students went on exchange program to 39 partner schools - Aarhus School of Business, BI Norwegian Business School, Bocconi University, Catolica Lisbon School of Business and Economics, Copenhagen Business School, ESC Rennes School of Business are some the schools visited by our outgoing students. The STEP started in 2017, when one student from our Institute spent 3 Terms at ESCP-Europe (Parix Campus). This program is coupled with student exchange program with globally well-known business schools. Currently, this exchange program is gaining momentum every year. In 2017-18, 133 STEP students from our institute participated in an exchange program, while 87 students from partner schools spent their term at our institute. In 2018-19, our 111 STEP students went on exchange program to 39 partner schools and 46 incoming exchange students visited our institute.

b) Tie-ups with Foreign Institutions: CEMS

For internationalisation, the institute became a member of the Global Alliance in Management Education (CEMS) in 2012. As a result, the institute became the member of the elite club comprising 30 premier international business schools in the world. The CEMS has created a global standard of management studies for students to become true global managers with excellence in performance and ethical conduct and understanding of cultural diversity. Since 2013, the institute has been offering the CEMS Masters in International Management (CEMS-MIM) degree. In this program, our selected students from the PGP program who qualify for the CEMS program are given the option of taking the CEMS-MIM as an additional degree. Our Institute is India's only business school to be a member of the CEMS.In CEMS-MIM, global rank for IIM Calcutta has climbed to 4th position in 2015 and it was up one in 2014 and three positions higher than its 2013 ranking (IIMC Sandesh, 2015).

i) CEMS and MIM Program

The Global Alliance in Management Education (CEMS) was formerly known as The Community of European Management Schools established in 1988 between Università Bocconi, ESADE, HEC Paris and the University of Cologne. Started as a Pan-European beginning, it has now grown to become a truly global organization consisting of 33 leading European, Asian, Australian and American schools of business, over70 multinational companies and 7 NGOs. Through the prestigious "Masters in International Management" (CEMS MIM) degree become a global institution, and as a step towards achieving its vision of becoming an 'International Centre of Excellence in Management Education'. So, our institute joined CEMS, which grown to become a truly global organization.

The CEMS-MIM program is a one-year program which can be taken up simultaneously with the 2 year flagship PGP program. The qualifying students have to spend one term in any of the CEMS member schools abroad before returning to the institute for the final term. During the CEMS terms, students will interact and build networks with their peers and professors globally. Through the collaboration with CEMS corporate partners, students are exposed to real-life business situations thereby gaining insight into management best practices and learn key practical skills required to function effectively in an international organisation. It also provides the privilege of furthering international job prospects through interactions with these multinationals. It has been playing a pioneering role in professionalising Indian management. Today, the institute continually evolves to meet its goals in an ever-changing business environment.

The vision of the Institute is to emerge as an International Centre of Excellence in all facets of Management Education, rooted in Indian ethos and societal values. Over the past seven decades, the institute has blossomed into one of Asia's finest Business Schools. Its strong ties to the business community make it an effective mechanism for the promotion of professional management practices in Indian organizations. The CEMS considered other parameters in the rankings include value for money ranking, involvement of women in the Institute's board, international student in-take, international mobility ranking of alumni, faculty with doctorates and other languages known etc. The prestigious CEMS-MIM created a global standard of management studies for students to become true global managers.

ii) Benefits of CEMS-MIM Program

The CEMS MIM Program at our institute offers a wide range of courses imparting student's critical analytical skills and global perspectives on management of organisations in varied settings. The courses particularly bring in the experiences of the emerging economies like India and China. The overall objective is to foster cross-cultural understanding and dialogue in relation to different types of organisations- corporate, public and the third sector. The courses are oriented towards underlining the social embeddedness of organisations and highlighting the robust growth of social entrepreneurship in contemporary context. Alliance with CEMS gave our Institute access to cutting edge developments in the area of management education, recognition of being among the elite in the sphere of management research and education and opportunities of collaboration with the very best schools around the globe.

Our students who undergo the 10-week summer internship as part of PGP satisfy the CEMS requirements. Additionally, students who at the end of our PGP join overseas companies can show first 10-weeks of their job as international internship for CEMS. The institute will also be eligible for participation in the Global Ranking Survey conducted by the Financial Times. One of the requirements for joining the CEMS MIM program is a 10-week international internship at CEMS schools. In CEMS-MIM, our institute ranked 3rdglobally in 2012, 7th in 2013, 5th in 2015 and improved further to 4th in 2015 (Table 1.7.1). The Institute made some plans to improve our ranking globally and wish to come in the top 50

c) Pan American Board Members

In 2009, the Bhargava Committee recommended the establishment of a pan-India IIM board to protect the "IIM Brand" which in effect would drastically reduce power and autonomy of each individual IIM, ruled out their establishing centers beyond their 'regions' within the country and made them subject to supervision by a 'super board' rather than leave them free to develop their own institutional personalities. The Bhargava Committee report was criticized by Directors of the IIMs, because it replaced MHRD interference with even closer supervision by the proposed pan–IIM super board, prompting a whistle-blowing special report feature titled "Bitter Medicine for IIMs".

d) The Future Plan

The Institute believe that today's managers need to inculcate in themselves an analytical orientation to understand and analyse complex business situations while at the same time possess an action orientation and an administrative point of view.Our educational and training programs are anchored around this philosophy. So, our programs and activities are guided by our vision, mission and core values.The Institute's mission is to develop innovative and ethical future leaders capable of managing change and transformation in a globally competitive environment and to advance the theory and practice of management.The Institute strives to develop and sustain the following values to provide the context for all our programs and activities.

The Institute's philosophy has been to develop leadership qualities through not only classroom teaching and learning but also equally importantly through participation in co-curricular activities. The Institute has a vibrant and talented student community comprising students from all parts of the country who are actively involved in seminars, business school meets, business plan competitions, sports and cultural events and social and community work. The premier management institute is continuously strived to remain at the cutting edge of research and enquire in the various functional areas of management and related disciplines.Research is at the heart of our intellectual activities and the Doctoral Program offers a unique opportunity to engage in high quality research and develop the qualities needed to become top class academics in management and related fields.

2. ACCREDITATIONS JOURNEY

a) AMBA Accreditation in 2014

The Institute bagged a global accreditation status by the Association of MBAs (AMBA) for its PGPEX and PGP programs for five years in 2014. The AMBA is based in London in United Kingdom and it focuses on individual program. Its rigorous assessment criteria ensure that an AMBA accredited program has demonstrated best standard in teaching, curricula and student interaction.

b) AACSB Accreditation in 2015

The Institute bagged the accreditation of the Association to Advance Collegiate Schools of Business (AACSB) for 5 years in 2015. The AACSB international is the longest serving global accrediting body for business schools that offer under-graduate, master's and doctoral degree in business and accountancy. There are 716 business schools in 48 countries that maintain AACSB accreditation. The chief accreditation officer of AACSB said that "It takes a great deal of self-evaluation and determination to earn AACSB accreditation and I commend the Indian Institute of Management Calcutta for its dedication in management education, as well as its leadership in the community…Through accreditation, our institute has not only met specific standards of excellence, but has also made a commitment to ongoing improvement to ensure that the institution will continue to deliver high quality education to its students."(Economic Times, 2016)

Our Institute became the first IIM to receive accreditation from AACSB and joined an elite group of global institutes that received this accreditation – considered the gold standard in business education and earned by less than 5% of the world's business programs. Our Institute became the only B-school in India with both AACSB and AMBA accreditations. Benchmarking our Institute against the best in the world will not only further the institute's global ambitions but also help it tie up with better known international counterparts for offering these programs, carrying out student and faculty exchanges and promote better research. The AACSB accreditation is a process of rigorous internal review, evaluation, improvement and can take multiple years to complete. The AACSB evaluated our institute according to 19 parameters including the quality of faculty, research, student quality, infrastructure, financial stability and assurance of learning. They also judged whether we are aligned to our overall mission and vision statement. The institute received the accreditation of AACSB for its dedication to management education, as well as its leadership in the community. Through accreditation, the Institute has not only met specific standards of excellence, but also made a commitment to on-going improvement to ensure that the institution will continue to deliver high quality education.

c) EQUIS Accreditation in 2016

The institute was accredited by the EFMD Quality Improvement System - EQUIS, (European Quality Improvement System) for 3 years in 2016. Accreditation by EFMD, the globally recognized international organization for management development with over 800 members from academia, business, public service and consultancy in 81 countries. The EQUIS Accreditation Board voted to confer EQUIS Accreditation to us. With the EQUIS accreditation, the institute became the first Indian business school to achieve the 'Triple Crown' in accreditation. Our Institute asserted its reputation over the decades. Thanks to strong leadership and faculty, active student involvement and timely innovative intervention in placement, curricula introduction or faculty selection, research, academics or industry interaction. The institute's achievement through innovation and changes made learning teaching experience keeping up with the times. Our faculty members, administration, Board of Governors have always tried to bring in new things to the system for better teaching learning. Our institute is India's first triple accredited management school to receive accreditation from the all three agencies of the world. The Institute was accredited by Association of MBAs (AMBA) for 5 years in 2014, the Association to Advance Collegiate Schools of Business (AACSB) for 5 years in 2015 and European Quality Improvement System (EQUIS) for 3 years in 2016.

d) Triple Crown

The Institute has been awarded all the three most sought after international accreditations agencies in the world for management education. These accreditations are a big step towards internationalisation. Our institute became the first and only B-school in India with Triple Crown", as being recognized by three globally reputed b-school accreditation organizations. This achievement has rendered our institute to join the league of only 5 other business schools in Asia and 73 business schools around the world are currently 'Triple Accredited' (HindustanTimes 2016). Accreditations from all three reputed international agencies involve international benchmarking of the programs offered and of the Institute as a whole. Accreditation processes review institutional strategy to see if they are in sync with the pace of change in the global environment and in the corporate world. They also review the learning environment, academic quality of programs, efforts to develop ethical leaders, impact of faculty research, quality of students, societal and professional relevance and assurance of learning. Our Institute is one of the best business schools in the world.

All three agencies help their members to work towards continuous improvement of their academic programs. The peer review services and accreditation awarded by them is acknowledged globally as the hallmark of excellence. As a result, the institute become a model of educational excellence and continues to face challenges and on the course of evolution. The institute believes to take stock of what have been able to achieve in last 60 years. The institute is going to celebrate our Diamond Jubilee in 2020 to 2022. The Institute is focusing on excellence in teaching and focus heavily on research as well, and looking at developing collaboration relationship with other IIMs along with international institutes.

3. THE GLOBAL ACCREDITATION AGENCIES

World-wide, the most important Accreditation Agencies are AMBA (Association of MBAs), AACSB (Association to Advance Collegiate Schools of Business) ant the EQUIS (Quality Improvement System).

a) AMBA

Our institute has already been accredited by Association of MBAs (AMBA), based in London. Our institute won AMBA accreditation that accredits just 1% of the world's MBA business schools. Our institute has been able to achieve this accredits within the initial 5 years of its commencement.This achievement is an epitome of the quality of their MBA program offered by them and place Indian management education on a different landscape in global scenario. The institute received this recognition and reaffirms the commitment to academic excellence and marks a significant step towards our journey to be a global leader in management education. As organization became global, they create new opportunities for talented leaders.To capitalizes on opportunities; practicing managers need cross-functional skills, strategic vision and superior management expertise. Managers and Executives of modern day organizations need to continuously hone their skills and upgrade their business acumen, to stay abreast of industry trends and leverage upon emerging opportunities. Our EDPs have been designed to effectively spread quality management education among practicing managers at all levels. These programs equip experienced professionals with powerful knowledge and tools to tackle the most complex today's business challenges.

b) AACSB

World-wide, the most important Accreditation Agency is AACSB (Association to Advance Collegiate Schools of Business).The Institute was awarded AACSB accreditation; the hallmark of excellence in business education. The AACSB is based in the Tampa, Florida in United States The AACSB is a global non-profit membership organization of educational institutions of businesses and other entities devoted to the advancement of management education. Established in 1916, AACSB International provides its members with a variety of products and services to assist them with the continuous improvement of their business programs. AACSB Accreditation is the hallmark of excellence in business education. Since less than 5% of the world's business programs have earned AACSB Accreditation therefore it can be summarized that AACSB-accredited schools have the highest quality faculty, relevant and challenging curriculum and provide educational and career opportunities that are not found at other business schools.

There are 716 business schools in 48 countries that maintain AACSB accreditation. Only, 181 institutions maintain an additional specialized AACSB accreditation for their accounting programs. The IIM Calcutta is the first IIM and third institute in India having AACSB accreditation. The AACSB found at our institute a very high quality in a significant number of areas. Our Institute supports a continuous improvement of environment. Worldwide AACSB accreditation represents the highest standard of achievement for business schools. The AACSB grants internationally recognized specialise accreditation for business programs at the bachelors, masters and doctoral level.

c) EQUIS

The Institute was accreditited by the EFMD Quality Improvement System - EQUIS, (European Quality Improvement System) in 2016. The EFMD Accreditation based in Brussels in Belgium.

d) CEMS

The Institute is the only member in India of Community of European Management Schools (CEMS), which is an elite club of 29 premier business schools from across the world. Therefore, our Institute is the only Indian business school that is a member of the CEMS. Our Institute has jointed a grouping of 30 premier global business schools that offer the Masters in Management (MIM) Program Accreditation Board voted to confer EQUIS accreditation on our Institute. Hence, the globally recognized international organization for management development which has over 800 members from academia, business public service and consultancy in 81 countries entitled our institute with such prestigious accreditation to its account. All these accreditations will further help the institute to get into many more partnerships with other esteemed institutions. It would also open up opportunity to collaborate with foreign faculty members on research projects, publications, etc.

The institute will have the scope to get more foreign faculty members to teach our students and help them to be acquainted with global practices in business environment.In this institute,faculty members individually and collectively are committed to this continuous improvement environment and are supportive of any strategic changes that the school has implemented for the betterment of quality. The school showed an overall ability to achieve desired outcomes across wide range of activities. TheInstitute is committed to excellence and will remain to do so and the accreditation process helped us to take a holistic view of all its activities. The process encompasses various parameters like quality of students, faculty quality and research output, infrastructural facilities and financial stability of the institute. The institute is guided by its mission and vision and this quality assurance process will continue the institute to achieve its mission and vision by providing a qualityframework.

4. THE INSTITUTE'S RANKING: GLOBAL AND INDIAN

None of the vintage IIMs - A,B and C have featured in the top 200-500 league tables of the world's best universities published annually by the London-based rating agency Quacquarelli Symonds (QS), *THE (Times Higher Education Supplement)* or the Shanghai Jiao Tong University. The only top-ranked Indian education institution is the IIT - Bombay, ranked 187 in the league table of the QS World University Rankings 2010. However, absence of the IIMs and India's B-schools in the league table of the world's top varsities is probably they are not 'universities' but specialist institutions of professional education. Although none of the IIMs figure in the 2010 league table of the world's top 100 business schools of the London-based *Financial Times.* The pre-requisite for inclusion in the FT B-schools league table is affiliation with European Quality Improvement System (EQUIS).

A) Global Ranking

There are three major ranking agencies for b-schools in the world. Those are Financial Times Ranking, CEMS MIM ranking and Quacquarelli Symonds (QS) ranking. Financial Times publishes Global MBA Ranking and Global, Asian and Indian Master in Management (MM) rankings. The CEMS publishes Global Master in International Management (MIM)ranking. The QS publishes Global, Asian MBA ranking and World UniversityRanking.

i) Financial Times: Global MBA Ranking

The Financial Time Ranking is based in London. FT global MBA Rankings is considered the gold standard in B-school ranking.It published both

Global MBA and Global MM Ranking for b-schools around the world. The rank of MBA course in our institute was considered in the FT Global MBA Ranking. A valuable factor in the ranking methodology is Careers Rank under the alumni career progress section of parameters for which the batch of 2011 had been considered. The Institute ranked number one the careers rank signifying that the alumni has registered the best career growth, which was calculated in terms of seniority and company size and employee strength over the last three years in comparison to all other participating B-Schools. The rankings will help us network with the top European B-schools.

FinancialTimes publishes worldwide annual rankings related to Management Schools called Global B-School Rankings. This ranking features the world's best 100 full-time MBA programs. The broad parameters on which the institutes are ranked include value for money, career progress, female faculty, female students, international faculty and students. The institute is exploring the possibility of entering into new partnerships for student and faculty exchange programs and engaging closely with its alumni and to undertake a review of the curriculum for PGP program. Our Institute has upped its global ranking and is working on a strategy to improve further. The FT Rankings demonstrate that ourMBA program is powerful. In line with our vision ofglobal eminence, our continuous endeavour is to further promote curricular relevance, international engagement and diversity for a dynamic learning experience that positions our students as global leaders. Categories considered in the rankings include alumni career progress, school diversity and international experience and research. Our institute excelled in criteria of salary percentage increase and career progress of alumni.

The FT Rankings demonstrate that the institute's MBA program is a powerful launching pad for its graduates to contribute to business and society in leadership positions. According to the FT Global MBA Ranking, the institute's rank improved to the 42nd position in 2020, from 49th in 2019, 78th in 2018 and 95th in 2017. But, in 2021 and 2022, its ranks stepped down to 44 and 56 respectively. Our Global MBA Rank moved upward from 78 in 2018 to 42 in 2020. However, the average global rank of the institute in last six years was nearly 61 in FT's Global MBA Ranking. In theFT's Global MBA ranking, ranked 42nd to 68th during last six years, 2017 to 2022. The Institute ranked highest 42 in 2020 from 95 in 2017, while decreased to 68 in 2022(Table 1.7.1).

ii) Financial Times: Global Master in Management (MM) Ranking

The FT's MM Global ranking reached the milestone of 100 B-schools, as the MM degree continues to grow in popularity worldwide. Keeping internationalisation in focus, our institute is committed to offer the best management education in the country. This ranking features the top management degrees for students with little or no previous work experience. Based on the 2015 graduates' ratings of their own program, subject-wise, our institute ranked at number one in Economics and number seven in Finance as subjects being taught at the business schools. The FT has devised a concept of clustering of the top 14 schools form the top cluster. Categories considered in the rankings include Alumni Career Progress, School Diversity, and International Experience and Research. Our Institute excelled in several individual criteria within these categories, including the salary of graduates three years' after graduation, salary percentage increase and career progress of alumni since graduation, and the effectiveness of career services with jobs upon graduation. Our institute did well in terms of diversity like the percentage of female faculty and female students, international faculty, international board members and international course experience.

In FT's MM Ranking 2020, the Institute secured 21st rank globally in for its flagship MBA program.This two-year course has climbed up to the 13th position from that of 19 last year in the FT's MM ranking 2014. The institute posts an impressive debut at 19 in the list of 70 B-schools in 2013. It has improved its position by six places from 2013. But, that does not mean that our institute has been ranked as 13th best B-school in the world. FT's MM ranking recognizes our PGP as the 13th best MM program globally. However, this is no way recognition of our institute as the 13th best B-School in the world. In 2018 FT's Global ranking of MM, the institute ranked at 23 by improving its rank from 28 last year 2017. So, the Institute climbed five places from 28 in 2017 to 23 in 2018 (Table 1.7.1).

The Institute was at the top 13 in 2014, but stepped down to 28 in 2017. During last seven years, our ranks in FT's MM Global Ranking varied from 13 to 28. The average global rank of the institute in last six years was nearly 20. In 2018, FT's MM ranking, our institute featured as the number two B-Schools in the country and number three in Asia. In FT's MM Rankings 2020, the institute secured the second spot in Asia and also in India.In FT's MM Asian Ranking, our Institute ranked 3rd in 2018 but stepped up to 2nd in theyears 2019 to 2021. The average Asian rank of the institute was nearly 2 in FT's MM Asian Ranking. In FT's MM Indian ranking, our Institute was 1st in 2019 and 2nd in last three years during 2018 to 2021. Our average rank was nearly 2 in FT's MM Indian Ranking

iii) The Quacquarelli Symonds Ltd (QS)

The Quacquarelli Symonds Ltd (QS) is a London based higher education information and research company which organizes the largest business education event in the world. The company publishes its annual QS World University Rankings of Global 200 Top Business Schools Report. The QS Global Report 2010 ranks 200 B-schools in North America (80), Europe (67), Asia-Pacific (36), Latin America (10) and Africa & Middle East (7) on the basis of employer preference. Globally our institute ranked 94 in 2018, 79 in 2021 and 76 in 2022. So, our average rank was 83. In the Asia Pacific regional rankings, our rank was 12 in 2020 and 2021 but 14 in 2022 out of 200. In the Asia Pacific region, our rank in QS Global MBA ranking was about 13. The QS World University Rankings is an annual publication of university rankings which comprises the global overall and subject rankings amongst Top 200 B-schools in the World. In this ranking, our rank improved from 94 in 2018 to 76 in 2022. Moreover, in the QS World University MM Ranking, our ranked was 46 in 2017.

iv) CEMS –MIM Ranking

The CEMS has created a global standard of management studies for students to become true global managers with excellence in performance and ethical conduct and understanding of cultural diversity.Our Institute is the only Indian member of this renowned alliance of leading global business schools and multinational corporations, through its prestigious Masters in International Management (MIM). As a member of the CEMS, our institute offers the CEMS – MIM Degree, a Double Degree Program since 2012. In CEMS-MIM, global rank for our institute has climbed to 4th position in 2015 and it was up one in last year 2014 and three positions higher than its 2013 ranking (Sandesh, 2015). The Institute ranked 3, 7, 5 and 4 in 2012, 2013, 2014 and 2015 and our average rank was 5.

B) Indian Ranking

At the national level, the management schools has been ranked by - NIRF (National Institutional Framework Ranking) and the Business Magazines like - OUTLOOK-ICARE, Business Today, India Today, Jagran Josh and Shiksha etc.

i) NIRF Ranking

National Institutional Ranking Framework (NIRF) was launched by the MHRD (Minister of Human Resource Development) in 2015. It outlines a methodology to identify the broad parameters for ranking various institutions across the country. There are different parameters on which the institute is given a score and ranked accordingly. Our institute has been ranked 3rd for past six years at a stretch from 2016 to 2021 (Table 1.7.2).

ii) OUTLOOK-ICARE Ranking

The Outlook-ICARE India MBA Rankings survey is a 100 per cent outcome-based assessment, developed with inputs from the industry and supported by strong research. The parameters used by Outlook MBA Rankings are - Full time Faculty and Student Ratio (FSR), Research as an indicator of Paper productivity and citation per paper, Employability as an indicator of Student placement percentage and the median salary, Faculty quality as an indicator of Faculty qualification and corporate experience and the Inclusiveness & Diversity as an indicator of Regional and Gender diversity.In 2020, the score of our institute was 100 in FSR, 86 in Research, 96 in Employability and 95 in Faculty Quality, 82 in Inclusiveness & Diversity and 89 was the overall score. In 2021, the score of the Institute was 100 in FSR, 49 in Research, 83 in Employability 87 in Faculty Quality, 57 in Inclusiveness & Diversity. In the Outlook-ICARE India MBA Rankings, our institute ranked 3rd in last three years 2020 to 2022. In Outlook India, our institute holds 3rdposition in the total 75 top management colleges in India. The institute also ranked 3rd by the Outlook India's Top 25 Public MBA Colleges in 2021 and 2022.

iii) Others Ranking

The Business Today ranked our institute in first to third positions during 2017 to 2022. The India Today ranked the institute in first position in 2021 and Jagran Josh ranked the institute in 3rd position in 2020 among Management Institutes, while Shiksha has ranked us in 3rd positions during 2021.

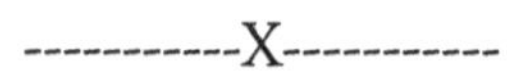

CHAPTER 1.8

THE GROWTH OF THE INSTITUTE TILL 50TH BATCH: 1961-2013

ENROLMENT IN PGP, FPM, FACULTY STRENGTH AND FEES

INTRODUCTION

This chapter delved into the growth of the Institute during last fifty batches. The growth of the Institute has been discussed in five sections. In Section – A, the growth in number of Programs introduced so far has been discussed. In Section – B, the growth in enrolment in PGP and FPM program till 2013 was discussed. The growth in enrolment of Women students in those programs has also been discussed. In Section - C, the growth in number of faculty members in different groups and representation of Women faculty members was discussed. In Section D, the growth in Total Fees for PGP in current and constant prices and growth of fees by items has been discussed. Finallyin Section E, the growth of the Manpower in the Institute during last fifty years has been discussed.

SECTION – A: GROWTH IN NUMBER OF PROGRAMS INTRODUCED

The Institute started with a solo program Advanced Management Program (AMP) in 1961 at Barrackpur Campus. After shifting to Emerald Bower (EB), the AMP was started as EDP, currently named MDP. The Core Program PGP along with EDPs, In-Company Training and Consultancystarted. in 1964 and FPM in 1971 at EB Campus. The Institute moved to Joka campus in 1975. After six years, in 1981, an evening program Certificate Programme in General Management (CPGM) was introduced in our City Office at Calcutta. After eleven years, a two year PGDCM was introduced in 1992. In 1994, the evening program was upgraded to three years PGDBM course. After thirteen years in 2007, two new programs PGPEX and PGPEX_VLM were introduced, while LDP was introduced in 2008. Of late, a two years Course PGDBA was introduced in 2015(Exhibit 1.8.1).

The CPGM stopped and renamed as PGDBM in 1994. The PGDCM has stopped in 2014 and renamed as PGDBA in 2015. Finally, the PGP, EDP, In-Company Training, Consultancy, FPM, PGDBM, PGPEX, PGPEX-VLM, LDP and PGDBA are still running. The AMP started in 1961, PGP, EDP, In-Company Training and Consultancy in 1964, FPM in 1971, CGM in 1981, PGDCM in 1992, PGDBM in 1994,PGPEX and PGPEX_VLM in 2007, LDP in 2008 and lastly PGDBA in 2015, The institute started with one program, now ten Programs are still runningand number of residential students increased from 200 to 5000. These programs are discussed below.

1. Advanced Management Programme of MIT

The Institute started with a solo program - Advanced Management Programme (AMP) in 1961 at Barrackpur Campus. The Ford Foundation provided the professionalised managerial expertise at the top and middle level through this annual Advanced Management Programme of MIT. The Ford Foundation organised the visit to American business school by a selected group of influential Indians. To ensure the support of the Industrialist, the Ford Foundation sponsored "Advanced Management" seminar at a picturesque resort of Srinagar in Kashmir. Initially staffed by MIT, the seminar helped further towards American style professional management to Indian industrialists. The participation of Ford Foundation and the Sloan School of Management at MIT was most direct. The purpose was to develop professional management in business and industrial organisations, as well as in the Government through education and training of working executives and officers. The main aim was to develop a cadre of young professional managers who would transform the Indian business and industry through high quality knowledgeable professional managers.

2. Post-Graduate Programme in Mangement (PGP)

The academic activities prescribed by the MIT were - a) Post-Graduate Programme, b) Executive Development Programme, c) Fellowship Programme, d) Research and e) Consultancy.In 1962, the Post-Graduate Programme in Management was accepted as a Core Programme. This program should cover the following four major areas - i) Management Concept and Practice, (ii) Major Operational areas of enterprises - Marketing, Production, Finance and Personnel. iii) Tools for Management Analysis and (iv) Environmental influence in Social, Culture and Governmental Change. The MIT's technical assistance transferred its own curriculum biases to this Institute. Traditional lecture base methods were prescribed for classroom teaching, but the evaluation system vastly different from Indian University system. Performance of students should not determine by marks in final examination but on the basis of all Semester examinations.

Evaluation should use along with reports, term papers, class performance etc. Instead of marks, grades of 9 points were suggested to be awarded. The PGP was a two year full time compulsory residential programme. The MIT transferred its own curriculum and the course of PGP is designed to train students as excellent managers and decision makers. The PGP was to develop a global perspective while responding effectively to changes in the economic, political, cultural and technological environments. A set of specific skills be taught to students in the sphere of finance, accounting, marketing, operations etc.

3. Executive Development Programme

The Executive Development Programme (EDP) started at Barrack pore campus. The EDPs was a especially renowned feature of MIT, as it involved in the annual "Advanced Management Programme". Later, the AMP of MIT was replaced by EDP in 1964 at Emerald Bower Campus. The EDPs were meant for executives at the top and middle level. These EDPs will lead to: i) Important service to present managers, ii) Spread the Institute's values, iii) Enhance the acceptance of Institute's graduates and iv) Encourage the faculty members for both money contribution and opportunities. Thus, the stress on EDP was a direct outcome of MIT's influence. Initially, the Institute planned for four EDPs, as it lacked the physical facilities for starting the PGP. The EDPs aimed to spread the value of the Institute and to enhance the acceptance of our graduates. Over the years, EDPs were continuing as original plan and the Institute took over the staffing of annual AMPs offered by MIT in 1964. The EDPs were designed with the objective of providing practicing managers the insight into managerial concepts and implementing strategies in functional areas. After 1980, in Joka campus, most of the EDPs were held in our own EDP Center at Tata Hall. The EDPs have been designed to effectively spread quality management education among practicing managers, across all levels. These programmes equip experienced professionals with powerful knowledge, tools and resources to tackle the most complex business challenges.

4. In-Company Training

The Institute offers the Executive Education through– In-Company Training. In this program, our faculty members will go to the Company's office and train the managers of the Company. The number of participants will be fixed by the Company and a few faculty members will take classes by rotation.It is a customized Training Programme in tailor-made modules created around specific mandates from discerning corporate clients.

5. Consultancy

All the preparatory documents on the establishment of IIM Calcutta suggested Consultancy as a supplementary activity. It was adopted to attract more talented teachers, who may not be available due to restricted pay scale.Consultancy was aimed to attract more talented faculty for additional income, keeping in touch with current problems in business and administrative problems. Each faculty was allowed one day in a week or 54 days in a year on consultancy work. Such efforts were for enhancing the research base as well as keeping faculty members in touch with the real business world.

6. Fellowship Programme inManagement

The Meriam-Thurlby placed the priority for teachers training in management education. The Fellowship Programme in Management (FPM) was aimed at fulfilling the shortage of management teachers in India and to help Universities in India as well as in Asian countries. This training of teachers of business administration would lead to a Ph. D. degree. Not the Thesis, but the research training in a broad basis on realistic materials on Indian management problems. Initially, the FPM was not started because of shortage of faculty and resources. After the Institute moved from Barrackpur to EB Campus, the FPM was planned to start in 1968 but it started late in 1971. The first batch of our Fellows came out in 1975.

7. The Certificate Programme in General Management (CPGM)

Atwo year evening course-"Certificate Programme in General Management" (CPGM) was introduced in 1981 at the City office. This programme was meant for working persons who could join classes after office hours. The classes were held at our City Office at Harrington Mansion in central Calcutta, The classes were held at 6 p.m. to 9 p.m with 30 to 40 students. Our faculty members were provided transport from Joka to City Office for taking classes. This city office had a library and other facilities like Fax, Xerox and Typing. About ten staffs were deputed there by rotation from the existing employees at Joka campus. Some employees were eager to join there, as the office starts at 12 noon and close at 9 p.m. After passing this CPGM program, some students have joined our Institute as Assistant Professors.

8. Post Graduate Diploma in Computer Aided Management (PGDCM)

A two years residential full time Post Graduate Diploma in Computer Aided Management was introduced in 1992 to cater the needs of the Information age. This course was given additional emphasis on use of

Information Technology in Management. The fifty seated PGDCM was in addition to existing PGP. The students of PGDCM will sit with PGDM students in the first year, but they will sit in CAM center in second year.

9. Post Graduate Diploma in Business Management (PGDBM)

The two years evening Certificate Programme in General Management (CPGM) started in 1981. It was upgraded to a three years evening diploma program - PGDBM in 1994, with an intake capacity of fifty students. The classes will held in our City Office at Harington Mansion and the timing will be same 6 p.m. to 9 p.m. as before.

10. Post-Graduate Programme for Executives (PGP-EX)

The "Revenue Maximising Committee" suggested introduction of some new academic programs. The Institute introduced four new courses – PGPEX, PGPEX-VLM, PGDBA and LDP. They also suggested the introduction of a one year full time programme on International Management. The PGPEX was started in 2007 with the aim of developing experienced and ambitious executives for leadership positions. It was of one year full time residential programme and for working executives having more than five years of professional experiences. The courses started with intake capacity of 40 students. It started to provide mid-career professionals the ideal platform to augment their existing skills. The PGPEX was to endeavour for senior and top management roles in industry. Under the guidance of leading management faculty, a passion for continuous learning synergizes with experiences from diverse backgrounds is to enrich learning environment. Learning beyond the classroom is an equally important, while case discussions enrich the practical experience of unravelling real life business puzzles. The PGPEX is a "One-Year Miracle" and many executives are using this as stepping stones to life-changing mid-life career switches.

11. Post Graduate Programme for Executive for Visionary Leadership in Manufacturing

The programme PGPEX-VLM was also started in 2007 with the mission to develop future visionary leaders for the manufacturing sector in India, so as to enhance the global competitiveness in manufacturing sector. This is one year full time residential program with the focus to appreciate an industry's metamorphosis in competitive times. The PGPEX-VLM was for working executives having more than five years of professional experiences. The course is conducted jointly by three premier institutes – IIMCalcutta, IIT Kanpur and IIT Madras and it is designed by these Institutes in consultation with industry and MHRD. Concurrently, the PGPEX-VLM was started in collaboration with the Government of Japan.

12. Long Duration Programme (LDP)

The Institute realized it had to develop a programme of longer duration. It intended to develop a six month to one year tailor-made program.In 2008, a one year Long Duration Programme (LDP) was introduced in the Institute. The LDPs were conducted on the distance learning format and was disseminated through satellite-based learning platforms, interspersed with brief in-campus sessions. The LDP is an Online and classroom based programme.

13. Post Graduate Diploma in Business Analytic (PGDBA)

In 2015, a new two years full time course PGDBA was introduced in lieu of old PGDCM. It was a two year residential full time programme that focuses to develop skills for business analysis.

SECTION – B: GROWTH IN ENROLMENT OF IN PGP AND FPM

1. GROWTH IN ENROLMENT IN PGP

i) Annual Growth in Enrolment

The Post Graduate Programme in Management (PGP) was introduced in 1964 with 40 seats, but the enrolment was only 39 in first batch. In second batch, the enrolment rose to 70 and 80 in next two batches, 90 in next two batches but increased to 100 in 7th and 9th again reduced to 90 in 10th batch (Table 1.8.1). The enrolment in second decade varied from 90 to

128 and reached its peak in 16th batch, when the Institute moved to new Joka campus. In third decade, the enrolment increased from 105 to 150, as the PGDCM was introduced in 1992. In fourth decade, the enrolment varied from 148 to 272. In 1997, the Central Government directed to double the intake from 105 to 210. So, enrolment increased to 263 in 34th batch. Lastly, because of reservation of OBC candidates in 2006, the enrolment jumped to 322 in 43rd batch and reached a peak of 462 in 50th batch.

ii) Decadal Growth in Enrolment of PGP Students

During first decade (1964-1973) covering first ten batches, total enrolment in PGP was 819. In second decade covering 11 to 20th batches, total enrolment was 1048 while 1133 in third decade, 2290 in fourth decade and 3361 in last decade (Table 1.8.2). The decadal enrolment increased gradually and reached high in fifth decade. The enrolment increased by 229 in second decade, 85 in third, 1157 in fourth and 1071 in fifth decades. In the entire period of fifty years, a total of 8651 students have enrolled. On an average, 82 students enrolled annually in first decade, 105 in second, 113 in third, 229 in fourth, 336 in last decade while. 173 enrolled annually in all decades combined.

In relative term, student enrolment increased by 28% in second, 8% in third, 102% in fourth and 47% in fifth decades. So, enrolment increased most in fourth decade. The year to year growth in enrolment was highest 78% in 1997 and 41% in 1992. The main reason was introduction of PGDCM in 1992 and the Central Government's direction to increase student intake in 1997 and further in 2008 due to reservation of OBC student. So, student's enrolment increased most in recent years, 1998 to 2014. We divided the entire period into two equal parts of 25 years duration. Student's enrolment was 2387 in first half and 6264 in second half.So, the enrolment of students became more than double in second half. In the first half, the Institute was under the full control of the Central Government and the growth in enrolment was meagre. In second half, the

Central Government drastically cut its grants and institute started under market economy, it resulted enrolment increased exponentially.

iii) Log Normal Trend in Enrolment in PGP

We have fitted exponential trend of Log-normal values on enrolment of students during different time periods. The annual growth in enrolment was 6.5%, 1.3%, 3.7%, 7.3% and 6.1% in successive five decades and 3.7% in all decades combined (Table 1.8.2). The growth rates were higher in fourth, firstand fifth decades, while lower in second and third decades. But, we found no significant growth in second and third decades. So, a significant growth in enrolment was in last two decades. We divided the entire period into two equal parts of 25 batches each. The annual growth in first half was 2.1%and 5.7% in second halfwhile 37% in entire period. So, the growth in enrolment was more in last two decades.

iv) Reasons for Slow and High Growth in Enrolment

The number of student intake was solely depended on Central Government's direction. Initially, the Government sanctioned 40 seats, then to 80 again further to 100 till first 20 years. But changes in Government policies have induced changes in intake. In 1992, the introduction of Computer Aided Management (PGDCM) has increased the intake by 50. So, intake in PGP (both PGDM and PGDCM) increased from 105 to 148 in 29th batch. In 1997, theCentral Ministry directed the Institute to increase the intake, unless the Government's grant be restricted. Thus, in 1997 student enrolment increased further from 148 to 263. In 2009, the enrolment increased more due the implementation of reservations for OBC students. As a result, student enrolment also increased further. Because of the OBC reservations in 2009, enrolment rose from 278 to 383 (Table 1.8.1). Moreover, in 2005, 2% reservation was introduced for Physically Disabled (PWD) students and in 2009, 10% reservation was introduced for EWS (Economically Weaker Section) of the Society. Thus, enrolment increased from 383 to 462 in fiftieth batches. Lastly, the Government took initiativeto empower women, a new policy was adopted for enrolment of more women. So, the average enrolment of women was 30 in preceding years but it jumped to 107 in 2013.

The enrolment of student also depended on placement of pass out students. In initial years, our faculty members have to lobby to corporate leaders for recruiting our graduates. In second decade, the corporate leaders and Public sector enterprise were eager to recruit our graduates. In later years, the sluggish placement seasons that lasted for more than a week, as we failed to provide placements to our students. In 2006, our placement seasons became dull and we fail to provide employment of our students. So, enrolment of students in next year was dependent on following sluggish placement. But, in current years, it has changed, and our placement finished in two days and our graduates are employed abroad.

v). Enrolment of Women Students in PGP

In the first batch of 1964, there were only two women students to whom we could not provide hostel in our EB Campus. They were housed in hostel of Indian Statistical Institute, about 3 kilometres away from EB campus. In next years, we provide only three women in our hostel in EB Campus till 1975. In 1976, when we moved to unfinished Joka Campus, the Institute had six women in awing of Menes' Hostel. Afterward, the crisis for women hostel was solved and enrolment of women increased from 10 to 24. The numbers of women students were 24, 56, 98, 194 and 394 in five decades respectively (Table 1.8.2). Thus, the average number of women enrolled was 2, 6, 10, 19 and 39 annually in successive decades. But, more women started to enrolledin last decade from 2004 to 2013. We divided the entire period into two equal parts covering 25 batches; the enrolment of women was 122 in first half and 644 in last half. So, more women were enrolled in second half. The representation of women in PGP was very poor around 3% in first, 5% in second, 9% in third, 8% in fourth and 12% in fifth decades. But, it reached a peak at 23% in 2013 (Table 1.8.1).

2. ENROLMENT IN FELLOWSHIP PROGRAMME

The Fellowship Programme started in 1971 and the first Fellowship was awarded in 1976. Gradually, the number of Fellows started increasing annually by 2 or 3 in first twenty years and by 30 to 80 in last twenty years. Till 2013, the Institute has awarded Fellowship to 161 students. Some of our Fellows have been recruited as Faculty members in our Institute and other Institutes locally and globally. We will study the progress of our Fellowship Programme in last 40 years, 1971 to 2013. The Institute's website does not publish enrolment data for FP students, but provide data on FP awardees by year, groups, supervisors etc.

During first ten years, 1975 to 1984, only 24 students were awarded Fellowship. In next decade, another 26 students were awarded Fellow. In next decade ending 2004, 31 students were awarded Fellow, while in last decade till 2014, as much as 80 students were awarded Fellow (Table 1.8.3). So, in successive decades, numbers of Fellowship awardees were 24, 26, 31 and 80. The number of Fellows was stagnant at 30 in first three decades. On the other hand, a half of the Fellowship was awarded in last decade 2005-2014. The recent hike in enrolment in our FP was due to Policy changes introduced in 2005. Out of total 161 FP awardees, 50 were awarded Fellow in first half while 111 have been awarded Fellow in last half.Only, 2 to 3 students were awarded Fellow annually in first 30 years but it increased to 8 in last ten years. During the entire period, only 22 women were awarded Fellowship. Among them, mostly were in last two decades. The representation of women was 14%.

In the first two decade 1975-1994, most Fellows were in OPR, FIN & CON and Economics groups. In the last two decades, most Fellows were in MIS, FIN & CON and OPR groups. The Strategic Management was introduced in last decade but it produced 8 Fellows. Most of the Fellows in MIS and OGBH were in last two decades. The FIN & CON and OPR have produced Fellows uniformly in all decades, while Economics and Marketing have a few Fellows in all decades. The supervisors of these Fellows were senior faculty member of the concerned groups. In the entire period, the Institute produced a total of 161 Fellows. Among them, 38 were in MIS group, 27 in Operation Research and 9 in its allied group Operations Research and System Analysis. So, the Operation Research and its allied combined had 36 Fellows. The Finance & Control group had 25 Fellows. Thus, a majority of Fellows were in these three groups which combined shared two-third of the total Fellows (Table 1.8.4). The Organisational Behaviour OGBH, Economicsand Marketing groups have 14, 12 and 10 Fellows respectively. Similarly, Strategic Management, Regional Development and HRM groups have 8, 7 and 6 Fellows respectively. The Sociology group had 4 Fellows and Mathematics in Management had only one.

Among 161 Fellows, 141 were supervised by individual Faculty and rest 20 by two or more faculties. Individually, Prof. S K Chakraborty of Finance & Control group and Prof. S Ray of Strategic Management group had supervised six students each.Prof. A K Chaudhuri and Prof. M N Pal supervised five students each. Four Professors - Prof. A K Chatterjee, Prof. B K Sinha, Prof. N K Chandra and Prof. L Chatterjee supervised four students each. Eight Professors had supervised the Thesis of three students each. They were - Profs. A Bagchi, A Bhattacharya, B N Srivastava, K K Bhattacharya, N K Rao, N Ramchandran, S K Basu, and S Bhattacharya. Moreover, the eighteen Professors had supervised the Thesis of two students each.Moreover, thirty five faculty members supervised the Thesis of only one student each.Thus, Prof. S K Chakraborty, Prof. S Ray, Prof. A K Chaudhuri, Prof. M N Pal, Prof. A Mohanti, Prof A K Pal, Prof. A K Chatterjee, Prof. B K Sinha, Prof. N K Chandra and Prof. L Chatterjee have supervised the Thesis of most of the Fellowship awardees.

a) Women Students in Fellowship Program

In the entire period, only 22 women were awarded Fellowship. Among them, one each in first two decades, 6 in third decade and 14 in last decade. The share of women was 4% in first two decades, 19% in third and 18% in last decade. So, most women Fellows were in last two decades. Among the women Fellows, 7 were in Organisational Behaviour, 5 in HRM, 3 in FIN

& CON and one or two each in MIS, Sociology, Economics, Marketing and Operations Research. So, most of them were in Organisational Behaviour and HRM.

SECTION – C: GROWTH IN FACULTY STRENGTH BY GROUPS

1. THE GROWTH IN FACULTY STRENGTH

In early days at EB Campus, the teaching community was very small in number but vast in knowledge and intellect. Initially, the faculty members were a few but gradually increased to nearly hundred today. In 1964, there were only 24 faculty member which reduced to 12 in next years, as the early recruited members left for joining more responsible positions. The faculty strength increased to 24 in next year and gradually increased to 38 in 1974, 50 in 1984, 60 in 1995and 60 in 2005 and 92 in 2014 (Table 1.8.5). During last fifty years, the strength of faculty members increased from 24 to 92, while total students in PGP I and II combined increased from 80 to 866. So, total students increased by ten times, while faculty strength increased by four times. Thus, the teaching strength was low compared to that of student. Thus, the Institute started suffering from the acute scarcity of faculty members.

2. CHANGES IN FACULTY STRENGTH BY GROUPS

In 2014, out of total 92 faculty member, a maximum of 14 were in Operation Research including Statistics and System Analysis. The Management Information System and Economics groups have 12 faculty members each, while 11 faculties in Marketing group. So, a majority of faculty members belonged to these four groups – OPR, MIS, Economics and Marketing. The Public Policy Management group had 9 faculties while Finance and Control, Behavioural Science and Strategic Management groups have 8 faculties each. But, the PMIR/HRM and Business Ethics groups have 5 faculties each (Table 1.8.5). .

The Faculty strength in Operations Research including Statistics was 8 in 1974 and increased to 10 in 1984, 12 in 1994 and 14 in 2004 and 2014. The number of faculty members in Economics group remained stagnant at 6 to 7 since 1974, but jumped to 12 in 2014. The number of faculty members in Management Information System was 4 till 1984, but increased to 8 in 1994, 10 in 2004 and 12 in 2014. In Finance and Control, the number of faculty members was 4 in 1974, 8 in 1984, 9 in 1994, 7 in 2004 and 8 in 2014. The faculty strength in Marketing remained stagnant at 4 till 2004 but jumped to 11 in 2014. The Faculty strength in PMIR including HRM was highest 6 in 1974, but it reduced to 3 in 1984, 4 in 1994 and 5 in 2014. The faculty strength in newly formed PPM group increased from 3 in 1974 to 6 in 1984, 8 in 1994, 7 in 2004 and 9 in 2014. The newly group Strategic Management has only 2 faculties in 1994 but increased to 8 in 2014. New Business Ethics group started with one faculty in 2004 but increased to 5 in 2014(Table 1.8.5).

In mid-1970s, faculty strength was strong in Operations Research, Economics and PMIR groups. While, in mid-1980, Operations Research, Behavioural Science and Finance & Control was strong. In mid-1990s, Operations Research, Finance & Control and MIS became strong. In 2004, the Operations Research and MIS became strong. Finally, in 2014, MIS, Operations Research and Economics became strong by numbers. So, different groups became strong in different times. Till 1984, the Operations Research group was strong in most time. The MIS group became strong since 2004. Through out the time, Economics group was a powerful lobby but lost power as they are newly recruited young faculty members. The Finance & Control group remained dim after an eminent Professor S K Chakraborty detached from this group and formed the Management Centre of Human Values. Later, Prof. Asok Banerjee of Finance & Control group became involved in Institute's non-academic matters.

3. STUDENT TEACHER RATIOS

Because of scarcity of faculty member, the student teacher ratio increased from two in initial years to ten in recent past. During first decade (1964-

1973), since the inception of PGP, the student teacher ratio was 5.7. In successive decades, the ratio decreased gradually to 4.6 in second and 4.1 in third but increased to 7.5 in fourth and 9.4 in last decade. During last 50 years, the student teacher ratio was low in second and third decade, while high in first, fourth and fifth decades. In last decade, the student teacher ratio exceeded 10 in last five years since 2006. The student teacher ratio in some bench mark years (Table 1.8.6) indicated that the ratio began to increase since 1999.

These findings are based on students enrolled in PGP I & II. But, two more programmes were introduced since 2007. The annual enrolment in PGPEX varied from 39 to 51, while that in PGPEX-VLM varied from 29 to 38. The same faculty members have to teach all these students too. By considering the students in both these programs, the student teacher ratio reached a maximum of 11 in last few years (Table 1.8.5).By adding the students in both the courses along with PGP, total student was 954 in 2013. Besides them, these teachers had to supervise about ten Fellowship students. The teachers had to conduct Management Development Programme and Consultancy throughout the year. So, increased student teacher ratio hampered quality of education, as a faculty member has to teach more students in a fixed time. In 2007, the Ministry of HRD admitted a severe shortage of faculty in all IIMs. In that year, IIM Calcutta has 88 sanctioned posts where only 70 faculties were in position.

SECTION – D: GROWTH IN TOTAL FEES FOR PGP

1. TOTAL FEES FOR TWO YEARS PGP

Initially, the Total fees charged consists of six items like - Admission fees, Tuition fees, Accommodation charges, Course materials charges, Association fees and Caution deposits. These items were continued till 24th batch. In 25th batch (1988-1990), Computer Charges were introduced, while Library fees and Alumni fees were introduced in 29th batch (1992-1994). The Medical Insurance was introduced in 36th batch (1999-2001) and the Development fees introduced in 42nd batch (2005-2007). During the entire period, Admission fees was discontinued after 36th batch (1998-2000) and Computer charges, Library charges and Caution deposits were discontinued since 49th batch (2012-2014). Finallyin 50th batches, the total fees consists of seven items – Tuition fees, Accommodation charges,Association fees, Course materials charges, Alumni fees and Medical insurances.

2. THE TOTAL FEES FOR PGP

The total fees consist of tuition fees, course materialscharges, room rent development fees etc. The tuition fees are charged for providing teaching activities and course materials charges covered the cost of new text books, study material prepared by the Institute. The room rent is charged for accommodation in a well furnished room. The Association fees and Alumni membership fees are charged for students' activities. The medical insurance charges collected for medical needs during illness. Moreover, the medical facilities are provided free of cost by Institution's medical consultants available in our Health Unit close to our Hostels.The Development fee is charged for development of infrastructure like new classroom etc. Till 28th batch in 1991, the total fees to be paid by two annual instalments. After that, total fees are payable in six instalments prior to each semester. The tuition fee, academic charges and room rent be paid by instalments. But, development fees, Medical Insurance, Students Association fees are to be paid once in a year. The refundable caution money be paid once during registration and be refunded after completion of the program.

3. DECADAL INCREASE IN TOTAL FEES

i) At Current Price

The total fees for the entire two years PGP courses were Rs. 1,090 in the first batch in 1964. These fees were paid in two annual instalments of Rs. 670 in the first year and Rs. 420 in second year. The total fees remained static for next two years. It increased to Rs. 1,290 for next two years and then increased to Rs. 1,550, Rs. 1,800 and Rs. 2,100 in 10th batch. So, in the first decade covering 1st to 10th batch, the total fees increased from Rs. 1,090 to Rs.2,100. Thus, the total fees have been doubled in the first decade. In second decade covering 11th to 20th batch, the total fees increased from Rs. 2,350 to Rs. 3,650(Table 1.8.7)..The total fees hiked most form Rs. 2,700 to Rs. 3,300 in 1978, when the Institute moved to its incomplete Joka Campus. In third decade covering 21st to 30th batch, the total fees increased by more than nine times from Rs. 3,650 to Rs. 35,750.

The total fees hiked most from Rs. 5,460 in 1991 to Rs. 25,250 in 1992, as the Central Government started cutting of our Grants. In fourth decade covering 31st to 40th batch, the total fees increased from Rs. 51,250 to Rs. 2,54,000.During this period, fees were hiked by five times. In fifth decade, it increased most from Rs. 3,02,000 to Rs. 13,50,000. Thus, the total fees increased by four times in this period. We observed that hike in total fees was not a regular phenomenon but followed a cyclical pattern. Such peaks were reached in 1992, 1998, 2008 and 2010. During the entire period of fifty years, the total fees increased from Rs. 1,090 to Rs. 13, 50,000. The growth rates of total fess were 8% in first, 6% in second, 25% in third, 19% in fourth and 25% in fifth decades (Table 1.8.8). So, the total fees increased most in third and fifth decades. During last fifty years, total fees increased by 17%.

ii) At Constant Price

The inflation is the main reason behind the high growth in total fees in last fifty years. We compared the total fees at the constant price at the base price 1990. The total fee for the first batch was Rs.1,090 at current price. If we adjust the same at the price level of 1990, it became Rs.8,059. Similarly, in 10th batch the total fees of Rs. 2,100 became Rs.8,053 at constant price. So, during first decade covering first ten batches, the total fees remained static, as it increased merely 2% in constant prices(Table 1.8.8).In second decade, (11th to 20th batches), the total fees at constant price reduced from Rs. 7,037 to Rs. 6,285. Hence, the total fees at constant price reduced marginally by one percent. Thus, in first two decades, total fees at constant price remained stagnant. In third decade (21st to 30th) batches, the total fees increased much from Rs. 5,813 to Rs. 26,707 at constant price. So, the total fees hiked annually by 14% at constant price. Thus, the actual increase in total fees occurred in first time in third decade. In fourth decade, (31st to 40th batches), the total fees increased from Rs. 34,473 to Rs. 95,886 at constant price. The total fees hiked by 12% at constant pricein fourth decade. In fifth decade, (41st to 50th batches), the total fees increased from Rs. 92,928 to Rs.2,36,990 at constant price. So, total fees had been hiked by nearly 15% at constant price. During the entire period of fifty years, the total fees increased by 9% at constant price. The significant increase in total fees at constant price was in last three decades.

4. COMPONENTS OF TOTAL FEES

The total fees includes the tuition fee, academic charges, room rent, development fees, computer charges, library fee, students' association fees, alumni membership and medical etc. In the first batch (1964-1966), the total fess was Rs.1,090, of which, Rs. 100 for admission, Rs. 200 for tuition, Rs. 400 for course material, Rs. 240 for accommodation, Rs. 100 for caution deposit and Rs. 50 for association fee.Out of total fees, 37% was for course material, 22% for room rent, 18% for tuition fees, 9% for each of admission fee and caution deposit and 5% for others. Similar trend continued till 24th batch.Gradually, new items were added which resulted further increase in total fees. The Computer Charges was introduced in 25th batch, Library fees and Alumni fees were introduced in 29th batch, Medical Insurance was introduced 36th batch and Development Fess introduced in 42nd batch.

In 25th batch, computer charges of Rs. 1,000 were introduced and total fee rose to Rs. 4,910. The share of course materials and room rent was 24% each, tuition fee and computer charges 20% each and 12% other charges. In 29th batch, Library fees of Rs. 7,200 and Alumni fees of Rs. 350 were introduced and total fee rose to Rs. 25,150. In this year, tuition fees alone increased from Rs. 1,000 to Rs. 12,000. The share of tuition fees increased to 48%, library fees 29%, computer charges 10%, course materials and room rent 5% each and others 3%.In 36th batch, Medical Insurance of Rs. 1,000 was introduced and total fee rose to Rs. 1,67,500. In this batch, the tuition fee increased by ten times from Rs. 12,000 to Rs. 1,20,000 (Table 2.3.3). The share of tuition fees increased to 72%, computer charges 9%, room rent 7%, library fees 6% and others 6%. (Table 2.3.2)

In 42nd batch, Development fess of Rs. 4,000 was introduced and total fee rose to Rs. 3,02 Lakh. In this batch, the tuition fee increased by 50% from Rs. 1,20 Lakh to Rs. 1,86 Lakh. The share of tuition fees reduced from 72% to 62% in earlier years. The computer charges and library fees was 10% each; course materials 8%, room rent 6% and others 4%. In 50th batch, the total fess increased to Rs.13.5 Lakh, of which, the tuition fess was Rs. 8.52 Lakh, course materials Rs. 3.40 Lakh, development fee. Rs.1.0 lakh and room rent Rs. 0.54 Lakh. The other fees like - Association fees, Alumni membership fees and Medical Insurance charges combined was only Rs. 4 thousand. Thus, out of total fees, 63% was for tuition fees, 25% for course materials, 7% for development fees, 4% for room rent and rest 1% for other. In this year, there were no separate charges for computer and library and it seems that these fees were merged with academic charges.

The total fees increased by 8% in first, 6% in second, 25% in third, 19% in fourth and 25% in fifth decades at current price. In constant price, the total fees increased by 2% in first, (-) 1% in second, 14% in third, 12% in fourth and 24% in fifth decades. So, total fees increased most in third and fifth decades in both the prices. Similarly, tuition fees increased most in third decade, the course materials charges increased most in third and fifth decade, the accommodation charges increased most in fifth decade, all at both the prices. During the entire period covering fifty batches, all fees have not increased uniformly. The total fees increased by 18%, tuition fees by 21%, course materials charges by 16% and room rent by 12% in current price. On contrary, the total fees increased by 9%, tuition fees by 12%, course materials charges by 8% and room rent by 4% only in constant price, So, the tuition fees and course materials charges increased most in both the prices.

5. HIKE IN TOTAL FEES BY ITEMS

The Total fees consists of items like - Admission fees, Tuition fees, Accommodation charges, Course materials charges, Association fees, Caution deposits, Computer Charges, Library fees, Alumni and the Medical Insurance for students. During the entire period covering 50 batches, the share of Tuition fees was 64%, Course materials charges 27%, Accommodation charges and other charges share 5% each in Total fees. The major items in Total fees were - Tuition fees, Course materials charges and Accommodation charges. The share of Tuition fees was at a peak of 70% in third decade and reduced to 63% in fifth decade. But in earlier three decade, the share of Tuition fees was 22% to 36%. On the other hand, the share of Course materials charges was 27% in entire period, but it reached to a peak of 42% in third decade but reduced to 19% in fourth decade while varied from 28% to 38% in rest decades. The share of Accommodation charges was nearly 5% in entire period, but it reached to 31% in second decade from 23% in first decade. Gradually, it reduced to 13%, 7% and 4% in successive decades. So, share of Accommodation charges reduced over time.

The average Total fee in first decade was Rs.1,566, which increased to Rs.3,040 in second decade and tripled to Rs. 9,757 in third decade then to Rs. 1,59,285, in fourth decade to Rs. 8,23,520 in fifth decades at current price(Table 1.8.10).. On the other hand, the average Total fees remained stagnant around Rs. 8,000 in first three decades, but it increased to Rs. 71,191 in fourth and Rs. 1,94,154.in fifth decades at constant price.The average Tuition fee in first decade was Rs.340, which doubled to Rs.760 in next decade and reached to Rs. 3,500 in third decade. It jumped to Rs. 1,11,000 in fourth decade and Rs. 5,18,000 in fifth decade at current price. So, Tuition fee increased much in last two decades. But, the Tuition fees at constant price was stagnant at Rs. 1,800 in first two decades, while increasedto Rs. 3,000 in third, to Rs. 48,950 in fourth and to Rs. 1,22,428 in fifth decades.

The average Course materials charges was Rs. 600 in first decade and Rs. 900 in second, Rs. 4,000 in third, Rs. 31,000 in fourth and Rs. 2,27,000 in fifth decade at current price. While in constant price, the Course materials charges was Rs. 2,300 to Rs. 3,700 in first three decades. It increased to Rs. 14,000 in fourth and to Rs. 53,000 in fifth decades. Thus, the Course materials charges increased much in fourth and fifth decades both at current and constant price. The Accommodation charge in current price in first decade was Rs.356, and Rs. 940 in second, Rs. 1,300 in third, Rs. 11,000 in fourth and Rs. 33,000 in fifth decades. So, Accommodation charge increased much in last two decades. The accommodation charge at constant price were Rs. 1,800 in first, Rs. 2400 in second decade, but reduced to Rs.1,400 in third, increased to Rs.5,000 in fourth and Rs. 7,700 in fifth decade. Thus, this charge increased slowly in first four decades but increased most in fifth decade.

6. THE TREND IN HIKE OF TOTAL FEES

We have fitted Log-normal distribution to estimate the growth rates of Total Fees (F) over the periods and whole period.

The curve is:Fn = Exp (b^*m^n),

Where, Fn is the total fees for the n-th batch, b is the Constant and

m is the Coefficient.

The growth rate (r) in total fees was given by the equation:

r = Exp ((Coefficient)-1)*100.

Total fees (F) for n-th batch,

(Fn) = Exp {Constant (b)*(Coefficient (m))^Batch (n)).

The Log linear Trend is

Ln (F) = {Ln (b) + n*Ln (m)}.

For the entire fiftieth batches,

The Constant b = 5.803, Coefficient m = 0.1600. and

Growth rate r = 17.35 at current price

The Constant b = 7.282, Coefficient m = 0.0834,

Growth rate r = 8.69 at constant price

The fitted Lognormal Curve is given by:

$$F50 = Exp \{(5.80311) *(0.15998) \text{^}50\}.$$

The decadal growth of total fees, at current and constant prices are given in Table -1.8.9. We found that growth rate of total fees, at current price was more (25%) in third decade and fifth decades, while low 6% in second and 8% in first decade. That growth of total fees, at constant price was more (15%) in fifth, 14% in third and 12% in fourth decades while least (-) 1% in second and 2% in first decade.

7. GROWTH RATES OF DIFFERENT FEES

During the entire period, the total fees had increased by 17% in current price and 9% in constant price. In order to gauge, which fees has increased more and which has increased less, which have discussed growth rates of those fees in different periods. The Tuition fee is a major component in Total fees as it shares more than 66%. In the entire period, the Tuition Fees increased by 21% while Total fees increased by 17% in current price. While, it increased by 12% compared to 9% increase of Total fees in constant price. So, in both prices, the Tuition fees increased more than the Total fees. during first two decades (1964 to 1983), The Tuition fees increased by 8% to 12% in current price and 2% to 5% in constant price. But, the Tuition fees increased most by 29% in current price and 18% in constant price during the third decade of 1984 to 1993. This increasing trend continued in fourth and fifth decades. It increased by 24% in current price in both decades while by 17% and 14% in last two decades in constant price. (Table 1.8.11).. Thus, the Tuition fees increased marginally in first two decade but it increased most in third decade and continued till fifth decade.

The second major component in Total fees is the Course Materials Charges. In the entire period, the Course Materials Charges increased by 16% in current price and by 8% in constant price. It grows as well as the growth of Total fees. But, the Course Materials Charges increased most by 31% in current price and 20% in constant price during the third decade. Similar trends continued in fifth decade, when it increased by 27% in current price and 17% in constant price. While, in first two decades and fourth decade, the Course Materials Charges increased by only 5% to 11% in current price and (-) 1% to 4% in constant price. The Course Materials Charges in constant price reduced by 1% in second decade. Recently, Computer charges and Library charges were included in Course Materials charges. And it increased further. In first two decade, the Course Materials Charges remained stagnate and increased marginally in fourth decade while itincreased more in third and fifth decades.

The reasons behind the hike in Course Materials Charges were technological changes as well as changes in outlook of faculty members. In the initial years, the Course materials were distributed in Cyclostyle format copied by Gestetner Machines. The Course Materials were first typed in Stencil Papers, and then rolled in Gestetner machine for more copies. Finally it simple stapled and distributed to students. When the Xerox machines were introduced, the Cyclostyle became obsolete and Xerox Copies were supplied. The need for Typist reduced as more and more Xerox Machines were introduced. In recent times, the Course Materials were not being prepared by faculty members. Now printed Text Books mostly authored by them are being supplied. The lose bundle of Cyclostyled papers turned into printed books might have escalated to cost of Course material over time.

The third major component in Total fees is Accommodation Charges collected from students for staying in Hostel rooms. In the entire period, the Accommodation Charges increased by 12% in current price and 4% in constant price. So, the Accommodation Charges increased less than that of Total fees. Across the years,. In the first decade, it increased most by 12% in current price and 5% in constant price. But, in second and third decades, it increased by 3% to 5% in current price whilereduced by 4% in constant price. In second and third decades, this charges increased by 8% in current price and 1% in constant price. In fourth decade, this charges increased marginally. While, the most impressive rise was in fifth decade (2004 to 2013), when it increased most by 19% in current price and 10% in constant price. This high increase was due tothe nature and size of hostel rooms have changed abruptly as fully air-conditioned environment and marble finish floor, glossy tile etc. The belongings in hostel rooms have changed from a shabby look to crystal clear look with several amenities. The Development fees started in 42nd batch in 2005. It was only Rs. 6,000 in initial year, but it has increased to Rs.1,00,000 in 50th batch of 2013. During 8 years, the Development charges increased annually by 50% in current price and 37% in constant price. It was introduced to augment financial resources for increasing needs of infrastructures - classrooms, educational devices etc. for more students in future.

During the entire period of fifty years, the Total fee increased by 17% in current price and 9% in constant price. So, the Total fee increased more despite ignoring the inflation. Moreover, the Tuition feeshave increased by 21% in current price and 12% in constant price. Thus, the Tuition fees increased more in real terms than the Total fees. The Course Material fees have also increased by 16% in current price and 8% in constant price. The Accommodation chargeshave increased by 12% in current price and 4% in constant price. So, the Accommodation charges increased less in real terms. The Development Charges introduced in recent past during 2005, but increased rapidly. In last ten years, the Development Charges increased by 51% in current price and 38% in constant price. The Development charges introduced to augment resources of development for coming years.

8. OTHER REASONS BEHIND THE FEE HIKE

The main reason behind the current hike in tuition fees was stoppage of Central Grants since 1992. To meet the current operating expenses, the

Institute began to raise tuition fee since 2000.The Government has been gradually reducing the subsidy given to the IIMs from 1992 onwards on the basis of Kurien Committee Report. This Committee proposed that IIMs stop depending on Government for their operating expenses. The Varghese Committee in 1992 framed the basis for cutting subsidies to the IIMs and raising their tuition fee. The Committee suggested "Every Institute should pursue a policy of progressively moving toward full cost recovery in its education and training" (Frontlines, 2004). It also suggested limiting the Government's role to just Block contributions.The Supreme Court had to hear a PIL regarding reduction of tuition fee on February 15, 2004. The petitioner demand the annual fee be Rs. 30,000 instead of prevailing Rs. 1.5 Lakh on that time. The Moily Committee in 2007 recommended raising their annual intake from 1800 in 2008 to 2800 in 2010 in all IIMs. A 52% increased intake will be reserved for SC, ST and OBC candidates.

After passing of IIM Act 2017 by the Parliament, IIMs have gained much greater autonomy in fee regulation, student intake and infrastructure expansions. In recent time, fee hike in unregulated IIMs elucidated a grave concern. The autonomy played a significant role in incentivizing the IIMs to hike fee. "The management of these premier institutions attributes fee restructuring to prevailing inflation and the associated cost of faculty and infrastructure. However, no quantitative assessment as such was provided to justify this argument. Lack of accountability owing to the absence of Government interventions leads to more questions than answers: (Soni and Ganesaraman 2021). Even though, the IIMs provide high placements, higher money offered and higher was their demand. Does high demand translate in higher fees. This resembles typical pricing structure of a market economy. But, education is not a market commodity. Education serves a larger purpose of social upliftment and nation building. The fundamental objective of education aims to provide accessibility and affordability to the prospective persons.

The then Director Prof. Chaudhuri said "IIMC will refund course fee of students, if they join Public Sector Undertaking or Voluntary

Organisation.The initiative is primarily aimed to make such jobs attractive to students, who prefer corporate jobs for higher compensation and paying off their education loan" (Economic Times, 2011).In 2016, A Balkrishan, Chairman and our alumni justified the fee hike to cover the cost increase and capital expenditure on additional infrastructures for the increased intake, cost of providing on-line access to journals, subsidized Ph D and providing fee waiver to poor students.He also told "We have decided to increase fees after a gap of four years. We decided to occasionally calibrate the fees. The Institute runs on profit, we have 15% more surplus than other IIMs. The entire money is spent on providing better infrastructure and in development of students (Times of India, 2014). The then Director, Prof. Chattopadhayay said "we have substantially increased the Scholarship to students. We have allotted Rs. 5 crores every year towards scholarship and fee waiver to candidates from humble background".

SECTION – E: GROWTH IN MANPOWER IN THE INSTITUTE

1. MANPOWER IN THE INSTITUTE, 1965-2015

i) Growth of Manpower Since Inception

The Institute started in Barrackpur Campus in 1961 with only one program – Advanced Management Development Program (AMDP). There were only three Professors, one Officer, two typists and a Steno along with six Groups –D staffs.So, there wereonly 13 staffs, mostly were Ex--Servicemen belonging to Gorkha Regiment. They were short in height but fluently spoke English. When the Institute moved to Emerald Bower in 1964, several Mallies (Gardeners) were recruited and batch of six Library Assistants were recruited for processing the newly acquired huge books and Journals. Moreover, several attendants were engaged in Students Hostel and their Mess. An EPBX was installed for Inter-Com services and it was maintained by three women. A group of Typists and Stenos were recruited for typing course materials, which was cyclostyled in Gestatener Machines for multiple copies, as there was no Xerox Machines. In 1965, there were 66 man powers - of which 24 Professors, 2 Research Assistants and 40 administrative staffs.

After ten years in 1975, the manpower increased to 100 as more and more Typist and Stenos were recruited for increasing number of new faculty members. During this time, out of total 100 manpowersin which, 38 were Professors, 2 Research Assistants and 60 administrative staffs. During this time, only 14 professors and 20 administrative staffs were added. In EB Campus, there was a dozen of Project Assistants on contractual basis and not included in manpower engaged in the institute. I was such a Project Assistants attached to Prof. Chandra and others were attached to Prof. Kamini Adhikari and Prof. Satyesh Chakraborty.

Even though the Institute moved to incomplete Joka Campus in 1975, but stated full functioning in 1977. In this time, more gardeners and security staffs were recruited for maintenance of the vast 135 acre campus. The Professors recruited at the initial stagesuper annuated or left and a bunch of new faculty member recruited. To assist the newly recruited Professors, more Typist and Stenos were recruited in 1980, So, the institute started fully functional, the manpower increased to total 348, in which, 48 Professors, no Research Assistants and 300 administrative staffs.Because of regularisation of Project Assistants, canteen staffs, hostel staffs and also recruitment of wards of land losers, the manpower reached to its peak around 462 in 1985. Mr Samir Banerjee a leftist trade union leader forced the then Director Prof. Aiyer for regularisation of these staffs. Another Employees Union under Congress banner led by Mr Asit Dutta, organised agitation for wards of land losers.

Our manpower increased to 550 in 1990. Among them, there were 53 Professors, 12 Research Assistants and 485 administrative staffs. The number of Professor increased by only 3, ResearchAssistant by 12 and administrative staff by 85. During a span of five years, the manpower strength increased by 88.But, in 1992, the Central Government informed that IIM Calcutta is over staffed in terms of "Staffs per Faculty' ratio, compared to other IIMs. So, we have to reduce the staff strength.The then

Director Mr. Subir Chowdhuri has taken several measures and banned the trade union activities in the institute. Since then, there was no recruitment of general staffs except faculty members and a few Executives.The manpower decreased by 79 and reduced to 471. The number of Professors increased by only 2 while that of administrative staff reduced by 81. Among them, there were 55 Professors, 12 Research Assistants and 404 administrative staffs (Table 1.8.14).

In 2005, the strength reduced further to 409, by increasing Professor's strength by 14 while Research Assistant reduced to 11 and general staff reduced to 329. In 2010, manpower in the Institute reduced to 325, of which, 75 Professors, 5 Research Assistants and 245 administrative staffs. In 2018, manpower reduced to 189, of which, 90 Professors, no Research Assistants and 99 administrative staffs. Finally, permanent general staffs were getting reduced gradually to only 99 in 2018 from a maximum of 485 in 1990.In order to cope up with shortage of manpower, the Institute started hiring contractual staff with low salary and without job security, In 2005, a bunch ofTrainee Teaching Assistant (TTA) was recruited on annual basis with a consolidated salary. Year after year, the TTAs are coming and going. Some Administrative Officers were hired on contractual basis. The house-keeping staffs were engaged from service provider agencies.

In 2020, 170 employees were contractual, 97 hired from Agencies. To cope up with shortage of Officers, the Institute hired Executives and Managers on contractual basis and annual renewal.The manpower strength increased from 16 in 1963 to 550 in 1990. But it reduced gradually to 189 in 2018. When the Central grant was available, the manpower increased at exponential rate. After reduction of Central grants, the manpower started decreasing and there may be no permanent general staff as more and more manpower supplied by Agencies. Gradually, number of staffs in Central Government pay scale started reducing since 2000 and it will vanish in next few years. The initial contract in 1960 with the Central government was that salary budget for boththe Teachers and Staffs will be born by them, while the State Government will provide land and buildings. Now, the institute has to bearthe salary budget, andoptimising the salary cost by paying them lower scale. When the number of Teachers and Students were growing exponentially, the number of general staffs is getting reduced.

ii) Changes in Manpower Pattern

During last fifty years, journey from Barrackpur to EB then finally to Joka, a lot of changes occurred in work culture and office environment. In the EB Campus, employees were mostly relatives (brother, sister, wife etc) of the senior staffs, mostly typists and stenographers. All were a small and well knitted group of young generations. Faculty members were also small but distinct groups. The Professors were busy in preparing study material, both by dictation to stenos and by hand written notes given to typists. These notes were cyclostyled in Gestetner machines and distributed to students before the classes. In the typist-pool, a dozen of typists were placed in a room. The supervisor of the typist pool distributed the materials to different typists. After few hours, the Professors have to collect the typed pages. So, most of days, typist pool was busy and full of hammering sound of typing machines. Most of the time, Professors were busy in Library in collecting study materials for the classes. The accounts section was in a corner with five six accounts assistants and the Accounts Officer. The canteen was placed in a corner room, where tea, coffee and snacks were available in lunch hours only. The Canteen was supervised by Mr. Rathin Pal No.2.

When we moved to Joka Campus, myself and Accounts office was placed in Staff quarters. The branch of the State Bank of India was also opened in a staff quarter. After completion of the Administrative building, all office was shifted there. Mr. Hiten Bhaya officiated as Director in third of B Block and Mr. Nepal Ram served tea for Director and his guests. As I was moved to B Block, I also go to Nepal Ram for a cup of good Tea. Sometimes, Prof. Nirmal Chandra called Nepal Ram for tea, for both of us. Now, the Canteen was running in an Asbestos shaded hall with more staffs and Rice, Vegetable, Fishetc. were available in lunch hours

When the Library moved from Asbestos shaded godown to newly constructed Library building, a batch of library assistants was recruited, most of them were women. After the MCHV was established in 1994, a set of new employees were recruited for maintenance while subordinate office staff was placed among old staffs. So, by this time, the office is full of employees. During the second term of Prof. Aiyer, the plenty of staffs started agitating for their permanency. The office became a mela ground full of crowd. The next blow came from the Central Ministry in 1992, when Mr. Subir Chowdhuri wasthe Director. The Ministry wrote that the proportion of non-teaching staff to teaching staff is highest in IIMC compared to other IIMs. So, the Institute has to reduce the non-teaching staffs. The Director called all employees and informed the observations of Central Ministry. The Director attempted to reduce daily expenses like Electricity bill, Telephone bill, Post office bills, Daily Newspapers bills etc. The payments to supplier of Books ton Library, Stationary supplied to office etc were restricted their payment on fortnight basis instead daily.

The rumour was rolled that one employee from one falsify norm be introduced. So, brother, sisters, wife and sons of existing employees may be terminated. The age old Malis and Sweepers may be terminated to reduce staff strength. In view of the growing demand for highly skilled professionals in IT Sector, the Institute introduced the PGDCM in 1992. The introduction of PGDCM helped the Institute financially. In this time, Prof. S K Chakraborty established the MCHV solely with his own efforts without any help from the Government. He established the Center with the help of corporate leaders.After Dr. Subir Choudhuri; our Prof.Amitava Bose became the Director in 1997. He introduced two posts - Dean (Planning & Administration) and Dean (Program Initiatives), to lighten his day to day duty. Since then, the general employees have no interaction with the Director. In earlier days, general staffs met the Director as and when need arises, with the permission from Mr. S B Dey.

iii) Changes in Work Culture and Office Environment

Mr. N Krishnaji, as a Research Fellow in 1965 at EB Campus and promoted to Assistant Professor in Economic in 1967. He left the Institute in 1973 to joins as Director of the Canter for Development Studies in Trivandrum.

Krishnaji in his autobiography "The Best for Past" mentioned that the Institute at EB campus was as a best place to work with.He also wrote that, "I was on very friendly terms with not only academic colleagues but also with the administrative staffs and those working in the library.......I must conclude my IIM story with a sad note.In 1986, I opted to go back to IIMC for a year. Then I found that, I no longer felt the sense of belonging that I used to experience earlier during my first spell 1965/1973. Another loss was my good links with the non-academic staff, the composition of which has changed during the 13 years, when I was away from the Institute. I also felt that there was no sense of belonging of the staffs recruited on contractual basis since 2000.

v) Recent Trends in Work Culture

The Institute started recruiting employee on contractual basis in academic administration. The posts are - Manager, Assistant Manager, Secretary to Deans, Program Secretary, Administrative Executives, Accounts Executives, Trainee Teaching Associates, Research Executives etc. A survey was conducted by 'Indeed', a placement organization on experience of working in the Institute. Most of the respondents said the it was a low pay salary, minimum benefits, long duty hours, without extra pay, stress work to met deadlines, hectic jobs etc. (indeed.co.in) during 2020.They also receive ill treatment from permanent employees of the Institute.

In recent times, some faculty members are sharing cut-money from the agencies who are supplying manpower to the Institute.As on March 2018, out of 24 Trainee Teaching Assistants, most (21) were females and only 3 were males. The house keeping service for about a dozen of Hostels is being maintained by 45 personnel supplied by Agency. Among them, one was Manager and one Head cleaner and 43 cleaners. They were paid minimum wage as per Central Government's rate for contractual employees. The manager of Housekeeping cell is paid Rs. 3782 per month, while Head cleaner is paid Rs. 1000 per month along with 12% Provident Fund and 3.5% for ESI contributions. The cleaners are paid Rs. 60 for uniform. As on 2020, as much as 170 employees are contractual and 97 are outsourced through Agencies. So, a total of 267 employees are not regular while only 90 staffs are regular employees of the Institute. So, among current staffs, three-fourths are non-regular (IIMC Website on Mediclaim).

-----------X-----------

SECTION – II

CONFLICTS, CHAOS, COURT CASES AND GOVERNMENT INTERVENTIONS IN RECENT TIMES

CHAPTER 2.1

RESERVATION POLICIES FOLLOWED FOR PGP STUDENTS: CONSEQUENCES OF OBC RESERVATIONS AND COURT CASES

In recent times court cases arises due to reservation of OBC students in IIMs. Moreover, the crisis arose due to reservation of OBC among Faculty members and Fellowship students. The Studies on reservation in IIMs have been justified the reservations. But, most faculty members oppose it in Faculty positions, while they were up in arms over "Restructuring Proposal" by the Central Government.The government ordered to follow reservation policies among faculty members as well as students in Fellowship program. The Institute was following reservation policies for students in PGDM, PGDCM, PGPEX and PGPEX-VLM courses. The reservation policies followed so far are discussed below.

1. THE RESERVATION POLICIES FOR PGP STUDENTS

a. Introduction

The Institute followed a quota system, as per the provisions of the Indian Constitution. As per the provisions, 15% of the seats are reserved for students belonging to Schedule Castes, and 7.5% for Scheduled Tribes. Since 2008, the Other Backward Classes have also been given 27% reservation, after the Supreme Courts. The provisions for OBCs are being implemented in a phased manner due to resource constraints. All aspirants have to take the Common Admission Test which consisting of objective type exam, group discussion and personal interviews, with the cut-off for reserved category candidates being lower than for general category candidates. There are reservations for the underprivileged section of the society. This is done looking forward to people who are talented but do not have the resources to complete their education.

With the benefit of the reservation policy, a lesser percentile candidate can also admit in IIMs.Now, in all IIMs have 15% seats reserved for SC, 7.5% for ST and 27% for OBCs belonging to 'non-creamy' layer (NC-OBC). Moreover, 3% seats are reserved for Persons with Disability (PwD) since 1995. This category was considered for reservation with low vision blindness, hearing impairment, loco motor disability or cerebral palsy. Candidates suffering from not less than 40% of these disabilities are considered for reservation. Now, 10% seats are reserved for the Economically Weaker Section (EWS). In sum, 15% seats reserved for SC, 7.5% for ST, 27% for OBCs, 3% for PwD and 10% for EWS.

b. The Drawbacks of the Reservation Policies

These reservation policies have some drawbacks. Because of these policies, a lot of students who deserve but the entire general category became unable to get admissions (Singh 200?). The process of selection of candidates for an IIM is a very rigorous process but due to the reservations, certain candidates get through the process just for the sake of it and hence the quality of the batch declines. The decorum of the classes also gets hampered because the students entering through reservations are unable to catch up with the rest of the class and students who have meritoriously gained their seats in the college. Not only students but also the teachers start losing interest in teaching the class because of the ambiguity in the quality of the students. The government is concerned about the quality of students which receives it blowback because of the reservations. Also, if the quality degrades then the reputation of the institute receives a setback. Since these Institute have been marked and one of the best institutes of the country, they are bound to maintain their reputation. For this, a check has to be kept on the reservation policy of the institute.

The Board members of the IIMs and the government should come to a pact that not only benefits the underprivileged section of the society but also maintains the quality of the students in the IIMs. To combat with all these issues and efficient reservation system should be developed that does not hurt the sentiments of any of the stakeholders of the institute and it also maintains the dignity that the institute has earned over the years. The main scope of reservation in the field of education is to provide the students belonging to SC, ST, OBC, PwD and EWS, with an opportunity where they can overcome their poor status and compete to others. On the contrary, it has been observed that the students are being provided with the opportunity where they are kept in the place as the creamy lot of Indians. This unjustified reservation and proposal from the government is sure to have several negative effects on the education and the quality of pass out from such elite institutes as IIMs (Gupta 2018).

While giving an opportunity to the potential and deserving candidates, reservation also introduces certain candidates who reach the final stage just for the sake of it. This limits the number of seats that can be offered to others who are the real claimants. Furthermore, with the easy entry, several of these students are least interested in being serious about their studies and also affect the concentration and devotion of others. The IIMs are the best business schools of the country and getting into IIMs mean that you have to go through a tough screening process wherein it is mandatory that you get the highest score. These institutes are known by the quality of their education that they provide and if that gets questionable, it will lead to a long-term disaster.

2 RESERVATIONS POLICIES IN DIFFERENT PERIODS

a) Reservation for SC, ST in Initial Years (1964-1995)

During initial years, in response to the directive of Central Government the policy on reservation was enacted.The institute reserved 15% seats for Scheduled Castes (SC) and 5% for Scheduled Tribes (ST) students. For them, the stringent admission standard was relaxed (Sanchetti 1986).

The SC and ST students were automatically waived tuition fees and were paid additional allowance for their maintenance. In mid 1970s, the reservation of ST was increased to 7.5%. So, the institute reserved 15% seats for SC and 7.5% for ST students. Historically, reserved seats for SC were nearly filled up but reserved seats for ST were not fulfilled in most years. There were only two women out of 40 in the first batch and there was no reservation for women. Initially, there was a restriction that only six women be admitted per year due to scarcity of their Hostel facilities. Gradually, women hostels were built and thenumber of women increased from 10 to 15 since 1985 and now crossed 100 in 2013.

b) Reservation for PwD Students in 1995

"Person With Disability" (PwD) ACT (1995) was enacted to improve lives of people with disabilities. In 2003, only four students were admitted in DA (Dis-Ability) quota. The number of students in DA quota gradually increased to 12 in 2009 and 18 in 2023. The IIMs have now 3% reservation for PwD students. In reply to an Unstirred Question in Lok Sabha about SC/ST reservation, the Institute disclosed that during last five years 2001 to 2005, among 1310 students, 163 were SC, 67 were ST and 10 were in DA quota.So the representation of SC, ST and DA students were 12%, 4% and 1% against the norm of 15%, 7.5% and 3% respectively. So, the gaps were 3%, 3.5% and 2% respectively for SC, ST and PwD students. So, the reservation policies were not being followed properly.

c) The Reservation for OBC in 2006

The Central Educational Institutions (Reservation in Admission) Act, 2006, is an act of parliament passed in the year 2006 and enacted as a parliamentary law in 2007. It provides the reservation of seats to the students of SC, ST and OBC category with a share of 15%,7.5% and 27% respectively in admissions. Annually in each course of study the respective students are admitted accorded to their share of reservation percentage. In any central educational institution, out of 100 seats sanctioned, 49.5 seats should be reserved for ST, SC and OBC respectively according to their percentage. Therefore, the institute should reserve, half of its sanctioned strength of seats to reservation students through this Act.

As per all IIMsare concerned, they are registered as societies under theSocieties Registration Act, 1860. According to Section 2 (d) (v) of the Central Educational Institutions (CEI) Act, 2006 states that The Central Educational Institution means, an educational institution set up by the Central Government under the Societies Registration Act, 1860.This section of clears the position of all IIMs as central education institutions. According to Section 3 (i), (ii) & (iii) of the CEI Act, 2006 states that the reservation of seats in admission shall be provided in the following manner. The Central Government directed the Institute for implementation of Mandal Commission (1990), which prescribed reservation of seats for Other Backward Classes (OBC). After more than a decade, the reservation for OBC came into effect in Centrally funded institutes.

The institute has planned to increase the intake in a phased manner to reach the desired goal of 27 % intake of OBC candidates in three yearsInitially, the institute reserved 18 seats for students belonging to Non Creamy OBC in 2007, but it increased to 74 out of the total intake of 408 in 2009. In 2013, the number of NC-OBC students in PGP increased to 120 and their representation was 27.4%.The IIMs not sure about filling all OBC seats on the Supreme Court ruling on OBC quotas in educational institutions (Mohan and Nichenametla, 2013). Even the IIMs get set to implement the 27 per cent reservation for OBCs following the Supreme Court go-ahead. Instead of a 15% are reserved for the SC and 7.5% ST, in most IIMs, nearly 30 per cent seats for STs remain vacant as suitable candidates are not found

The MHRD constituted a **"Group"** (2006) to discuss the appropriate strategies and to develop a plan of action for implementation of reservation for OBCs in all IIMs. The Group was under the Chairmanship of Prof. Paul of Public Affairs Center in Bangalore and the Director of IIMCalcutta and some other IIMs. Two major policy decisions were announced; firstly, reservation of 27% seats for OBC from 2007 and secondly, to ensure that total seats for General category students be maintained. Based on the above two, it was understood that the intake would have to be enhanced by 54%. The Group felt that implementation of the OBC quota should be phased out over three to four years. Under the capacity expansion plan, an additional intake of 162 in IIMC was spread over successive years as 18 in 2007, 90 in 2008 and 54 in 2010. So, the intake capacity has to be increased from 300 to 462.

Our Institute took decision to increase the number of seats although it did not receive any order from the MHRDto that effect. From the coming session, the total number of seats for PGP should increase from**265 to 431.** The Group members for Management Institutions on OBC Reservation met to discuss the appropriate strategies and to develop a plan of action for implementation of reservation for OBCs in management institution during June 2006. Appropriate formats for seeking relevant information from various institutions were designed by the group. The information like data on intake, sanctioned and existing faculty strength, norms on teacher to student ratio, cadre ratio, infrastructural facilities and basic amenities. All the institutes were asked to provide estimate of additional requirements of recurring and non-recurring expenditures for the seat increase based on the following two policy decisions.

The policies were a) Reservation of 27% seats for OBCs from 2007 and b) ensuring that the total number of seats available for the general category students is maintained. Based on the above two premises, it was understood that the intake would have to be enhanced by 54%. The Directors explained to the Group about their programs, the sanctioned and actual intake, and sanctioned and actualfaculty strength of their respective expansion. All the above considerations point to the serious risks to excellence and quality that may follow any attempt to force the pace of expansion. Given the limited time available for expansion and the difficulties and constraints underscored above, the Group felt that implementation of the OBC quota should be phased out over at least a few years. The Chairman of the Oversight Committee has very clearly mentioned in that the infrastructure should be placed in 2007. The Group felt that this is an unrealistic goal since only less than a year is available to deal with the complex constraints cited above. The Institute expressed readiness to implement reservation for OBCs coupled with 54% capacity expansion in a period of three years.

d) Reservation Policy for Economically Weaker Section in 2019

In 2019, the Union Government tabled a constitution amendment bill to provide 10% reservation in jobs and education to economically backward sections from all communities. The MHRD informed that the government will increase seats in educational institutions by 10%, to ensure that meritorious students do not get harmed by the government's decision to provide 10% reservation to economically weaker sections (EWS). This reservation will be inadditionto the existing 50% reservation provided for people from SC, ST and OBC. The 124thConstitutionAmendment Billwas cleared by the Union Cabinet which seeks to extend to benefit of reservation to those people not covered under existing reservation for SCs, STs and OBCs. The economical backward section was defined as anyone with an annual income below Rs. 8 laths, apart from other clauses. This limit is at par with the existing limit for the creamy layer of OBCs. Taking additional 10% reservations, the total reservation raised to 60%. So, a fewer seats will be available for meritorious who do not come under reservations.

The worry about educational institutes has been taken care of, as the existing level of unreserved seats will be maintained by creating additional seats to accommodate the newly reserved seats. The Bill will benefit economically backward people from the upper caste also. The Bill will cover upper caste but also cover everyone people from communities ignoring their caste. The Institute hikes seats to start EWS Quota since 2019. The Institute is set to introduce a 2 to 3 per cent reservation for PGP to implement quota for economically weaker sections of the general category. The institute intends to raise the EWS quota to 10 per cent by the 2021 when, by which time the total number of seats will be capped at 578. In order to increase the intake of students, in the next few years will focus on setting up new academic infrastructure including construction of adequate number of hostels, additional classrooms and faculty offices. Our Institute was the first to implement the EWS quota.

After assessing our available facilities, the institute is in a position to implement the EWS quota from 2019. Moreover, the government had been pushing for implementing the 10% increase under the quota within two years. To increase student intake, in the next few years, will construct an adequate number of hostels, additional classrooms and build faculty offices in order to enhance the academic infrastructure. The Institute will start the expansion within this year and faculty vacancies will also be filled. The students can avail the EWS quota, who has a gross family income of less than Rs 8 Lakh, any candidate whose family does not own agricultural land of 5 above and does not own a plot of 200 square yards or above in areas other than notified municipalities can apply for consideration under the quota. The increase in intake means more aspirants will be able to study. Also, the institute will have an opportunity to provide more resources of top talent to the recruiters. Now, 27% seats are reserved for NC-OBC, 15% for SC, 7.5% for ST, 5% for PwD, and up to 10% for EWS along with 10% extra seats reserved for foreign nationals.After all these reservations, IIMA added 151 seats while IIMC add 142 more seats.

e) Concessions to Reserved Categories

In2009-10, the minimum graduation score for different categories were different. For CAT examination, the minimum graduation score was 50% for Open Category and NC-OBC, but it was 45% for SC, ST and PWD candidates. For admission, minimum percentile in CAT score requirement varied for different categories (Table 2.1.2). The students of Open category required 98.97 percentile, while it was 94.44 for NC-OBC, 86.60 for SC category and 71.29 for ST and PWD categories. For OBC, the minimum percentile requirement was lower by 4 percentile from Open category. For SC categories the minimum percentile requirement was lower by 8 percentile from Open category. However, for ST and PWD categories the minimum percentile requirement was lower by 23 percentile from Open category.

f) More Women in IIMs Since 2019

An extremely low women representation in the major IIMs was a concern all these years. Women have been under represented inIIMsover the years and it is high time the issue is addressed, besides putting an end to all the misogyny about women in all IIMs. (Benue, 2019). Our Institute made the semi-historic decision of creating additional seats exclusively for women. This decision has been made at a time when even after the implementation of a gender-based reservation of 30 per cent for women. The IIM A, B and C have managed to have less than 25 per cent enrolment of women. The IIMC was the first to introduce 30 per cent reservation for women. If the nation isn't totally represented in the campus, there is something wrong in the system. It is nothing like women aren't intelligent or on par with men in terms of their capabilities, This batch will not affect the chance of other candidates since we are creating 60 supernumerary students, hoping that this will open up a lot more opportunities for women.The NIRF data tells us that the percentage of women students is a paltry 23%, 23% and 24% in IIMB, IIMC and IIMA respectively. But, IIML however, stood out with a 45% female representation while IIMK currently has a 36% women representation and aimed a record of 54% women in 2012.

More precisely, Chetan Bhagat protagonist describes his first tryst with his IIM classmates and eventual love interest and wife; this is how he has chosen to do it. He said, we had only twenty girls in a batch of two hundred. Good-looking ones were rare; girls don't get selected to IIMs for their looks but get in because they can solve mathematical problems faster than 99.99% of India's population and crack the CAT. Most IIM girls are above shallow things like make-up, fitting clothes, contact lenses, removal of facial hair, body odour and feminine charm.If you were to browse through interactive portals you would very quickly realize that men in IIMs have very little regard for the women inIIMs.

Many IIMs were now giving extra weight age in the selection to women candidates (Mohanty 2019). This move to lower the cut-off has triggered a debate. Lastly, the IIMs introduced a special relaxation for female candidates.While the CAT cut-off for the general category students is 95 percentile, the institute had lowered it to 90 percentile for general category women. The newly introduced model was likely to increase the pool of women for selection at first stage.The efficacy of both the models should be evaluated with more data points. But, it would be interesting to see the impact of the lowered cut-off model in terms of performance of students and the societal good. The relaxation was unprecedented, as we do not discriminate between students based on gender. Moreover, women candidates were allowed 12% lower marks in eligibility criterion. To remove gender inequality, the admission standards for women were further relaxed and resulted an increase in number of women. During first 25 years (1965-1990), there was a restriction that only six females be admitted per year due to scarcity of Hostel facilities. Gradually, women hostels were built and their number increased from 15 to 35 per year in 1990 to 2010, but it reached at 107 in 2013

3. INSTITUTE'S POLICY ON EQUAL OPPORTUNITIES

Around 2015, the Institute declared their Policy on Equal Opportunities. The Institute is committed to a policy of equal opportunities and inclusion of all social groups including people belonging to Minority groups, Scheduled Castes, Scheduled Tribes, Other Backward Classes and Persons with Disabilities (PwDs) (IIMC website). The students are encouraged to connect with the Equal Opportunity Cell with a view to ensuring their continuously expanding access to the entire range of academic and social activities in the campus. To this end, the Institute will work to adjust the academic, administrative and infrastructural configuration of campus life so that PwDs can strive to attain their potential.

The Institute will undertake a series of initiatives that aim to develop the administrative apparatus required to oversee and facilitate the policy on equal opportunities; create awareness in the community of students, staff, and faculty about the differences in the ways in which PwDs communicate with the world; enhance quality of physical access to institute infrastructure and work towards a barrier-free environment, in ensuring access to tuition, equipment, counselling, placement facilitation, etc. The Institute will seek not only to abide by the applicable national legal stipulations including the Persons with Disabilities Act, 1995. India is continuously evolve in tune with global conventions, but to go beyond the legal requirements in order to proactively provide a supportive environment for, and prevent discrimination against PwDs.

The Institute will work with governmental agencies as well as non-governmental and corporate organizations that can support the institute's efforts. Efforts in this regard will be coordinated by our Equal Opportunity Cell that will also arrange for the assessment of needs for PwDs, communicate the same to the relevant officers and faculty, and coordinate the fulfilment of the identified needs.Sensitisation Workshop is arranged on for students, faculty members, officers and staffs to enhance inclusiveness and help with meaningful integration of students with disabilities. The Institute provides - Equal accessibility of course materials including e-Books or hardcopy of reading materials, as per the student's preference. Additional time to write during examination Accessible Exam Papers, including use of bigger fonts in the question papers and other study materials as and when needed Provision of writers/scribes during exams Support for state-of-the-art assistive devices

Providing augmentative communication devices and text-to-speech software packages Arranging special tutorial sessions for students with disabilities Information shared with faculty members in each Term regarding the students in their respective sections Buddy system for students, where first and second year students are mapped, so as to create an inclusive infrastructure not only for academic but also for extracurricular, placement and hostel requirements. Equal Opportunity Cell addresses issues related to equal opportunity and inclusion of all social groups including students with disabilities and students' accommodation requirements. Most class rooms and the common areas have been renovated with ramps for barrier free movement. Students are provided preferred seating arrangement with suitable chairs for supportive movement. The program office facilitates access to motorised wheelchairs to facilitate movement around the campus.

A dedicated vehicle has been engaged in the campus for students with disabilities for attending classes, going to the library and other barrier-free movement within the campus.

4. STUDIES ON RESERVATION IN IIMS

A: Bangalore Study

A study on reservation was undertaken in IIM Bangalore for studying the impact of reservations. The Central Government proposed a bill to reserve 27% seats in premier institutions for OBCs students.This reservation is over and above the 22.5 % reservation for students of the SC and ST categories. The announcement from the Government was followed by widespread protests by students and proponents of anti-reservation all over the country. A survey about reservation brings forth strong arguments both for and against reservations. Besides, many of their arguments are based on perceptions rather than actual.

Thus the arguments though logical, may not reflect the ground realities. It is these perceptions that are influencing key government policies on the reservation issue and are going to affect educational institutes like the IIMs. The IIMB endeavoured to study -: a) Effects of reservation in uplifting the SC/ST community, b) Effects of reservation on the quality of students and c) Role of IIMB in training students of reserved category. An analysis of the reservation will be incomplete without an understanding of the ground realities. Even today, large parts of India are still plagued by caste discrimination and the resultant atrocities like untouchability and exploitation. There is a need to uplift the affected sections of the population through effective actions. The Indian government used reservation as an instrument of affirmative action

Prof. Mohant's Study on Expanding Reservations to OBCs

This paper (Mohanty, 2006) brings to debate around expanding reservation in centre of excellence in higher education. This paper attempts to put the issue of reservation in context and to respond to some of the issues that have been raised in the ongoing debate around expanding reservation in centres of excellence to cover OBCs. Agreeing to implement OBC reservation from this year (2007), heads of more than 80 central educational institutions (CEI) voiced concern about the problem of faculty and they would face in expanding seats. It is also clear that these institutes would have to start implementation from their own resources. The government would compensate them only after the cabinet clears the extra funding to these institutes. After meeting with head of CEI, HRD minister said we know institutes have problem of faculty and resources, we will do everything to help them.

But all of them are implementing the quota from this year. Heads of IITs and IIMs voiced maximum concern about implementation. They had resource related issues like setting up of more laboratories and classrooms. However, reservation was a national policy and would be implemented. There was no resistance from any institute about implementation, as all have started the process of OBC reservation. And to ensure that quota-driven unequal access does not become another tool in perpetuating inequality, we also have to invest in reasonably good quality, compulsory school education for all. As Mao had said long ago, one needs a policy of walking on two legs.

5. CONSEQUENCES OF OBC RESERVATION: STUDENTS PROTEST IN INDIA

i) Mandal Commission Protest in 1990

The Mandal Commission was set up in 1979 to identify the socially or educationally backward classes to consider the seat reservation to redress caste discrimination. To determine their backwardness, the Commission used eleven social, economic and educational indicators. The Commission submitted the Report in 1980 recommending 27% reservations for Other Backward Classes (OBCs). As a consequence, it resulted in 49.5% reservations in government jobs and public universities. The government tried to implement its recommendations in 1990 which led to protests. The protesters were against giving jobs to certain castes, rather than merit of the candidates. This commission snatched away the right of upper castes to get the job. The protesters closed the roads, highways, transportation services, schools and business in India. The incidents of destruction of public property, looting and intimidation came in from the protests and riots. The government had to mobilize army units against the riots.

The protest began when the government tried to implement the reservation policy based on Mandal Commission in 1990. The failure to effectively control the protests had escalated in many parts of India. This led to accepting the resignation of the then PM. As a Consequence of the Mandal Commission Report, a series of self immolation attempts sparked in Delhi. Rajiv Goswami was the first student to attempt self immolations in 1990 to protest against the implementation of Mandal Commission

ii) Anti Reservation Protest in 2006

In 2006, a series of anti Reservation Protest took place all over India. The protest was in opposition of the Central Government decision to implement reservation for the OBCs in central and private institutes of higher learning. The reservation for the OBCs in the premier institutes like - AIIMS, IITs, IIMs, NTIs and IISc etc. was in order to help them gain higher level of representations. The massive protest movement was from the students and doctors belonging to General Category. They claimed that the Government's proposal was discriminatory, discarded meritocracy and was driven by vote-bank politics. The first Anti-Reservation Protest began in March 2006 with medical students protesting in New Delhi. Next month, another protest was carried out by medical students in New Delhi and also held by medical students in Mumbai, In all these protests, police *lathi*-charged and detained the agitators for a few hours. The Bombay High Court has already banned the protest.

Most forward castes students across India took to the streets, boycotting classes In IIT Delhi; a human chain rally was organized in May 2006 by the students to protest the OBC reservation. A resolution signed by 2500 IIT Roorkee students expressing their opposition to the OBC reservation was sent to the then PM and others. Lately, many anti-reservation protesters now began to group under the aegis of 'Youth For Equality', which suggested some measure.The Protesters called for a Civil Disobedience Movement in Delhi. A massive rally was organized in Delhi with participants numbering over one Lakh from all over India. The Supreme Court sought the Government to clarify the basis on which the reservation policy was being implemented. At last, the Government set up an Oversight Committee under the Chairmanship of the Union Minister Mr. M V Moily. The Committee was entrusted to "prepare a road map with a time bound program to implement 27% reservation for OBCs without compromising merit and addressing apprehensions aired by students propose an affirmative way to implement reservations keeping the interests of all sections of society in mind." The Committee submitted the Report after three months.

In 2006, the Supreme Court upheld the law for the provision of 27% quota for candidates belonging to the OBC in premier educational institutions. But it directed the government to exclude the "creamy layer" among the OBCs. The 93rd Constitutional amendment was passed unanimously in the Lok Sabha and most of the parties supported the move to extend the OBC reservation to premier educational institutions. The Left parties supported the move and called for exclusion of creamy layer. The BJP supported the move but asked for extending the reservation to economically weaker section of the forward castes. The Shiv Sena was the only party opposing the OBC reservation.

6. COURT CASE ON OBC RESERVATION

a) Calcutta High Court stays OBC quota in IIM Calcutta

The Calcutta high court stayed a memo (or order) issued by the MHRD on 27% reservation for OBCsin the IIM Calcutta, paving the way for more litigation and confusion over the already contentious issue. The immediate casualty could be admissions to the PGP program at all the IIMs. The court's stay came in response to a petition filed by a student, who had appeared for the CAT to the IIMs for admission to the PGP program in 2008. In his petition, the student argued that graduates could not be considered backward in keeping with the Supreme Court's ruling on the issue of reservations. That would mean the proposed 27% reservation is not applicable to PGP program that the MHRD has consistently denied.

After the court order, MHRD said there was no confusion about reservation in PGP. The judgment would impact all postgraduate courses. A lawyer in the Supreme Court, argued against the 27% reservation on behalf of "Youth For Equality'. In a recent case, the Supreme Court gave the go-ahead to reservations. The MHRD said that the stay could delay the quota implementation in IIMCalcutta not others. The IIMs, meanwhile, are not clear on their course of action. IIMA has finished provisionally admitting OBC applicants and we will take legal advice about the impact of this stay order from Calcutta High Court. The Calcutta HC sent notices to the MHRD and IIMC but none responded. The order might stall ongoing interviews of OBC candidates. So, the Institute has to stop interviewing OBC candidates. The Delhi high court issued a notice to the Centre asking it to reply to a petition filed by an association of IIM alumni challenging reservation for OBCs in PGP course. The stay could delay the quota implementation in IIMC, but it would not affect the process. The IIMs are not clear on their course of actions, as IIMA has finished provisionally admitting OBC applicants and take legal advise about the impact of this stay order from Calcutta high court.The order might stall ongoing interview of OBC candidates.

b) Court Case on OBC Reservation

The Calcutta HC stayed interviews of candidate in IIMC under the 27% OBC quota. The order was passed by the Justice, who was hearing a writ petition by a general category candidate. His counsel said while the apex court had directed that graduates would not be considered for reservation, the HRD ministry violated the order by passing an office memo to the effect that OBC students would get reservation in PGP. MHRD may move Supreme Court over Calcutta HC stay for clarification. If the apex order does not allow 27% OBC reservation in PGP courses said an MHRD official. The Centre would move Supreme Court to transfer all cases pending in high courts in Delhi and Mumbai to itself. MHRD also said if it were not applicable to PGP courses, Supreme Court would have struck down HRD's order of April 20 asking central educational institutions to implement OBC quota in PGP courses. HRD Minister said, we will put our views across. It would have no effect on reservation for post–graduate classes. The Delhi HC issued notice to the Centre on a petition challenging the implementation of the OBC quota in IIMs and higher educational institutions. It sought Centre's response to the petition filed by alumni association of IIMs. The association said the government had misinterpreted the SC judgment, while upholding the OBC reservation policy, had said it would not be applicable to higher educational institutions.

The SC/ST of IIM grads earn 15-22% less than general category (Financial Express, 2008). The scheduled caste and scheduled tribes graduates of IIMs get salaries that are 15-22% lower than their general category peers in 2006. The IIMs, however, say the salary difference mirrors the performance grades which are also 15-20% lower for SC/ST student. Interestingly, the SC/ST student average score at the CAT stands at 64 percentile opposed to general category student 98 percentile. Pro-quota lobbyist says, its the job of IIM directors to narrow these salary gaps. The findings will be cannon fodder for the anti-quota lobby which fears the proposed reservation will lead to a fall in the quality of graduates and the brand of these premier institutes.

-----------X-----------

CHAPTER 2.2

RESERVATION IN FACULTY POSITIONS, FELLOWSHIP PROGRAMAND COURT CASES

SECTION A: THE RESERVATION POLICY FOR FACULTY POSITIONS

The Institute followed different reservation policies for students in PGP since the inception in 1964. But, the reservation policies for faculty members and fellowship students have not yet been introduced. Now, the Central government ordered to follow reservation policies among faculty members as well as students in Fellowship program in all IIMs.The issue of IIMs not implementing reservation is being raised in Parliament. A committee on the welfare of OBCs had recently raised several questions on non-implementation of reservation in educational institutions. The MHRD has often nudged the IIMs to introduce reservation but never issued a binding directive. The IIMs maintained that reservation did not apply to them in recruitment but make a positive discrimination in favour of candidates from deprived sections. The ministry had compiled teachers from general categories occupied 545 of the 699 posts in the six older IIMs, as against 10 OBCs, three SCs but none from the STs.

1. SOCIAL STATUS OF EXISTING FACULTY MEMBERS IN IIMS

According to the MHRD data, teachers from general categories occupied 545 of the 699 posts in the six older IIMs, as against ten OBCs, three SCs and none from the STs (Table 2.2.1). So, in six older IIMs, 97.7% faculty belongs to General category, 1.8% to OBC while 0.5% to SC and none from ST categories in 2018-2019. Another study in Indian Express (Table 2.2.2) show social status of existing faculty members in seven IIMs in 2019. In these seven IIMs, among 533 existing faculty members, 524 belonged to General category, 6 to OBC, and 3 to SC but none were ST. So, 98.3% faculty belongs to General category, 1.1% belongs to OBC while 0.6% belonged to SC and none from ST. A broad study covering 13 IIMs by the WIRE (Table 2.2.3) in 2018, found that out of 642 faculty members, 620 belonged to General category, 17 from OBC, 4 from SC and only one from ST. So, 96.6% faculty belongs to General category, 2.6% to OBC. 0.6% to SC and 0.2% to ST.

The MHRD data submitted to Parliament in 2022, that all IIMs had 784 sanctioned posts, of which only 2 posts were filled up by ST, 8 from SC and 27 from OBC category. Around 590 faculty posts were occupied by General category while the remaining were vacant. The latest report in *the Print* (March 2023) showed that the members of SC, ST and OBC constitute just 6% of total faculty members across 18 IIMs. According to MHRD in 2023, more than half the faculty positions reserved for SC, ST and OBC in IIMs are vacant. In 20 IIMs, 62% of SC, 79% of ST and 63% of the OBC faculty posts are laying vacant. Among the Centrally run higher education institutions, the IIMs faring the worst. Despite reservation of SC and ST after 70 years of India's Independence, what a pathetic scenario! Why are there still such few OBCs, SCs and STs at IIMs?

There are only 11 faculty members belonging to the Scheduled Caste and Scheduled Tribe categories in the country's 20 Indian Institutes of Management (IIMs), The government had asked all IITs and IIMs to implement reservation in teaching positions. All government institutions are mandated by the Constitution to provide 15 per cent reservation for SCs, 7.5 per cent for STs and 27 per cent for the Other Backward Classes (OBCs). The IIMs - Bangalore Sirmaur, Rohtak, Udaipur and Lucknow had only one faculty each from the reserved category. The IIMs - Kozhikode, Shillong and Jammu have two faculties each from the reserved communities. Among top and oldest three IIMs (A, B, C) only the IIM Bangalore has one faculty from reserved category.

a. Faculty Members Opposing Reservation in Teaching Posts

The IIMs put up a defiant note, say they stress only on merit in faculty recruitment. These IIMs might be on a warpath with the government over implementing reservations in teaching staff. The IIMs are opposing the caste quota in selecting faculty (HT May 2016). The top IIMs haven't yet responded to a MHRD's letter asking if they followed SC, ST and OBC quota policy in faculty hires. Some other IIMs stressed only on merit in staff recruitment. Another IIM-Rohtak said "You cannot be giving non-deserving candidates preference just because they are SC/ST/OBC". The IIM-Trichy may extend reservations provided the candidate measured up to qualification sought. Reservation in IIMs faculty positions has a controversial history.

An IIM Director said quotas in teaching positions will hurt the quality of education that 'brand IIM'. The reservations to fill the faculty positions on the basis of caste at IIMs are centres of excellence is foolhardy. India extends reservations for SC, ST and OBCs for social empowerment of the communities that have been historically marginalized. But critics say the quota system hurts quality of education and is unfair to upper-caste candidates. The IIM controversy comes as the Central Government faces intense criticism over caste discrimination and the absence of SC/ST/OBC faculty members. The suicide of a Dalit PhD student sparked a storm of protests. He was a Dalit Research scholar at the University of Hyderabad, which stopped paying his monthly stipend. He was targeted for raising issues on campus under the banner of a Dalit student organization. After his suspension, he committed suicide. His death sparked protests and outrage across India and gained widespread media attention as a case of state sponsored discrimination against Dalits. Most IIMs recruited teachers on merit and not on the basis of their caste. A combination of meritocracy and affirmative action is the solution and if all things are equal, we would certainly give preference to a candidate from SC/ST community. After getting the status Report on reservation policy in these institutions, the government will work out a strategy to enforce it.

In 2008, the MHRD directed all centrally funded institutions to implement faculty quotas, triggering protests. The IITs toed the government line but the IIMs were defiant. Faced with protests, the minister proposed a bill that would exempt 47 premier higher educational institutions, including IITs and IIMs, from reservations. The bill was passed in 2008 but it lapsed after the Lok Sabha dissolved. A letter dated in 2013 was a follow up. In this letter MHRD asked the IIMs to implement quotas in faculty positions. The letter asked IIMs if they implement quotas in faculty hires and if they didn't, why they should be exempt from a constitutional provision that requires every centrally funded institution to follow. Only the SC/ST teachers, staff and graduates praise Government push for faculty quota.

b. Welcome Change: Alumni and Academics

Academics and alumni from the IIMs, who have earlier raised the issue of reservation while hiring teachers, feel this new directive will bring a positive change and diversity of castes in the IIMs. A Professor of Public Policy at IIM Bangalore published a paper and the paper argues that "diversity deficit at IIMs is a 'wicked problem', but one that should not be wished away. It is a good thing that the government has issued such a directive, but I hope that the IIMs follow the spirit of the order and recruit people accordingly. What the government has done is signal a normative intent that needs to be followed intelligently.The IIMs have been citing a 1975 order by the ministry of education to IIM Ahmadabad, where the institute does not give caste-based reservation.

They openly defy constitutionally mandated reservation till now. Thedeficit of caste diversity in the institutions has affected teacher-student interactions. IIMs have a huge diversity deficit, and it manifests in teacher-student interactions. Some teachers have bias towards students from the reserved category and at times it comes out very strongly. They create a line of discrimination- reserved category students are non-meritorious and non-reserved aremeritorious.

An IIM alumnus, also detailed how people at IIMs often judge those from the reserved categories on "the basis of how they speak, dress, whether they are able to speak good English or not". An alumnus of IIM Calcutta had advocated for a non-discriminatory environment in the institute during his student days. Even institutions like IIM Calcutta did not have a very conducive environment for students from the reserved category. They had to fight to create awareness and did counseling of students. In the lack of faculty from reserved categories, students from the same category sometimes miss a role model to look up to.

2. SOCIAL DIVERSITY DEFICIT IN IIMS

The diversity deficit among faculty in IIMs is mostly due to clubbing them in to "Other" category. As public institutions, these bleak pictures severely undermine the legitimacy of IIMs. Over last five decades of omissions and commissions and skirting of constitutional and statutory provisions had contributed to "missing scholar". Most IIMs chosen to massive under reporting of faculty belonging to SC, ST and OBC, who have chosen to mask their social group identity. The under reporting of faculty members might be due to the stigma of belonging to socially marginalized groups. It resulted in to the pernicious consequences of socially monochromatic faculty bodies. The IIMs have an effective arsenal to defend against pressure for social inclusion and diversity. The biggest driver of the diversity deficit is the lack of a sufficiently qualified faculty pool from under-represented groups. The IIMs are both producers and consumers of faculty talent. Nearly a third of existing faculty members are trained from any one of the IIMs. The Fellowship Program in Management (FPM) has produced a vast pool of doctoral scholars. But statutory mandate of reservation in admission at FPM must be taken as an affirmative action to produce prospective faculty from the socially under-privileged groups.

a. Reservation for Faculty Position

An IIMC alumnus Anil Wagde (Wagde 2019) asked that less than 10% of Indian social groups account for over 95% of all faculty members at

IIMs. This might be generous, for anecdotal accounts suggest that an even narrower pool of upper castes accounts for the vast majority of faculty positions. If the so-called self-governing market forces are not catering to the 97% of the population, then the government must intervene to correct these imbalances. This restatement had to be made, despite it being the law. These "elites" have deliberately not implemented the law. Of late, the government has ordered these institutes. Only when we widen the catchment area will the result of the competition will improve. We need to make sure that everyone has an "equal" chance of winning.

This same argument needs to be extended to the other side in the classroom. Until and unless teachers also represent society, how will classroom discussions become wholesome? If the classroom is not inclusive (diverse students and teachers), then we run the risk of forming elitist institutions cut off from ground realities. The IIMC Director's address to our batch, he said, the gap between the poor and the rich is continuously increasing. He warned that if this gap continues to grow, it can lead to a catastrophic event, which severely disrupts the progress of the nation. Democracy is a means of achieving change in a peaceful way. The democratic forces have acted to ensure inclusivity in teaching staff.

The faculty members of IIMs have deviated from the "common good" to "protecting their salaries and seeking independence from the government. Unless the teaching staffs come from the deprived sections of society, there will be no one to fight for them. Incidentally, these "elites" had opposed access to education for women and to the SCs and STs for centuries to keep it meritorious. After reservation, these same "elites" worried about the dilution of merit. However, there is no proof of dilution of merit due to reservation. The IIMs placement reports found no difference between the placement packages of reserved and non-reserved students. Hence, this dilution of merit argument is a bogus. We have to either correct these factors or else provide corrective action in the form of reservation to girls, whose situation is exactly like that of SC/ST. By not enabling girls, we are denying 50% of the population to participate in the national discourse. Look at how elites come up with "instruments of exclusion".

Till development reaches everyone, the government must make a conscious effort to include the deprived – rural, women and lower castes. This will benefit the society and the nation. Unfortunately, the bias and discrimination attitude of some faculty members was the standard practice on Indian campuses, resulting in lower seasonal and practical marks. These elite institutes will find ways to defy such orders. To deal with wilful defiance, the government should invoke the SC/ST Atrocity Act. We are seeing rules similarly being flouted by IIMA's PhD program. This institute remains the only one to oppose reservation for its PhD course. The government must issue a directive to all IIMs that they must follow reservations in their PhD program as well. If reservation in PhD is not provided, how will they get candidates for faculty positions?

b. Faculty Reservation Order to IIMs

The government has decided to direct the IIMs to reserve post for candidates from socially and economically deprived backgrounds. The IIMs were superseding a 44-years-old order that the B-schools have so long cited to evade quota based recruitment. The MHRD sprang into action after several MPs and Parliamentary Forums put the government in the dock over this continued evasion by the IIMs while hiring faculty.The ministry has now decided the 20 IIMs to set aside 15% of the posts for SC, 7.5 % for ST, 27% for OBC and 10% for the EWS. The MHRD would cite this Central Educational Institutions (Reservation in Teachers' Cadre) Act. The MHRD's official order said that this ACT in July 2019 to give reservation in teaching positions. The Act came into effect and provides for reservation of SC, STs, OBCs, and EWS candidates in direct faculty recruitment by clubbing vacant posts of the same rank across all departments in an institution.

SECTION – B: THE RESERVATION IN FELLOWSHIP PROGRAM

The Fellowship Program in Management (FPM) in IIMs is a full-time doctoral program in different fields of Management. This program focuses on training outstanding scholars for advance management education. The IIMs look at the FPM students as a pool for potential faculty. The specializations in FPM were available in different specialised groups. Time to time, the Government decided for increase in the stipend for FPM students. Students were also provided a one-time grant for field study, laptop grant and a fully supported international conference attendance anywhere in the world. The Institute also revised various rules and policies related to the FPM students in order to ensure a more enriching academic experience. The increase in stipend has attracted more students, especially those with industry work experience to get into an academic career. Currently, the Reservations are sought in Fellowship Program. This move comes at a time when IIMs are grappling with a faculty crunch coupled with a serious problem in attracting quality faculty.

As all IIMs were not established at one time and their FPM was introduced accordingly. The FPM was introduced 1971 in IIM Ahmadabad and Calcutta and in 1976 at Bangalore. The FPM started in 2000 at IIM Lucknow, 2006 at Indore, 2007 at Kozhikode, in 2017 at Raipur and Ranchi.Till 2022, the number of Doctoral scholars at IIM Ahmadabad was 408. Calcutta was 248, Bangalore 279 and Lucknow 102. Those numbers at Indore was 87, Kozhikode 41, Raipur 17 and Ranchi 13. So, a total of 1195 scholars had been produced in these eight IIMs (Table 2.2.4). The number of existing scholars pursuing doctoral program was 134 in IIM at Ahmadabad, 89 at Calcutta, 105 at Bangalore, 119 at Lucknow, 89 at Indore, 83 at Kozhikode, 27 at Raipur and 39 at Ranchi. So, a total of 663 students were pursuing doctoral program in those IIMs. So far, all these IIMs have produced a total of 1858 scholars may full fill the vacant pasts of teachers in IIMs.

2. RESERVATION IN FPM FOR PROSPECTIVE FACULTY FROM RESERVED CATEGORY

An IIMC alumnus Anil Wagde, a functionary of the Global IIM Alumni Network has been fighting for reservation in faculty posts and admission in FPM. The reservation in faculty posts will bring diversity. Classroom discussions will touch ground situation and address the problems of common people. The institutions will be more inclusive, but warned against tricks the IIMs might employ to evade quotas. The government must state that the IIMs cannot recruit faculty on contract or guest faculty against regular posts to avoid reservation. The IIMA has already implemented reservation in its PhD courses. The IIMs are already trying to recruit more candidates from socially and economically deprived sections. But quality and excellence should not be compromised. There were not enough suitable candidates from the socially deprived sections to be hired as teachers and expressed fears that many of the posts reserved for SC, ST and OBC might remain vacant. The government is talking about excellence and good quality faculty is the key to excellence. Reservation in FPM will produce prospective faculty from the socially under-privileged groups.

By resisting the implementation of reservations in their doctoral programs and faculty appointments, the IIMs are not fulfilling their mandate of acting as socially responsible public institutions (Thakur 2017). The issue of reservation in faculty appointments and in Doctoral/ FPM has brought the IIMs back to the centre of public discourse. The IIMs, though public institutions, have emerged as canters of excellence in professional education with appreciable global recognition. The number of IIMs increased to 20 and covering a wide geographical area, to cater the felt needs of access to management education by the increasing numbers of aspiring youths. So, the IIMs can be seen as trend setters in an otherwise not so encouraging scene of higher education in India.

Expectedly, what happens in the IIMs has wider ramifications for higher education in particular and the country in general. This is equally applicable in the present case of reservations. The 27% quota for the non-creamy layer of the OBC is in operation since 2008 for PGP students. The reservation debate about IIMs boils down to extending similar reservations to their FPM students. As s matter of fact, the IIMs have managed to do without reservation despite continuing demand from the government and other stakeholders. Recently, the enduring issue of reservation has been to the centre stage by the MHRD, who reminded the IIMs of their constitutional obligations at the coordination committee meeting of the Chairpersons and Directors of IIMs in 2016.

The IIMs are not politically and ideologically neutral institutional reeling out innocuous professional managers and business leaders for the furtherance of the efficiency need of business and related organizations. The IIMs do bestow status and credentials to individuals and preselect and socialize them for certain kinds of elite roles. Through their socialization process they contribute to the production of a shared cultural code that is the hallmark of elite. However, the IIMs do not appear to have done much to fulfill their mandate of acting as socially responsible public institutions. They operate in a self–contained cycle of virtuous excellence where much of energy is expended on maintaining their so-called brand value. They appear to be convinced of the longevity of the brand image and are reluctant to come out of their institutional comfort. Such complacency propels the IIMs to be scattered islands of excellence amidst general mediocrity. This probably explains their studied indifference to the ideals of social justice and equity.

The historical resistance towards reservations in the IIMs emanates from the old hackneyed argument that the introduction of reservations will dilute quality and standards that they have so assiduously promoted. Very often, they bring up the much-debated issues of quality, merit and excellence in elite higher education institutions to bypass the constitutional mandate of affirmative action for the backward classes. They also have a tendency to cry hoarse about their loss of academic autonomy as and when such demands for reservations in faculty appointments are made. In the contemporary context of increased global integration, the IIMs are also likely to use the possible decline in their ability to compete globally if such undesirable social constraints are imposed on them. Some of the older IIMs may equally advance the glib argument of their financial independence and non-dependence on government grants to evade reservations.

2. B. GUJARAT HIGH COURT: NOTICES TO IIM AHMADABAD: SEEKING QUOTA IN PHD

Gujarat High Court issued a notice to the IIMA on a plea seeking implementation of reservation for the SC, ST and OBC candidates in its PhD program.An alumni association, Global IIM Alumni Network, has filed public interest litigation (PIL) stating that although IIMA was governed and funded by the Union education ministry, it was violating the Central Educational Institutions (Reservation in Admission) Act, 2006 while carrying out the admission process for the PhD programme. The division bench issued notices to respondents IIMA, the Central and state governments, UGC and others. The court, however, refused to "interject with the admission process, which has already commenced", while turning down the petitioner's request to the current admission process for the program ends. The PIL states that 15 out of 20 IIMs across the country provide reservation for the same program as per the CERA Act. All the IIMs are governed by the IIM Act, 2017, which makes IIMA and other IIMs as central institutions under the CERA Act.

The petitioner claimed that the IIMA had been carrying out an admission process in gross violation of the 2006 Act and Rights of Persons with Disabilities Act, 2016. The CERA Act provides for the reservation of students belonging to the SC, ST, and OBC, in Central educational institutions. Despite being a Central institution under the Act, IIMA has not provided reservation for its PhD programme. The institute should be directed to follow and implement Article 15 (5) of the Constitution by providing reservation to the SC, ST and OBC candidates as well as persons with disabilities.

3. COURT CASE DEMANDING RESERVATION IN DOCTORAL PROGRAM

Members of the Global IIM Alumni Network – a group of people across the world who have graduated from various IIMs have filed a petition in the Gujarat high court against IIMA alleging that the institute has failed to follow the constitutionally-mandated reservation policy in its doctoral programme. The matter was heard by the Gujarat High Court. However, the court asked IIM Ahmadabad and the Centre to respond to the petitioners' demand and the outcome of the application process would be subject to the results of the writ petition. So if the court rules in favour of theGlobal Network, IIMA will have to implement the reservation policy from this year itself. The Network groups persuade the board and director of IIMA to change the way admissions are conducted to the FPM and implement the reservation policy went unheeded.

The MHRD had also written to IIMs asking that they implement the reservation policy and address the lack of social diversity on campus. The issue of the lack of diversity within IIMs wasfirst raisedby Joshi and Malghan of IIM Bangalore. They had pointed to the dismal diversity records and very low number of SC, ST and OBC at the faculty level in various IIMs. They traced this lack of diversity in the faculty back to the doctoral program, since a large number of those hired to teach at IIMs are graduates of this FPM. The IIMA chose to stick to their ways and not implement the reservation policy in their doctoral program. The Global Network says in the press release announcing their decision to go to court: The Network had written to all the Directors of IIMs urging them to address the stark under-representation of historically marginalized SC, ST and OBC communities on the faculty body of IIMs. Choosing to ignore its legal obligation, IIMA went ahead and published Notice of FPM Admissions 2018-19 without provisions of reservations mandated by Central Educational Institutions (Reservation in Admission) Act 2006.

The Global Network met Director-in-charge of IIMA and urged him to implement SC/ST/OBC reservation in their Doctoral program and faculty positions given the utter lack of diversity. The Global Network had written to the Hon'ble President and Prime Minister calling on them to ensure implementation of Constitutional provisions in all IIMs. The letter was also copied to MHRD and the Members of the Parliament. Since then, multiple IIMs-Bangalore, Lucknow and Indore have implemented reservations in the admission notices to their respective Doctoral programs.

But IIMAcontinues to deny reservations to students from marginalized sections of the society. Faced with complete disregard for diversity in IIMAeven after years of denial of due representation to students from SC, ST and OBC communities. Having exhausted all avenues of persuasion, the Global Network has filed a Petition against IIMA asking for reservation provisions to be enforced. The recently enacted IIM Act, 2017 further puts the onus of implementation of reservation policy on the respective institutes. The top IIMs have the moral obligation, beyond the legal requirement, to ensure adequate diversity on the campus.

The IIM Ahmadabad objected to a public interest litigation (PIL) filed in the Gujarat High Court demanding reservation for PhD courses. The nation's top business school said in a recent declaration submitted in response to the PIL that the **IIMA** continues to be an autonomous and independent institute without support from the government despite being a statutory organization under the IIM Act, 2017.Earlier, this week, the case was heard by a division bench. The institute rejected reservations for its PhD programme on the grounds that it was a "super-specialized programme" and that neither the Indian Constitution nor any other statute contemplated reservations for highly specialized courses or programs.

The Global Network filed the PIL, which contests the lack of any form of discrimination in the PhDprogram. The IIMA was established as a facility to be run by a society established in accordance with the Societies Registration Act. IIMA was designed as a board-managed organization that was not under the sole power of any one constituency. The IIMs were designated as Institutes of National Importance under the IIM Act of 2017. All IIMs controlled by the IIM Act remain independent and autonomous, under the control of their Board of Governors (BoG). The BoG has comprehensive supervision, direction, and control over the business of the institutes, including the authority to create policies and regulations, it stated. The institute argued that by not including any reservations in its PhD program, there was no illegality or violation of other laws or the norms of the Indian Constitution.Even candidates from the reserved category would profit from the reservation policy by the time they apply for PhD programs. Therefore, no additional reservations are required for such advanced specialization programs, Due to the reduced number of seats that may be available for PhD programand the lack of number of seats.There is no practical way to reserve seats because the selection was entirely merit-based. Such a reservation may be counterproductive and might cause injustice to other eligible meritorious candidates.

a: The Missing Scholars

In 1990s, Prof. Amartya Sen coined the term "missing women" to describe lower sex ratio for women due to sex-selective abortion or female infanticide. In IIMs, five decades of omissions and commissions at their doctoral program (FPM) is akin to cultural prejudices that lead to "missing women". The deliberate circumvention of constitutional and statutory provisions by IIMs had led to "missing scholar". The IIMs have produced about 1200 doctoral scholars and 700 were in the process in last fifty years. So, a total of about 2000 doctoral scholars existed in IIMs. But, these IIMs failed to use a diversity deficit proportion of 20%. So, the number of missing scholar is at least 400. The IIMs do not collect social group data on doctoral program applications. The diversity deficit among doctoral students is just as acute as in faculty positions. Currently, as much as 208 faculty members across IIMs received their doctoral degree at one of the IIMs. The normative structure of exclusion has directly engendered documented social exclusion in management praxis.

b. Dilution of Quality?

The IIMs have accomplished the task of elite reproduction. In fact, upper caste groups are preponderant in IIMs at all levels. The IIMs are public institutions and endowed with scarce public resources could have been productively employed elsewhere. Even when some of them have ceased to receive grants from the government, it does not necessarily mean that they can abdicate their larger national goals. The argument about the decline of quality and standards owing to reservations also does not stand to empirical test. And in no way can reservations be held responsible for the deterioration of academic standards in the IIMs. On the contrary, these institutions are academically vibrant precisely because their governance structures have internalized an ethos of inclusiveness.Even if reservations are not the sole and the best way of dealing with existing inequalities, they do hold the promise of making our public institution more representative and inclusive.

The Mandal Commission report reminds us, reservations are not about the distribution of handful of government jobs across different social groups. It is about political empowerment and representational justice. The IIMs must partake of this socially responsive ethos of our times. They should proactively implement reservations in their doctoral program and faculty appointments. As more and more sections of Indian society come to these institutions, their diversity and plurality of world views will impart the IIMs an epistemological vitality. The reservations are not going to be a drag on the IIMs, but these are a pathway towards an effervescent future for IIMs.

4.A ADMISSION PROCESS HALTED AS IIMS WAITS FOR MHRD ORDER

It now depends on how far back the IIMs would have to go in their admission process and how much time the government will take to clarify matters.For the IIMs, the Supreme Court judgment upholding OBC quotas in higher educational institutions means virtually going through the admission process for the academic year 2008-09 all over again. The final admission list was due to be out but given that the Supreme Court has decreed the implementation of the new reservation regime. There is also no clarity on whether IIMs, could be brought under the purview of the Central Educational Institutions (Reservation in Admission) Act. The IIMs are waiting for clarifications from the MHRD. However, the IIMC try best to ensure that the academic year and the preparatory classes that start before the session begins are not delayed.

Delay was the word from IIMs, who will wait for the MHRD to send us notification and then decide. Some Directors of IIMs were waiting to see the Supreme Court order. IIMs had requested the government to apply the quota in a phased manner, rather than all at once. We are yet to see what the final verdict is. So, the final list for the fresh batches of the six IIMs will take a while in any case. It depends on how far back the IIMs would have to go in their admission process to source candidates and how much time the government will take to seek clarification on whether the IIMs are required to adhere to the reservation regime.

Each IIM will now have to now re-work admission lists to separates Non Creamy layer OBC students who quality to be considered under the quota. The IIMs will also need to refer to an earlier shortlist from the 2007 session, forms required that student specify whether they belong to SC/ST or OBC category to select the rest of the OBC quota, and a corresponding number for the general category. These students may have to go through admission processes, especially group discussion and interviews, some institutions may find a shortage of candidates for the OBC quota from the non-creamy layer. The IIMs will also have to deal with issues like additional infrastructure as the number of student will increase. The number of seats at IIMC has been increased to 378. New hostel should be ready in the next two months. The construction of new and bigger classrooms is in progress too.

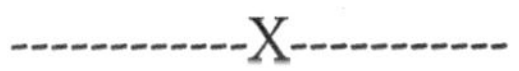

CHAPTER 2.3

MHRD ORDER ON FEE CUT AND ITS CONSEQUENCES

In order to reduce its financial burden, the Central Government constituted the Kurien Committee to look into ways to reduce its financial burden. The committee filed its Report in 1992 and recommended some steps. Those were - a) Creation of a Corpus fund, b) Reduced dependency on the Government, c) Upward revision of fee structure and d) Provision of scholarships and loans to needy students. These recommendations were accepted by the Government and the IIMs. Fees in IIMs have been gradually increased and correspondingly the Government reduced its grant by 30% in 2004. During six years, 1997- 2002, the fees for PGP increased from Rs. 1.03 Lakh to Rs. 2.54 Lakh.So, the total fees were more than double (2.5 times) in a span of six years. The fees in those years were Rs. 1.03 Lakh, Rs. 1.56 Lakh, Rs. 1.67 Lakh, Rs. 2.07 Lakh, Rs. 2.25 Lakh and Rs. 2.54 Lakh respectively. Other IIMs also followed the increasing trend of raising the fees. The IIMs increased the fees unilaterally and abruptly to compensate the reduced Government Grants.In this situation, the Central government asked the six oldest and premier IIMs to slash its fees by 80 %. The MHRD directed the IIMs to reduce the fees to Rs. 30,000 from the existing Rs. 1, 50,000.

1. MHRD'S ORDER ON FEE CUT

The MHRD vide the impugned Order dated 05.02.2004 directed the IIMs to reduce the fees charged to Rs. 30,000 per student from the academic year 2004-05 (Lype 2004). The impugned Order is bad in law and is vitiated for several reasons. The IIMs spent Rs. 4 Lakh on each student, whereas the fees collected were only Rs, 1.5 Lakh. Initially, the fees charged by the IIMs were negligible, as a result of which they had to wholly depend on the Central grants. In 1992, the Central Government reduced their financial burden to the IIMs. The Kurien Committee also recommended upward revision of tuition fees. This recommendation was accepted by the Central Government and IIMs were gradually increasing their fees. The total fees increased exponentially since 1992. On the contrary, the Central Government reduced its grants to IIMs by 30% in the year 2004-05.The MHRD asked the IIMs to sign a MoU with the Government, based on which annual grants would be made. Most IIMs refused to sign the MoU as they are autonomous body registered under Societies Act and free from government interference.If the Order is implemented, it would adversely affect the excellence of the IIMs. In this situation what will be the fees at the IIMs now (Lype 2004).

TheIIMs have been embroiled in controversy over a cut in its fee structure and interference from the MHRD. The Central government asked the six premier IIMs to slash its fees by 80 per cent. While many management experts ridiculed MHRD's aggressive stand, some agreed with the minister, saying it was the government's prerogative to reduce fees at the IIMs. The MHRD's insistence of a fee cut led all four IIMs (Calcutta, Kozhikode, Lucknow and Indore) to accept the government decision. While IIMA argued against the fee cut while the IIMB did not take a decision on the issue. But the change of government has now ensured that the IIMs need not change its fee structure. The new MHRD's decisions were to undo earlier controversial fee cut decision. After a meeting with the all IIMs Directors, the present MHRD issued a directive ordering the immediate withdrawal of the ruling of cutting fees. The new directive has a rider: that the IIMs should provide scholarships to poor students that may amount to a full tuition fee waiver. Accordingly, all the students, whose annual gross family income is Rs 2 Lakh and below, be eligible for receiving financial assistance amounting up to full tuition fee waiver.

The IIMC's Faculty Council has requested the government to initiate a process of mutual consultation and discussion with different stakeholders before imposing such a drastic fee cut. The IIMC decided to accept the fee cut order and it inserted a clause in the decision that a final resolution to the matter would be made subject to the Faculty Council's concern on autonomy. Now that the controversy has been resolved, IIMC decided to take the existing fee: Rs 1, 27,000 a year. The credit for the IIMs' fight against the fee cut decision goes to the country's leading IIM. The fee at IIMA was Rs 150,000 and increased to Rs 157,000 in next year. The premier IIM does not take government assistance to fund the education of poor students. The IIMB also consistently argued that a fee cut would considerably weaken a well functioning world-class institution. It will retain its old fee of Rs 150,000 per year and decided to increase the value of scholarships.

The wholly unsolicited reduction in the PGP fee was decreed by the MHRD and has drawn an unprecedented storm of protest from industry, academia, students and the media. A ministerial bolt from the blue has thrown to the old IIMs, the national proud of world class institution of management education scattered across the country into disarray, anguish and confusion. It directed these IIMs to slash all fees payable by students in this year (2004-05) from Rs.1.5 lakh to a uniform Rs. 30,000 per year. Describing the existing annual fee was exorbitant while stressing that the IIMs are fully funded central government institutions. By invoking the observations made by the Supreme Court. The recommendation of the Rao Committee decreed that the revised fee structure will be effective in next year.

The IIMs are India's only world class Institutes in business education. The government seems bent upon removing that autonomy is the basic issue. The fee reduction is only one of a series of actions in recent years. The Bharat Shiksha Kosh was set up to 'channel' all funds to IITs and IIMs through the government. This had the desire effect of drying up all alumni and industry support and grant to these Institutions. The process of appointment of Directors was suddenly changed. In the old system, the board of each IIM recommended a few names to the government. But, now the government has a standing committee headed by a bureaucrat and directors have to 'apply' and go for 'interview' to Delhi. Recently, the Government issued orders that CAT will now be conducted by them.

3. CORPUS FUNDS

The MHRD Order has generated widespread indignation because it common knowledge that even the annual fee Rs.1.5 lakh per year currently payable by the students. The actual cost of training and developing a graduate from India dumped down higher education system into a globally accepted business manager is over Rs. 3 Lakh per year. In the circumstances, the order is clearly a case of arbitrary and irrational exercise of power. The fear of no money being made available to the IIMs to make up the shortfall is baseless. These institutes have huge corpus funds which are upward of Rs.85 crore, which these IIMs are not supposed to have such huge reserve funds. The MHRD suggested that they keep Rs.25 crore as reserve and then utilize the rest and the IIMs will never starve for funds. Far from assuming public apprehensions, these utterances of the minister have only served to fuel them. Informed opinion within academia and industry is almost unanimous that the issue is not of calibration of tuition fees but of administrative control of these autonomous institutes of professional education.Therefore they have succeeded in raising their academic standards and reputations to be reckoned among the best B-school in the world.

There is a growing awareness within academia and industry on the fate of these IIMs. The MHRD called upon each IIM to sign a Memorandum of Understanding (MoU), under which the institutes would surrender surpluses in excess of Rs. 25 crore to the ministry in exchange for guaranteed funding according to need. The three major institutes (IIM-A, B and C) followed Government's adoption of the Kurien Report for accumulated corpuses of Rs. 60-100 Crore demurred. On the financial independence, their managements quite naturally were bowled over by the prospect of going cap in hand to the ministry every year. Nor are the huge Corpuses at three old IIMs accumulated as sinful. These Institutes of higher education need to build up corpuses to encourage and finance research and development, attract top-grade faculty and provide state-of-the–art infrastructure.

Regardless of the verdict of Supreme Court in this case would be all to the good if this unsavoury episode also prompts some introspection within the faculties and boards of governance of the IIMs. The managements of IIMs need to reflect upon the extent to which their *brahmanical* and too superior management styles and attitudes at public expense have contributed to arousing the hatred, ridicule and contempt of the Minister, the educracy at the centre and the states. The government has also asked three oldest IIMs - A, B and C, to reduce their corpus to Rs 25 crore. This clearly shows that they do not want these institutions to be autonomous. The fee reduction, which most probably will not be compensated by an increase in grants, will force these IIMs to eat into their corpus.

4. MEMORANDUM OF UNDERSTANDING (MOU)

In 2003, the MHRD had been attempting to destroy the autonomy of the IIMs by asking the IIMs to sign a MoU (Memoranda of Understanding), based on which annual grants would be made. The MoU sought to gain more control over IIMs and made the signing a condition to grant of funds. The Government sought to change the MoU and giving arbitrary powers of interference to the government. But, three old IIMs (A, B and C) have so far not signed the MoU. They are now being told that, unless they do this, they cannot get government funds. These IIMs refused to sign the MoU, in order to function as autonomous institutions and free from Governmental interference.

The IIMs were started as Societies registered under the Societies Registration Act. The impugned Order has been passed with a view to gain control over the IIMs and is therefore mala fide. This Order is a retrograde step and adversely affects the excellence of the IIMs achieved over the decades. Admission to the IIMs is based on merit and students with humble economic background easily get admission. None of them has been declined admission on the ground of their inability to pay fees. The numerous scholarships are sponsored by the Industry, IIMs and the government for needy, SC and ST meritorious students. The Banks are extending educational loans to them, who after passing out get gainful employment with good salary package. The government also said that the class size in the IIMs must be raised. There is also a strong move to do away with interviews and group discussions in the admissions process. Apparently that is for selecting IAS officers, but not for management graduates. In the next year, there will be interference in the academic curriculum.The fee reduction has completely paralysed the IIMs. They cannot raise funds because of the Shiksha Kosh and cannot charge appropriate fees. Some arguments have been used to buttress the government position.

The government said that poor students cannot join IIMs with the 'high' fees. However, scholarships and loans are very easily available to them. If the government is really interested in poor students, they can directly give scholarships to these students. When there is a fund crunch for primary education, how can we justify subsidy to IIMs students who will work for multinationals? The government argued that faculty student ratios are very high in these IIMs. The class sizes are too small, that faculty teaching loads are very low and that research at the IIMs is not up to the mark. The government has not taken into account the teaching in the PhD programs, in the executive programs in public policy, software management and the agriculture programs. If we take into account all this additional teaching, the faculty–student ratios are all right and so are the teaching loads.

There is, however, some merit to the argument that student batch sizes are too small and that research needs improvement. On batch sizes, there are two problems- one is placement for the extra student is likely to be a problem and in long run will erode the brand image. There is scope for increasing the number of seats. Second, there is already a severe problem in attracting and retaining good faculty. With all the negative publicity and erosion of autonomy, the IIMs will find it very difficult to recruit top quality faculty. The IIMs needs to improve their research record, but the current moves by the government will ensure that they go in the opposite direction. Teaching in IIMs is distinctive as the quality of the faculty, some of them are outstanding and could be placed anywhere in the world. Student in honour of some professors used adjective like 'legend' or 'God' to describe some of them. The core value is the quality of teaching, which is nurtured and supported at the IIMs.

5. THE NEED BASED FINANCIAL ASSISTANCE (NBFA

The Institute justified the fee hike as it need money for more infrastructures for future needs of growing students. The Need Based Financial Assistance is provided to many students to continue their studies for payments of exorbitant fees. There are many scholarships available to our poor students. They are provided fee waiver schemes. So, every poor student is being protected, so nobody left the institute for their inability to pay total fees. The Need Based Financial Assistance in 2013-14, of Rs. 4.09 crores was provided to 132 students out of total 900 students(Table 2.3.1).The assistance was provided to 52 first year and 80 second year students, out of 438 first year and 462 second year students. The financial assistance to each of the recipients in first year was Rs. 2.86 Lakh, second year was Rs. 3.25 Lakh and Rs. 3.1 Lakhin both years combined. Among 52 first year students, Rs. 1.48 crores was provided and Rs. 2.60 crores was provided to 80 students in second year. Only 12% of the first year, 17% of the second year and 15% students of both years received the assistance.

In both (first and secondyears) combined, 29% of NC-OBC, 23% of DA, 19% of ST, 16% of SC and only 5% of Open Category and 15% of all categories combined received the financial assistance (Table 2.3.2). Among the recipients, the share of NC-OBC was 54%, SC and Open category was 16% each, ST was 9% and 5% of DA category. So, among the recipients, the NC-OBC was more. Out of a total of 900 students, 436 belong to Open Category, 245 to NC-OBC, 130 to SC, 63 to ST and 26 to DA category. Among all students, 49% belong to Open Category, 27% to NC-OBC, 14% SC, 7% ST and 3% to DA category. The share of Open category was 49% in total students, but their share was only 16%. The share of SC student was 14% in total students, but their share was 16% among the recipients. The share of ST student was 7% in total students but their share was 9% among the recipients. The share of NC-OBC student was 27% in total students but their share was 55% among the recipients. The share of DA student was 3% in total students but their share was 5% among the recipients. So, the recipient of NBFA was more among NC-OBC, DA and ST category students while meagre among Open category students.

6. FOR AND AGAINST FEE HIKE

a. Justification of Fee Hike: Views of Corporate World

Several captains of corporate Indian, which is the major customer of the IIMs particularly Mr. Murthy[1]has prompted. The reduction of tuition fees is the Trojan horse for eliminating autonomy of all IIMs, felt Mr Rao[2] The MHRD's infamous order came as a bolt from the blue for all Directors of the six old IIMs. It measure of minister desperation and ministry ineptitude that the Order cites the Supreme Court judgment in the historic TMA Pai Foundation Case (2003), in which the apex court decreed greater administrative and financial autonomy for institutions of professional education and upheld their right to earn reasonable surpluses. The ministry cited unaffordable fees as the reason for fee revision at the IIMs. However the reality is that even poor students from low income families can afford the fees charged by the IIMs. The starting salaries of IIM graduates are high enough to allow them to easily repay loans taken to finance their education which are easily available. IIM students can always avail of education loans which are liberally dispensed and pay them back within a short while after they begin their highly paid careers. Far from reducing the fees at the IIMs, was raising them to eliminate all subsidies. The minister asked - for how long cans the IIMs walk on the crutches of government support? The huge subsidies annually allocated to the IIMs need to be canalized to other institutions which are desperately short of money.An IIM graduate earns Rs. 6-8 Lakhper year and it makes easy to service education loans.

b. Views of Student Community

The student community in IIMs agitated against the Order but also against the incremental erosion of the autonomy of the IIMs.A comprehensive survey conducted by the union of IIMC students indicates that 90 percent of students are opposed to the proposed fee reduction. They believe this will translate into loss of autonomy which in turn will lead to a fall in the academic standards of globally renowned IIMs. The media has fallen in line with industry, academia and the student community and trenchantly condemned the ministerial harassment to the IIMs. The MHRD has unleashed a new wave of ministerial interference in education which goes against the spirit of liberalization pervading in every sector of the Indian economy. The elitism of IIMs is their credibility for their Brand. The policies of cutting fees will end up damaging the Brand, when mediocre Central Officials will instruct qualified academicians to run the IIMs. The glaring consequence of the perennial shortage of resources for education and the learned Justices of the apex court need to take judicial notice is that 20% of rural primary schools are of single teacher, 33% do not have proper buildings, 58% have no drinking water and over 70% are bereft of toilet facilities. In these circumstances, enhancing the subsidy of IIM students is tantamount to criminal negligence.

c. Fees Cut For More Government Intervention

The decision to cut fees will only bring down the quality of education offered at the IIMs. Also this whole issue of taking in more students does not make sense. Personalised, individual attention will not be possible and this can only end up bringing down the high standard of IIM courses. Nobody will approve of any drastic cut in fees at IIMs that are centers of excellence. No student who been admitted into an IIM has ever faced any problem about either getting or repaying loans. But with the government deciding to slash fees of the IIMs and curtail their funding, it will definitely make these institutions weaker. And once this is done, the government can easily step in and intervene in their functioning.

6. AUTONOMY TO FACULTY MEMBERS FOR EXCELLENCE

Peer esteem rather than administrative rewards from Directors or Deans drives faculty to strive and maintain excellence. The IIMs facilitate active interaction with the industry through case writing, executive education, workshop and conferences. This brings a richness and variety to the classroom that students and recruiters value. Another very important issue here is faculty autonomy. Faculty decides the curriculum, the pedagogy, the teaching material, the evaluation and the grading of students. The sense of ownership and pride that faculty have makes or breaks the quality of the course they deliver. The teaching materials are not always standard text book, but include cases studies, teaching notes of faculty, papers and articles chosen by the faculty concerned, which is strongly-felt culture of these IIMs.There is no boss: the Director cannot give orders to faculty. Those who have tried have found to their cost that is does not work. The culture can perhaps be best described by the term faculty governance. This faculty governance is tied to a higher standard by peer culture. Someone who slackens off becomes a bit of an outcast.

Today, the external opportunities also act as a spur to excellence. Those who do not perform well lose out on teaching, research and consulting opportunities within the country and overseas. Autonomy is desirable because higher education is a specialized field and cannot be left to generalists. Autonomy is also important to decide the mix of teaching and research, the different programsthe IIMs run. Autonomy also allows the IIMs to enable faculty to interact with industry through travel, workshops, conferences and consultancy. Without that interaction, the IIMs would become text bookish, dry and conceptually outdated. It allows faculty to do research in collaboration with colleagues at the IIMs and overseas. Under the new dispensation, this has to be cleared by the government. If we are to attract and retain the brightest and best in academics, we need to give that degree of freedom.

In any case, academics in India are underpaid compared to the industry and to teaching assignments overseas. Without that freedom, the best will simply leave and that trend has already started and will continue.No one can argue that the IIMs are a law unto themselves. They are part of the society, get taxpayers' money and are accountable to the society at large. However, accountability with control of a few individuals in the control by the government as it pays grants. Government money does not mean government control. Currently Government is giving prescriptions For improvement of the IIMs, the current prescriptions will have the opposite effect. The simple method of monitoring outputs and performance, the best method of ensuring improvement needs inputs like salaries, teaching loads, class size, fees etc.

7. THE COURT CASES FOR FEE REDUCTION

A writ petition was filed in public interest as a last resort to save the IIMs from being destroyed by their arbitrary action and irrelevant considerations by the Respondents (MHRD). The write Petition was approaching the Honourable Court directly in Public interest under for breaching their fundamental right guaranteed under the constitution against the arbitrary and ill conceived action of the Respondent. The MHRD's impugned Order directed the IIMs to reduce the fees charged to Rs.30,000 per student from the academic year 2004. This order is bad in law and is vitiated as the fees charged by the IIMs from each student are already subsidized by more than 60%. The IIMs spend Rs.4 Lakh on each student, whereas the fees collected per student is only Rs.1.5 Lakh. In initial years, the fees charged by the IIMs were negligible as a result they wholly depend on the Central Govt. Thus, the decision for fee reduction is ill conceived and having been arrived on irrelevant consideration as well as gaining more control over IIMs. The petitions were to save these IIMs of international repute from being destroyed by the Central Government.

a) IIMCMoves Supreme Court Against Fee Cut

In 2004, the Faculty Council (FC) of IIM Calcutta filed an application before the Supreme Court praying for an order imploding it as a respondent in the fee cut case already pending before the apex court. The FC expressed its opposition to the Board of Governors' (BoG) decision to accept the fee cut as recommended by the Centre, decided to make the application independent of those which may be made by the BoG. The faculty feels that some members of the BoG may not be exercising their independent judgment in the interest of the institute. It has therefore become incumbent upon the faculty to take up the interest of the institute, its faculty and its students. The Supreme Court has already issued notices to the six IIMs in the case filed challenging the government decision to slash the fees by 80%.

b) Cases in Supreme Court on Fee Cut

The board of the IIMA filed an affidavit before the Supreme Court stating that the Centre's decision to cut fees could encroach on its autonomy (Roy 2013). In an almost simultaneous action, the faculty council of IIMC filed an application before the court for impeding it as a respondent in the ongoing public interest litigation against the fee cuts. IIMB filed an affidavit in court that speaks of our stand on the fee cut and autonomy issues. The affidavit mainly contains the position paper published by the faculty of IIMA and resolutions by the society and the Board. The affidavit also mentions that the institute has set up a committee to discuss the issues with the MHRD. The Supreme Court had asked all six IIMs to express their interest to become a party to the ongoing litigation. The court had told all six IIMs to take "notice that in default of appearance, the matter will be decided and determined in your absence". The boards of IIM Lucknow and Kozhikode will emphasise their consent to the fee cut. But there is confusion about IIM Indore because its board is split on the fee cut. The IIMC faculty seeks to be made party in case and the Board is likely to file an affidavit in court that is not expected to differ with the government order.

c) Case in Calcutta High Court by Faculty Council

The IIMC's resolution was to abide by Calcutta HC decision. The Calcutta HC observed that any decision taken by the IIMC authorities on a resolution taken at its Board meeting would abide by the result of the case filed by the faculty council ((Zee News 2004).Justice Ghose, after hearing the contention of the parties in the case, directed them to file affidavits and adjourned the case till summer vacation. Appearing for the central government, Additional Solicitor General (ASG) opposed the writ petition claiming that the petitioner had suppressed material fact that they had already made an application on the same cause of action before the Supreme Court and as such the writ was not maintainable. ASG stated that there was no illegality in appointing six members on the board of governors at IIMC, claiming that according to rules, the Centre before appointing new members, should consult the issue with the state government. He submitted that this consultation had been made long before in 2000 and claimed the question of illegality was not tenable. Counsel for IIMC board chairman submitted that the memorandum of association of the premier management institute empowered him to adopt the resolution and as such there was no illegality on the part of the Chairman in adopting the resolution. The faculty council had in its petition challenged the appointment of six new members on the BoG of IIMC by the MHRD, claiming that the appointments were illegal and the 164th board meeting was also illegal.

The IIMs are not in agreement with the Central government regarding a provision in the draft rules that seeks to put a condition on the fee charged by the management institutes (Srivastava 2018). The MHRD shared the draft rules, with the IIMs for their feedback.The ministry wants to bring in a set of rules which may allow it to have a say in the fee structure, student intake capacity, gender equation, degrees offered and the amount of the corpus the IIMs can maintain. Some IIMs have objection to the clause in the draft rules that allows the Board of Governors to ensure that the fee charged from the students shall be commensurate with the overall expenditure for maintenance and expansion of the institute. The reason behind older IIMs' objection to this is the fact that the old IIMs do not take funds from the government for maintenance and expenditure. Also, these institutes fear that this may become an issue of disagreement between them and the government in future.

The MHRD on the other believes that a check on fee hike is just to ensure that the students do not suffer due to arbitrary fee hike which is why the clause has been proposed. The ministry assured there is no restriction on increasing the fee.The IIM Act passed last year in the Parliament, gives the elite institutes more autonomy in matters related to day to day activities, administrative decisions as well as decisions related to academic and financial aspects of the institute; besides allowing them to offered degrees instead of diplomas. Some of the older IIMs also do not approve of the provision of MoU with the government on performance parameters like student intake, expansion of institute and output targets.

The government has sought feedback from the IIMs are: a) The process of appointment of the institute chairperson should begin three months before the term ends and should be completed a month before his/her retirement. In case a new chairperson is not selected within the time frame, one of the board members will be appointed as the acting chairperson by the government. b) The chairperson's term will end as soon as he/she turns 74 years or on the completion of four years. c) No person shall be director of an IIM for over two terms. The retirement age of directors has been extended from 65 to 70 years, d) A chairperson can be removed only through consensus of the BoG. Such action can be taken only if it is approved with two-third majority. e) Neither the chairman nor any Board member should have a conflict of interest with the institute. If a conflict of interest is discovered later, then the concerned person will have to resign. f) The government has the power to issue directions to the IIMs if they are found to be acting in contravention of the Act. Such directions shall be binding. g) The new IIMs can co-opt alumni of older IIMs as board members and h) In case of any doubts regarding any provisions of the rules, IIMs may seek clarification from the government and the clarification provided shall be final.

The faculty council of the IIMC filed an application before the Supreme Court praying for an order impeding it as a respondent in the fee cut case already pending before the apex court (Zee news 2004). The faculty council, which had earlier expressed its opposition to the Board of

Governors' decision to accept the fee cut as recommended by the Centre, decided to make the application independent of those which may be made by the board. The council said "The faculty feels that some members of the Board of Governors may not be exercising their independent judgment in the interest of the institute. It has therefore become incumbent upon the faculty to take up the interest of the institute, its faculty and its current and future students," the council said. The Supreme Court has already issued notices to the six IIMs in the case filed by an IIM alumnus, challenging the government Decision to slash the annual fee of IIMs by 80 per cent.

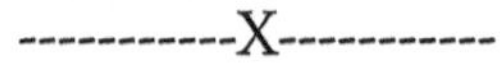

CHAPTER: 2.4

RECENT CONFLICTS, CHAOS, CRISIS AND GOVERNMENT INTERVENTIONS

Three important events have resulted the conflicts and crisis in our Institute in recent time since 2017. Those were the Restructuring of IIMs, the IIM Act 2017 and Introduction of Code of Conduct for faculty members in view of termination of our Director before her term ends. The faculty members were not consulted in coming up with the recommendations by the Bhargava Committee.The Directors of several IIMs have expressed disagreement towards the Centre's consideration of the proposal seeking greater control over the IIMs, through the IIM Act 2017. Of late, the Central government introduced Code of Conduct for faculty members after the rift between the then Director and faculty members. The Code of Conduct for the faculty was introduced to curtail their academic freedom.

1. RESTRUCTURING PROPOSALS ON IIMS: BHARGAVA COMMITTEE

i) Views of Faculty Members

The recommendations by the Bhargava Committee (2008), the faculty members need to cut on management development programs (MDPs) and increase time allocated to classroom teaching. Our faculty members have gone on the offensive for restructuring at the IIMs. The discontent of the faculty was on issues of governance, teaching hour, size of the governing board etc. The faculty was left out of consultations in coming up withthese recommendations for change. The faculty members were not consulted when arriving at this decision. Among the primary issues,our Professors are opposing the teaching hours. According to one teacher, the accusation of limited time to classroom teaching is baseless.The recommendation also disregards singular requirements for time that the faculty has to allocate for classroom teaching and comes up with a blanket must do for all.

The Bhargava Committee proposed a work norm of 160 hours of classroom teaching, which has been accepted by the MHRD and now under fire from our faculty members. The faculty members were not consulted in coming up with the recommendations. They are now complaining over a unicameral method of decision-making. There is the communication gap, given that the faculty was not consulted and opinions were excluded. A majority of these recommendations are to do with them. They were also miffed at this exclusion in light of the fact that they had earlier raised concerns with the Report of IIM Review Committee, which dealt with restructuring as well. In bicameral governance structure, decision making is formally divided between the faculty and the Board. The teachers believe that such attempts to exclude the faculty are to silence voices of disagreement and violate the established norms and practices of our governance. Also under contention is the restructuring of the governing board, the Committee's recommendation of reducing the size of the Board from 30 to 14.

As per this recommendation, Board members would be selected by a nominations committee comprising government representative and corporations that made donations. The institute is a property of the public and placing this kind of a power in the hands of a corporate is dangerous and lead to privatisation. Our Chairman had earlier shot down any possible chances of privatisation. The recommendations took into account the fact that IIMs were in different stages of evolution. Recommendations have kept in place a condition of flexibility depending on faculty talent and inclination. Our faculty presented a set of recommendations of flexibility which are under consideration.

ii) Attempt of Reversal of Powers to Attain Greater Control

The heads of the IIMs have criticised the Centre's consideration of the proposal seeking greater control over the IIMs and reversing the powers provided under the IIM Act 2017. The Directors of several IIMs have expressed disagreement towards the Centre's consideration of the proposal seeking greater control over the IIMs. The MHRD is considering a proposal empowering the Government to initiate an inquiry against the Board. According to MHRD, any difficulty arises in giving effect to the provisions of this Act. The Central Government may make such provisions not inconsistent with the provisions of this Act, as may appear necessary or expedient for removing the difficulty.

The Centre's move goes against the public stand on the autonomy of educational institutions. After granting autonomy to the 20 IIMs under the IIM Act, this current reversal erodes the autonomy of the institutes of national importance. Under the Act, the Board is the executive body, comprising 19 members, including nominated 17 members and alumni and two nominated from Centre and State governments. The Board appoints its Chairperson and the Director of each IIM. Under this Act, students are awarded the MBA degrees instead of PGDM. The IIMs have violated the provision and the Centre had issued a letter to the IIMs, instructing them to 'act in conformity with the UGC Act 1956'. It is the Government's attempt to give itself more powers to move against the Board. As far as checks and balances are concerned, our alumni, who have a decent representation on the Board, will never allow the institute to do something that will hurt the IIM brand. The Ministry's reason to reverse the powers provided to the Board. The risk of being summoned and investigated had prompted many independent directors to resign no one would want to be part of an IIM Board. The Government is not the only responsible agency and they will have to trust the Board members. It is an unnecessary attempt at centralization and will destroy the institutes.

iii) Failure of the Government

The problem with IIMs is that the central government not equipped to discharge their functions properly. Our Institute have been established jointly by the Central and State. The funding for capital expenditure has always come from the Central Government and the State provided the land. In the initial years, the deficit in revenue expenditure is met by the Central government. The MHRD is answerable to Parliament for proper utilization of the funds and it was controlling key financial and administrative powers relating to IIMs, which have full academic freedom. The IIMs are governed by a society whose members are appointed by the government. The Chairman, Directors and Board members are selected by the MHRD, while pay scales, faculty and administrative staff strength are determined by the government. The government has the power to give directives to the IIMs and also carry out an external review of its functioning.

Over the years, many IIMs have felt that their functioning is impaired by the lack of financial and administrative autonomy. This feeling grew stronger in the older IIMs, which had started generating a surplus on the revenue account. The Bhargava Committee found that the existing system needed considerable modifications, partly due to the growth in the number of IIMs as well as much larger number of higher educational institutions. The management of IIMs was fragmented between the Government, the Board and the Director and was not leading to excellence. It was recommended that the Boards should be professionalised and given full powers to manage the institutes. This had to be accompanied by a system that made the Boards accountable and also enabled the government to fulfill its obligations to Parliament. While proposing powers for the Board and the Director was easy, but devising a system of accountability was not.

The MHRD expressed their willingness to make IIMs fully autonomous provided there was a satisfactory system of accountability. The government is not equipped to discharge the functions. Hence, the committee recommended that the IIM society should be so constituted that it can have a genuine and long-term interest. This would require some society members remaining as such for long periods of time and having a stake that could be either financial or of reputation. While this matter is under debate, the IIMs have already become more autonomous.

2. THE INDIAN INSTITUTE OF MANAGEMENT ACT, 2017

The Indian Institute of Management Act, 2017is an Indian legislation. The Act declared the Indian Institute of Managements institutions of national importanceand enabled them to offer degrees and further make substantial changes in their administration. The Bill was approved by the Union Cabinetin 2017 and was passed by the Lok Sabha and Rajya Sabha. After receiving the President's assent, the bill became an Act on December 2017. The Act declaresIndian Institutes of Management as institutions of national importance and grants them the power to give degrees. The Act provides for the creation of a Board of Governance (BoG), Academic Council (AC) and Coordination Forum (CF).The Act provides for the creation of a Board of Governors (BoG) which would act as the principal executive body for each IIM and would appoint onedirector for each IIM. The Board would have a maximum of nineteenmembers including one Chairperson of the board; one nominee each from central and state governments; two members of the faculty, four eminent personalities from fields including education and industry, one of whom has to be a woman and the director of the institute.

The Act provides for the creation of an academic council (AC) for each IIM, which is the principal academic body under the act and which would decide the: (a) academic content; (b) criteria and processes for admissions to course and (c) guidelines for conduct of examinations. The academic council would comprise: (a) the director; (b) deans in charge of academics, research, student affairs etc.; (c) Chairman's and coordinators of various areas, programs, faculties, centers, departments and schools of the institute; (d) all full-time faculty members at the level of professor and; (e) members, by invitation of the board — on the recommendation of the director —

who are eminent in the fields of industry, finance, management, academics and public administration.

The Act provides for the creation of a coordination forum (CF), which would discuss matters pertaining to all IIMs. The coordination forum would comprise: (a) Higher Education Secretary, (b) two secretaries in charge of management education of state governments,(c) four chairpersons of institutes, to be nominated by the chairperson of the coordination forum, by rotation for two years; (d) the director of each institute, (d) fiveeminent personalities - of whom onehas to be of a woman—in the fields of academia and public service.The bill also proposes to incorporate many other changes like audit of institutes by the CAG. Even after the commencement of the Act, not all IIMs granted degrees.Five IIMs including IIMC were granted degrees while otherIIMS granted PG diplomas. The IIMs were asked to chalk up their action plan and outline their long term strategy.

3. IIM ACT 2017 AND ITS IMPLICATIONS

The government has come out withthe IIM Act 2017 to assure independence of the IIMs. But, IIMC gone to the other extreme and come up with a code of conduct for the faculty that curtails their academic freedom. The draft code of conduct prohibits faculty members from criticizing the government or the institution, organizing to sign petitions, joining protests that hurt public order interacting with the press, approaching higher authorities till a matter is not decided by appropriate authority. Ironically, the code was originally circulated among the faculty by then director who, later had a big run-with the faculty which led to her resignation before her term ends. It is true that management institutes are different where questioning existing practices/beliefs are at the heart of learning. If the right to question is taken away from teachers, what example does this set for students?

Apart from the fact that IIM professor will also have a view on political or social developments. The value of the academia is realized as much in critical thinking, debate, dissent and activism as it is in pedagogy. Forbidding criticism of the government means that professors must be silent about policies. Had professors not been allowed to join protests that violated "public order" Ironically, while the IIMC code probably belief that the rules have to mirror the ones that apply to bureaucrats since both get paid by the government? The judgments of the Supreme Court and High Court both make it clear that the government university professors should not be treated as government servants. Indeed, the judgment states that university professors are neither members of a service nor do they hold a civil post. Indeed, the National Education Policy itself recognizes the importance of autonomy. The board of a prestigious institution would have tried to ward off government pressure.

a) Against the IIM Bill

The IIM Bill 2015, as well as articles in the mass media today, along with the incisive letter by the current Chairman of the BoG of IIMA to the MHRD, and ask the mandarins to tear up the current Bill. If a Bill is needed as higher education really needs to be radically reformed, restructured and revamped. It was the formative experience and unparalleled expertise the IIM alumni. The alumni owe to these IIMs and all of us care very deeply about their future. And if you probe deeper to ask about the IIMs they will all point to some outstanding faculty members, academic freedom and autonomy. Those faculty members and the students, enjoyed at those IIMs. And to the initiative those faculty members took to launch some very innovative courses. At the IIMs, become just as innovative about the way we analyzed problems, arrived at alternative solutions, made our decisions, and launched new products and services.

Those faculty members rewired our brains and our way of thinking completely, and we are always remaining utterly beholden for all that we have achieved in life. Our professors always taught us not to accept the *status quo ante*, to free our minds from the fetters of conventional thinking, and to break with traditions. That is what makes the IIMs different and that is what makes their students different. The bill wants to declare certain institutes of management as institutes of national importance with a view to empower these institutes to attain standards of global excellence in management. But it ends up being all about rules, regulations and Government. Now, thetime has come to unfetter the IIMs completely. Just as our government appar at chiks and mandarins learnt the hard way that they knew very little about higher education. India cannot afford the luxury of having these bureaucrats who have been itching, to get the IIMs under their control.

The government ought to focus on the National Institutes leaving the IIMs. These National Institutes can expect to be upgraded once they have established a reputation for excellence. The new council structure could be designed to dovetail seamlessly with the existing institution-specific society and Board of Governors. The council members could serve terms on the boards for any of the IIMs once they are done with their stints on the national councils and*vice versa.* The directors of the respective institutes would be accountable to the boards, the boards would be accountable to the national councils and the national councils would be accountable to the people of India.

The national councils may have captains of industry, high flying alumni and academic representatives. The government representatives could ensure that the government's voice is not being ignored, but they should not have veto rights on the council's decisions. These councils be self-policing and self-governing, to ensure that all of the councils' decisions are always transparent and in the nation's best interests. They would always put the nation before self. Take on the responsibility of making sure that the councils would have members just like them: selfless, brilliant and very capable? The people of India would not have to worry because they could rest assured that their IIMs are in safe hands, free from any petty interference and meddling by anyone. All IIM alumni care very deeply about IIM's future.

4. POWER STRIFE BETWEEN FACULTY MEMBERS AND DIRECTOR

a) Director Indulged in Academic Council

It is also alleged that the Director indulged in selective recording of Council Minutes and decisions in her capacity as Chairperson of the Academic Council (AC), where all permanent teachers being its members. The minutes of a main AC meeting did not reflect the decision that input from the faculty should be shared with the Board on regulations under the IIM Act. The new Act granting all 20 IIMs sweeping powers, including the appointment of directors, chairmen and members of the board. Each IIM has to draft its Regulations under the new IIM Act, which will supervise and direct the administration. The teachers at IIMC have argued that the Regulations tend to minimize the duties of the AC, which will only be able to elect one delegate to the Board. The Chairman of the Board will pick the second one. The faculty also claims that, without their participation and consultation, the formulation and adoption of the proposed IIMC Regulations was carried out. The Academic Council was given only five days to send proposals on the draft and Director did not consider the faculty's input on the centralization of powers.

The faculty also wrote separately its concerns about the Regulations. After writing to the MHRD against the leadership of the institute, asked the government to hold off its notification. Regarding faculty's concerns, the Chairman wrote that as a practice we do not discuss internal matters related to our Institute and the Board in the public domain. The Board is fully committed and aligned to the best interest of our Institute. The faculty members are pained by the reports instigated by the small group to sully the prestige created over decades in the Institute. The faculty member's commitment to the success of talented students;as they are working at much greater efficiency and effectiveness. They march into the future with honesty and loyalty to the promise of "IIM First," Blessed by the good wishes and their supports have turned challenges into opportunities to improve our resilience.

b) IIM Calcutta Experience

The Institute is in the midst of a battle for supremacy (Nambier, 2021). Recently a power struggle has brewing up within the institution. The faculty is locked in unprecedented standoff with the Director, arguing that she has consolidated powers in her possession and usurped their role in administration and decision-making. The conflict was attributed by Director to "a small group of people" angered by her attempts to encourage a culture of openness and accountability. Most faculty members wrote to the MHRD urging it to step in Director's style of functioning, arbitrary, discriminatory and having a very narrow vision. The message sent to the government after internally exhausting all redress avenues. The IIMs are skeptical of government intervention in the past. Any action by MHRD is impossible and cannot begin to interfere with the internal affairs of the institute. The MHRD met Director and Chairman and asked them to resolve the standoff internally.

c) Faculty Member's Protest Against The Director

Amid conflict with our Board of Governors, the first woman director stepped down from the post before her term ends (Yadav 2021). The development was noteworthy as it surfaced amid an unprecedented standoff between the Director and the Board. The director accused the Chairman of infringing on her executive powers. In contrast, the Board accused her of inappropriate conduct. The clash escalated into a full-fledged crisis, after the Board passed a resolution against her. Denying of her authority to make appointments and take disciplinary action. The faculty members are locked in an unprecedented standoff with the institute's director alleging that she has centralised powers in her hands and usurped their role in administration and decision-making (*Chopra 2021).*This is unusual given that the IIMs, in the past, have always been critical of government interference and any interventions. The MHRD cannot start interfering in institute's internal affairs when they granted autonomy to the IIMs. The crisis is seen more as an ego clashes as much as a turf war.

There's a lot of micromanagement by the director. For instance, the doctoral research program committee is almost defunct because the director insists on having the final say on attending international conferences. Some alleged her role as chairperson of the Academic Council (AC), the highest body of the faculty members. She indulged in selective recording of minutes and decisions of the Council Members. The minutes of a crucial AC meeting did not reflect the decision that faculty feedback on Regulations under the IIM Act should be shared with the Board. The new IIM Act came into effect in 2018 and grants sweeping powers including in the appointment of directors, chairpersons and Board members. Teachers have alleged that the Regulations seek to reduce the AC's remit. The AC in future will only be able to elect one representative to the Board instead of two as has been the norm. Now, the Board chairperson will select the second.

The faculty also claims that, the formulation and adoption of the proposed Regulations of IIMC was done without their engagement and consultation. The AC was given a short time to submit suggestions on the draft and that the faculty feedback on centralisation of powers in the Board. The Director was not considered by the Board while passing the Regulations. After writing to the ministry against the institute leadership, the faculty also wrote separately on its concerns and requested the government to hold off its notification. Our faculty members are committed to uphold the requirements of the IIM Act to firmly set the Institute on the path to global excellence, fostering a culture of transparency, accountability and meritocracy. These aspects of the Act may cause disruption and discomfort to a small group of individuals with dissimilar values and interests. Their baseless stories to sully the Institute's reputation built over decades.

We are excited to march into the future with integrity and commitment and blessed by the good wishes and support of valued members of our faculty and extended community. About the faculty's concerns over the new Regulations, the Chairman wrote: As a practice we do not discuss internal matters related to our Institute and my Board in the public domain. We on the Board are fully committed and aligned to the best interest of IIMC. The allegations are without context and baseless. We have a unique faculty-driven academic culture and our Teachers pride themselves in their role in the day-to-day decision-making. The teachers there have always elected two representatives to the Board. To change this legacy without taking the stakeholders will obviously cause problems. The resignation of the Director comes almost a month after the Board of Governors clipped her powers (Roy 2021).

The Director and the board accused each other of trying to snub the other party. Her resignation comes after the Board of Governors clipped her powers. The Director had accused Chairman of eating into her executive powers and the board had accused her improper conduct. A section of our faculty wrote a letter to the MHRD, where they alleged that the Director had centralised powers and infringed the decision-making role of the board.. A draft code of conduct for our faculties that calls for a bar on public expression of their views on government policies and actions has stirred a row with teachers writing to the Board voicing their dissent. During this time, a cocas group of faculty member have used public money for private gains. The attempt of the then Director failed to control such activates, that might be resultedin recent conflicts.

5. CODE OF CONDUCT: A RETROGRADE STEP

a) Faculty Members Face New Code of Conduct

The faculty member faced new code of conduct - no criticism, no protests, nopetitions. The code, circulated in 2021 by the then directoron behalf of the Board. But, the code met strong resistance from the faculty members. Most of the teachers have argued that the code, borrowing heavily from the Central Civil Services Rules (CCSR) goes against the understanding of an academic institution that promote critical thinking and academic freedom. It also infringes on their constitutionally protected rights and goes against the idea of considering academic institutions different from government departments. Aside from prohibiting criticism of the government and the institute and its policies, the code expects teachers to seek prior approval of the competent authority to pursue any academic interests outside the institute. It forbids them to any joint representation addressed to the authorities for redress of any grievance and forwarding their plea to higher authority.

Unless the lower authority rejected the claim or refused relief, or the disposal of the matter is delayed by more than three months. No employee shall, except with the previous sanction of the competent authority, have recourse to any Court of Law or to the Press for the vindication of any official act which has been the subject matter of adverse criticism or an attack of defamatory character. There is the expectation of maintaining political neutrality and not taking part in politics or being associated with any party or organization that participates in political activity. Participation in demonstrations that can be considered prejudicial to the interests of the sovereignty and integrity of India, the security of the State, friendly relations with foreign States, public order, decency or morality or which involves contempt of court, defamation or incitement to any offence is a no-go area.

Ironically, this code comes shortly after the faculty approached the government directly against their Director and the Board. By reposing its immense faith in the efficacy of CCS Rules was the foundational governing policy for an academic institution. The faculties said this is a departure from policies at best institutes worldwide. The stakeholders in an organization have the right to speak out against any wrong policies. The teachers have referred to court judgments to argue that CCS Rules should not apply to academic institutions since teachers are not government servants. The service rules of IIM Bangalore carry the provision on criticism of the institute, government and their policies. The conduct rules in IIM Ahmadabad make no mention of the same but expected to maintain political neutrality.

The Institute has circulated among teachers anofficial's a code of conduct that says that members of the institute are not expected to publish anonymously, pseudonymously or in the name of any other person or organization, materials that may bring disrepute to the institute. The teachers will try to avoid criticism of the institute in any media that may bring disrepute to the institute. The codewas approved at a meeting of the BoG, the highest decision-making body. The code of conduct has articulated the institute's resolve to gag dissentTeachers then written back to the institute about their opposition to the code. The approval of the code suggests that apart from undertaking a few modifications or tweaking a few words. The clause pertaining to unauthorized communication of sensitive information, no member of the institute will except in accordance with general or specific order of the competent authority, communicate directly or indirectly any official documents or information with any person with whom he or she is not authorized. A majority of faculty members had written to the Union education ministry, expressing the fear that the board was mulling restrictions on their freedom of expression. Teachers said the final code was in sync with recent efforts to destroy the atmosphere of plurality on campuses.

b) Content of the Letter to Ministry of Education

According to the faculty members, there is an alarming decline in the academic environment. There is faculty and staff shortage and reduction in spending on research. The director has sought to run the Institute with complete disregard for extant norms, rules and processes, thereby attempting to erase the legacy of IIM Calcutta, institution of higher education of national and international repute. Moreover, the director being away from the institute for almost 50% of days has also contributed to the slowdown. Consequently, only one faculty member has been recruited despite several resignations and retirements of faculty. The student-teacher ratio has worsened significantly and the Institute has 20-30 full-time faculty members, fewer than IIM Ahmadabad or Bangalore. It may be noted that IIMC has more students in PGP, compared to both IIMA and IIMB. The general morale of faculty and staff of the Institute is at an all-time low. There have been at least eight resignations from among regular and contractual non-teaching staff members, most of whom have not been replaced. This has adversely affected the quality of teaching and research. The director is unilaterally and arbitrarily short listing candidates for faculty positions. Not all applications for faculty positions are forwarded to the concerned academic groups for their consideration.

-----------X----------

SECTION – III

MY LONG ASSOCIATION WITH THE INSTITUTE

CHAPTER 3.1

LONG ASSOCIATION WITH THE INSTITUTE: AN AUTOBIOGRAPHICAL ACCOUNT

My work in this prestigious Institute was successful and the knowledge I acquired reflected in the development of the Institute. The Institute maintains a peaceful academic environment by producing highly trained Managers. The Institute is a platform of learning and growth. It is left for us to choose our path and give and get the best during the long association with the Institute. This is a narrative of my thirty six years of association with the Institute. It intends to portray the Institute as centre for learning. It is a platform to learn from the various roles in one's performance there while assisting different faculty members in connection with different Research Projects. During my long association, I have participated in various programs, doing my own research activities and attending seminars in Calcutta, Bhubaneswar and New Delhi. My narration of personal experiences, learning and accomplishments are being described here. I continued to be associated with the Institute and shown in the chronological account of some significant events. I like to recall the contributions made by the Professors who worked here for long years.

1. MY JOINING IN THE INSTITUTE

I was delighted after facing an interview with Professor Nirmal Kumar Chandra of Economics Group in IIM Calcutta at Emerald Bower in north Calcutta. He called me for the post of Junior Project Assistant in connection with his ongoing Research Project on "Agrarian Change and Peasant Organisation"in Burdwan district of West Bengal. After the interview that lasted for more than an hour, he called me to wait outside. Having lost hope, I was ready to go back home in my village to work in our agricultural field. As I am pure Science Graduate having no education in Economics, all he asked about my direct experience in agricultural work and the productivity of major crops in our area. After an hour, he called me again and asked to join next day. In November 1974, I joined the Institute and started data tabulation job and calculation using hand operated FACIT calculator. In Burdwan district, three villages has been already surveyed, I have to tabulate those data in a large spread sheet with large squares printed in red ink. During 1976 to 1980, I was carrying out the survey in 18 villages in 10 districts of West Bengal. Earlier, Mr. Kanchan Mukherjee was doing this job, but he left to join at the Canter for Development Studies at Trivandrum. After one month, I was selected for "One Year Evening Course in Statistical Methods and Applications" in Indian Statistical Institute. This program started in January and completed in to December in 1975.

The first three months was a contractual appointment as Junior Project Assistant, next two years on daily wage basis. In 1976, when the CMDS (Canter for Management and Development Studies) was formed I have to appear in informal interview in presence of Mrs. Kamini Adhikari, Chairperson of CMDS. Now the CMDS Rule was followed and all Project Assistants have to sign attendance Register kept in the room of Dr. K K Chowdhuri, Secretary of CMDS. Now, the Institute gave me second appointment as junior Project Assistant on annual contract basis and continued till 1982. After that, we were regularized in a regular pay scale. Instead of regular attendance, a monthly attendance system was introduced. After each month, the attendance sheet had to be concerned faculty members and be submitted to Personnel Section. Since 1987, I was appointed as Research Assistant on regular basis and enjoyed all the benefits along with other staffs.My association with the Institute continued till December 2010 (36 years) in diverse roles.

Many professors with foreign degrees from best Universities in the world chose to remain here and made a mark. I joined the Institute just after some eminent Professors like - Asoke Mitra, Barun De, Paresh Chattopadhya, Iswar Dayal and Dharni P Sinha etc. left out for more prestigious and more important positions. Still, many eminent Professors existed there at that time. All the outgoing and existing faculty members made valuable contributions for the Institute.As the Institute culture was designed to make every Professor a Man on Mission and an Institution Builder. Their contributions in research, writing, teaching, dissemination was of more values. My journey showcases how the Institute offers a platform for an interested person to learn,grow and contribute to its growth in different forms. In the process, it helps me to grow and even make a mark in my little way.

But, I focused on the opportunity to make impact in life. Whatever the jobs, I have enjoyed the process of working.A chronological account of some significant events of my education and professional journey is in Exhibit 3.3.1. In conclusion, I would like to reiterate that our Institute was platform for actions and learning. Academic institutions provide many avenues for growth. Besides learning from books & Journals, I have learnt a lot from my own actions with Professors, Administrative Officers, Colleagues, SeniorStaffs and one's self through reflection. Growth requires initiative commitments and inquest for learning. The last 36 years of my enriching relationship with this institute is my humble point of view - from "a sapling to the forest" is the saga of the development of our institute.

2. HUMBLE BEGINNINGS

a) My First Day in Emerald Bower for Interview

Prof. Chandra called me for an interview in connection to some village survey. I reached the office after getting down at Kantakal stoppage on B T Road. I crossed a football ground where some cattle were grazing. I entered in a row of asbestos shaded rooms meant for office work. I was waiting in a room, as my classmate entered Prof. Chandra's room to inform about me. He told me to wait till he asked to enter in his room. After an hour, he asked me to appear in his room. He enquired about my result of B.Sc. examination. I told that I have obtained more than 70% in each subject – Mathematics, Physics and Chemistry. He enquired what I was doing. I replied, as a son of marginal farmer, I used to do all agricultural operations – sowing, weeding, harvesting etc. he asked -Do you Plough?I replied, we have no bullocks instead, we used to hire ploughman. The only cash crop in our field was jute and Potato. Do you wash jute in waist deep rotten water? Yes, I do. Moreover, I have a small grocery shop in my house. To run this shop, I have to add prices of around twenty items by counting fingers.How correct was the addition?It was cent percent correct. So, he was impressed to me. After sometime, he called me again and asked me to join next day. But it was second Saturday, a holiday in this office. So, I joined the Institute in November 16, 1974.

As it was two months contract, my friend said you will get Rs. 400 per month. I replied for the two months in total? He said no, no, it is for each month. I don't know the name of the office and what are the activities. Few days later, Prof Chandra asked me to collect my appointment letter from the Director's office in the adjacent old building. I was appointed for two month (December 1974 to January 1975). For the month of November, I received Rs. 216 for 12 days @Rs. 18. From the appointment letter, I came to know that the name of the office was Indian Institute of Management Calcutta and Prof. Chandra is a Professor in Economics. Around 40 students across the country came here for studying Management.

The campus is known as the Emerald Bower. This was the palatial building of Pathuriaghata Tagore family. It is also known as '*Marakat Kunja*', a two-story Mansion built by the Tagore families. Mr. Pradoot Coomar Tagore beautified the splendid interiors and outsides of the Emerald Bower. The huge hall in the ground floor was used for musical performance and was known as '*Jalsa ghar*'. The mansion and huge parklands around Emerald Bower stands for pleasant retreats under the shades of green wood trees or climbing plants. The nostalgias of the Emerald Bower were the cast Iron gate, dry fountains, undecorated statutes, the ponds full of grass, pathways flanked by hedges and shrubs. In this time, students have makeshift classrooms, old borrowed building and hostels. The infrastructure was basic and the building was infected with mosquitoes and no proven reading materials. The EB campus housed the Library and Administrative office. There were two hostels - Tagore Hall and Ramanujam Hall.

The campus was in a traditional Calcutta neighbourhood. For coffee, drinks, tea, we have to go '*Sinthee More*' and for exotic meal, we have to go to Shyambazar. The makeshift campus at Emerald Bower was awfully short in amenities but long in history. Prof. Barun De, the Marxist historian served the Institute recalled the old days in EB Campus with his old colleague Prof Ashok Mitra, who "introduced me into the Indian Institute of Management and I had the privilege of working in the same room as his in our old EB Campus.Prof. Ishwar Dayal wrote his experience of IIMC at EB Campus, where he stayed for few years.

I joined the Institute in November 1974 on a two months contract to work with ProfessorChandra to complete the project 'Agrarian Change and Peasant Organisation' in West Bengal. Mr. Rathin Pal (1) was a good typist attached to Prof. Chandra and used to type non-stop and completing almost 300 pages manuscript of the two volumes of the final Report on: "Agrarian Change and Peasant Organisation" in just one month. I was offered the appointment by Prof. Chandra as Junior Project Assistant to do tabulation and statistical analysis of the just completed village survey data from three villages in Burdwan district. After completion of the Report on Burdwan Survey, sponsored by FAO and ILO, Prof. Chandra submitted the Report to those foreign agencies. By this time, I was attending the evening program on Statistical Methods and Applications in Indian Statistical Institute. After completion on this program, Prof. Chandra engaged in a similar Survey in ten villages around Kheyadaha village in Sonarpur Block of undivided 24-Parganas. In this time, I spend one week in the village and next week in the deserted Office at EB campus, as most part of the office has moved to Joka, about 20 kilometres away from the City centre.

b) My First Day in Joka on Truck

In 1977, Prof. Chandra came to my office in Hostel room at EB and asked me to be ready in the next mooring around 7 a.m. I reached the EB

Campus in early morning and found a Truck waiting for me. The entire filled up village schedules, computation sheets, files and folders along with the Almiraha, Chair, Table and FACIT Calculator etc. were loaded in the truck. The Truck followed the Conspore railway yard, Strand Road on the bank of river Ganges and passed under the Hooghly Bridge, Princep Ghat to reach Khidirpore, then followed the Diamond Harbour road and finally reached Joka at 11 a.m. So, my first journey to Joka campus was on Truck by sitting in driver's cabin. I can remember a travelogue titled '*Truck Bahane McMohane*' by Prof. Nabanita Deb Sen, wife of Dr. Amartya Sen.

I reached an unknown place full of trees, grass and lakes and uneven kutcha roads. By passing a lake, I reached near a building built for residential purpose. I was allotted a room and I stored the goods which I have carried from EB Camus. When I reached Joka for the first time, the new office was under full construction. There were no '*pucca*' roads with rough roads full of brickbats. Arranging all items in my room, I went to meet Prof. Chandra, in B Block first floor (B-203). Opposite to my room, a Branch of State Bank of India was opened at the top of our Accounts Office in the Residential Building. As Joka was more than 60 kilometres from my village, I have to travel daily about 120 kilometres of to and fro journey. I have to start at 7-30 AM and reached Joka village around 10 AM

After a few months, I was again evicted to third floor of the newly constructed Administrative Building in 1978. Here I met Miss Nalanjana Kundu, a Research Fellow attached to Prof. Kumar. Within a year, she left for joining the Psychology Department of Calcutta University as Professor. The whole floor was shared by three Research Fellows of Prof. Kumar and Ms. Nilanjana Kundu. Most of the time, I was alone in that floor as Ms. Kundu came around noon and left early. She asked for my help in analyzing data collected this morning while she was in her Psychiatric Counselling chamber. Within a year, she married and became Mrs. Sanyal. She left for joining as Professor in In 1980, I was again evicted from Administrative Building to B Block Ground floor room no B-102. I have to share this room with eight people, including three Research Fellows, three Project Assistants, one typist and the Security Officer Mr. Nag. Around 1982, I was again evicted to ground floor of C Blok room no. C- 103. I have shared this room with six Project Assistants. So, I have moved to different rooms in different buildings.

3. CHANGES IN SITTING ARRANGEMENTS

During long journey in the Institute, I have moved from here and there in ten places. In EB Campus, my initial sitting arrangement was in a single floor Asbestos shade low lying room with one window and one door. I was provided wooden chair and table with a steel almirah and a hand operated FACIT machine. I was given a bundle of Square Sheets, like graph papers with large squares printed in red ink. I have to use wood pencil for entering data on Square Sheets. I was given a box of wood pencils, erasers and writing Pads for calculations. My small room was shared by Prof. Chitta Mitra, me and Atul babu.When I moved from EB to Joka in 1977, I was placed in the proposed Director's residence, across the lake. There was no change in furniture and stationeries, but the room was very large and shared by me, Atul babu and Asit babu. The village survey in ten villages around Kheyada in Sonarpur was completed. So, we dump our filled up household schedules on the floor.

In 1978, I moved to third floor of newly built Administrative Building. My other colleagues attached to Prof. Chandra were busy in field survey in Bankura and Medinipur districts. During this time, an important change came in for Project Assistants. Ms. Krishna Chatterjee won the case which we were fighting against illegal retrenchment of her. Mr. Tarit Dutt has just been retrenched. Atul babu asked Prof. Chandra to appoint him in our Project, to help me in entering village data. Most of the he loitered here and there by riding his bicycle in our vast campus and was retrenched after six months.In 1980, I had a demotion from third floor of Administrative Building to first floor of B-Block room No B103, where at least seven staffs were sitting. Within a year, the security Officer Mr. Nag was placed in this room in a make shift chamber. Mr. Kabiraj, the horticulturist and typist Akshoy Roy used to come in his chamber. So, my room became cowshed and lots of hue and cry. Moreover, construction of classrooms L3 and L4 was in full swing. The sound of construction machineries and shouting of labours make this room horrible. In this room, I have prepared a Paper on Panchayats in West Bengal for ensuing National Seminar at our Institute. I wrote an article on Miseries of Rural Life *(Gramer hatasha o Andhakar Dik),* which was published in Bhumilaxmi, a publication of Ananda Bazar Group. I also wrote some Features and were published in PTI Features from Bombay.

After completion of classrooms L3 and L4, we were evicted and shifted to C block ground floor room No. C104, where were five project assistants – I, Atul babu, Tarit, Arun and Amal were accommodate. After few days, our colleague Mrs. Mamata Dutta was added next to me. So, the room became congested and Bhubanesh'da used to come for gossiping with Atul babu. Our Next door neighbours were - Shyamali, Prithwis, Ajoy and Gomes, who were attached to the Rural Development Management, who's Chairman was Prof. Mishra, a faculty member in Sociology group. In this period, I spent most time in our Library for jobs assigned by Prof. Chandra. In 1990, when Dr. Asoke Mitra engaged me in his Primary Education Commission, I was shifted to B block top floor room already occupied by Mr. Poromesh'Acharya. I used his computer in connection with the work of Education Commission, where he was a member of it. When he took voluntary retirement, I became the only occupant with an old Computer. Till 2008, I have two seats one in C block and other in B Block. Just before retirement, the Office allotted a well furnished air conditioned room in C block with an old and inoperative computer and a revolving chair. I have used it for a week just before retirement.

4. Computing Machines: FACIT, Pocket Calculator and Personal Computer

Till 1980, I was using the hand operated FACIT Machines weighing about 10 kilogram for arithmetic calculations like summation, subtraction, multiplication and division. In 1981, I purchased an electronic Pocket Calculator from Capital Electronics at Calcutta. I used this calculator for computing concentration of land holding in different States and All

India for Mrs. Rohini Nayar, wife of our Prof. Deepak Nayar. She was a regular contributor in People's Daily, a mouthpiece of CPI (M) published from New Delhi.In this time, Prof. Subratesh Ghosh gave me some data on industrial statistics. I analyzed those data with the help of this pocket calculator. There after my office provided a Desk Top Calculator, which worked as pocket calculator with large Key Board and bold figures.I have used this in analyzing village survey data on rural households in 18 villages in ten districts.

In 1980, I attended a ten week program in ISI (Indian Statistical Institute). The program was on Application of Electronic Computers and Mathematical Analysis. The participating students were engaged in any organization related to research activities. Most of them were Engineers from Geological Survey of India. There were no Personal computers at that time. The IBM business machines were called Computers. The communication between the Computer and the user was possible through Punch Card. The punch card is a stiff paper card having printed 0 to 9 vertically in 80 rows. The card has to be punched by Punch Machine like typing in Type Machine. The punched cards have to be verified by a Verifier Machine. After putting these cards in the deck, these cards will drop in the appropriate box and defectives card were stored in Reject box. Prof. Raha taught us Punching, Sorting and Verifying of the data in Punch cards. After this, we have to write the PROGRAM either in FORTRAN, COBOL languages. To analyse these data, we deposited a bundle of Punch Cards, loaded with the PROGRAMME and the DATA, to the ground floor of the main building of ISI. The IBM machine operator will run the data serially. After some hours we have to collect the result printed on broad papers marked with light and deep blue lines.

In 1987, I attended a MCA Teacher's Training program in our CAM centre under Prof. Ambujaksh Mohanty. I along with my partner, Prof. Pal of BE College, developed a software on Railway Reservation System for Mail/ Express trains. In doing this, I first used the modern Desk Top Personal Computer PC). These Personal Computers were run in DOS (Disk Operating System) as the present Windows System was not yet introduced.

Prof. Chandra called me to test how I have learnt the Computer. He gave me a hand written paper and asked me to present it in Word Processing (Typing). It was question paper of PGP 1 for next day examination. I type this paper in Word Processing and make a print out in Leaser Printer inside CAM centre. He has advised me to delete this document immediately, unless a student may look at it in CAM centre. I delete the document after a print out. Prof. Chandra submitted it in clear laser printout, while others submitted in typed form in PGP office.

In 1997, I booked a PC from Partech Computers Limited, who advertised in daily News Papers. Initially, I have deposited Rs. 5000 to an agent in Ezra Street in central Calcutta. It was declared that the PC will be delivered in six months but the Company failed. Due to this delay, the company announced that they will supply PC of higher configuration. At that time the only producer in market was HCL (Hindustan Computers Limited). Our office purchased about eight PCs - three Pentium-386 and five Pentium-486 in our DPC (Data Processing Canter). My computer delivered by PCL was Pentium-486.To install my PC at home, I have made a wooden Cubical in my bed room, to protect from smoke and dust. After a few months, I purchased a Dot Matrix Printer of TVS Electronics. For printing, I have to purchase a bundle of 1000 perforated sheets having round holes along the borders to fit in printer's spoke. The ribbon of the printer was very cheap and can be replaced easily. While printing, the printer makes noises as it was mechanical device. For storage of data, we used Verbatim Disc similar to Gramophone disk.

During this time, Internet was in introductory stage. In our DPC, out of 8 PCs, only one has internet connection. It was used mainly for using reading daily newspapers. At home, I have internet connection from Satyam Computers in Calcutta. I have to purchase a pack of around Rs. 50, after calling them over phone, the company send a peon to hand over the pack in my home. It was available in a disk, which has to be inserted for installation. Later, Calcutta Telephonesprovided the internet service through my landline. Earlier, the speed was very slow but it became faster.

5. OLD COLLEAGUES IN EMERALD BOWER AND JOKA

In the initial period at Emerald Bower, I met Mr. K K Chaudhri and Sushil Panja the Research Assistants attached to Prof. Kamini Adhikari's Center for Entrepreneurship Development. Besides them, there were Ms. Vaijayanti, N Natarajan, K Seetaraman and L Sridharan, who were alumni of Indian Statistical Institute and all hailed from South India. There was Atul Manna and Asit Misra, both hailed from Midnapur district, while Rohitaswa and I were from Hooghly and Dhruba Ghosh from the adjacent area of E.B. Campus. All six were attached to the Prof. Chandra's Project. Mr. V Nagi Reddy a Research Assistant was attached to Prof. Chandra. Ratan Ghosh was attached to Prof. Ranjit Sau. All these staffs were on contractual basis. Mr. M N Pal was associated with Prof. Arun Choudhuri in second West Bengal Project. Mr. Swaraj Bandopadhyaya, Swapan Bhattacharya and Arun P Sinha were attached to the Canter for Management Education, headed by Prof. D P Sinha, who left for joining ASCI Hyderabad. Now, Prof Kumar became the next Chairman of the Canter.

Among the administrative staffs, Mr. D C Bhattacharya was the Chief Administrative Officer and Mr. S C Dasgupta was the Senior Administrative Officer. Other Administrative Officers were - C P Massey (EDP), Dipak Chatterjee (PGP/FP) and Ashok Sengupta (Placements and Publications), In our Library, Ashok Mukhopadhyay was the Librarian and Ranjit Mukherjee was Deputy Librarian and some Library Assistants, The Telephone exchange was operated by three women. Other typists were Supti Chatterjee, Protima Nayek. Mr. Rathin Pal (Senior) and Rathin Paul (Junior) was canteen supervisor.

When the Institute moved to Joka campus in 1975, there was many security staffs and gardening staffs for planting trees of different varieties and maintain flower gardens. A folk of Stenos were recruited in mid-1980s, as more Professors were recruited at that time. Those Stenos were - Bijan, Tapan, Amiya, Udayan etc. along with Typist like Kashi, Jadab, Kamal, Ananta, Swapna etc. The Project assistants were Atul Manna, Asit Msra, Poromesh Acharya, L Sreedharan, K Seetaraman, Abdul Halim, Swapan

Bardhan etc. Around 1977, a few of Project assistants like Santwana, Tridib, Arun, Prithwis, Prosenjit, Shaymali, Krishna, Mamata, Tarit, Amal etc. joined. In 1987, 12 Project Assistants were placed in Permanent category of Research Assistant. In mid-1980s, the staff strength increased to about 500 and there were chaos in the Campus because of two rival Unions in the regime of second term of our Director Prof. Aiyar. The left-oriented Union was led by Mr Samir Banerjee and Mr. Tarak Nath Naskar while the Congress dominated union was run by Rathin Pal (Junior) and Asit Dutta. The officers who dictated by the administration were – S B Dey, Ashok Sengupta, Sudeb Mukherjee, Deepak Chatterjee, B B Kartgupta etc.

6. OUR DIRECTORS DURING MY DAYS

When I joined the Institute in 1974, my appointment was issued by the then Director Prof. Jati K Sengupta at EB Campus. He served the Institute as Director from 1974 to 1976. I have not seen him after the Institute moved to Joka Campus in 1976. Mr. Hiten Bhaya, Chairman of SAIL (Steel Authority of India), joined as Director in 1977 and served till 1982. He was very active and dynamic person regarding Indigenization of the Institute from the clutch of American boss. ProfessorsNirmal Chandra, Sitangshu Chakraborti, Gouranga Chattopadhayay etc. were his close associates. He considered the plea of Project Assistants who were working on contractual basis. While leaving at the end of his term, he wrote a note for considering our case sympathetically. Prof. R P Aiyar, a faculty member from our MIS group became the next Director for 1983 to 1988. By this time, the disturbance at our Campus for slogan shouting in the Lunch time and placards everywhere. The staff association was also demanding permanency of casual staffs in Students' Mess and Staff Canteen. Moreover, about 30 Stenos and Typist were recruited to support increasing Faculty members. So, this time there was chaos in the Campus and he took voluntary retirement in 1992. All the Project Assistants were absorbed as Research Assistants in regular pay scale during his tenure

The Faculty members felt that Director being an internal candidate was unable to settle the chaotic situation in the Institute. They thought for a

Director from outside the Campus. Mr. Subir Chowdhury, having 15 years of Industrial experience and five years of administrator as Ex-Director of ISWBM (Institute of Social Welfare and Business Management) Calcutta joined as Director. He tried his best to manage our Institute form 1992 to 1997. The bolt from the blue came in from the Central Government, which curtailed our Grants drastically. He started small measures for cutting our daily expenses. Moreover, he thought of retrenchment of old *Malis* (Gardeners) and *Durwans* (Security Staffs) etc. Once he called all Research Assistants to earn money for the Institute. Two of us started MDP (Management Development Program) with the help of our faculty members. Some, faculty members objected to their venture, because it may lower the image of the Institute. Finally, those MDPs organized by our RAs were great success.

Prof. Amitava Bose, our Professor in Economics group became the next Director in 1997 to 2002. During his time, two new Posts of Dean (PI) and Dean (Educations) were created to deal with day to day problems. The Director was only looking external matters with the Board and Central Government. We were engaged in Invigilation duty in PGP I and II examinations in his time. He run the Institute smoothly but declined the offer for second term. Prof. Shekhar Choudhuri of IIM Ahmadabad became the next Director and stayed for two successive terms of ten years from 2002 to 2013. During his time, the reservation of OBC students was implemented. He introduces several new Programs like PGP-Ex, PGPEX-VLM, and Long Duration Program (LDP) etc. He undertook several initiatives for Internationalization of the Institute. As a result, the Institute won triple accreditation from International Agencies. In 2007, he offered me a Memento in my hand for my 25 years of service in the Institute.

CHAPTER: 3.2

ACTIVITIES: ASSISTANCE TO PROFESSORS, INVIGILATION DUTY, ACTIVITIES IN ADMINISTRATION, CMDS PROJECTEtc.

INTRODUCTION

My activities during last thirty sixyears of servicewere –Assistance to different Professors in connection with different projects, Invigilation duty in PGP, PGPEX and PGPEX-VLM examinations and Assistance to the Secretary to the Board of Governance for a forthcoming Board meeting to be held at New Delhi. I have assisted the M Phil and PhD students of Calcutta University's department of Education. Moreover, I have assisted one faculty members in her PhD, two Research Fellows in doing their PhDs and also one Research Assistant in her PhD. I also assisted a Professor of Zoology in Kalyani University. I have fitted Gompertz Curve on the research trend on traditional Medicinal Plants in Biology at Calcutta University. I have assisted a researcher in doing his PhD on Use of Drugs Among Call Centre employees in Sector – V in Calcutta. Of late, I have assisted a researcher in his PhD on Job Satisfaction Among Professors in Private Engineering Colleges in West Bengal. I have assisted many of our faculty members like -Profs. Nirmal Kumar Chandra, Dr. Ashok Mitra, Raghabendra Chattopdhyay, V Nagi Reddy, Uttam Sarkar (presentDirector), Saibal Chattopadhya (Ex-Director),Subir Bhattacharya, Rahul Roy, Hrishikesh Bhattacharya etc.

1. ASSISTANCE TO DIFFERENT FACULTY MEMBERS

a) Prof. Nirmal Kumar Chandra

In November 1974, I was appointed as a Junior Project Assistant with a monthly salary of Rupees 400. Prof. Chandra engaged me in his Project on "Agrarian Change and Peasant Organization". During 1972-73, the field survey has been completed in three villages of Burdwan. Before my joining, Mr. Kanchan Mukherjee was working as a Research Assistant to Prof. Chandra. He left for joining at the Centre for Development Studies in Trivandrum. I was appointed to analyse the data collected in the survey of three villages in Galsi Block of Burdwan (undivided) district. I spent a lot of time at work hammering away at the hand operated FACIT calculating machine. The objective of the Project was to calculate the inequality in land holding and annual income among of all the households in those villages. Then, we estimated the extent of hunger among landless agricultural labourer households. We estimated the amount of "Levy" that can be imposed on rich peasants. The levy system was in practice by the State for procuring excess paddy from the landlords.

We also measured the extent of exploitation among varies types of agricultural labourers. The children of the landless labourers were engaged by rich peasants as 'Bagal', (cowboy) to herd the folk of cows of the landed gentry. They were paid a meagre amount in cash and kind, their plight has been written by Prof. Chandra. The "Bagals of Bengal", was chapterised in the book: 'Subaltern Studies' edited by Mrs. Nirmala Banerjee, mother of Nobel Laureate Avijit B Banerjee. I was acknowledged in this book. When my first appointment expired in March 1975 at EB Campus, Prof. Chandra engaged me on daily wage basis @ Rs. 18 per day, on no-work-no-pay basis. It was a monthly exercise that, after each month Prof. Chandra had to issue an IOM (Inter Office Memo) to the Director for payment of my salary and it took another week to receive my salary.

After completion of the project, Prof. Chandra left for a foreign trip for presentation of the Report on Agrarian Change and Peasant Organisation in Burdwan district. He has classified the peasant on the basis of contribution of their labour in the whole agricultural operations. Traditionally, farmers were classified by their size of land holding and they were classified as Small, Medium and Large farmers. But Prof. Chandra classified them as Landlord, Rich Peasants, Poor Peasants and Landless Agricultural Labourers. The landlords contributed no labour in agriculture but received half or one third share of the total crop, The Rich Peasants only supervised the agricultural operations but donot work on their fields but employ agricultural labourers in their farms. They were mainly service holders or business men. While Poor Peasants mainly work in their own field and sometimes engage as labour to Landlords and Rich Peasants. The landless agricultural labours were engaged in Landlords or Rich Farmers land on daily wage basis or as *Nagare* (Monthly contract) basis. The womenfolk of the Landless labour families were engaged as housekeeper in Landlord or Rich Farmer families. The children of landless families were engaged as Bagal (Cowboy) in Landlord or Rich Farmer families.

The main office of the Institute shifted to Joka in mid-1975, but some Research staffs were still working in EB Campus till 1977.I used to go to Kheaydah village in Sonarpur Block of Twenty Parganas (undivided) district, for one week and next week to my office at EB Campus. By this time, my room was demolished and I have been lifted to the first floor of the Hostel. In this time, a person used to come in my room and enquire about Prof. Chandra. Later, I recognized him as Mr. Sushil Khanna, our alumni, who. joined later as Research Fellow and became faculty member in Economics group. In the same way, Mr. Ramanuj Majumder, ISI alumni also used to meet Prof. Chitta Mitra, who shared my room at EB Campus. Here, I met a gentleman Dr. K K Chaudhuri, Research Fellow sitting in my next room.

When Prof. Chandra has not returned from abroad, his all four Project Assistants were engaged in the survey on ten villages around Kheyadah. The objective of the survey was enquiring land tenancy system prevailing in that area. The vast track of Vidyadhari Char has been occupied by the local landed gentry. Among them, Mr. Naskar of Kheyadah village was a sitting MLA in Dr. B C Roy Ministry. To reach Kheyadah from my village was a long journey. Generally, I went to Kheyadah on Monday and returned at Friday. We lived in a poor Bargadar's *kutchha* house and Atul babu cooked our food. While we were conducting field survey in Kheyadah village, Atul babu listened from his Radio on April 1977 that 'President's Rule' has been imposed in the State. He was much disappointed but I know nothing about 'President's Rule'.

During 1977-1982, I was engaged in surveying eighteen villages in ten districts of West Bengal from Digha to Darjeeling. Generally, I spent one week in the field survey and next week in Joka Campus to assist Prof. Chandra in his research work and academic activities. The academic activities were reviewing the student's answer scripts, to put total marks, checking if he has missed to put marks, final tabulation of marks and submit to PGP office. In 1978, he was studying the existing monopoly practices followed by Indian Large Business Houses. He gave me a book 'The Corporate Private Sector: Concentration, Ownership and Control" by R K Hazari. The Report on MRTP by Subimal Dutt (1966), has estimated that, 48 Large Industrial House having assets above 21 cores each, collectively own Rs. 4000 cores. The Birla family owns 280 companies, Tata family owns 84 companies and so were others. (Forum, 2007). The Dutt Committee report consists of business statistics like value of fixed assets, working capital, number of employees etc. of those companies.

He asked me to up to date the relevant data from the National Library, Commercial Library and our own Library. After collection of relevant data, he asked me to compute some statistic. Finally, it was resulted as an article, "Monopoly Capital, Private Corporate Sector and the IndianEconomy: A Study in Relative Growth 1931-1976." It was published in EPW in 1979, where he observed that 'under Indian conditions, it is quite possible that the companies are not 'legally' inter-connected, but are in fact controlled by one business family. The widespread practice of '*benami* shareholders, where by the de facto owner for a variety of reasons has the shares recorded in the member of a relative or a protégé helps to underscore this above lacuna.'

In 1980, Prof. Chandra took me to the National Library to compile various data on Indian economy. Next, I visited CSO library and Commercial library. After one year of frequent visit to these Libraries, I have collected a huge data. Prof. Chandra directed me to do some calculations. By this time, he also directed me to evaluate the cost of maintenance and new buildings in my own village. After completing this task, he was delighted by seeing the extent of value addition in rural housing sector. It was quite different from the Central Government's estimates in calculating National Income. Lastly, it gave birth the article "Long Term Stagnation in the Indian Economy, 1900-1975, published in EPW in April 1982. In 1988, Prof. Chandra published his first book the "Retarded Economics", a collection of his articles published earlier in EPW during 1980s. The book has been published by Oxford University Press. I have done the "Index" pages at the end of the book with the help of Mr. Ghosh, Librarian of CSSSR. I have put the corresponding page number in the index and EPW paid me for this job.

I have helped him in more than a dozen of his Papers published in EPW. Those were -"Export-Oriented Growth", "North and South Hemisphere", "Cost of German Unity","Peasantry as a Single Class", Notes on Bukharin, Peasants and Soviet Industrialisation", "Planning and Foreign Investment in Indian Manufacturing", "Was the Collapse of the CPSU Inevitable?,Russia's Sinking Economy: "External Dimensions and India's Rubble Debt and the Depreciating Rubble", China's Tryst with Globalisation", "The Political Economy of Consumer Subsidies"and "Trade, Technology andDevelopment" etc.

b) Dr. Ashok Mitra

In 1990, Prof. Chandra accompanied me to meet Prof. Ashok Mitra in his Sonali Apartment in Alipore. Prof. Mitra had some data analysis job relating to the RBI sponsored project on agricultural financing in different States. It was my regular job to attend Prof. Mitra in the morning in his Apartment before going to Joka. After showing him the result of calculations that I have done, I returned to office around noon. As the main data was in a Disc supplied by RBI, our CAM centre personnel have to be involved to run the data by Main Frame Computer in our office. They charged excusably, so Prof. Mitra could not pay any honorarium to me. After this job, in 1991 he asked me to meet at Rainy Park for another job. I was engaged in analysing data on Primary Education, in connection with the Education Commission headed by Prof. Mitra. It was continued for about two years. My colleague, Mr. Poromesh Acharya was a member of this education Commission. While doing my job at Rainy Park, I heard that film maker Satayajit Ray passed away just now in Bell ViewClinic close to Rainy Park. The transport service was halted andI had to walk upto Exide More.

c) Prof. V N Reddy and R. Chattopadhayay

After Prof. Chandra's retirement in 1976, Prof. Reddy engaged me in his research activities. Since then, I was assisting Prof. Reddy in his project "Socio-Economic and Educational Survey" in four districts of West Bengal. I surveyed a dozen of villages in Hooghly district. In 1977, I was supervising the field survey of the Project "Status of Primary Education in West Bengal", sponsored by the UNICEF and the State Government. Prof. R Chattopadhayay was the team leader and I was entrusted for supervising the survey in seven districts in and around Calcutta. For this, I have temporary offices in Board (WBBPE) office, Women Studies Department at room shared by Prof. Jasodhara Bagchi and my residence. I have to go to Board office frequently to make liaison with the then Chairman Prof. Bhabesh Moitra. In 1999, the project was completed and I personally carried two sets of final Reports in two volumes weighing about ten kilos to submit those in Board office.

In 2000, Prof. Chattopadhayay asked me to collect ASI (Annual Survey of Industries) Data on Factory Sector in West Bengal and India for the period 1979 to 1997. This project was jointly with Prof. A B Bandopadhaya of MIT. As our library had no current volumes of ASI publications, I went to CSO office for about a month.The librarian was on leave and no desk assistants. So, I have to use wooden ladder to bring down the publications stacked up in racks. I completed the collection and analysis and submitted in 2001. In 2002, the MHRD sponsored a project on evaluation of literacy Program in some States of East and North-East Region in India. As data from Assam were available, I prepared two reports – "Financing of Universal Elementary Education in the State of Assam" and "Evaluation of District Primary Education Program in Assam". In continuance to the same project, I have analysed the literacy data on the state of Orissa. As, the data was available in Oriya language, I need the help of my colleague Jaganaath Patra, who hailed from Orissa. Finally, I wrote the report "Evaluation of Post-Literacy in Khurdah district of Orissa" in 2005.

d) A Group of Professors

In 2004, the Central Ministry of Food Processing Industry sponsored a project on the scope of food processing industry in India and West Bengal. The team leader was Prof. R Chattopadhayay along with S Chattopadhayay and U Sarkar. Prof, S Chattopadhayay provided me the data on Agriculture in different Eastern and North Eastern States. I have analysed the data and wrote the Report on "Agricultural Development in the States of East and North-East Region".He sent my write up directly to the Ministry. In this project, I have to visit those food processing units for physical verification of the use of the assistance. I wrote the report - "Modernisation of Indian Food Chain and The Status of Food Processing Industry in India".

e) **Profs. R Chattopadhayay and S Bhattacharya**

In 2002, a team of Professors R Chattopadhyay and S Bhattacharya undertook a MHRD sponsored project. The Project was evaluation of literacy Programme in some States of East and North-East Region in India. Data from Assam were analysed and prepared two reports – "Financing of Universal Elementary Education in the State of Assam" and "Evaluation of District Primary Education Programme in Assam". In continuance to the same project, I have analysed the literacy data on the state of Orissa. As, the data was available in Oriya language, I need the help of my colleague Jaganaath Patra, who hailed from Orissa. I wrote the report "Evaluation of Post-Literacy in Khurdah district of Orissa" in 2005.

Profs. Chattopadhayay and Bhattacharya undertook a MHRD sponsored project on evaluation of Post Literacy Program (PLP) in 2006. The Total Literacy Campaign was organized by the Central Government across all the States in India. The PLP started in 2005 for new literates to achieve functional literacy. The Institute was entrusted to evaluate the PLP in two North Eastern States – Assam and Arunachal Pradesh. The team selected one district from each state. The Cacher district of Assam and Kurung Kumey district of Arunachal Pradesh were selected for evaluation. The team studied whether a significant difference exists among new learners belonging to different gender, caste and religions. To evaluate the success of TLP in Cachar District, an evaluation test was conducted to judge the Reading, Writing and Mathematical skills. The performance of learning centres has also been judged. The evaluation of PLP was also conducted the same test in Kurung Kumey district. The Reports of both the districts were completed in 2007.

The Central Government initiated many programs to attain the goal of Universalisation of Elementary Education. The launching of Sarva Shiksha Abhiyan (SSA) in 2001 was a most significant step in achieving it. To bring about qualitative change in education under SSA, the Block Resource Centres (BRC) and Cluster Resource Centres (CRCs) were formed in each Block in every district. The BRCs and CRCs were established to improve the quality of education through regular in-service training for teachers. The academic support was provided to them through BRCs and CRCs. An important role of BRCs and CRCs was to visit schools and on the spot academic support and guidance to teachers. The MHRD entrusted our Institute to evaluate the 'Effectiveness of BRCs and CRCs in Elementary Schools' in Assam and Mizoram in 2007. The study was to assess the performance of BRCs and CRCs in those states. Prof. Chattopadhayay studied the Mizoram while Prof. Bhattacharya studied the Assam State. We completed made suggestions for more effective functioning of BRCs and CRCs and wrote the Reports for both the States.

Profs. R. Chattopadhayay and S. Bhattacharya undertook another Study on Elementary Education in Andaman and Nicobar Islands and West Bengal during 2008. The study was based on DISE (District Information System for Education) data, receiving from schools from time to time. Based on that, we delved into the status of elementary education in those states. Prof. Bhattacharya was engaged in studying the Status of Elementary Education in Andaman and Nicobar Islands, while Prof. Chattopadhayay was engaged in Studying the Status of Elementary Education in West Bengal. We explored the status of Primary, upper Primary and elementary education in both the States. The Primary education was imparted almost entirely by government schools in both the States. We have also assessed the impact of the recent initiatives like - distribution of School Development Grants to schools, TLM grants to teachers and the distribution of free textbooks, uniforms and scholarship to students. We completed the Reports on Elementary Education in both the States in 2008.

f) Profs. R Chattopadhayay and U Sarkar

Monitoring under the SSA program was envisaged at three levels - at the local community level, State level and the National level. At the local level, the Community based monitoring was done by Village Education Committees (VEC) in rural areas and Ward Education Committee (WEC) in urban areas. They were entrusted of ensuring that the schools are functioning effectively. The community-based monitoring will ensure the properly functioning of the system. For State level monitoring, the MHRD identified two Academic Institutions for each States – IIM Calcutta and Viswa Bharati for West Bengal. Our Institute was entrusted for monitoring and evaluation of SSA in ten districts of West Bengal under the supervision of Profs. R Chattopadhayay and U Sarkar. I was supposed to analyse data and writing the Report. We have to cover ten districts, but failed to complete it in Darjeeling district for political disturbances. Finally, we completed monitoring and evaluation of SSA in nine districts. The Viswa Bharati conducted the monitoring and evaluation of SSA in rest districts. We evaluated the impact of SSA in selected sample schools in nine districts. The Evaluation Reports for each district were submitted to MHRD.

During 2009-2010, Prof. R. Chattopadhayay was engaged in studying the Half-Yearly Monitoring Reports on SSA in four districts. The Reports were based on data submitted by concerned District Project Director, who provided data on the recent SSA activities in sample schools. After receiving the data, we analysed them and wrote the Report. We have discussed the Mid Day Meal (MDM) program in those sample schools. We found that 98% schools were serving hot cooked food and 2% schools were serving dry food or ration. The most common items were - rice, pulses, vegetables, soya beans and eggs, while a few schools served some fruits. The cooked hot meal in MDM Program started in 2003. During 2006-07, 92 Lakh children in 70 thousand schools participated in MDM in West Bengal. In this year, Rs. 299 Cr. of Central Assistance was utilized, of which, Rs. 223 Cr. for cooking costs, Rs. 59 Cr. for kitchen shed, Rs. 10 Cr. for kitchen devices, Rs. 6 Cr. for management etc. and Rs. 3 Cr. for transport subsidy. Moreover, the State also contributed Rs. 299 Cr. So, the total expenditure for MDM was Rs. 598 Cr. The cost of midday meal per child was rupees five.

g) Prof. Rahul Roy

In 2007, aproject was to "Study on the Central Sector Schemes on the Development and Strengthening of Infrastructural Facilities for Production and Distribution of Quality Seeds". Prof. Roy was the Project Coordinator along with others. I prepared the Questionnaire for the field survey on different stakeholders and agencies in seed industry. Those were producers, distributors and transporters of quality seeds and the state government departments dealing with different seeds. I sent the Questionnaires to them and after receiving the filled up questionnaire, I have assisted him by sending the questionnaire, and entered data that were sent by the stakeholder. But no honorarium was paid to me.

h) Prof. R Chattopadhayay in MIT Collaboration Project

In 2006, IIM Calcutta had housed two prestigious research projects in collaboration with MIT and Yale University. Profs. R. Chattopadhayay and A V Bandopadhayay of MIT were involved in these projects. The first project dealt with the impact of women's leadership in Panchayat and the second one was on good governance. Total project cost had been paid by MIT, Yale and UNICEF (The Economic Times, July 24, 2006). The first part of the first project had started with Prof. Esther Dufflo of MIT along with Prof. Chattopadhayay. They looked into the distribution of public goods in villages with women Pradhans in Birbhum district. The second was on Rajasthan police for good governance. In 2000, Prof. Chattopadhayay asked me to collect ASI (Annual Survey of Industries) Data on Factory Sector in West Bengal and India for the period 1979 to 1997. This project was jointly with Prof. A V Bandopadhaya of MIT. As our library had no current volumes of ASI publications, I had to go to CSO office for about a month. The librarian was on leave and no one on desk assistance. So, I used wooden ladder to bring down the publications stacked up in racks. I have completed the collection and analysis of ASI data that submitted in 2001.

i) Profs. Hrishikesh Bhattacharya and Mousumi Ghosh

The day I was shifting from the rented house to own house in Serampore, both of them visited myunder construction new home at Serampore in 1990. They went to me for data analysis job on Small Scale Industries in the State. The project was sponsored by the Government of West Bengal. I have to analyse the performance of small and medium Industrial units spread all the districts of the State. I have analysed the data delved the problems of those units by industry groups as well as by districts. In 2000, Prof. Bhattacharya engaged me in his Project on Financing Fishery Companies in South India. This project was sponsored by the Central Ministry of Commerce. I have analysed the financial data of about five hundred companies engaged in catching fish in south Indian Sea. The voluminous Report was published as a book from Oxford University Press in Calcutta. He has duly acknowledged me in this book.

2. THE INVIGILATION DUTY IN PGP AND PGPEX AND PGPEX-VLM EXAMINATIONS

In 1997, when Prof. Misra was Chairman of PGP, he asked the Mr. Ashoke Sengupta, AO (PGP) to call his team from his Rural Development Management (RDM) Center , adjacent to the examination halls. In addition to RDM staffs, Mr. Sengupta also requested us who were working in next room for invigilation. In the next years, Prof. Anup K Sinha became the Chairman of PGP and he called us in a meeting to co-operate with the Institute by providing invigilation duty. He issued a circular endorsed by the Director on this issue. In the roaster of invigilation duty, names of Research Assistant were included along with faculty members. Some faculty members became furious by seeing our names with them. The next roaster came in two sets - one for faculty members and other for Research Assistants. One faculty member, have not permitted one of us in examination hall as her name was not mentioned in his roaster. He became angry asked her to show her allotment in invigilation duty in this room. With the help of AO (PGP), the problem was solved. Initially, the circular of our invigilation duty by day, date, time and venue were issued by the Chairman PGP. But, later on, this circular was being issued by AO (PGP) instead of Chairman.PGP. Gradually, the circular was issued by Secretary of AO (PGP) lastly to others staffs. We have not paid a penny except a cup of Tea/Coffee in the examination hall. We objected, but Chairman PGP paid no hear. Alas, we became assistants to academic administration.

By PGP, we meant students of both PGDM and PGDCM. The PGP I mean students of first year and PGP II means that of second year. For PGP I, there were three terms (I, II and III), and for PGP II, the terms were IV, V and VI. Each term have two examinations - Mid-Term and End–Term. Generally examinations were held in a week and for a consecutive five days. In an academic year, the examinations hold for (3X2X2) 12 weeks i.e. 60 days.As, both the Mid-Terms of III and VI were held jointly. In a year, the total number of days for examinations was 55. In a total of 240 working days in a year, 55 days were spent on invigilation duty. So, one-fourth of the annual workings days were spent in invigilation duty. Moreover, in a day, the examinations were held in two shifts – Morning and Evening. Thus, we have to perform invigilation duty in total 120 shifts of two to three hours duration.

In the initial years, we have to perform three to four shifts in a week, but gradually it increased to ten. The examinations were not hold uniformly by months. In the Academic year 2004-05, as much as ten days were spent on August, nine days in March and eight days in December for invigilation duty while 5 days in other months. So, the months of August, December and March have more invigilation duty. While performing invigilation duty along with Professors, I have met some arrogant Professors. But, invigilation duty with Prof. Amitava Bose, the then Director, was pleasant, as I met mostly in examination hall L2.

Our invigilation duty was initiated only for PGP in 1997, but extended to PGPEX and PGPEX-VLM also since 2007. During examination week, we have to attend five to six slots of one to three hours and in different Halls spread over the Campus. Not only in L1 to L4, A101 to A105 in A Block, C1 and C2 in New Teaching Block, MCHV Hall and Conference room in Library Building, Seminar room and Computer Hall in CAM centre and also in Finance Lab at the top of State Bank Building. So, we have to travel from Finance Lab. in the west to MCHV on the east covering half a kilometre. In the rainy seasons, PGP does not arrange for transport. The PGP office allotted the nearest venues to female colleagues,while I was allotted far away examination centres. Initially, we have to perform three to four shifts in a week. Now we have invigilation duty of eight to nine shifts in a week. In 2009-10, I spent as much as 55 days out of 220 working days for invigilation duty. I spent 8 to 10 days in invigilation duty during the months of August, March and December.

In 2008, Prof. Sudip Chowdhuri, Chairman FPR called all the Research Assistants (RA), for a meeting with other Committee members. The academic council felt that the services of RAs are being grossly underutilized. So, the Committee will look after the matter and have to come up with a concrete proposal for better utilization of RAs. Alas, this initiative came in, when all RAs were on the verge of retirement!By this time, the number of RAs had been halved from 12 to 6. He called all existing RAs for future job allocation. But it failed for further jobs except more and more Invigilation in PGP I, PGP II, PGP-Ex, PGPEX-VLM examinations.

3. ACTIVITIES IN ADMINISTRATION

a) Assistance to EDP Chairman

In 1988, after completing the MCA Teachers Training, I started the use of Personal Computer. Prof. Reddy took me to MDP office in the ground floor in Administrative Building. Prof. Joe Ezikel, the Chairman of EDP, asked me to analyzing Feed Back study of all EDPs held last year. They discussed with me for the job. There was about 30 EDPs with average 40 participants. So, I have to analyse feedback of around 1200 participants.

b) Assistance to Prof. Srivastava for Ranking of our Institute

I have assisted Prof. B N Srivastava by "Assimilating Data on Research and Publication" of IIM Calcutta. It was done for Ranking of our Institute in Indian Business Schools in India for Outlook Magazine in 2000-2002.

c) Assistance to Chief Administrative Officer (CAO)

The then CAO of our Institute served a Notice Vide IIMC/PERS/036 in 2006 on all Research Assistants with some Job Allocation in Administration. To fulfil the Institute's Administrative requirements and giving adequate exposures, I was posted in Board Office and had to report the Secretary to Board (CAO) and Dean (P & A). I was allotted to the Board Office under the CAO and the Reporting Officer was Dean (P&A), Prof. Mohanty. I have compiled the important Agendas from Board meeting held during last three years. I was entrusted to write a Report on "Changes in IIMC Governance During 2004-2005".It was completed it in 2006 in my own PC at home, as the office failed to allot a PC to me. For printing the Report, I have used my own Papers.

The Office had not paid a single penny as my honorarium for this job. Not only that, neither the CAO nor the Dean (P&A) discussed with me on this matter. I have read the Agenda and Minutes of all the Board meetings held in last two years. I observed some noteworthy changes in the administration. Those were – Establishing our Institute as a World Class Institute, Reforming the PGP curriculum, Maximisation of Institute's Revenue, Implementation of CMP, RTA, Government Directives and e-Governance, Joint Ventures of BSNL & TTSL etc (Singha 2006). I have assimilated the relevant information and submitted my report to the CAO and Dean (P&A), but none of them discussed me about my report.

d) Academic Assistance to PGP Students

I have assisted Prof. Chandra in evaluation of answer sheets in PGP Examination for some years. I have tabulated their scores and submitted to PGP Office. Except the Invigilation duties, I have assisted one student, who has broken his leg in the bathroom and cannot move. So, I went to his room in Hostel along with a Question Paper and Answer Sheet. I have written the answers that he dictated me. Moreover, I have assisted a foreign female student in our STEP Program by explaining herin English, which she was weak.

4) Own Project Completed

I have completed a Project "Policy Level Constraints in Universalising Primary Education in West Bengal". The project was funded by CMDS (Centre for Management Studies) of IIM Calcutta in 1999. As Director of my Project, I submitted the Project Report to Prof. Anup K Sinha the then Chairman of FRP (Fellowship and Research Program).

5. ACTIVITIES OUTSIDE OFFICE

a. Research Assistance to Scholars

I purchased a Pentium-486 Desk Top Computer, assembled by PCL (Partech Computer Limited) in 1997. A lot of assignment poured in from the students of Calcutta University's department of Education. Those who are doing M Phil and PhD in education used to come to me for analyzing their data and statistical testing of hypothesis. I have assisted more than 100 students of education department of Calcutta University. Moreover, I have assisted one of our faculty members in her PhD, one of our Research Fellow in doing his PhD on Management of Student Unrests in academic institution. I have also assisted another Research Fellow in doing his PhD on Production and Area of Tea Cultivation in Darjeeling district. I also assisted on of our Research Assistant who done her PhD on Industrial Disputes in some organizations. I also assisted a Professor of Zoology in Kalyani University. His research was on difference of mean weights of different types of fish. I have fitted Gompertz Curve on the research trend on traditional Medicinal Plants in Biology at Calcutta University.Of late, I have assisted a researcher doing his PhD on Use of Drugs among Call Center employees in Sector – V of Salt Lake. I have assisted a researcher doing his PhD on Job Satisfaction of Professors in private Engineering Colleges in West Bengal.

b. Teaching Experiences

1) I have taught 'Use of Statistics in Social Science' to DPM (Diploma in Personnel Management) students at National Institute in Personnel Management (NIPM) for a Semester in 1993. The classes were held at NIPM Office at Apeejay House in Central Calcutta.

I1) I have taught 'Economics' to DPM (Diploma in Personnel Management) students at NIPM for a Semester of six months in 1994 The classes were held at NIPM Office at Apeejay House in Central Calcutta.

6. VISIT TO MANY LIBRARIES

During my entire service period, I have frequently visited more than a dozen of Central and State Libraries in Calcutta. Those were - Commercial Library, CSO (Central Statistical Organisation) Library and Census Library, while NSSO Library in CGO Complex at Salt Lake and the National Library at Alipore in South Calcutta. Moreover, I have visited State owned libraries at State Statistical Bureau, Writers' Buildings, State

Planning Board, and Education Departments at Bikash Bhavan. I have visited the National Library for several months for collection of data for Prof. Chandra. I have to sit in Annex Building and in Asbestos shaded single floor rooms near Bhabani Bhaban. Now all those materials mainly FOD (Foreign Official Documents) have been shifted to New Building near Hospital Road.

7. MY EMPLOYMENT STATUS

a) Finding a Permanent Job

When the CMDS was formed in 1976, I was offered second appointment by the then Director, Prof. Ayer. Then, I was placed in the consolidated pay scale of Rs. 400 – 30 – 700, without any allowances. I was placed with two increments at Rs. 460 per month. In 1980, the Business Standard Research Bureau (BSRB) of ABP group advertised for a post of Statistical Assistant. I have applied for the post and they send me a call letter for interview. As the letter reached via Bishnupur Post Office, it reached after a few days. I met Mr. Kuruvilla, who gave me some calculations. After an hour, he asked me to meet Mr. T K Mohanti, head of BSRB. I met him and discussed about my publications in '*Bhumalaxmi*'. But, I received no response from them. After a few months, my colleague Miss. Krishna Chatterjee joined there, but she left the job and was re-instated in the Institute after a Court Order.

In 1981, the State Government advertised for recruitment of 17 District Evaluation Officers in Panchayat Department. I appeared for the examination conducted by the State Public Service Commission. I was very much exited, as I have stood first in the written examination. A few days later, I appeared for an interview in front of the Government officials and showed them my paper "Panchayat and Management of 'Rural Economic Growth' that I presented a few days ago in our seminar. Within few days, I received the Appointment letter and sowed to Prof. Chandra. I was eager to leave the Institute for a permanent job. But, Prof. Chandra insisted me not to join, as our case is being considered for permanency. In 1982, the Board of Governors started considering us in regular pay scale.

b) Regularisation of Project Staffs

The process of regularization started in 1982. After an informal interview, the Project staffs were regularized as Research Assistant in 1987. Now, we were entitled for Dearness Allowances, House Rent and Medical facilities, etc. We became entitled to avail office transport service. The sufferings of public transport for last ten years have been reduced

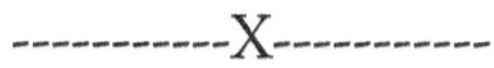

CHAPTER 3.3

ACADEMIC AND PROFESSIONAL ACHIEVEMENTS

ATTENDING DIFFERENT COURSES AND SEMINARS, WRITING OF WORKING PAPERS AND PUBLICATIONS

1. MY ACADEMIC ACTIVITIES CHRONOLOGICALLY

i) Three Years at EB Campus (1974-1977)

During my first appointment at Emerald Bower Campus, my job was to tabulate data on Household Survey for the Project ACPO (Agrarian Change and Peasants Organization) of Prof. Chandra. Three villages had already been surveyed, Prof. Chandra appointed me to analyse data of three villages in Burdwan district. I was at EB Campus for three years, of which I worked as Junior Project Assistant in the Pay Scale 400-30-700, for three months. After that, my appointment was not renewed, but worked on a daily payment @ Rs. 18 per day with no work no pay. After completion of Burdwan study, I was sent to Kheyadah village in Sonarpur block for surveying ten adjacent villages. During this time, I have completed one year Certificate Course on "Statistical Methods and Applications" from ISI.

ii) First Ten Years in Joka Campus (1976 – 1986)

In 1976, I was re-appointed as Junior Project assistant in the same scale and my basic wasfixed with two increments at Rs. 460 per month. During this time, I had surveyed the villages around Kheyadah. As most of the time,

I was visiting those villages with Atul babu and Asit babu. Sometimes, Prof. Chandra asked me toassist him in connection to his research papers in EPW. I have helped him a lot for printing of his first book "Retarded Economics" and helped him to prepare Index section of his book, for which, the EPW paid me some honourium.Despite above, I attended a 10 week full time course "Programming and Applications of Computers" from Indian Statistical Institute.

At that time,I have presented a Paper in the National Seminar organized by our Institute. My article – Panchayat and Management of Rural Economic Growth was chapterised in the book "Research Gaps in Management' edited by Prof. A K Chowdhuri, Prof. Binod Kumar, Prof M S Misra and Dr. K K Choudhuri and it was published by our Publications Division. Moreover,I have published 18 Articles in Bengali and 2 in English. Among these, nine were in Bhumilaxmi, a ABP group of publications, four in Dainik Basumati, five in Curtain and two in PTI Features published from Mumbai. My research interest was on rural poverty, indebtedness of rural poor, wage of agricultural labour etc, along with newly introduced Party based Panchayat Raj Institutionin West Bengal.

iii) Ten Years After Regularisation (1987 -1996)

All the existing Junior and Senior Project Assistants were promoted to the Permanent Cadre of Research Assistant posts with higher pay scale along with admissible allowances. During this time, I have assisted Prof. Chandra in connection with his research papers being published in EPW. In 1989, Professor Chandra accompanied me to Dr. Ashok Mitra for assisting him in some data analysis job for a RBI sponsored Project. Before office hour, I used to meet him in his residence in Alipore. Later in 1991, I have assisted Dr. Mitra in connection with the Education Commission on Primary Education in WB. The Education Commission was officiating at Rainy Park near Birla Technology Museum at Guru Saday Road. I worked here for about six months.

After completion of my MA in Economics in 1989, Prof. Chandra asked me to attend PGP classes in Economics with PGP Students. I have attended all classes in Economics and appeared at all Term examinations. I obtained highest marks in Development Economics, which war taught by Prof. Anup Sinha. My article "Liberalisation, Bio-Technology and Third World Agriculture" was published in our House Journal DECISION in 1995. Moreover, my two articles - "Winds of Change: Agriculture, Part I and "Market Limits Reforms Success: Agriculture, Part II" were published in the Business Standard, a daily of ABP Group. During this time, I published six Working Papers, of which two were jointly with Atul Manna. In this time, I have presented my paper "Globalisation and Its Impact on Indian Agriculture" in Indian Institution of Social Science in Calcutta. This seminar was inaugurated by Prof. Ashim Dasgupta, the then Finance Minister of West Bengal.

iv) After Retirement of Prof. Chandra (1997 - 2010)

As Prof. Chandra retired in 1996, I was attached to Prof. V N Reddy till his retirement in 2003. Officially, I started assisting Prof. Reddy in his research projects - Socio-Economic and Educational Survey, State Finance for primary Education, Assessment of Poverty and Elementary Education in West Bengal. Moreover, I helped him in the project "Rural Retail Price of Tea in India". I have also assisted both of Profs. Reddy and R Chattopadhyay in their projects. Those were "Status of Primary Education in West Bengal" sponsored by UNICEF.Other project was "The Study on Role of PRI and Local Bodies in Planning and Management of Primary Education in West Bengal" When Prof Reddy left, I was associated with Prof. R Chattopadhya, to whom I have assisted him in his projects – Cost and Financing of Elementary Education in Assam, Industrial Growth in West Bengal (Factory Sector), "The Status of Engineering and Technical Education in west Bengal" and Macro Mode Management of Agriculture".

After that, I have to assist a group of Professors - Profs. S. Chattopadhayay, U. Sarkar, S. Bhattacharya etc. Those projects were on "Prospects of Food Processing in Eastern States", Evaluation of Post Literacy Program in Orissa, Assam, Arunachal, Meghalaya, Andaman and Nicober Islands. For last five years, I have assisted Prof. Chattopadhayay in the MHRD sponsored project – "Evaluation of Sarva Shiksha Aviyan" in ten districts of West Bengal. The evaluation of SSA for rest of the districts was done by Viswa Bharati, Shantiniketan.During this time, I completed my own project "Determinants of Non-Enrolment at Primary Level". This study was financed by our CMDS and sanctioned by the then Chairman Prof. Anup K Sinha. I have read a part of the report in the "South Asian Conference on Education" organized by the Central Institute of Education at Delhi University in Delhi. Moreover, I read my paper on Common School System in the National Seminar organized by the NCERT in New Delhi. In this year too, I read my paper Anandapath (Joy in Learning) in the regional seminar of NCERT in Bhubaneswar, Orissa. Before that, I read my papers in the seminars organized by Agri-Horticulture Society, Calcutta Chapter and Jadavpur University.

I have published three articles in -The Economic Times, The Statesman and one in Bengali Daily Aajkaal. By this time, the Institute had published about a dozen of my Working Papers. Three were on Reforming the Engineering and Technical Education in Market Paradigm, School less Villages and Illiteracy, Primary education and Role of Panchayat Leaders, Floriculture Industry in India, Floriculture and Rural development through Tissue-Culture etc. Significant Events of Academic and Professional Journey has been presented in Exhibit 3.3.2.

2. ACADEMIC ACHIEVEMENTS

As my appointment was for two months only, I decided to continue my studies after leaving this job. The salary for 12 days in the month of November,1974 was Rs.216. Takeing the entire amount, I went to the Institute of Cost and Works Accounts and took admission there. They provided the Study Materials for the first Term. In December, I was selected at Indian Statistical Institute for "One Year Evening Course in Statistical Methods and Applications" with a course fee of Rs. 400.I have applied for that course before joining this Institute. I decided to jointhe ISI and left studying of Cost Accountancy. I took admission at ISI in the evening program where classes held from 6 p.m. to 8-30 p. m. I returned home at mid night and my father come to the station with a hurricane lamp. My friends asked me to stay in their Mess and I stayed in their Mess just opposite to ISI Campus. After returning from office, I started reading daily notes till 6 p.m. then walked to ISI for classes.

In December 1975, I appeared for the entrance examination of our PGP. I followed the book "Aptitude Test" authored by Professors Chaterjee and Chaterjee of ISI. The admission test was on paper and pencil based on a particular date all over India. My seat for the admission test was in a Cossipur Multi-Purpose High School, just opposite to our EB campus. A heavy booklet of more than 50 pages was the question paper with multiple choice type. I was puzzled by seeing the questions in English test, but I did fairly well in Mathematical and Quantitative Reasoning. Later, I received a regret letter, which I shown to Prof. Reddy. He replied that it could have a few Cinemas. The PGP Booklet cost of Rs. 100, one fourth of my monthly salary.

During this time, Director Prof. Aiyar insisted me for a Masters Degree. So, I met Prof. D K Sinha, VC of Jadavpur University to allow me in their evening course of M. Sc in Mathematics. As the course was solely for working school teachers, he cannot help. Then, I took admission in the Correspondence Course M. A. in Economics at the Rajasthan University. The University provided me the Study Materials, but within a month they asked me to appear at the examination at Jaipur. I could not go there and studying of MA at ended.In 1978, I appeared in an admission test for the Post Graduate Diploma in the Institute of Rural Management, Anand (IRMA) in Gujarat. The venue of the examination was in the Presidency College at Calcutta. I received no letter from the IRMA.

In 1978-1979, I appeared two times for the 'Statistician Diploma' examination in ISI. As I could not succeed, I requested our Prof. Ambuja Mohanti, but he could not find time, I approached Prof. Sujit Basu, who advised me to attend his PGP classes and have done so. By that time, my friend accompanied me to Prof. Rahul Mukherjee of Calcutta University at his Netaji Nagar residence. I was attending tuition after four hours journey from my village home. After two months, he joined ISI and could not continue my tuition. So, studying of Statistician Diploma ended. Later, Prof. Mukherjee joined our Institute as Professor.

In 1981, I joined a six week full time program 'Programming and Applications of Electronic Computers' at ISI. The Computer at that time was only Mini Frame Computer of IBM, but no Desk Top Computers. In this Computer, a user can put command not by pressing a key but through Punch Cards. I have learnt Punch Card operations and data processing along with Mathematical Analysis. I have attended classes of Prof. B P Adhikari and Prof. J Roy etc, the eminent Professor of ISI. I received the 'Certificate of Merit' after completing the course. During that time, I could not go to Joka, as the course was full time. I have taken permission from our Director and the course fee of Rs. 200 was disbursed by the Institute.

In 1987, I have attended the Central Government Sponsored ten weeks MDP held at our CAM centre. The course was organized by Prof. Ambuja Mohanti and was meant for the Professors who will teach MCA (Master of Computer Applications) in their Institutes. The participants were from the Technical and Engineering Institutes in different States including BE College, Sibpur. It was full time course from 10 a. m. to 5 p.m. and the classes were taken by our Professors as well as Professors from Jadavpur University and ISI. My colleagues - Baldeb Da and Krishna also joined this course. I have developed a railway reservation system with my partner, Prof Pal who teaches at B E College, Shibpur.

i) Statistical Methods and Applications

In 1975, just after joining the Institute, I was admitted in the course - 'Statistical Methods and Application" at ISI. In this program, I studied the Descriptive Statistics, Probability, Sample Survey, Design of Experiments, Statistical Quality Control, Time Series, Index Numbers, Inferences and Official Statistics etc. I have attended the classes of Prof. Hanurav, Kanan and Rao along with Nikhilesh Bhattacharya, Rabin Mukherjee, Deepak Condoo, Taresh Moitra, I S Roy and B P Adhikari. I was attending classes while working in E. B. Campus. This was an evening program from 6 p.m.to 8 p.m. and attended classes after office hour. Attending classes from my village became difficult; I started staying in a Mess.

ii) Programming and Applications of Electronic Computers

After six years, I attended a Program - "Programming and Applications of Electronic Computers". It was 10 weeks duration full-time program at 10 a.m. to 5 p. m. at ISI. The course fee was Rs. 200 was reimbursed from my office by the then Director, Prof. Ayer, who kind heartedly sanctioned my leave of absence. By this time, our office has been shifted to Joka Campus. Here, I studied Numerical Analysis, Computing Equipments and FORTRAN language. In Numerical Analysis, I studied Interpolation and Extrapolation. Among the Computing equipments, I used Punch Card Operation, Verifier and Sorting of data through Punch Cards. I wrote the Program in FORTRAN language and was run by a large size Electronics Computer of IBM make spread over the ground floor of ISI. Profs. J Roy, B P Adhikari, Raha etc taught us.The teachers organizes a tour to Regional Computer Centre at Jadavpur University Campus, to show how a Computer was drawing a Circle. They also organized an excursion tour to Badu Snake Park, 10 kilometres east of ISI Campus. We found several types of Snakes were being reared for supplying of Venom to Hospitals. We saw a Tiger Cub, on which one Prof. Brahmachari of I.S.I. was conducting experiments of Cancer Drugs.

iii) MCA Teachers' Training

In 1986, I was offered a 10 weeks"MCA Teachers Training Program" at our CAM Centre. It was Central Government program, organized by Prof. Ambuj Mohanti for faculty members of Engineering Colleges and Polytechnic across India. There was no tuition fee but Daily Allowances, Travelling costs etc. were paid to out-station candidates. I, Baladev Da and Krishna were internal candidates. I learnt Data Structure, Pascal language, Operating Systems, UNIX, System Analysis and Design, and Managerial Decision Making. Besides these, Prof. Binod Kumar taught us Inter Personnel Relationship and Conflict Management.Prof. Mohanti and Prof Ashim Pal took major classes, but faculty members from Jadavpur University and ISI took other classes. I along with Prof. Pal of B E College developed a Railway Reservation System. For the first time, I used Desk Top Computer (known as PC- Personal Computer). After completion of this Program, Prof. Chandra asked whether I have learnt Word Processing. I replied yes and he gave me a sheet of handwritten paper and asked me to type in Word Processing. (not MS Word). He asked me do this in a corner side Computer, so that no students look into. After, typing this, he insisted me to delete the file as it was a PGP Question Paper meant for next morning Exam.

iv) M A in Economies

To complete my Masters Degree, I have to pass B A (Special Honours) in Economics and completed M A in Economics from Rabindra Bharati University in 1989. I joined the Institute with a mere B Sc Pass with Distinction and completed M A. after 28 years of Graduation. Academic achievementsafter joining the Institute are in Exhibit 3.3.2. To attend the classes at EB campus, I started at 4 p.m. from Joka then to reach Dharmatala by private bus that took one hour. After getting down at Sahid Miner, I have to board North Bound bus. That time, the Central Avenue became congested as Metro Rail Project stared just. So, after spending more than hour in full loaded bus, I reached EB campus around 6 p.m. for my M. A. classes. After the classes finished, I have to board Serampore bund Bus No 3 to reach Serammpore. I reached around 9-30 and have to get down in eastside of the rail, as the construction of Railway Overbridge in Serampore was going on. I reached home around 10 p.m. After three years of extensive journey via Serampore to Joka, Joka to Sinthee again Sinthee, I reached at Serampore home. So, I had to spend 14 hours a day for Master Degree.

3. PROFESSIONAL ACHIEVEMENTS IN RESEARCH

I) Working Papers

i) Initial Stage

A total of 17 Working Papers have been published by our institute during 1990 to 2004. The first two Working Papers were with my colleague Mr.

A. C Manna.The first one was "On the Realm of Prosperity" in 1990 and the second was "An Essay on Social Justice" in 1993. These papers delve with the development of Indian economy as well as development of the society. The first one was on the problem of "Butter or Gun? The Central Government was increasing Defence expenditure by reducing budget on food production. The second one was on social justice in the light of Mandal Commission Report. By analyzing our village survey data, we found that implementation of the Mandal Committee's Report was most urgent need in reducing the social inequality. Later, the paper on social justice was published in a political mouthpiece in Hindi language.

a) Working Papers on Agricultural Reforms

Later, I individually published Working Papers on various issues relating to Economic Reforms. The impact of New Economic Policy in Indian Agriculture was discussed in the Working Paper "Agricultural Reforms in the New Economic Policy" in 1993. Next year, I published "Structural Deterioration in Indian Agriculture", and "Impact of Globalisation in Indian Agriculture" in 1995.I have discussed the impact of Biotechnology in Indian agriculture in the Paper - "Liberalisation, Biotechnology and Third World Agriculture" in 1995. Consequently, this paper has been published in our House Journal DECISION in 1995.

In the Reforms of Agriculturesector, use of Biotechnology, Greenhouse Technology, Tissue Culture and Corporate Farming etc have been discussed. My research interest grow was on the Floricultural Industry, a highly Biotechnology based cultivation with modern technique of drip irrigation and Greenhouses. This was a sunrise industry having potential in earning more foreign exchanges by exporting floricultural products. The floriculture industry flourished in South India and many Corporate Sector companies have invested there. My working paper "Export Oriented Floriculture in India" was published by our Institute in 1997. In the same year, "Floriculture and Rural Development" was published and presented in a seminar organized at the Jadavpur University. As the Floriculture industry did not flourish in the Eastern India, I have suggested the production of different ornamental plants in Nursery for creating rural employment, especially for women. The biotechnology based Tissue Cultural plants are very small and need great care that can be easily done by women.

b) Agriculture to Primary Education

In 1998, the NCERT called for papers relating to Common School System. My paper, "Economic Reforms and Education Through Common School System" was accepted for presentation. For this, the NCERT provided the train fare for to and fro journey by Rajdhani Express and free accommodation in their hostel. Later, it was chapterised in the book - "Common School System: Retrospect and Prospect" - Edited by Prof. Sharma A A and Arora G L. and Published by NCERT, New Delhi, 2000.Next year, the NCERT was arranging another seminar on Community Participation in Management of Primary Education. Because of shortage of time, I could not attend the seminar. I have studied the role of local stake holders like - Primary Teacher, Guardians as well as Gram Panchayat Members in the management of primary schools. The Working Paper "Management of Primary Schools by Community Participation" was published in 1998. Till date, I was interested in Indian Agricultural reforms, but had to shift towards the problems of Primary Education in West Bengal. By this time, Prof. Chandra retired and I became associated with Prof. Reddy.

A group of seven Professors jointly undertook a survey on the "Status of Primary Education in West Bengal". As I was associated earlier with the Education Commission under the Chairmanship of Dr. Ashok Mitra, they insisted me to be a part of them. I was conducting the Survey on Primary education in Calcutta and adjoining districts of Howrah, Hooghly, and North 24 Parganas. We have completely enumerated the households and the Primary Schools in the selected sample villages in rural areas and Urban Sample Frames in urban areas. I had engaged about firry investigators and officiating in Primary Education Board at Sarat Bose Road, Women Study Centre at Jadavpur University and at my residence.

In 1999, the West Bengal Primary Board was thinking about different measures through a program called ANADAPATH (Joy in Learning) to attract small kids in primary education. I was interested to evaluate the success of the program. So, I have investigated how the schools were implementing those schemes in some schools in Haripal Block of Hooghly. My working paper "ANANDAPATH in West Bengal: A Resume" was published by our Institute in 1999. This paper has been presented to the "Regional Seminar on Researches in School Effectiveness at Primary Stage" held at the Regional Institute of Education in NCERT at Bhubaneswar. They provided me second class AC train fare by Jagannath Express and free boarding and lodging in their hostel.

In 1998 I have taken a Project which was financed by our CMDS. Prof. A K Sinha was the then Chairman of CMDS sanctioned the Project.So, I was the Director of the Project and completed it in due time and submitted the Report to CMDS. The Report was in the form of two Working Papers - "Policy Level Constraints in Universalisation of Primary Education in West Bengal" and "Determinants of Non-Enrolment: Myths and Realities at Primary Education in West Bengal".

That time, the Central Institute of Education in the University of Delhi called for papers in their "South Asian Conference in Education at the Central Institute of Education".I submitted the just completed Report as two Working Papers. One Paper - "Policy Level Constraints in Universalising Primary Education in West Bengal" was presented in this South Asian Conference on Education. Within a few days, Prof. Anil Sadgopal rang me in my residence and sent the Acceptance letter to our City Office in Central Calcutta. The organizer provided me to and fro Air Fare from Calcutta to Delhi and provided my accommodation in Ashoka Hotel. In the seminar hall, I met Prof. Anil Sadgopal, the Convener of the seminar along with a dozen of Nobel Prize winners including Dalai Lama and Amartya Sen. I also meet Andre Bettie, J B G Tilak, Tapas Majumdar, Manabi Majumdar and many educationists. This was an International Seminars with participants from Sri Lanka, Maldives, Nepal, Bangladesh, Bhutan, Pakistan etc.

In 2000, Prof. Reddy observed that primary education was neglected in villages having low female literacy. In this paper, I have calculated various indices of literacy. He collected list of villages by female literacy from NSSO Office for All States including West Bengal. In order to highlight the axiom, I have undertaken a survey in all villages of Dhaniakhali Block in Hooghly. I have identified villages with low female literacy and observed that the low literacy was due to non-existence of primary schools in those villages.

c) Primary Education to Engineering & Technical Education

In 2002, the Government of West Bengal initiated computing of Human Development Index for all districts. Prof. R. Chattopadhayay was entrusted for studying the status of Engineering and Technical Education in West Bengal.I have investigated the Institutes which were offering those educations in five districts. I surveyed the Engineering Colleges, Polytechnics and Technical Schools run by both Public and Private sector. I had to go to Bikash Bhaban and met Directors of Technical Educations. After surveying those Institutes, I published three Working Papers during 2002 to 2004. Those were "Genesis and Growth of Engineering and Technical Education in West Bengal: Colonial Period to Market Paradigm" and "Reforming the Engineering and Technical Education Market Paradigm" and lastly the "Engineering and Technical Education in Market Paradigm". It is to be noted that the last Working Paper was in the form of a Booklet printed from the Press, while earlier Working Papers were in A4 size bound volume of Xerox Copies.

4. PAPERS PRESENTED IN THE SEMINARS

I have presented eight Papers in Seminars organized by different Institutions. Among those, two in Delhi and New Delhi, one in Bhubaneswar and rest five in Calcutta. The first one was is in our Institute, second one in Indian Museum, third was in Indian Institute of Social Science at Calcutta, fourth was in Agri-Horticulture Society of India (Calcutta Chapter) and last one in Jadavpur University. My research interest was impact of New

Economic Reforms introduced in India since 1991. These papers on Agricultural Reforms, Structural Deterioration in Indian Agriculture, Impact of Globalisation in Indian Agriculture, introduction of Bio-Technology etc. When, I started supervision of the UNICEF sponsored project – "Status of Primary Education in West Bengal", my research interest shifted to the problems of Primary Education in West Bengal. My Paper, "*ANANDAPATH*"in West Bengal was presented in the Regional seminar at NCERT, Bhubaneswar. The "Common School System: Elitist Education for Privileged Class?" was presented in NCERT in New Delhi.

i) My First Seminar in the Campus

In 1977-1978, the Left front came to power in West Bengal. On the basis of our village survey data, I have collected socio - economic profile of the elected Panchayat Members in just completed party based Panchayat election in the State. I completed a write up on the class character of the newly elected Panchayat members in different villages in different districts. To collect the names of elected members, I went to Government Press at Alipore to purchase the Gazettes, which mentioned the names of newly elected Panchayat Members in all the districts of West Bengal. On the basis of our field survey data, I found that the Panchayat representatives were mostly from poor and middle class, who may serve the Panchayat well. In 1980, our Institute was going to organize a National Seminar on Research Gaps in Management. The Chairman of the Seminar was Prof. Arun K Choudhuri who asked me to explain the relevance of my paper in the seminar. Dr. K K Choudhuri, a Research Fellow, the Secretary of the seminar also helped me to explain. My paper was selected for the seminar. In the first seminar in our Institute, I was a young rural boy of 30 and studied in Bengali Medium village Schools. I was afraid to talk in presence of the audience gathered from many Cities like Bombay, Pune etc. Prof. Kaman Adhikari helped me a lot to answer their quarries and questions about the subjects. This article was chapterised in the Seminar proceeding - "Research Gaps in Management" Edited by Prof. A K Choudhuri et el, and was published by our Publication Department.

As my employment was on contractual basis, I appeared in a Public Service Commission (PSC) examination for the Post of District Evaluation Officer. In the written examination, I stood first as the questions were mostly on rural survey, which I am doing for last seven years. I was called for an interview at Bhabani Bhavan and I was present with this Paper presented in our Institute seminar. The members in Interview Board were puzzled by seeing my paper and asked me to join as early as possible. Firstly, my appointment letter reached to me and I saw that to Prof. Chandra. He has no interest to release me. As I have not accepted this offer, the PSC dispatch another Appointment Letter to Prof. Chandra in his office and also to my father in our village home. Finally, I did not join ther with a hope of my permanency in this Institute. That process started in 1982 and finalized in 1987.

By this time, the Comprehensive Area Development Corporation, a Govt. of West Bengal Undertaking called for Papers on Rural Development. The CADC was headed by Mr. Kalyan Dasgupta and some of my colleagues have already joined in Binchee Centre in Hooghly and Ajodhya Centre in Purulia districts. My paper 'Management of Rural Credit Towards the Upliftment of Rural Poor' was selected for the seminar. They informed that my paper was displayed in the seminar hall of Indian Museum.

ii) Seminars Outside Joka Campus

After a gap of 15 years in 1995, I presented my paper "Globalisation and Its Impact on Indian Agriculture" in Indian Institute of Social Science, Calcutta. This seminar was inaugurated by Prof. Ashim Dasgupta, the then Finance Minister of West Bengal. In this paper, I have delve into the impact of Dunkell Draft in Uruguay Round of New Economic Policy. Use of Bio-technology based hybrid seeds, use of Green House technology and Corporate Farming were the main issues. Along with this paper, I have presented two more papers on New Economic Policy (LPG), liberalisation, Privatisation and Globalisation. In 1997, I read my paper "Biotechnology in Indian Agriculture" in the Seminar organized by Agri-Horticultural Society of India, Calcutta Chapter. Here I meet, different companies dealing with

Floricultural materials, Suppliers of Green House Technology and Tissue-Culture companies in and around Calcutta. I have seen cabbage size Roses, large size Gerberas produced in Green Houses. In this seminar, I meet a few Professors of Jadavpur University, who formed an NGO, ELABS (Eastern India Agriculture and Biotechnology Society) in Baharu village at Joynagar Block of South 24 Parganas district. I presented my paper "Floriculture and Rural Development" in their seminar held at Jadavpur University and Institute of Chemical Engineering opposite to the University Campus.

iii) Seminars Outside Calcutta

Till date, all the seminars were held in Calcutta . Next year in 1998, I presented my Paper, "The Common School System: Elitist Education for Privileged Class?" in the Seminar organized by the NCERT in New Delhi The NCERT provided me to and fro journey by Rajdhani Express, which I was seen from childhood passing though my village in the evening and returned in next morning to Howrah. I boarded the train and reached first time in Delhi. I took a reserved Auto-Rickshaw to reach NCERT, but the driver took me to IIT Delhi, where from a journey of ten minute, I reached NCERT. I was looking for Prof. Arora and reached his cabin and accompanied a person to reach Student Hostel, for my boarding, close to Qutub Minar, whose picture I saw in school text book. I was only representative, while another one from SCERT reached next morning for second day.

In 1999, the West Bengal Primary Board was thinking about different measures through a program called *ANADAPATH* to attract small kids in primary education. They have introduced certain measures like painting of class rooms, drawing there on by students, supplying of learning materials etc. I was interested to evaluate the success of the Program. So, I investigated how the schools were implementing those schemes in some schools in two Panchayats of Haripal Block in Hooghly district. This paper has been presented to the "Regional Seminar on Researches in School Effectiveness at Primary Stage" This was held inthe Regional Institute of Education in NCERT Bhubaneswar. They provided me second class AC train fare of

Jagannath Express and accommodation to their hostel.A Headmistress of a Primary school in Bolpur Block in Birbhum district discussed her experience in a Tribal village where dropout is a common problem.

In this year, I have presented two papers on Primary Education in the seminar "South Asian Conference in Education at the Central Institute of Educationin the University of Delhi at Delhi. The organizer provided me the Air Fare for to and fro journey and provided accommodation in infamous Ashoka Hotel. That time, I have completed my Project financed by the CMDS and I was the Project Director. I have met Prof. Anil Sadgopal, the Convener of the seminar along with a dozen of Nobel Prize winners including Dalai Lama and Amartya Sen etc. I meet Andre Bettie, J B G Tilak, Tapas Majumdar, Manabi Majumdar and many eminent educationists. This was my last seminar and feels proud to be by participating in an International Seminars with participants from Sri Lanka, Maldives, Nepal, Bangladesh, Bhutan, Pakistan etc.

6. CHAPTERISATION IN BOOKS

In the National Seminar on Research Gaps in Management was organized by our Institute in 1980, In this seminar, I presented my paper "Panchayat and Management of Rural Economic Growth". Later it was Chapterised in the Seminar proceeding - "Research Gaps in Management" Edited by Prof. A K Choudhuri. Prof. Binod Kumar, Prof. M S Mishra and Dr K K Choudhuri and was published by our Publication Department. In 2000, the article "The Common School System: Elitist Education for Privileged Class?' was presented the Seminar organized by the NCERT, New Delhi. It was Chapterised in the book - "Common School System: Retrospect and Prospect" Edited by Prof. Sharma A and Arora G L. and Published by NCERT, New Delhi, 2000. Moreover, my article "Globalisation, Biotechnology and Third World Agriculture" was published in our House Journal DECISION, Volume 22 and No. 4 in October-December 1995

7. ACHIEVEMENTS IN PUBLICATIONS

i) Publications in English Newspapers

I have published seven articles in different English dailies. Two each in the *Business Standard, the Economic Times and* 'PTI Feature', while only one in *The Statesman.* All were from Calcutta while 'PTI Feature' was from Mumbai. I published two Features in 'PTI Feature', published by Press Trust of India. Those were the "Importance of Invalid Votes: Analysis of West Bengal Election" in 1982 and the "Role of Panchayat Members in Rural Development" in 1983.I have written some features in the *Business Standard,* a daily Newspaperof ABP group. The articles "Winds of Change: Agriculture, Part I" was published on August 26, 1993 and "Market Limits Reforms Success: Agriculture Part II"was published on August 27, 1993 in the *Business Standard.* These articles were based on my Working Paper "Agricultural Reforms in the New Economic Policy".

When my research interest shifted from Agriculture because of my highly involvement in the Survey of Primary Education in connection to the UNICEF sponsored project the "Status of Primary Education in West Bengal". In connection to the problems of Primary Education in the State, I published the article "A Fools Paradigm: Bengal's Primary Education" in the *Economic Times* in 1997. In the same years, when I was studying the problems of Child Labour in different districts of West Bengal, I published "End of Innocence: The State of Child Labour in West Bengal" in the *Economic Times* in 1998. The *Economic Times,* a English daily published from Calcutta. In 1998, another feature the "Primary Education: Role of Panchayat Leaders" in *The Statesman,* a daily newspaper published from Calcutta. This was an abridged version of my Working Paper "Management of Primary Schools by Community Participation" published in 1998.

ii) Publications in Bengali Newspapers

During 1977 to 1983, I published nineteen Features written in Bengali script. Among these, nine were in *Bhumilaxmi,* a bi-weekly of ABP group, five in *Dainik Basumati* a Bengali daily and one in the *Ajakal,* a Bengali daily. All the dailies were published from Calcutta. The rest four articles were published in *Curtain,* a fortnightly magazine published from Hooghly. During 1977 to 1980, I wrote nine articles in the *Bhumilaxmi.*I have discussed the topics –*Gramer Hatasha O Andhakar Dik* (Economic miseries in rural life), Khet Majoor O Nunyatama Majoori (Agricultural labourers and their minimum wages*), Krishite Kit Nashak Oushadh* (Pesticides in agriculture), Paschim Banglar Graam (Small and large villages by population), *Grraame Daridra Bereche* (Increasing Trend of poverty in the villages of West Bengal.In The CURTAIN, a Fortnightly Political Magazine from Hooghly, I have written a lengthy article, which has been published in four parts in 1981 on 'Peasantry of West Bengal' *(Banglar Krishak*). I delved into the problems in land distribution, Domestic animals like Cow, Buffalos, Goats etc. and rural transports like – Boat, Hand pulled Cycle Vans, Bullock Cart etc.for transportation of agricultural produces. In the *Dainik Basumati* (1982-1983), I have written the topics on *Phasaler Daam (*Prices of Crops), *Gramer 50 shatansgh Loker Aay Mote Aiyer 14 Shatnagsh* (Fifty percent household earn14% of total income), *Gramer Loker Sangshar Kharach* (Consumer expenditure of rural household),*Gramer Loker Reen o Sanchay (*Indebtedness and Savings of rural households). In 2001, after returning from the South Asian Conference on Education in Delhi, I wrote "Biswayan O Prathamik Shiksha" (Globalisation and Its Impact on Primary Education) in the Bengali in the *Aajakaal*, a Bengali daily published from Calcutta.

CHAPTER 3.4

PROFESSOR NIRMAL CHANDRA'S RESEARCH AND ME

1. INTRODUCTION

He was a renowned economist and socialist thinker who encouraged many individuals to undertake the path of research in the field of economics. He offered a very distinct insight towards economics to his pupils. He was a great inspiration to those who received his able guidance. He joined the Institute in 1966 as an Assistant Professor and was one of the early recruit professors of the institute. He played a pivotal role in shaping not just the Economics Group, but also the perception of management education as a whole.He emphasized on the need for management education to be implemented towards development of the society and not just remain confined to the corporate world. The diverse and heterogeneous group at initial stage of the Institute would shape the values and objectives of India's first management school.To them, "management" was not to be confined to the narrow realm of corporate or business life, but encompassed the entire challenge of managing development and modernisation of a post-colonial economy and the society.

2. HIS EDUCATION IN UK AND EASTERN EUROPE

Descended from a rich North Calcutta family with land and property, he described his background as "semi-feudal" and comprador. He was immersed in what in his view was an adventure in intellectual pursuits. He wanted to tear himself away from his family moorings. He was born with an innate sense of rationality, which could instinctively ferret out the superior from the inferior – and distinguish the exploited and under–privileged from those who terrorized and tormented them.He had stints at Universities in London, Warsaw and Paris. With an easy flair for picking up languages, he read essential classics in the original at all the three seats of academia, listened to discourses and participated in substantive polemics with felicity and comfort.It took him hardly a couple of years in England before he joined the Communist Party of Great Britain as a card–carrying member. His ideological convictions did not interfere in any manner with his steady, but most remarkable, maturing into a full–fledged, well-honed, technically impeccable economist. His exposure to different schools of thought at London, Paris and Warsaw certainly helped, but what explains his emergence as one of the founder of the Indian economists and his intuitive ability to separate the rational from the irrational. He had plenty of private means, he hated newspaper and TV eminences and therefore he had no need to join the vulgar rat race.

He left for the UK immediately after his graduation from Presidency College in 1955. Although, he came from a wealthy family, he financed most of his research trips in Poland, Russia, France and London by earning money as research scholar, lecturer or translator. Upon completing his undergraduate studies in economics at Kolkata, he undertook graduate and doctoral studies at the London School of Economics.Such studies and researches took him a decade in Europe.Mainly in England, France and Poland – he even joined the CPGB and the PCF (PartiCommunisteFrancais) – before his head back home to Kolkata and joined our Institute.He followed an extraordinary routine by shutting himself up in his residence and cut himoff from the world.He lived with the theme, concentrate on the analysis, collate the data, and alter the draft of a paragraph a number of times if it had yet to attain perfection and put down his conclusions with care and deliberation, sometimes taking a full day to compose it when it would fully satisfy him. And once the completed the text and mailed to the EPW.

Prof. Chandra was referred to by his dear friend, Ashok Mitra as "The Complet Economist" and "An Economists' Economist". In AM's words, he was one of India's "very best economists". It must have detested the works he produced was alongside one of this country's leading radical economists. The scholarly paths he charted were concerned with Political–Economic aspects of post-revolutionary societies, the Soviet Union and China, in particular; agriculture and the peasant question; and retarded economies, andthose with "organic and structural impediments"to their "normal growth" as a result of "the link between foreign domination and the balance of class forces inside the country.

a) His Researches Topics

In 1986, Prof. Chandra wrote on "Export-Oriented Growth" and "North and South Hemisphere" of the globe. In 1990, he was engaged in "Cost of German Unity". In 1984, he was working on "Peasantry as a Single Class: A Critique of Chayancy. This article was published in EPW and adapted in Ashok Mitra edited book "The Truth Unites" in 1985. In 1986, he studied a "Notes on Bukharin, Peasants and Soviet Industrialisation" and "Bukharin's Alternative to Industrialisation 'Without Forced Collectivisation'. In 1991, he studied the problems of foreign investment in India in - "Planning and Foreign Investment in Indian Manufacturing". In 1992, he wrote on the collapse of Soviet Unionin the article - "Was the Collapse of the CPSU Inevitable?:A Political Essay". In 1993, his studied the Russia's Sinking Economy: External Dimensions and India's Rubble Debt and the Depreciating Rubble. He wrote "China's Tryst with Globalisation". His article "The Political Economy of Consumer Subsidies" in view of World Bank and IMF prescribed New Economic Policy in India. He also wrote "Trade, Technology andDevelopment".

b) Monopoly Capital

In the paper "Monopoly Capital, Private Corporate Sector and the Indian Economy, 1931-76", he found, that "monopoly capital in India is a very different species from its counterpart in the West". The monopoly capital in India bears a closer family resemblance to pre-industrial monopolies than to contemporary monopoly capitalism in the West. In the early 1990s,when the debate over the Dunkel Draft of GATT's Uruguay Round was at its peak. Prof. Chandrawas really outstanding, for the focussed quite a bit on the implications as regards the likely negative impact on indigenous technological development, discussing the C-DOT and C-DAC cases, and the development of Indigenous technological capability in the Pharmaceutical industry post the 1970 Indian patents Act, and the likely impact the Uruguay Round of the GATT might have on these technological successes.

In 1977-78, he worked on Monopoly Capital and Private Corporate Sector in India. At that time, India's top 20 business groups by assets were – Tata, Birla, Martin Burn, SahuJain, Bird Heielgers etc. Each of these groups had 100 to 400 companies. I have to calculate assets of these companies for different years, to assess the changes in their assets over the years. I have followed the Report of the Hazari Committee (1951-1967) and Dutt Committee (1969) appointed by parliament. In this article he delved how our Corporate Sector was getting richer by avoiding Monopoly Trade Practice Acts. He also found that Multinational Companies[1]were exploiting us. As an example, a tooth paste Company invested only Rs. 7 crores in India but has remitted Rs. 700 cores to its country of origin in last few years. This MNC has killed numerous indigenous dental care producers in India.

I helped him in all the Papers published in EPW. I assisted him in preparing Index pages of his first book - Stagnation in Indian Economy, published by Oxford University Press.One day in the afternoon, he told me to stay in his room after office hour. He was editing a paper and asked me to recalculate the calculations that I have done for last few months. As the paper is going to Press, I have to check errors and omissions if any. It was around 8-30 PM, he completed the task and took his old car. In Behala Chowrasta, the car broke down. He started the car for three four times but it did not move. I suggested him for a new car? The Car was gifted by his father after passing MetricExamination at Rs. 10 thousands. He lighted a Cigarette smoked slowly and the Car started at last, He replied that the car knows that I have not smoked for a long time? Then at around 9 P.M, we reached the GPO and he ran inside to post by last mail to Bombay. After that, I reached

Howrah station and home at mid-night. Within a few days he handed over an Offprint of that paper published in EPW in that week[2].First I saw my name printed in this article as acknowledged by him.

c) Economic Development of India, USSR and China

During the next 40 years he published more than 120 articles and two books.His attention was focused on three broad themes: (i) the problems and contradictions of building socialism in USSR and China; and the relationship of both USSR (and later globalising China) to developing countries like India, (ii) the question of an agrarian transition in India, and (iii) market reforms in China.The first and third themes were discussed by Bagchi. According to him, Prof. Chandra's the critical scrutiny of the Marxist corpus of class analysis of agriculture from the early writings, the strategy of collectivisation under Stalin.Some of this analysis also carried over to his work on agrarian relations in Burdwan district. The largest number of his papers was published in the pages of EPW. Those articles published there up, he considered worth preserving were put together in his book "The Retarded Economies; Foreign Commination and Class Relations in India and other Emerging Nations".

Arguments and discussions for him did not just happen in seminars or other academic events; they happened above all in an adda where even research agendas, what needed to be "looked into" were decided. Having made the decision that he mustlook into" something, He would retreat into his study for days on end, emerging from it with a paper that was as detailed and erudite as it was definitive. He did not write much in terms of the number of publications. But almost every paper he wrote was a very substantial contribution, the last word on the subject until that time. They were meticulously researched, extraordinarily erudite, very careful in assessing the statistics they used, and of course articulated a clear position. His paper "Western imperialism and India Today" was a milestone.

His calculations about the control exercised by foreign capital over the Indian economy were path-breaking and generated a large literature. Whatever he wrote became a standard reference, as is evident from the set of papers of his on the long term growth of the Indian economy brought together in a volume published by the Sameeksha Trust. It is a volume of extraordinary richness and eminently worth possessing. But he was by no means a prolific writer.Had he been so, the quality of his work would not have been of the same order.He not only took great pains over what he wrote, but also devoted much time to discussing and commenting on the work of his students, friends and associates. His time was generously available to all.He spent long hours reading and thinking, chasing up obscure references and visiting libraries to look up specific things.

He was also a remarkable proficient linguist, a rare trait among Bengali intellectuals.He not only knew several languages, notably English, French, Polish, and Russian, apart from his native Bengali, but had actually a facility with languages.I certainly found his insistence that burgeoning subsidies were the cause of the economic crisis of the East European socialist countries somewhat unconvincing. But he was somebody one could always turn to for intellectual guidance, for discussions, for testing one's ideas.He was literally a *dada* to so many of us as we shall sorely miss him.

He joined the Institute and in a way, continued to work out of there to the very end. The Institute "took in bright young men and women and trained them in the obscene art of making money, but even these managers-in – the – making, admired the great teacher in Prof. Chandra. He began the first-year, third-semester course on the Indian economy by tracing the roots of underdevelopment, moving from the orthodox view to the radical. For him, the breakaway from imperialism and the doing away with semi-feudalism were the preconditions of development. Data and the handling of data were particularly given their due. He goes on: "The difficulty, at bottom, steams from the fact… that the peasant possesses "two souls', one of the proprietor, and the other of a worker."In the Indian context was the combination of the proprietor and the worker – the peasant – is imbued with caste consciousness, which drives him to strive to give up the use of family labour in tilling the soil and in other manual tasks.How they will the Indian peasant, even the poor and middle one, develop solidarity with the landless labourer, who, is most probably a dalit? In the Indian case, the institution of caste impedes class solidarity and class consciousness, and as far as the rich peasant goes, it induces him to behave like the landlord does.

A heterodox economist and socialist thinker, he was first and foremost a legendary teacher who inspired his students to take the "road less well travelled". He also belonged to a generation of heterodox scholars who encouraged students and researchers to publish in Indian journals rather than those in the west which were hegemonised by liberal and then new-liberal academia". As he was fondly called Nirmal'da - by his numerous students and younger colleagues.Even after his retirement, he had a small room where he would beaver away on his computer, producing another two dozen papers, most of them published in the EPW.Over the 10years that he lived in UK and in other parts of Europe, he picked up French, Russian and Polish. In UK, he met and was influenced by Maurice Dobb and Michal Kalecki. After brief stints in Paris and Delhi, he joined our Institute and never left.

He soon turned to writing and publishing on India as well as the challenges of development in neighbouring countries.One of the early articles he wrote in EPW was "Class Character of Pakistani State" (Chandra 1972) and on agrarian classes in both India as well East Pakistan (Later Bangladesh), in Now and Frontier magazines. One of his first works on the grip of foreign capital on the Indian economy ("Western Imperialism and India Today", 1973) became much quoted and the study of multinational corporations remained an abiding interest.To him, third world countries could only develop if they charter a successful path of technological development, independent of foreign capital and its grip on markets and technology. Market power and its use and abuse was therefore of great interest to him and another area of his research was the corporate monopolies and conglomerates and the nature of capitalist class in India.

d) Indian Agrarian Study

We discuss here his work on the agrarian transition. He was the organiser of an important seminar at IIM Calcutta and Presidency College on the Capitalist Agriculture in India in the 1970s, many of which were subsequently published in the pages of EPW. He was excited with the left Front's land reform policies, efforts to strengthen Panchayats and transfer resources for decentralised planning and travelled into the countryside with some of his students to see the actual process of implementation.

e) Industrial Development

He felt that the left could actually chart a new path of Industrial development (Chandra 1978).Related was his engagement with the constraints and possibility of an independent industrial development strategy for India – independent of giant multinational corporations that controlled global markets.This is where he asked his students to undertake doctoral studies. All his students worked on themes like foreign direct investment, both inwards and outwards from India, technology transfer and dependent industrialisation, role of the public sector in the struggle to establish a self-reliant industrial base in India, problems of small and tiny industry, and appropriate technology.

He celebrated both major and minor successes in development of indigenous technology, national and firm level R & D efforts and the challenges of absorbing these efforts. His students turned our studies on industries like steel, petrochemicals, electrical equipment and pharmaceuticals, spanning both questions of technology and market control. His contestation of hegemony and power meant that the nation state as it ranged against the hegemonic tendencies of globalising capital, but within the nation state he supported institutions of federalism, decentralisation and autonomy. His engagement with hegemony and power also led him in other directions: associations with efforts of contesting power from the margins.

This led to his lifelong association with two Calcutta's Political Weeklies – Now and Frontier, and with their Editor Samar Sen, with the Bengali cultural magazines - Ekshan and Arek Rakam, the magazines of political and cultural debate. He was with the association of third world economists founded in 1976; with various trades unions, small and large, both to contest capital and to devise alternate means of organising economic activity. A gravitational pull exerted by his ultimate desideratum of the construction of a socialist world, and the counter-push of rich-friendly globalisation which he detested. Such pulls and pushes produced a tension in his work, a tension that was sometimes revealed by some change of angle of vision for portraying a problem that had been visited earlier. He had his deep focus on the context of the problem.He was one of the most scholarly and insightful practitioners of what I call 'contextual political economy – said Bagchi.

When he discussed the soviet economic system, he did not simply describe the structure of the system at any given moment of time.He generally gave a sketch, based on the mostscholarly books and articles availableon the subject, of how the system came to be shat it was during that slice of time. His thesis was supervised by Alec Nove, and he interacted on a regular basis with R W Davies, the joint author of perhaps the most authoritative account of the developed Soviet system. He had also interactions with Moshe Lewis, when both of them were in Paris.Nove was a steady reference, but he did not hesitate to contradict his teacher, when more evidence and better reasoning convinced him of the validity of an opposite inference. His paper in the Journal of Peasant Studies (1992) is clear evidence of this.

While discussing the dynamics of the Soviet system, he studied closely the reasoning behind and the struggles conducted by the leaders of the movement. He also analysed in detail the views of Chayanov, who is often held up as the quintessential enemy of the Marxist view of the character and role of the peasantry in a socialist revolution. He also underscored that the tendency of the small peasants to split up as the proportion of workers to consumers increased, even when the land they could acquire was obtained on very onerous terms. He inferred that small peasants suffered from underemployment and this was a factor causing acute land hunger in Tsarist Russia, where the vast expanses of land were often uncultivable and rich peasants and landlords generally held the better pieces of land.

He delved into the strategies to be adopted by a communist party, which believed that it was the industrial workerswho would spearhead the socialist revolution even in a country in which such workers formed a small minority; he tackled the issue of the evolution of class analysis by the Marxists, beginning with Marx and Engels in the first place. He pointed out that already in the Communist Manifesto, Marx and Engels in the firstalready in the Communist Manifesto, Marx and Engels had called upon the workers to support the Anti feudal, nationalist movement among the polish peasants. He referred to Engels's writing on peasant movements in France and Germany, and the change of attitude of Marx.But he was also careful to underscore that neither Marx nor Engels had conducted a class analysis of peasants or an agrarian society.

He notices that Lenin was one of the first to recognise how poor peasants' choices are blocked by the inter linkage of markets in labour power, land, peasant produce and loans. He had made the very interesting point that the maximum sustainable rate of growth of the economy was not achieved by over-taut planning or capital outlays: His contributions were to the understanding of the political economy of India. Most of them appeared in the EPW.In these papers, he looked at the positive and negative effects of FDI on the domestic economy in different countries of the world, and related the inferences to the Indian context. He was especially concerned about the need generated by Indian governmentpolitics to attract debt-creating foreign capital.He was severely critical of the proposals related to intellectual property rights- the proposals that were substantially incorporated in the WTO agreement.

He then proceeded to sketch how developing countries such asIndia could develop their R&D and benefit from a strategic absorption of foreign technology. Many of these papers will still be useful if a student of the Indian economy wants to have a critical look at the way R & D policies and current account deficits are being managed by the present controllers of economic policies in India. This was a detailed study of the growth of monopoly houses in India since the 1930s.It provided a historical retrospective to the studies by R K Hazari, the Monopolies Inquiry commission and the SubimalDutt Committee and brought them forward to the middle 1970's.

Another massive inquiry into the growth of the Indian economy since 1900, published in EPW invites comparison with the estimates of national income in Sivasubramonian. There has always been a substantial proportion of guesswork in estimates of Indian GDP. However the proportion of guesswork to hard data has increased enormously. His articles - India's Rouble Debt and Depreciating Rouble assesses the India-Russia agreement on the size and modalities of repayment of India's rouble debt from two different angles.The first consists of examining the distribution of the gains of India's trade with the former Soviet Union.

The focus is on the unit values of the commodities exchanged, particularly our arms imports financed through Soviet credits.The other aspect concerns the nature of the rouble as a currency up to 1989 and after, on which score there appears to be very widespread mis-conception. The debate on German unification has deeper ideological implications. Contrary to the fond hope of innumerable socialists in the not-too-distant past, international capitalism today is not only vibrant, but also seems to be dusting in peaceful competition 'existing socialisms' from countries stretching from China through the USSR toEast Germany.

f) His Research Work and Me

I was deeply involved with the following papers of him. In 1977, I was assisted him in his paper "USSR and Third World, Unequal Distribution of: Gains". In 1979, I was associated with his paper "Monopoly Capital, Private Corporate Sector and the Indian Economy". In 1982, I helped him a lot in his paper "Long-Term Stagnation in the Indian Economy, 1900-1975". I have also helped him in publishing his book, "The Retarded Economies; Foreign Commination and Class Relations in India and other Emerging Nations", published by Oxford University Press for Sameeksha Trust. I helped him in preparing his paper "Costs of German Unity" in 1990 and "India's Rouble Trade and Depreciating Rouble" in 1993. I was deeply involved with Prof. Chandra in the following papers published in EPW:

a. Chandra N K (1977): USSR and Third World, Unequal Distribution of: Gains, EPW, Annual Number, February.
b. Chandra N K[1] (1979): Monopoly Capital, Private Corporate Sector and the Indian Economy, A Study in Relative Growth, 1931-1976: EPW, Special Number.
c. Chandra N K[2] (1982): Long-Term Stagnation in the Indian Economy, 1900-75, EPW, Annual Number, Volume – 17, Issue Nos.14 - 16, pp. 517 - 80, April 17.
d. Chandra N K (1988): The Retarded Economies; Foreign Commination and Class Relations in India and other Emerging Nations, Oxford University Press for Sameeksha Trust, Chandra N K (1990): Costs of German Unity, EPW, Volume-25, Issue No. 30, July 28.
e. Chandra N K (1990): Costs of German Unity, EPW, Volume-25, Issue No. 30, July 28.
f. Chandra N K[3] (1993): India's Rouble Trade and Depreciating Rouble, Volume-28, Issue No.27-28, July 3.

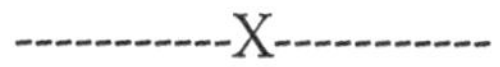

CHAPTER 3.5

TRIBUTE TO PROFESSOR NIRMAL KUMAR CHANDRA

INTRODUCTION

I like to offer my tributes to these entire great Professors who worked here for long years. As the Institute culture was designed to make every Professor a "Man on Mission" and an Institution Builder. Their contributions in research, writing, teaching, dissemination was of more values. I will talk about Prof. Chandra, who changed my life from a village boy to researcher in an institute of national importance. He was very affectionate to me and I also respect him as God. Prof. Ashok Mitra termed him as a Complete Economist while D'Mello termed his as a Radical Economist. But, I termed him a kind hearted and plain living and simple person with high thinking in social change. He has distinct insight toward economics as a great inspiration research in economics. He emphasized Management education not to remain in Corporate World but to the development of the Society

Even though, he was termed him as a Compleat Economist and a Radical Economist, I termed him as a kind hearted and simple living person with high thinking in social change. A PGP student described him as – "Probably the only guy to charm was Prof. Chandra but the Economics was "Bread and Guns" for this Jeans-clad Ecotheorist". He emphasized on the need of management education to be implemented toward the development of the society and not just remain confined to the Corporate World. He played a pivotal role in shaping the Economics group of the Institute. He spent all his life teaching at the Institute and even nurtured an institutional loyalty towards it.

Many scions of *Zamindar* families in Bengal had repudiated their inherited wealth to become lifelong followers of the Communist movement. He belonged to that list and would be among the last names on it. He was the Thesis supervisor of a FP student Mr. D'Mellow, who described him who encouraged on the unconventional path. He paid tribute by offering the book- "On Naxalbari" on him. He introduced the peasant question and there's no better way I know of to pose that concern. How can the mass of peasantry be drawn into a revolutionary movement spearheaded by the socialists, representing above all the proletariat? "The difficulty, at bottom, stems from the fact, that the peasant possesses 'two souls' one of the proprietor and the other of a worker. What came to mind when I read this was another difficulty in the Indian context. Here this combination of the proprietor and the worker- the Indian peasant – is imbued with caste consciousness, which drives him/her to strive to give up the use of family labour in tilling the soil and in other manual tasks.

a) Prof. Chandra and Me

I met Prof. Chandra in 1974 at Emerald Bower Campus. He was very perfectionist, as long as he satisfies with the study. He was also a miser; who write every inches of the paper of our office pad. Whatever calculation I did, he advise me to check again and again. After his retirement, he used to call me for computational assistance or teaching him "Excel" software. In EB Campus, he and I were housed in a single floor Asbestos shaded room. After 1977, I was housed in in different buildings at Joka Campus. Every day I used to meet him in early morning in his room. He asked to do the needful calculation on the data, which he had collected from different libraries. I used to enter data in the computer (PC) in his room, as I have not allotted any PC. I have a long association with him for last 22 years till his retirement in 1996. After that, he was engaged as a National Scholar of Indian Council of Social Science Research in India and was housed in our Institute in a smallest room.

b) Fondness forAdda and Sharing of Launch

For him an *adda* was not an indulgence, something separate from the serious business of life; it was an act intimately linked to his intellectual praxis.He was as choosy with his food as he was with friends. His political beliefs remained unwaveringly the same through the rest of his life. He would still not shout his beliefs from the rooftop, but he was never to be seen straying even accidentally with the wrong ideological crowd. The structure of his mind and his civilization was worth nothing. For the outstanding attribute of his nature was no question thequality of affection he chose to bestow on those whom he liked.His affection was not a free gift,it was not available to each and all. In many ways theBengal's culture of *adda (Gossip)*were an important part of his social world. He was truly in his element, even more so than while in class and teaching.

His fondness for *adda* had a quotidian avatar in the gathering of some colleagues for lunch every working day. Of this motley group which had a few regulars but whose composition changed over time, he was the fulcrum. Again if there were guests or friends from out of town visiting the Institute, they were invited to lunch where food from different kitchens was shared among members present for an abbreviated touch *adda.*In the common lunch time *adda*- Poromesh, Sudip, Sushil, Nagi, Raghab, Sailo etc. were regularly present. in the common table. I, Atul, Bhubanesh, Tridib, Gopal and Santawana were present. We also shared Prof. Chandra's lunch box containing – boiled and half-fried Soya Nuggets, Bitter guard, green leaves in vegetable oil. He is very fond of *adda* in leisure time and every day he shared his same Tiffin with us.

He used to pay for all who were accompanied him in tea. He was extremely generous and very much social. An intensely private person, he was nonetheless extremely generous and sociable and loved an *"adda"*extraordinarily helpful to students he was nonetheless meticulous and exacting in the standards he demanded in their work; utterly gentle. He was nonetheless a strict, unwavering and life-long adherent of the left ideology; a staunch Marxist. He spent all his life teaching at the Institute and even nurtured an institutional loyalty towards it.As many scions of *Zamindar* families in Bengal had repudiated their inherited wealth to become lifelong followers of the Communist movement. He belonged to that list and would probably be among the last names on it

c) Accompanied Me to Different Libraries

He accompanied me to Commercial Library and National Library for data collection. He used to borrow books from n the National Library and I have to collect or return those books. Once, I have not gone to office for about three months at a stretch, as I was daily visitor in the National Library Annex Building having regular Entry Card. Very frequently, I have to visit the Commercial Library and CSO (Central Statistical Organization) Library in Dalhousie area.

d) Learning of Russian Language

Once he brought, a book on India's Foreign Trade With Russia written in Russian Language. He advised me to a read the book on - How to Read Russian Language from our library. It was for my familiarity with Russian Language. Gradually, I became familiar with the Russian alphabets and made the computation as he directed. Then I realized the name of commodities exported from India and imported from USSR[3]. Then I have computed the trade statistics as directed by him. He told that, India is paying till 1980 the debt for machineries in our steel plants with the collaboration to USSR. We are exporting sugar at 30 paisa per Kg and Darjeeling tea at one Rupee per Kg, when domestic prices were Rupee one per kg of Sugar and Rs. 4 per kg of tea.

e) My Association with him in Both Campuses

In the EB campus, my first involvement with Prof. Chandra was in connection to the analysis of data on rural households in three villages of Burdwan district (undivided). This the first time, I used the "Square Sheet", a graph paper style large sheet of paper full with boxes and printed in red ink. Like graph paper, the square was larger than that of graph paper that I have used in school and college. The data was transcribed in these boxes with one letter or digit in each box and leaving blank space for clarity. I used wooden pencil for entering data. For each sheet of paper, a grand total was written by rotating "FACIT Machine". I have used earlier the"FACIT Machines" in the examinations at Indian Statistical Institute while reading in the course on Statistical Methods and Applications. After the tabulation was over, I have computed the number of households and amount of total land owned and operated by size class of land holding. I became familiar with the measures of inequality in land holding as well as annul income among landholders in each of the three villages and all villages combined. In final report, I draw the Lorenz Curve for distribution of Ownership and Operational holdings and on Income distribution of rural households.

In 1975, the Institute moved partly in incomplete Joka Campus but I shifted later in 1977. In Joka, I helped him in all his research work and academic activities like – summation of scores for each student, tabulating the grade sheet and submission to PGP office. I helped him in his all Research Projects and all Papers published in EPW.I assisted him in preparing Index pages of his first book - Stagnation in Indian Economy, published by Oxford University. The publisher paid me for this and Prof. Chandra acknowledged me in his book. Prof. Chandra officially retired in 1996, but consequently engaged as a National Fellow of ICSSR. Our administration placed him in a very small room, as he was not a serving faculty member. At that time, he called me for a few calculations, fitting of graphs in Excel. After my retirement, he engaged me for data entry job for Thalasemia patients of his wife Dr. Sharmila Chandra, a veteran Haematologist.

f) His Marriage and Mine

Once, he was absent for couple of days. After returning office, I asked for the reasons for his unnoticed absences. He said I went to bon (forest) I replied Bonn in Germany. No no it was Simlapal forest in Orissa. With smile he gave me an invitation card signed by his father for a marriage reception party at St. Pauls Cathedra; in central Calcutta. I told that it is a restricted area and they may not allow me to entry. He replied – show them the invitation card.I reached there around 5 PM but none except the Caterers were present. After a while, there came Prof. Ashok Mitra and enquired about Nirmal. I know Prof. Mitra earlier at Nirmal's Office. So, both of us were gossiping, while a tall, smart and handsome man came in. He started talking with Prof. Mitra. After seeing his face I realised, he is Soumitra Chattopadhayay, a veteran film actor of Bengali Cinema. As a Village boy, I have never been to Cinema Hall and seen any movies.

Meanwhile, our office bus stopped in front of the Gate of the Church and all from our Institute including Nirmal'da got down. He asked, I went to office despite my marriage but you wereabsent. After the dinner, I left for Howrah station to reach my home at mid-night. I got married after few months of his marriage. To attended my marriage ceremony in December 1982, Profs. Chandra, Sudip and half a dozen of Project assistants including Atul Babu and Poromesh'da attended the ceremony in my village home at Singur, infamous for left out Tata's Small Car Project. He reached around evening and he asked me to accompany him to tour my village. In front of a rich Peasant's house he stopped and watching the compost pit for making fertiliser from agricultural waste. At that time, New Delhi bound Rajdhani Express was passing with high speed above 100 kilometres per hour. The train crossed in a while and submerged in the dark.

g) I Was His Tutor

When a desk top personal computer (PC) was installed in his room, I became his instructor in operating the PC for *Word Processing* and *Excel* software for data processing. He frequently called me for help when he faced the problem in his PC. Moreover, he also called me for magic tricks when the PC and Printerwere not responding. I switch on the cables from the plug point and reset the connections. Once he gave me a set of huge data for regression analysis. After doing thousands of regressions, I was fade up and asked him what you are enquiring with these regressions. He said, I am trying to catch the cow lost in the forest. Do you know, *Gabesana* (Research) means "Go (Cow) plush Eshana" (searching)? After his retirement, he frequently called me for computational assistance or help in Excel.

h) His Bengali Literature

Even though he spentmore than twenty years in Europe, he does not mix English word in any Bengali discussion or conversations. He was very fluent in Bengali as well as other languages. Not only in English, he had written articles from time to timein Bengali.In *Anustup* - a leading cultural Magazine of Kolkata, he wrote *Paschim Banglar krshite dhanatantrer bikash* (Capitalist Development in West Bengal Agriculture) and *Unnayaner Jukti Tarko* (Pros and Cons of Development). He wrote the article–*Bamfronter panchis bachar* (25 years of Left Front) in the book "Paschim Bangalay Bam-Fronter Panchish Bachhar" published by the Left Front of West Bengal in 1982.

i) People Around Him

Since 1980, Prof Chandra's office was in B Block first floor Room number 203. I have a separate table in his room. In 1980, another table was added as Mr. Sudip Choudhuri joined as a Teaching Assistant to help Prof. Chandra's teaching in PGP. Sudip was doing his Ph. D. in JNU in New Delhi. After receiving Doctorate Degree, he was absorbed in the Institute as an Assistant Professor in 1984. Me and Sudip were in the same age group and became friend. Since 1975, a young man frequently visited Prof. Chandra's office at EB Campus. He was Sushil Khanna, our alumni. Later he joined our Fellowship Program under the supervision of Prof. Chandra. Later, he was absorbed as Assistant Professor in Economics. Around 1980, a young man frequently visited Prof. Chandra's office. He was Mr. Bernard D'Mello a Fellowship student under his supervision. He used to come regularly at the end of the day to discuss his academic matters with Prof. Chandra. He completed his Fellowship in 1988 and left. After a few years, he joined the EPW in Bombay as an Assistant Editor. Later, he came to visit Prof. Chandra, and I showedhim that I have completed a Bibliography on Agriculture on the basis of articles published in EPW. He encouraged me to do it for the entire period, but I failed.

j. An Institution (IDSK) Builder

The Institute of Development Studies Kolkata (IDSK) was promoted in 2002 by the Government of West Bengal as an autonomous centre of excellence in social sciences.It was a society with an autonomous governing body with one eminent historians in India, Professor Irffan Habib as President,Prof. Nirmal Kumar Chandra as Vice-President and Professor Amiya Kumar Bagchi as Director and Secretary. The Governing Council consists of the Vice-Chancellors of two Universities in Calcutta and eminent academicians like Profs. Suranjan Das, V. K. Ramachandran and Malini Bhattacharya as its members. The Instituteis devoted to advanced academic research in the area of Literacy, Education, Health, Women, Employment, Technology, Communication, Human Sciences and Economic Development. Other programmes of the Institute were - training of research scholars in the social sciences working towards a Ph.D.The Institute is committed to the dissemination of its research finding through workshops, seminars, publications in the media, and public counselling.

k. His Demise

On his death, the country lost one of its very best economists.The media made no mention of his passing as he preferred it that way. There was something unreal about him, the renowned economist who was totally free of any malice, totally devoid of any pettiness, and totally free of any desire to get into the limelight. I came to know it in the next mornig by daily News Paper, seeing the Obituary given by his wife and older sister. None of his associates organised any *shok sabha* on him.

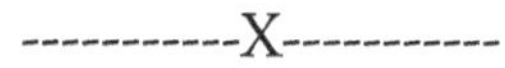
-----------X----------

CHAPTER 3.6

TRIBUTE TO FIFTY OLD AND EMINENT PROFESSORS

A: EMINENT PROFFSSORS IN EB CAMPUS (CHRONOLOGICALLY)

In this section, I will discuss our old and eminent Professors who worked during the first 30 years, 1962-1992 of the institute.They were recruited in early days at EB campus and others appointed after 1975 in Joka. I will discuss about fifty old and eminent Professors, of whom twenty fiveeach were recruited in EB Campus and Joka Campus. Our Professors were mostly with foreign degrees from best Universities in the World and they chose to remain here and made a mark. Here I met Professors Nirmal Chandra, Ranijt Sau, Ajit Biswas, Kamini Adhikari, Gouranga Chattopadhayay, Dilip Lahiri, Ramaswamy P Aiyer etc., I joined the Institute just after the eminent Professors like - Barun De, Ashok Mitra, Ishwar Dayal, Dharni P Sinha and N Krishnaji etc. left for important positions all over India.

1. Ashok Mitra (1962-1970)

Prof. Ashok Mitra became a Professor of Economics at the Institute, which was established as the first national institute for post-graduate studies and research in management. He was given freedom by the first director K.T. Chandy to build up a strong academic community. He was part of the young group actively associated with the India League spearheaded by Mr. Krishna Menon. Some members of this group later became important Communist leaders in India. His joining at our institute was really an offshoot of what could be called the "old boy network".By then, Prof. Mitra was very much a part of the Communist Party of India (Marxist), which led the Left Front Government in the State.

I have had the privilege of knowing Prof. Mitra since 1980, when he was anxiously waiting in the veranda of Prof. Chandra's office room B 202. As he was standing alone, I introduced me as an Assistant of Prof. Chandra and requested him to sit in Chandra's room. Next time I met him in the reception of Chandra's marriage at St. Paul's Cathedral along with Bengali film actor Soumitra Chatterjee. In 1988, I met him, when Professor Chandra accompanied me to his residence Sonali Apartment in Alipore. It was after office hour around evening; we reached in front of a tall building surrounded by large trees and row of waiting cars. By lift, we reached his residence at Sonali Apartment. Prof. Chandra introduced me as a master of calculations that appeared in EPW papers. Prof. Mitra carried a tray full of tea pot, milk, sugar, cookies and some biscuits. He made two cups of tea for me and Prof. Chandra.

After tea, Prof. Mitra carried a bunch of papers with some rough calculations. He discussed his propositions the can be analysed from these data sheets. After the discussion, he requested to come tomorrow around 9-30 AM to collect more data sheets. For about a month, I used to reach his home in early morning to show my calculations and results. By this time he was ready in clean shaved and wearing *Dhoti* and *Punjabi,* made of *khadi.* He prepared my tea and showed the progress of the calculations. When his data sheets exhausted, he collected a Computer Disc from Reserve Bank of India. The Disc is similar to a Film Tape and contained data. But, this Disc cannot be feed in Personal Computers; I sought the help of our Computer assistants in CAM Centre. They analysed those data but charged heavily. So, Prof. Mitra has no money left for me and told to wait for next assignment.

After a few days, my colleague Poromesh'da asked me to meet Prof. Mitra in Rainey Park close to Birla Industrial and Technology Museum. I went there in the morning; Prof. Mitra reached around noon and told me to take the assignment of data analysis for the just completed survey in connection with the on Primary Education Commission, under his Chairmanship. After that, some Officers of Education Department along with the Education Secretary were present. They crosschecked my performance and association with Prof. Mitra and Prof. Chandra. They asked how these huge data can be a tabulated, which they have tried but failed. When I presented the data in a sheet of paper they were amazed. For next three months, I continue my office at Rainy Park with some investigators who have collected those data in different districts of West Bengal. One day in the afternoon, Calcutta became standstill, as film Director Satyajit Ray passed away in Belle View Clinic close to Rainy Park. I walked up to Exide More and took a Taxi to reach Howrah station.

He was not just an administrator, a politician and an activist, but also a writer of amazing eloquence and insight in both Bengali and English (Thakurta 2018).In the mid-1990s he became a member of the Rajya Sabha and was Chairman of the Parliament's Standing Committee on Industry and Commerce.He was the Chief Economic Adviser to the Government of India from 1970 to 1972 when Indira Gandhi was the Prime Minister. His career was not an academic, but an administrator, politician, activist and above all, a writer of amazing eloquence and insight in both Bengali and English. Prof. Mitra was the recipient of the Sahitya Academy Award in 1996 for his contributions to Bengali literature. He has written 20 books in Bengali on diverse themes. At the ripe age of 85, he had the "cheek" to edit, print and publish a Bengali fortnightly, *Arek Rakam* (That which is different), which should hopefully continue publication. One May Day, former Member of Parliament, prolific writer, bureaucrat, economist and Marxist thinker passed away in a Kolkata in 2018.

2. Kamini Adhikari (1962-1994)

She joined the Institute in 1962 as Professor in Sociology group. From the very beginning, she was the Chairperson of the Center for Entrepreneurship Development till retirement. She was also the Chairperson of the newly formed CMDS (Center for Management and Development Studies) in 1976 and she served the Institute for 32 years. Her assistants -Dr. K K

Choudhuri, Suvendu Dasgupta, and Anjan Ghose etc. were bright scholars. She assisted me very much in presenting in my first Seminar at the Institute in 1980. Lastly, I met her in Park Hotel in the three day seminar organized by Prof. A Bose in 1997. She was wife ofProf. B P Adhikari, Director of ISI Calcutta. I have heard that she was the daughter of Nuclear Scientist Dr. Homi J Bhava, who died in a mysterious plane crash.

3. K.T. Chandy (1962-1967)

Mr. Chandy was the first Director of the Institute, who joined at the early stage of the Institute. He used to rub shoulders with Alice and Daniel Thorner, P.N. Haksar and a number of other left–leaning intellectuals. Academic freedom at the Institute was fostered by senior Professor like Ashok Mitra, Barun De and Surajit Sinha. He left the Institute in 1967 while I joined in 1974. So, I have not seen him earlier, but met him later in 2007, when he delivered our Foundation Day Lecture. He recalled that, he had to fight a Case in Calcutta High Court filled by land owners of Joka village against the acquisition of their agricultural land to build our Campus. At that time, Mamata Banerjee (then not CM) was on hunger strike opposing accusation of agricultural land for Tata Nano Project in Singur.

4. Bani Kumar Sinha (1962-2000)

He joined the Institute in 1962 at the early stage of the Institute. He joined as Research Assistant and became Research Fellow. After completing his PhD in 1970, he became Assistant Professor in Operations Management Group. He retired in 2003 and passed away in 2022. After retirement, he served as the Directors of the Heritage School of Management and the Calcutta Business School. He authored some textbooks on Operations Research and Linear Programming. He was kind hearted person and interacted with all of us.

5. Barun De (1963-1973)

He joined the Institute in 1963 as first Senior Professor of Social and Economic History. He was also the first Director of Indian Post-Graduate

Program (PGP) in management. His area of research was social and economic history of India in 17th and 18 century.Prof. Ashok Mitra seated jointly with him in a room in old EB Campus. Both of them met recently in 2004 on the occasion of 135th Anniversary ok Kolkata Port Trust, where Prof. Satyesh Chakraborty delivered the key note address. He had combined the excellence of and organizational ability. His teaching encouraged wide ranging ideas among students.He left our Institute in 1973 to join as Founder Director of the Center for Studies in Social Sciences in Calcutta. He was also associated with Moulana Abul Kalam Azad Institute of Asian Studies and the Asiatic Society. He was the Chairman of Bengal Heritage Commission. He delivered the Foundation Day Lecture at our Campus in 2008 and expired in 2013.

6. Ishwar Dayal (1963-1967)

The first Director, Prof. Chandy asked him to join the Institute in 1963 as Senior Professor in Organization Behavior group. He left our Institute in 1967 to join at IIM Ahmadabad (IIMA) on the request of his colleague Prof. Ravi Mathai, the first Director of IIMA. He worked there till 1973, after that he became Director of Indian Institute of Public Administration and served till 1976. In 1986, he became the first Director of IIM Lucknow. So, he was an Eduprenure as he headed several Institutes all over India. He contributed much for establishing management educations in India. His novel "Dayal: An Eduprenure", was published in 2011. He wrote his experience in IIMC in a book "Masters Speak: Management Education in India. He died in 2015, but he would be remembered for his uncompromising sense of quality and contribution to management education in India.

7. Paresh Chattopadhay (1964-1972)

He joined the Institute in 1964 as Professor in Economics. He was French trained Marxist Scholar, reported as a Maoist and was arrested in the EB Campus in early 1970s. After release from the jail, he left for joining a University in Berlin. The renowned Economist Prof. Y K Alagh wrote an article "Marx and Us" about him in Indian Express's Outlook Magazine in 2018. Prof. Chattopadhayay was a regular contributor in EPW.

8. Gouranga Chattopadhayay (1964-1991)

. He joined the Institute in 1964 as a senior Professor in Behavioral Science group and continued till retirement in 1991. He was very friendly with Prof. Chandra, Hrishikesh Bhattachary, Binod Kumar and Ajit Mathur etc. I was astonished by seeing him, a handsome, brighter, taller and fairest look like a Vedic Saint. He was a scion of the families of Raja Ram Mohan Roy, Pundit Ishwar Chandra Vidyasagar and Prince Dwarakanath Tagore. His father was great grandson of Vidyasagar and his mother was the eldest daughter of Surendranath Tagore, second eldest brother of Rabindranath. He spent his early life in Great Britain, spoke English fluently and pronounced as a Englishman. He started his career as an anthropologist and reinvented himself as a behavioral scientist. He calls himself a socio-analyst and worked as a teacher and consultant in 5 continents. He introduced Group Relations Conferences in India in 1973 and organized a series of conferences till 1991. In the development of group relations in India, Zahid Gangjee and D Banerjee were his close associates. I have no scope to help him.

9. N. Krishnaji: (1965-1973, 1984-1986)

He joined the Institute in 1965 as a Research Fellowand was promoted to Assistant Professor. Prof. J K Senguptaleft the teaching of Econometricswholly to him. In 1967, without a publication to his credit or a PhD, he was debarred from promotion. At that time, he observed factionalism among faculty members, who were divided on many issues but united in their freedom. There were two factions - one doing research in their own disciplines regardless of the relevance for management education. The other faction did consultancy and other types of work they thought appropriate for our Institute. In the initial stage of the Institute, he was on very friendly terms with all but mostly those working in the library. He played a significant role in building up the library collection of published material relating to the Indian economy.He left the Institute in 1974 and joined as Director of the Centre for Social Studies in Trivandrum. In 1979, he joined at the Centre for Studies in Social Sciences Calcutta and worked till 1989. After that, he rejoined our institute for a change. But, he no longer felt the sense of belonging that was experienced earlier. He was associated with Prof. Reddy as a consultant in a Project. That time, I used to go to him to assist him in that project.

10. Nirmal Kumar Chandra (1966-1996)

He joined the Institute in 1966 and I joined eight years later.Ihave a long association with him till his retirement. I met him first in 1974 at EB Campus. He was very affectionate to me and I also respect him as God, as he transformed me from a village boy to a Researcher in Economics. He had close friendship with Alice Thorner who involved in India for "Land Reforms Policy" in first two five year Plans. After his death, the Institute took initiative to honour him for his outstanding contributions in the Institute. A MoU was signed with the Jan Chetna Trust, established by him for organizing the "Nirmal Chandra Memorial Lecture" series.Now, it has been stopped and a Prize was initiated in his name for FPM students.

11. Ajit Kumar Biswas (1966-1979)

He joined the Institute in 1966 as Professor in Economics, but I knew him since 1974 after my joining. He and Prof. Chandra used to seat in the same room in EB Campus, where he asked me about my village in details. I could not find him in the Joka campus during his retirement in 1979, when I was busy in household survey different districts of West Bengal.

12. Arun K Choudhuri (1966-1994)

He joined the Institute in 1966 as Professor in Operation Research group. I knew him since 1974 at the EB Campus. He supervised the first Fellowship student M N Pal. I have seen them in EB campus as both were working on a "Second West Bengal" project. In 1980, he called me to describe the utility of my Article submitted for the National Seminar organized by our Institute. As, he was the Chairman of the seminar, I have a lot of discussion about just completed political based Panchayat Election in West Bengal.

Finally, I read the Paper in the seminar and it was published in the of the Seminar Proceedings – "Research Gaps in Management" edited by Profs. A K Choudhuri, M S Misra and Dr. K K Choudhuri.

13. V Nagi Reddy (1966-2004)

He joined the Institute in 1966 as a Research Assistant attached to Prof. Chandra. He took lateral entry in M Stat. at ISI and finally obtained Ph D from ISI. In 1977 to 1980, he left the institute for Post-Doctoral Research Fellow in the Commonwealth Scientific and Industrial Research Organization, Canberra in Australia. His area of interest was designing and analysis of large Sample Survey. I knew him since the first day of my joining. When I joined, I could not speak in English and he was not fluent in Bengali, so language became a barrier in communication. Just before the day of leaving for Australia, he offered us a dinner in a College street Chinese restaurant sitting on the floor. Prof. Chandra asked me are you eating worm, as the noodles look like and I am eating it first time. After returning from abroad, he joined our Institute as Professor in Economics. He asked me to collect a package of books and study materials from Customs Office. But, I failed to identify his luggage form the heaps at Custom's godown. When Prof. Chandra retired he absorbed me in hisprojects. He became Director of a Management Institute in Hyderabad after retirement in 2004,

14. Satyesh Chakraborty (1966-1991)

He joined the Institute in 1966 as Professor in the Regional Development group. He was the Chairman of the Center for Regional Development till retirement in 1991. He spends his whole life for the development of city of Calcutta. He elaborated the Sewerage Pipe line and Drinking Water pipe line of the City in the 1970s. He had about ten Project Assistants in his Center and Mr. Abdul Halima, known as a Maoist, was one of them.

15. Biswanath Sarkar (1966-1995)

He joined the Institute in 1966 as Research Fellow in Operations Management group. and promoted to Assistant Professor.He did his M Sc in Calcutta University and M Stat in ISI Calcutta.While doing his PhD in Calcutta University, he wasted a few years. He always maintained low profile, mostly due to his rural background and low economic status. I knew him since 1974 in EB Campus and made gossips with him.

16. Chandan Mustafi (1966-2000)

He joined the Institute in 1966 in the Operations Management group as Professor in Statistics. He was a very simple and learned man. He wrote a few text books on Statistics for Managers etc. He was the Editor of our house journal DECISION in 1985 to 1987. Once I met him in connection to an article, which has attracted me much. The article dealt on "No Response", "Not Mentioned" and "Don't Know" type responses in the large sample surveys.

17. Dharni Prosad Sinha (1966-1975)

He joined the Institute in 1966 and became Chairman of the Center for Management of Education System in India. This center was funded by the Ford Foundation. He left our Institute in 1975 and joined the ASCI (Administrative Staff College of India) in Hyderabad. He was the Founder President and Coordinator of AMDISA (Association of Management Development Institutions in South Asia), The AMDISA became a SAARC recognized body. I have heard that, he left the institute for a quarrel with the then Director, Prof. J K Sengupta and a Professor in Economics group. When I joined the Institute in 1974, he was conducting aManagement Development Program (MDP) on Management of Education System. He wrote his experience in our Institute in his book "Learning From Life". He recalled that, first two years in IIMC placed all resources and energy to bring business leaders in MDPs. to educate business leaders and create market for our students. He expired in 2007.

18. Jati K Sengupta (1967-1977)

He joined the Institute in 1967 as Professor in Economics and Operations Research. He became our Director in 1972 to 1977. My first appointment was issued by him in 1974. After that he left for teaching in a university in USA. He was member of Ford Foundation and the World Bank and Fulbright Scholar of United States Educational Funds.

19. Ramswamy P Aiyer (1969-1992)

He joined the Institute in 1969 as Professor in the Management Information System group. He became our Director for two consecutive terms, 1982 to 1992. He always asked me to do a Post Graduate degree. I did my MA in 1989, just after our absorption as regular cadre in 1987. I have met him several times in connection to the regularization of the Project Assistants. He took voluntary retirement in 1992 and joined as a Director of a Management Institute in the South India.He passed away in 2006 after prolonged suffering from Cancer. Our Alumni and our Ex-Chairman, Ajit Balkrishnan has lifelong connection with him.

20 Ranjit Kumar Sau (1970-1995)

He joined the Institute in 1970 in Economics group. Earlier he was a Professor in Jadavpur University. He was inclined to left politics and believed Marxism as social change. He wrote some books on contemporary issues in Indian Economy.He left the Institute in 1980 to join an University in USA and for education of his children. He was very reserved person and talked less. He was residing in Sonali Apartment in Alipore where Dr. Asoke Mitra also lived in. The Left Front Government in West Bengal asked him to take some responsibilities but he refused. But, Profs. Satyesh Chakroborty and Nirmal Chandra took some responsibility for Left Front Government during 1977 to 1984.

21. Chitta Mitra (1970-1982)

He joined the Institute 1970 as Professor in Marketing group. Earlier he worked in ITC in Cigarette Advertising. I knew him from the first day, as he was sitting in my room in EB Campus. He established his advertising firm C-Marc in 1977. He also founded IMRB (Indian Market Research Bureau). During 1977, he had undertaken a World Bank Sponsored Project – Economic Evaluation of Market Development in Agriculture in West Bengal. Next year, he undertook another Institute sponsored project

– Study of Market Information in Agriculture on Perishable Products. For these two projects, a batch of 30 project staffs was recruited and the Institute could not provide accommodation to them in the Campus. Thus, the team officiated in a rented building just opposite to our main gate. Some of his Project assistants were better placed outside and some joined in our Institute projects. Tarit Datta and Subal Manna joined in our Projects of Prof. Chandra. He resigned in 1982.

22. Sitangshu K Chakraborty (1971-2003)

He joined the Institute in 1971 as Professor in Finance and Control group. He had a huge contribution in Finance and Control of the Corporate World. Later, he was inclined toward teaching of Human Values and Indian Ethics. He was the most enthusiastic advocate of "Ethics of Indian Management" from our Hindu Epics. His colleague, Prof. Jacob Mankidy stressed on the Indian Cultural Heritage in Management. He established the Management Center for Human Values (MCHV) in 1992. It recognizes first to use *shashtras* in management education. In 1994, he was awarded "Best Management Teacher" by Association of Management Schools in India. I have no interaction with him thogh met daily.

23. Binode Kumar (1971-2001)

He joined the Institute in 1971 and became Chairman of the Center for Management of Education System in India in 1975. When, Prof Sinha left for joining ASCI, he became the Chairman of this Center and continued for long 15 years. He took leave for two years 1990-1992, for joining as Director of FORE School of Management in New Delhi. He was father founder of CAT (Common Admission Test). He was very jolly good fellow with smiles and jokes. He pertained that all the National heroes in Bihar were his close relatives. I have attended his classes in the ten week MDP on MCA Teachers, organized by Prof, Mohanti in 1987. He had three Research Fellows – Swaraj, Swapan and Arun, who shared my room in B-103. None of them was absorbed in our Institute and were placed elsewhere. Mrs. Nilanjana Kundu was recruited in his Center as a Post-Doctoral Fellow. After a few months, she joined the Psychology Department of Calcutta

University as Professor. I have a good relation and friendship with him till date.

24. Aloke Ray (1972-2006)

He joined the institute as Assistant Professor in 1972 and taught India's Foreign Trade. He was cool and calm person and never talked loudly. He stood second in Higher Secondary examination from a village school near Bakreswar in Birbhum district. In 1987, Prof. Ray was awarded V K R V Rao prize worth Rs. 25,000 for Economics Research in Social Science. He was a close relative of Prof. Bose, our Ex-Director. His father was a revolutionary and was jailed in Cellular Jail for five years in 1932 to 1937, as he transported Arms to revolutionaries in Bengal. His name has been transcribed in the walls of the Cellular Jail. Prof. Ray retired in 2006 and became Director of a Private Management Institute in Calcutta. I have no official attachment with him but met him daily in the office.

25. Amitava Bose (1974-2012)

He joined the institute as Assistant Professor 1974 and I also joined in the same year. I and Ratan Ghosh were making *adda* in a vacant room in EB Campus. We were informed that a Professor from America is coming to join us and he will sit here. He used to sit in my opposite room at EB Campus. He became our Director in 1997 to 2002, but turned down the second term.Both of us performed invigilation duty in classroom L2 in Joka campus.He invited me to attend a three day Seminar at Park Hotel in 1997. There I met Prof. Kamini Adhikari in this seminar along with the then Director, Subir Chaudhury. Prof. Bose taught Economics for long years.

Despite his popularity, he said, "I haven't been able to connect with my students the way my own teachers at the Delhi School of Economics. I wish to have more initiative."He simplifies concepts and never gets irritated and learning is a journey with him. His life has been interested with the development of IIMCalcutta, particularly during his years as the Director. His research interest was employment issues in India. He was already a legend in Joka and became the Institution builder. He donated Rupees two Cores for the development of our Economics group in the Institute.

B: EMINENT PROFESSORS IN JOKA CAMPUS (CHRONOLOGICALLY)

1. Manabendra Nath Pal (1975-2010)

He was our first Fellowship student of the Institute and awarded Fellow in 1975. I knew him since 1974 when he was assisting Prof. Arun Chaudhuri in his Second West Bengal Project sponsored by the Government of West Bengal. He became Assistant Professor in 1975 and was a very dynamic person. The students dared him very much, as he used to set tough questions in Operations Research. After completion of his paper in examinations, the students used to through garlands among themselves. A student described him as "The tools (Library, documents, images etc.) would be provided to you. But, these would always be the toughest Pal sirto intimidate the contents". He died in harness before retirement in 2010.

2. Sujit K Basu (1975-1998)

He joined the Institute 1978 and took voluntary retirement in 1998 for joining as Director in Army Institute of Management Calcutta. Nexthe joined as Vice chancellor of Viswa Bharati in 2001 to 2006. The Nobel Prize won by Rabindranath was stolen during his tenure. I have assisted him by providing our household survey data for testing some theory of probability distribution. I have attended his PGP classes in Statistics. He supervised the Fellowship student Dilip Roy, who stood first in the All India Statistical Service in 1984.

3. Sushil Khanna (1976-2017)

I knew him since 1975, when he used to come at EB campus to meet Prof. Chandra. He was a PGP student of 8th batch (1971-1973) and worked in City Bank. He joined the institute as Research Fellow in 1976 and completed Fellowship in 1984 and became Assistant Professor in Economics group. His area of research was the Transnational Corporation and Technology Transfer. He became the Consultant for Private and Public sector enterprise. He served as Consultant at World Bank, IBP, and Oil India etc.

4. Hiten Bhaya (1977-1982)

Former Planning Commission Member and Chairman of Steel Authority of India, Mr. Hiten Bhaya joined the Institute as Director in 1977 and continued till 1982. A few of Project Assistants met him for our regularization. He heard our grievances and asked not to stage agitation in the campus. While leaving the institute, his note on regularization of Project Staffs helped us a lot. At that time, the Administrative Building was under construction, and he used to sit in top floor of B-block, where Nepal Ram makes good quality of tea.

5. N K Rao (1977-2007)

He joined the Institute in 1977 as a Professor in Finance and Control Group. He was the supervisor ofour FP student N Ramchandran, who became Professor in the same group.He was a cool and calm person and always busy in taking PGP classes.

6. Nilkantan Ramchandran (1977-2011)

He joined our Fellowship Program in 1977 and awarded Fellow in 1983. I knew him since 1977 when both of us were sitting in our office across the lake in Staff Quarters. While, ferrying by boat, he taught me to row the Boat kept in other side of the lake. He became Professor in Finance and Control group since 1983 and left in 2011 to become Director of Kochi Business School in Kerala.

7. Deepak Nayar (1977-1983)

Initially, he was in Indian Administrative Service (IAS). He left this job for further studying of Economics at Oxford University in UK. He joined the Institute in 1977 as Professor in Economics group. He worked for six years and left to join as an Advisor to the Ministry of Commerce in 1983. During 1983 to 1991, he was Chief Economic Advisor of India

Government when Rajiv Gandhi was the Prime Minister of India. I have assisted him by analyzing India's export-Import data for those years. At that time, my employment at the Institute was not permanent, so he was eager to place me in LIC office at Delhi, provided I have own accommodation there. Later, he became the Chairman of Sameeksha Trust, publisher of Economic and Political Weekly. His wife, Mrs. Rohini Nayyar was also staying with him in New Alipore area of Calcutta and was doing her PhD. She used to meet me in our Campus for her research work. I have computed concentration of landholding in West Bengal and other States of India in mid-1970s. She was a regular contributor in the Peoples' Daily, a CPIM mouthpiece published from New Delhi.

8. Sudip Chaudhuri (1978-2018)

When Prof. Reddy left for Post-Doctoral studies in Australia, Mr. Sudip ChoudhurI joined the Institute in 1978 as Teaching Assistant to Prof. Chandra. Earlier, he was teaching at a Degree College in Central Calcutta and also doing PhD in JNU at New Delhi. He and me both were sitting in Prof. Chandra's room in B-Block. He was a very nice person and was associated with us, when we the Project Assistants were struggling for permanency. He became Assistant Professor in 1990, and his research interest was on Pharmaceutical industry in India. I have friendly relationship with him and he visited my upcoming home in Serampore, where his relatives reside. I went to attend his marriage ceremony at Tyagaraj Hall in South Calcutta. He also attended my marriage ceremony in my village in Singur.

9. Bharatendu Nath Srivastave (1979-2019)

He joined the Institute in 1979 in the Behavioral Science group. He was very much busy in conducting Executive Development Program (EDPs), In-Company Trainings throughout the year for many companies in both Public and Private sectors.He was awarded Escort Book award for his book – International Management: Concepts and Cases, which was adjudged the best Management book in 1997. Now, he is Founder of the MLEAD, a platform for management consultants. I have no academic connection with him, but met mostly in Canteen and Examination halls. I assisted him in assimilation of Institute's data for OUTLOOK Magazine. He became Director-in-Charge in 1997 and 2019 for a few months, when the term ended for Directors and new incumbent joined.

10. Ms Jainab Ahmed (1983-1999)

She joined the Institute in 1983 as Professor in Business Environment group. She was very affectionate to me and asked frequently about Atul Babu, who was known to him since their friendship in London. She was a regular smoker and sometimes asked me for a Cigarette. She was scholar in Business Law and was practicing it in London before joking us.

11. Ambujaksha Mohanti (1984-2017)

When Prof. Rahul Mukherjee left my tuition, I approached Prof. Mohanti for help. He was so busy, he cannot afford time. Then he selected me for a 10-week MDP on MCA Teacher's Training on Computer. He helped the Research Assistants very much. He was very much cooperative in implementing our Promotion schemes.

12. Leena Chatterjee: (1984-2015)

She joned the Institute in 1984 to teach Organisational Behaviours(OB), which issomething students tend to lose sleep over, because it is not considered 'hardcore' like strategy, marketing or finance.When, she is on the podium, the class turns into a theatre.Students have to make presentations based on various characters in novels and act our situations. She brings in examples to everything, she teaches by using a lot of poetry andliterature in her teaching and with a smile. She not only a teacher but also a friend and mentor to many of her students. She believes in enjoying, what she does. The wonderful interactions which she have with young intelligent people, She is refereed by her students as Joka's Jane Austen. She was very busy in conducting many MDP and In-Company Trainings. She retired in 2015 after a long service to the Institute and I have no interaction with her.

13. Hrishikesh Bhattacharya (1985-2005)

He joined the Institute in 1985 as a Professor in Finance and Control Group. In 1991, he came to my incomplete house at Seramporefor an urgent work in connection with the Problems and Prospects of Small Scale Industries in West Bengal. In 2001, he undertook a Central Government sponsored Project- Implementation of Reconstruction Funds for Revival of Indian Sea Food Export Industry. He engaged me in analyzing the amount of fish caught by about 700 companies from southern states – Andhra and Tamil Nadu. I have also analyzed financial data of those companies, to identify their prospect in coming years. The Report of this Project has been published in a book form. I was never been officially attached with him, but he seek my help in Mathematical and Statistical problems, while analyzing financial data for Corporate Sector. He acknowledged me in all his papers in EPW and his Book.

14. Mousumi Ghosh (1988-2002)

She joined the Institute in 1988 as a Professor in Finance and Control Group In 1991, she came to my incomplete home in Serampore with Prof. Bhattacharya. I have helped her in doing her PhD on Audits in Corporate World. I have no official attachment with her, but I helped her in joint projects with Prof. Bhattacharya. When she was Editor of our Institutional Journal "Decision", she asked me to submit my current Working Paper for publishing. It was referred to an expert, who advised for some correction and finally it was published in Decision.She took voluntary retirement in 2002 for establishing her own Future Institute of Engineering and Management (FIEM) in Narendrapur in South 24-Parganas.

15. Neelu Sancheti (1986-1988)

She joined the Institute as Professor in Behavioral Science group. She did her PhD in London University in 1984. Her Thesis was "Educational Dependence – An Indian Case Study in Comparative Perspective". She studied the IIM Calcutta's evolution since 1957 to 1984. Earlier, she was student and teacher in Loreto College in the city. She died in harness within two years of joining the Institute in 1988, under a tragic circumstance. The Loreto College still remembers her by organizing Neelu Singvi Sancheti Memorial Lecture and distributing Gold Medals in her name. I have not seen her, as I was busy that time for studying my M. A. course in the Evening at the Rabindra Bharati University at EB Campus. I heard her sudden demise in the next morning when I joined office after my leave of absence.

16. Rabin Ganguly (1987-2008|)

He joined the Institute in 1987 as Professor in Regional Development group, founded by Prof. Satyesh Chakraborty. He became the Chairman of the Center for Regional Development Studies till retirement. Besides academic activities, he have also done administrative duties for the then Directors. I have good relation with him.

17. Ajeet N. Mathur (1988-1998)

At the age 33, he was appointed as aProfessor at our Institutein 1988. He was our Alumni of 12th batch and was elected the Colloquia Secretary.At the night of the emergency, he invited newspaper editors to a colloquium on the campus to discuss freedom of the press, which caused a minor hiccup. He led a student strike against miss-management of our Institute. In 1977, he was awarded the Bharat Chamber of Commerce Gold Medal for the most balanced and progressive outlook on management by our institute. Initially as an economist with the Tata Group and studied the industrial potential of West Bengal. He worked for more than a decade with business firms like ITC, Dunlop etc. He received his PhD from the Indian Institute of Science, Bangalore.

In 1994, he was invited by the Helsinki School of Economics to relocate to Finland.Since 1978, he conducted Group Relations conferences in collaboration with Prof. Gouranga Chattopadhayay, his colleague since 1978. He interned with the Indian Society for Applied Behavioral Science. He became Director of the Institute of Applied Manpower Research and Secretary, Government of India in the Planning Commission.

He became Professor in Strategic Management and International Business at IIMA. While working in his room, he locked the room from inside to avoid out side disturbance. Once, he became lunatic and mental patient and his elder sister called from Delhi to take care of him. I knew him for a few years and have no interactions with him.

18. Rahul Mukherjee (1989-2021)

He joined the Institute in 1989, but I knew him since 1980, when he was my private tutor for the Statisticians Diploma (SD) examination of Indian Statistical Institute. Then he was a Professor at Calcutta University. As he joined the ISI as Professor, he cannot teach me for ethical reasons. So, my dream of passing the SD was unfulfilled. In the field of Probability Theory, he became world famous. I met him last at an outside auditorium, where my daughter and his wife were participating in a musical program. But when he is on campus,he maintains an open line.Students are free to call him or drop by at this office almost whenever they feel like. He has co-authored five books and more than 200 papers. He is a professor whom students love a lot and call him as an "Open-door Tutor". He retired in 2021 and remained my colleagues till my retirement in 2010.

19. Annapurna Shaw (1989-2018)

She joined the Institute in 1989 in the Regional Development group.Later, she was placed in Public Policy Management (PPM) group. Her research interests were areas of Urban Policy and Planning, the Informal Sector and Economic development. She has authored several books - Making of Navi Mumbai, Indian Cities etc.I sat next to her room in B-Block second floor. But, I have no interaction with her on academic activities. I first met her in 2004, when she was Chairperson of our Publication Division. I submitted a Working Paper on Status of Engineering Education in West Bengal under Market Paradigm. She published my Working Paper in printed format instead of earlier Xerox format.

20. Raghabendra Chattopadhayay (1990-2012)

He joined the Institute in 1990 as Assistant Professor in Environment group and teaches Business History of India. After Prof. Reddy retirement, I was attached with him for 1998 to 2010. He directed me to analyze the Sarva Siksha Aviyan (SSA) data for some sample districts of West Bengal. I have prepared the Report on Evaluation of SSA in those sample districts. Later, I wrote the Evaluation Report of SSA for the States of - West Bengal, Andaman Incober Islands, Assam, Mizoram, Arunachal Pradesh and Nagaland. I completed the Report on the Status of Primary Education in West Bengal for Profs. Uttam Sarkar (now Director) and Subir Bhattacharya for Assam and W.B.We have also studied the effectiveness of BRC and CRC in Elementary Education in Assam and West Bengal.

21. Sanjiv Damodar Vaidy (1990-2021)-

He joined the Institute as Assistant Professor in Management Information System group in 1990. He was our PGP Alumni and also our Fellow. He completed his Fellowship under the supervision of Prof. Ashok Agarwal in 1992. I met him in our CAM centre frequently whenever I used to go CAM center for using Personal Computers for Prof. Chandra. At that time, PCs were available only in CAM center and Data Processing Centre in B-block. He is a cool and calm person who resided whole life in our Campus with his family.

22. Anup Kumar Sinha (1991-2016)

He joined the Institute in 1991 by leaving Professorship in Presidency Collage, when Prof. Ashim Dasgupta, the then Finance Minister (FM) of the State. The FM curtailed the extra budgetary grant of the Presidency Collage, So, father of Nobel Laureate Prof Abhijt Binayak Bandopadhya and Prof. Sinha left the Presidency College. I knew Professor Sinha who used to meet Prof. Chandra and Raghab'da, with whom I was attached. I have attended his classes on Development Economics along with our PGP students. I obtained a high marksin his paper. Once, he was a referee in our house Journal Decision, he suggested some topics in my article "Bio-Technology in Third World Agriculture".He was most popular among the students and was awarded Best Professor for several years. Presently, he is serving the Bandhan Bank as Independent Chairman.

23. Subir Chowdhury (1992-1997)

A Company Executive with 15 years experience in Industry butwithout a PhD degree joined as our Director from 1992 to 1997. Before joining our Institute, he was Director at the Indian Institute of Social Welfare and Business Management (ISWBM) at Calcutta. After serving five years in our Institute, he became Vice-Chairman of the Indian Institute of Bank Management. A bolt from the blue came in during his time, when the Central Government started curtailing of grants to the Institute. To curtail Institute's daily expenses he took some temporary measure. Once, he called all Research Assistants and asked to earn for the Institute. Accordingly, two of us started conducting MDPs on their subjects.

24. Saibal Chattopadhyay (1997-2018)

He joined the Institute in 1997 in Operation Management group. He was Professor of Statistics in this group. He became our Director in 2013 to 2018 and retired thereafter. I have assisted him in a Project on Prospects of Food Processing Sector in Eastern Region comprising six eastern States. The Project was sponsored by the Ministry of Food Processing Industry, Government of India. In this Project, I have analyzed the progress of Agriculture in these States in recent past. I have written the Report, which he sent directly to the Ministry.

25. Mrityunjoy Mohanty (1999-2025)

He joined the Institute in 1999 as Assistant Professor in Economics group. He did his PhD under the supervision of Prof. Deepak Nayyar of JNU. He left the Institute twice, 2006 to 2008 and 2014 to 2016 for research in

Quebec and Montreal in Canada. His research interest was Development Economics. He was a regular contributor to EPW. I have no academic connection with him but I am an admirer of his Papers in EPW.

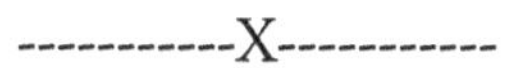

CHAPTER 3.7

SURVEY OF SOME UNCOMMON VIILAGES IN WEST BENGAL

I was born and bought up in a remote village in Singur Block of Hooghly district. The infamous Tata's abandoned car factory is just two kilometres away from my village. I have surveyed more than fifty villages in different districts of West Bengal, most of which was in plain areas but a few were in hilly regions, which I have never seen before. Villages in Hooghly, Howrah and Burdwan were close to my village home, but villages in Darjeeling, Purulia, Bankura, South 24 Parganas and Midnapore were far away. I have surveyed those villages in connection with the different Projects under different Professors from time to time. These Projects were 'Agrarian Change and Peasant Organisation', "Education and Social Change' and 'Status of Primary Education in West Bengal', sponsored by the UNICEF. I share my village experience of a few uncommon villages.

I will describe only six villages which have some peculiarities in comparison to other villages. The village Ladam Khas Mahal was on the top of a hill in Darjeeling (now Kalimpong) district. The village Paprahurum was also in a hilly area surrounded by some small hills and forests in in Khatra block of Purulia district. Among these villages, the poorest village was Bajeberia in Midnapore (now East Midnapore) district. This village was full of hunger and starvation, floods occurs most of the years. The village Kasipur was in hilly and forest area in Bankura district. This village was in a drought prone area with scarcity of water for drinking as well as bathing. The village Patihal in Jagat Ballavpur block of Howrah district, on the bank of river Kana Damodar. The village Chechera was near Bangladesh border in Tapan block of West (now Dakshin) Dinajpur district and close to river Punarbhaba. The elevation of these villages from Mean Sea Level variesfrom 8 meters for Patihal, 30 meters for Chechera, 90 meters for Kashipur and more than 100 meters for Paprahurum and Ladam Khas Mahal.

1. LADAM KHAS MAHAL: A VILLAGE ON HILL TOP WITH SCENIC BEAUTY

This village was on the top of a hill in Darjeeling (now Kalimpong) district. Reaching this village atop a hill was painful, as I had to walk upward for more than an hour after getting down from the Jeep that started from Kalimpong town. This village is at a very high altitude and very close to Sikkim boarder. In the evening, the areas in Sikkim part from the village looks very nice as dotted light in the dark sky. The day temperature was around 15 degree Celsius and it dropped to 5 degrees at night. For surveying this village, we stayed in the *Dak Bungalow o*n the highest point on hill top.Lying on bed, I have seen every morning the glowing and bright *Kanchenjunga* while woke up in the morning.

Cultivation practice was very poor as there were no irrigation facilities like ponds, Canals, dug wells or fountains. Only a small fountain flows with limited water that falls drop by drop for household use. This was the only source of drinking water. Ginger, Large Cardamom and Oranges were the main commercial crops while whet, ragi and makai (Corn) were staple food crop. These crops were cultivated in narrow tracks on the sides of the hills. People used to go to market once in a week or month. Among the vegetable, Squash and Radish etc. were produced in small scale for own consumptions.

I was at 30 and never gone to any villages in other districts, Prof. Chandra asked me to go this village alone, as others have left earlier. Atul babu asked me to buy an advance ticket to get front seat in the Rocket Bus that starts from Dharmatala at 6 p.m. every day and reached Siliguri around 9 a.m. in the next morning. I leave my own village in the afternoon and reached in Dharmatalaat 5 p.m. After loitering here and there, I reached at Dharmatala Bus Stand around 5:30 p.m. I got a seat just behind the Driver. I have to spent more than 12 hours in this bus. The first stoppage of the Rocket Bus was at Maldah town around 2 a.m. for a short break. After a break of half an hour, the bus started moving and after an hour, the Conductor requested the passengers not to light *Bidis* or Cigarettes, as we are crossing a dacoit prone zone. Half sleep half awoken night passed away and entered Siliguri Town by crossing congested area on Mahanada River Bridge, I got down at Sevak More around 9.a.m.

After getting down at Sevak More, I rode on a Kalimpong bound Mini Bus. The road was very narrow and zigzag on the bank of the river Tista. After crossing Mongpu, rest house of Tagore, the bus stopped, as a herd of elephants was walking along our road.Around noon, I reached at Tista bazaar, where the bus has to cross the river on a hanging wire bridge. Some village children were offering "Santara" (Oranges in local language). I procured the ripen Oranges from them, who have just plucked from the garden. I cannot forget the taste of those ripe Oranges in the noon after 20 hours of journey. I reached at Kalimpong Bazar around 2.p.m., where some young boys rode on the top of the bus and carried my language. I was afraid, but the conductor told me that no one steal your bags, they will carry to your hotels and pay them at your wish. Really, I did so and they smiled. Atul babu was waiting for me in the bus stand and accompanied to the hotel, where they were staying. In the next morning, we started from Kalimpong Bus Stand to the village Ladam Khas Mahal. The Zeep on this rout came in time and carried passengers including me to Sikkim Bound Terminal.

2. PAPRAHURUM: A HILLY VILLAGE WITH MINERAL WATER

This village is in hilly areas of Purulia district on the bank of river Subarnarekha bordering Bihar (now Jharkhand). The village is in Jhalda block and has some small hills and uneven typography. The villagers were poor and mostly were landless agricultural labourers. There were some tracks of agricultural land in the low laying bottom of the hills. In plain areas of districts Hooghly and Burdwan, uplands are costly, as that can grow three/four crops. Here, uplands were not fit for cultivation as water flown down. The low laying lands can hold water and favoured for cultivation. Except paddy, vegetable were grown in small areas. Instead of paper bag (*thonga*), *Saal* leaves were widely used in grocery and tea shops. 'Mahua' (liquor made from scented *Mahul* flowers) was available as soft drinking beverage.Drinking water from dug well was very cool and healthy. Most poor women collect wood for cooking and *Saal* leaves to make plates, which sold to traders in urban areas. The leaves of drum sticks (Sajane) were widely used as green vegetables throughout the year.Some labourers used to make Bricks by cutting the edges of stone. In 1980, price of a stone brick was only Rs. 2, while it took two to three days to make it. These bricks were used in in making pucca roads in towns.

We passed the chilled winter in Ladam Khas Machala and returned to Paprahurum in summer. To reach this village, I started in the evening from my village to reach Howrah station for boarding the Ranchi-Hatia Express leaving at 8 p.m. I have no experience of boarding Express trains as I used to journey in local trains. So, I have no ideas about reservation of seat in Express trains. t purchased an ordinary ticket from Howrah to Torang, the nearest station to the village.When the train reached to the Howrah station, passengers make chaos and I board the train when there were no vacant seats. So, I stand up asking the passengers, mostly poor '*Mitas*' (labourers) who used to come in the East for carrying paddy from field). They were discussing among themselves and looking at me as a helpless boy.

They arranged me a seat on the bunker above their head. I took dinner that I have taken from home and fallen asleep and requested them to wake me before the train reach Torang. In the mid night, the train stopped for a few minutes at Tata Nagar (Jamshedpur) station. The co-passengers told me to sleep again and the train will reach Torang in the early morning.The train reached around 5.a.m. and I got down in lonely platform. In the early morning after a long journey, I was looking for hot tea but no tea stalls. I found a man was collecting dried leaves and branches for making tea for passengers in the next train. He told me to wait as he will make tea. I waited about half an hour and drank the smokedtea flavoured with smoke with local snacks (*Jhuri bhaja*) served on a green *Saal* leaves.

There was no transportation to reach the village. I started walking and asking passers by about the village. This village was about half an hour of walking distance, there was no rickshaw except bullock carts for owners and it was the main means of transportation. When I was walking at the end of the village, a passerby asked me to stop as there was river ahead. I told him about our staffs who have reached earlier in this village. He took me to them, who were sitting around a Cowshed neatly cleaned and my colleagues have left for survey.

3. BAJBERIA: A VILLAGE OF HUNGER AND STARVATION

This village is in Bhagabanpur Block of Midnapore (now East Midnapore). From Howrah station, I board a Kharagpur bound local train and reached Kolaghat station and took a bus that will terminate its journey in the bank of river Haldi. I have to cross the river for another bus starting from opposite side. Haldi River was not completed as it was leaning in one side. The ferry service was stopped for Tide and had to wait till flood returns. They river became full of water and I crossed the river by boat. I was asking for a ticket, the boatman ordered to keep coins in the earthen pot lying on the bank. I asked the rate, the boatman replied five *Paise* or ten *Paise*.For five *Paisa* you have to enter in the mud and for ten Paise, some bricks were laid to cross by wearing shoes. After crossing, I board the Digha bound bus and get down after half an hour in Bajeberia, before the Bajkul bus stop. After completion of the bridge, now this road became Kolkata - Digha National Highway.

When I reached the village, it was around 3 p.m. in the afternoon. As I entered the village, I saw all dilapidated thatched rooms with half covered straw roofs; women wearing torn cloths, cattle with visible bones, under nourished village children. The children were bare footed, no clothing on upper body only a small pants in the middle. The sketches in History books on "*Chhiyattere er Manantar*" (Famine of 1176 Bangabda), became living in mind. The representation of poverty in this village was very shocking. The male adults used to go to Hooghly and Howrah for begging. Lack of irrigation facility makes this area of single crop and paddy is cultivated only in rainy season. The agricultural practice was different, as paddy was only to be sown not transplanted because of water level crossed over head in the rainy season. While we were in this village, we never ate fish, only vegetables with rice, as we have to feed 10 to 20 outsiders, who gathered before our meal. One of the village helpers were engaged in data collection job in the village. Later on, he was employed for data entry job at Joka. In this village, I surveyed a person, who makes money double. He used to come to Calcutta for exchanging the soil notes at RBI counter and returned with fresh currency notes. He has never blackmail any poor, while his target was Marwari's in Calcutta.

By hearing the miserable condition of this village, where fifty percent household lives on begging in the East – Hooghly and Burdwan. These beggars moved from door-to-door by chanting *Kirtan* or their miserable condition in floods every year. After 20 years, an NGO, was interested about this village and approached Prof. Chandra. We handed over all the village schedules to them.The re-surveyed this village to gauge the Socio-Economic Changes occurred during first 20 years of Left Front Government in West Bengal. They observed some positive changes in this village, as some deep tube wells have already been dug for irrigation. The begging practice reduced due to implementation of "Food For Work".

4. KASHIPUR: A VILLAGE WITH SCARCITY OF WATER AND LEPROSY PATIENTS

This village was in Khatra Block of Bankura district on the elevation of 90 meters and five kilometres from Khatra Town. The river Kangsabati flows on the one side of the village and remain full of sand and no water in summer. A reserved forest was being maintained by the State Government. This is a middle sized village with population of about 500, about one-fourth of them belong to SC and ST community but literacy rate was high. As in other villages, agriculture was the principal occupation and there exist the predominance of landless agricultural labours. Goatary is in practice, not only by the poor, but also by large farmers. Most households have folk of goats which graze on the foothills of small hills (tilas). A Professor of n Purulia College residing in this village had more than 100 goats. Agricultural labourers complained that the farmers gave broken rice as wages paid in kind, while cash payment was meagre. For drinking water, dug well and tube well was rare. There was scarcity of bathing water, as the village had only one pond, where all villagers including Leprosy patients also used this pond. When I seek another alternative, the village helper took me to the river, which has no water only sand beds. He dug a small hole of one foot deep and water started infiltration. The hole became full of water and I pour the water on my head.

To reach this village, I board the Howrah-Gomo Passenger at Howrah around 11 a.m. I reached Bankura station around 3 p.m. and approached to bus stand to board Khatra bound bus. I got down at Khatra town around 5 p.m. Then I took a Rickshaw to reach Kasipur village, but the rickshaw puller took me to another village. I returned to Khatra Block Office in the evening and asked for a shelter. The BDO was a young chap just joined from Calcutta. He suggested taking shelter in his office. The caretaker arranged my bed by connecting some large office tables under a fan. In the next morning, I found the same Rickshaw puller standing. I told him to go Kasipur village after consulting other rickshaw pullers for actual route. Finally, I reached Kasipur and found *Atul babu* working in a household.

5. PATIHAL: A VILLAGE WITH OLD COTTAGE INDUSTRIES: HANDLOOM AND LOCK

This village was in Amta Block of Howrah district, on the bank of river Kana Damodar, a tributary of Damodar river. This village is in flood prone area and altitude was just 6 meters from Mean Sea Level. This village was close to the village Gohalpota, where shooting of half a dozen of Bengali cinema starring Uttam Kumar was done fifty years ago. It was a populous village consists of a large population of more than 10,000. I went to the village by boarding Amta bound bus from Howrah station. The bus crossed Bankra, Dasnagar, Jhapardah, Domjure, Bargachia, Patihal rout. Sometimes I returned by Haripal bound bus starting from Bargachia. It crossed Jangipara, Dwarhatta, Gajar More and reached Haripal station, where from I boarded local train and get down at Kamarkundu.

The communication of this village was only through the private buses on Howrah-Amta route, as the narrow gage Howrah-Amta Martin Railway services has been closed. When we were surveying this village, the construction of broad-gauge rail was in planning stage. Later it started operation after ten years by originating from Santragachi station. This village was dependent not on agriculture but on household industries. Weaving of cheap *sarees* was popular along with the Lock and Key industry. The main market of these *sarees* was the *Mangala Hat* (Tuesday Market) near Howrah station. The Lock and Key of this village was very popular at all India level. These Lock and Key can compete with those of Aligarh in Uttar Pradesh. Both of the workers in weaving and Lock and Key industries were exploited by p*haria* (middleman), who sold these products in urban market.

By observing the extent of exploitation in Hand loom weaving, *Atul babu* formed two Cooperatives – one for weavers and other for Lock and Key industry workers. Initially, he collected donation from us and from some of our Professors. These Cooperatives ran for about two years. Later on, *Atul babu* arranged about one Lakh Rupees from the Cooperative Department of the State Government.The state official harassed him as usual, as he would not bribed them. Finally, after a couple of months, he as a Chairman of this Co-operative had obtained the cash in instalments. He constructed two asbestos roofed shed for two cooperative and purchased huge cotton thread from Calcutta for weaving *sarees*. For Lock and Key industry, he procured a large sheet of brass plate.In the morning, the workers joined at the shed and started working. The finished products are brought to Calcutta by the member of the societies. The *pharias* were angry, as they were not getting products for marketing. *Atul babu* started marketing of sarees in our office too. Those *sarees* were cheaper than market price. I have to go to their Cooperatives for checking the Files and Accounts book.

6. CHECHERA: A PROSPEROUS RICE PRODUCING VILLAGE

This village was in West Dinajpur (now Dakshin Dinajpur since 1992) district on the boarder of Bangladesh. The village is situated at the elevation of 30 meters from Mean Sea Level and 15 kilometres away from the CD Block Tapan and 30 kilometres from district town Balurghat. This village was of large size having more than 4000 population of which 20% were SC and 7% were ST. Agriculture is the main occupation of this village and Paddy was the principal crop. During our survey, we attended a village fair on the bank of Punarbhaba. Sitting on a bullock cart for about an hour, we reached the fair ground. There many shops selling local made Curds (*doi*) in soil jars (*Kalasi*) and platted rice (*Chira*). There were hundreds of Jackfruits, large and small, for sale. The villagers took bath in the river, then purchased Chira and Doi for meal. We consumed the same and returned from the fair.

Close to this village, there were some archaeological items lying here and there. The Government has placed only a sign board, but no initiative to preserve the site. Kajal Dighi and Dhabal Dighi are two large pre-historic lakes, named after Dark and Fair looked Queens. The Archaeological site BANGARH has numerous specimens of Maurya – Shunga - Kushan and Gupta periods.Bangarh has 2400 year old history. The excavation of this site has been started by the ArchaeologicalSurvey. Bangarh is also referred to as Devikota for millions of years. It is one of the most important ancient sites in North Bengal.

The city was protected by a fortified wall inside a deep moat. The walls of the fort were eight feet higher than the height of the city and there were eight guard camps at the entrance. Attached to the moat was a huge tank and the lake was connected to the river *Punarbhaba*. When the water level in the trench decreased, water was supplied from the tank, and the river was connected to the canal so that the water in the tank did not decrease. There was also an improved sewerage system, which is proof of a modern city. According to the archaeologists, Bangarh covered an area of 1,200 acres, of which 141 acres are forts area. Bangarh is one of the leading Ancient and

Early-Medieval City in Eastern India. Now,the ruined City is located at half mile to the north of GangarampurMunicipality. Now, there are several blogs on touring the Bangarh in the Social Medias. The day I returned from this village on a bicycle to reach nearest bus stand, he showed me the ancient birth place of Mr. Shibaram Chakroborty, a comic story writer living in a Mess in College Street. I reached Balurghat bus stand around 2 p.m., while the Calcutta bus will start at 6 p.m.I have nothing to do, as there was no train service from Balurghat at that time. The bus reached Calcutta at 10 a.m. after thoroughly and lengthy checking at Check Posts in Maldah and Barasat.

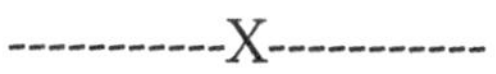

-----------X-----------

NOTES AND REFERENCES

SECTION - I

CHAPTER: 1.1

B B C (2005): On This Day: 13 January 1964. www.news.bbc.co,uk/onthisday/news/id..html

Balkrishnan A. (2012): Thought Leadership in IIM Calcutta, The 47th Annual Convocation Address of Indian Institute of Management Calcutta, 2012

Basu S. P.: West Bengal Food Movements: www.merg.ac.in

Chandy K T (2007): The Foundation Day Lecture delivered in IIMC Campus.

Das S. and Bandopadhyay P. (Ed.) (1999: Food Movement in 1959, K.P.Bagchi and Co.

Dogra Deepak (2010): Dayal an Eduprenure, Ane Books Pvt. Ltd. New Delhi.

IIMC Convocation (2012): The 47th Annual Convocation.

Indian Eagle, Travel Beats: Political Unrest in West Bengal during Mid-1960s.

MBAUniverse (2016): IIM Journey, the memory lane/June25 2016,www.mbaunverse.com/

Mitra A. (1960): Calcutta Letters: Mass Food Agitation, Economic Weekly April 2.

Nangia V K (Ed.) (2014): Masters Speak: Management Education in India, Bloomsbury Publications, New Delhi. Articles by Profs. Abad Ahmed of Delhi University and our Ex-Professor Iswar Dayal, who served the Institute for 1964-1968 and joined IIMA.

Samaddar R. (2018): Student Radicalism in Kolkata in the Sixties, February http://doi.org/10.1017/six_2018.288

Sancheti Neelu. (1986): Educational Dependency: An Indian Case Study in Comparative Perspective: The Ph D Thesis submitted to the Department of Comparative Education, University of London, Institute of Education http://discovery.ucl.ac.uk/id/eprint/..574.pdf

REPORTS

Hill R and Ensminger Reports (1957)

Indian Management Education Study Team (1959): Report of a Visit to the USA, Ministry of Scientific Research and Cultural Affairs, Government of India.

Meriam-Thurlby (1957): Recommendation for an All India Institute of Management Studies, Ford Foundation, New York, USA.

Robbins G (1959): Recommendation for an All India Institute of Management Studies, Ford Foundation, New York, USA.

CHAPTER: 1.2

Alagh Y K (2018): Marx and Us, The Indian Express (2018), May 21.

Bhattacharya Amit (2018): Spring Thunder and Kolkata: An Epic Story of Courage and Sacrifice (1965-1972).: Setu Prakashan, Kolkata.

Chowdhury Kamala (2000): Cited in Sancheti, 1986.

De Barun (2005): The History of Kolkata Port and The Hooghly River and Its Future, 2nd KoPT Anniversary Lecture on 135 Birth Anniversary of the Port Trust. 17 October.

Economic and Political Weekly (1977): 'Law and Order Killings' Kalyan Chaudhuri, July 16.

Goonaratne Mudliver E R. (2009) The Emerald Bower of Rajah of Tagore: The Complete Opinions, Forum, 28 Junewww.vijayvanni.com

Connection IIMC (2012): Balkrishna Ajit: Alumni (1969-71), Chairman (2002-2011).

Connection IIMC (2011): Roy Sudas, Alumni (1964-66) and Professor.

India Today (1990): Placements and Salaries of MBAs in 1970s and 1990s, 1 March.

Nangia V K (Ed.) (2014): As cited in Chapter 1.

Samaddar R. (2017): 50 Years of Naxalbari, The WIRE, 6th March.

Samaddar R. (2019): Student Radicalism in Kolkata in the Sixties, Cambridge Core, February http://.doi.org/10.1017/six-2018.288

Sancheti Neelu (1986): Ibid.

Sinha D. P (2004): Management Education in India, ICFAI Books, Hyderabad.

Sinha D. P: (2007) Learning From Life, Excel Books India, 2007. In this autobiography, he mentioned his IIMC Days (pp.105-142).

Times of India (2018): Kolkata Colleges: That Have Kept Their Heritage Alive, May 27. www.timesofindia.indiatimes.com/lifestyle/spotlight/Kolkatacolleges

Times of India (2002): Cossipore Massacre in 1970s,May 6, The Telegraph online (2002): Our Reading Angels: 19 march

The WIRE (2020): Why Mamata is sitting on Reports: Snigdhendu Bhattacharya, 13 August.

CHAPTER: 1. 3

CPIM website (2007): Thirty Years of the Left Front Government in West Bengal, 17 June.

De N R and Srivastava S (1967): Gheraos in West Bengal, I – IV: A Study in Industrial Conflicts, EPW, Vol II, Nos: 45 – 48, November – December, Forum (2007): The Indian Forum: How Not Fight Monopolies www.theindianforum/articles/how_not_fight_monopolies.pdf

Ghosh S and Ghosh P S: (2007) New Record of Birds from Kolkata Metropolitan Area and Its Environs, UGC Sponsored Project to Study in six Areas including IIM Calcutta Campus, Available at Rec.Zool.Surv.India: 107 (Part 4), 17-25, 2007.

Kohli Atul (1991): Democracy and Discontents: India's Growing Crisis in Governability, Cambridge University Press.

Mayer James (2001): Economic Reforms and the Rural Urban Divide: Political Realignment inWest Bengal, 1977-2000, Journal OF South Asian Studies, Vol -XXIV, No 1, https://doi.org/10.1080/00856400108723422

Nagar Parul (2017): IIM Calcutta: Life Beyond Placements

Nanda G L (1981): Report and Recommendations of the Review Committee for Indian

Institutes of Management (A, B & C) and Promotion and Developmentof Management Education.

Raj Bhavan (2006): Occasional Paper no. 3: Governor, Anthony Lancelot Dias. www.rajbhavankolkata.gov.in/writereaddata/PDF/occationalpaper-3

Sharma B R (1972): What Makes Managers: Merit, Motivation or Money?: Economic and Political Weekly, No 7 (22), pp. M51-M56

Sancheti Neelu (1986): Ibid.

CHAPTER 1.4

IIMC website: www.iimcal.ac.in/programme/doctoral/doctoral-dissertation

Kurien V (1992): Report of IIM Review Committee

Rmaswamy V (2011): It Does not Dies – Urban protest in Kolkata, 1987-2007. An interview with Ranabir Samaddar: South Asian Multi-Disciplinary Academic Journal, No. 5 http://journalsopeneditions.org/samaj/3230

Tilak J B G (2012): Higher Education Policies in India in Transition: EPW, March 31.

CHAPTER 1.5

IIM Calcutta, Academic Diary: 2004-2005

IIM Calcutta, Annual Report (2013-14)

IIMC website: www.iimcal.ac.in/programme/doctoral/doctoral-dissertation

CHAPTER 1.6:

Balkrishnan A (2007): The Annual Convocation Address, IIM Calcutta,

Business Today (2008), https://www.businesstoday.in/magazine/issue/july132008/story

This story based on an interview with Prof. B P Abraham, Chairman of PGPEX.

Chaudhury Sekhar: Management is not an esoteric discipline; An Interview with the Director, published in Business Standard, Kolkata, May 12, 2011.

Christopher Charles (2014): Description of Design of IIMC, Campus Development

http//worldarchotectures.org/Indian-institute-of-managementcalcutta/projectpages

Economic Times (2006): IIMC and MIT Collaborations, Calcutta, July 24,

Economic Times (2019): IIMC Satellite Campus 24.12.2019

IIM Calcutta, Annual Reports, 2015-16,www.iimcal.ac.in/annual-report-2015-16

Success2019.:http://www.sucesscds.net

Singha Akshoy (2006): "Changes in IIMC Governance during 2004 and 2005",

IIM Calcutta, (Unpublished)

CHAPTER 1.7

Das Riddhiman (2014-15 batches): Life Beyond IIM Calcutta Campus:

Economic Discussions:

www.economicdiscussion.net/essays/essay_on_the_the_monopoly_and_

Hindustan Times (2016): Global accreditations give IIM Calcutta an edge over others, April,

IIMC Sandesh (2015): Internal Newsletter for IIMC: Global Management Ranking

IIMC (2016): IIM Calcutta Acquires EQUIS Accreditation - Becomes India's First TRIPLE CROWN Business School.

IIMC (201?): IIM Calcutta Awarded Coveted AACSB Accreditation, The Hallmark of Excellence in Business Education

IIMC Wikipedia (2022): Ranking and Accreditation of IIM Calcutta.

Jagran Josh (2021): IIM Calcutta Ranking 2021, Apr 5,

Nanda G L (1981): Report and Recommendation of the Review Committee for IIM ABC and Promotion and Development of Management Education, Govt. of India.

The Business Standard (2022): India's B-schools fall in FT Global MBA ranking, Feb. 18.

The Economic Times (2015): IIM Calcutta becomes country's first IIM to receive AACSB accreditation,

The Economic Times (2016): IIMC wins EQUIS accreditation: First B-school in India to bag "Triple Crown."

WEBSITES:

https://www.business-standard.com/article/management/iim-calcutta-ties-up-with-cems-for- global-expansion-112111500596_1.html

www.iimcal.ac.in/iim-calcutta-awarded--coveted-AACSB-accreditation-hallmark-of-excellence-in-business-education

https://www.hindustantimes.com/education/iimc-collaborating-with-the-best/story-ioz1fptm3AoHzimofctqVK.html

https://www.business-standard.com/article/current-affairs/iim-calcutta-climbs-5-places-in- ft-masters-in-management-rankings-2018-118091200977_1.html

https://economictimes.indiatimes.com/industry/services/education/iim-calcutta-2nd-in-asia-in- financial-times-rankings/articleshow/78361230.cms

https://timesofindia.indiatimes.com/home/education/news/iim-c-number-2-b-school-in- country-ft-ranking-of-mim-globally/articleshow/65805661.cms

CHAPTER 1.8

Economic Times (2011): IIMC may reduce tuition fee, Views expressed by Director of IIMC November 15, 2011

Frontlines (2004): IIMs Fee Structure, Vol.21, Issue 6, March 2004

IIMC Annual Reports: 1979-80 onwards

Indeed (2020): New Employee Woes in IIMC http//:www.indeed.co.in

Soni S and Ganesaraman K (2021): IIM Fee Hike: What Arethe Consequence, Down to Earth, March 4.

The Economic Times, (2016): Fee Hike Justified, say Chairman and Alumni, Views of Balkrishan A, April 19,

Times of India (2014): IIMC increase tuition fee by 20%, Views expressed by Chairman and Director of IIMC April 6,

SECTION - II

CHAPTER 2.1

Benu Parvathi (2019): Women Have Been Under Represented inIIMs

http://www.edexlive.com/author=Parvati-Benu

Gupta Nidhi (2018): Reservations in IIMs, Sept. 27, Jagaranjosh

http://www.jagaranjosh.com/article/reservation-in-iims-all-you-need-to-know-1486727009

Group 2006, Final Report of Group for Management Institutes on Implementation ofOBC: http://nitigov.in/planningcommission/gov.in/docs/group/researvationpolicy.pdf

IIMC Annual Report: 2013-2014

IIMC Website, 2015

Mohanty B S (2019): IIM Experiment for Women, August 29

www.telegrphindia.com/iim-cut-of-experiment-for-women/cid/1701256

Mohanty M. (2006): Social Inequality, Labour Market Dynamics and Reservation, Economic and Political Weekly, Sept.2

Singh Rahul (200?): Reservation in IIMs, CATking May 05, https://catking.in/tag/exam-strategy

Sanchetti N (1986) :Ibid

CHAPTER 2.2

Hindustan Times: IIMs oppose Govt. over quota in faculty, say it will hurt quality - By Brajesh Kumar New Delhi May 01, 2016

In Defence of Reservation for Faculty members in IIMs

www.telegraphindia.com/india/faculty_reservation_order_to_iims/cid/1720266

Mohan Archana &Nichenametla Prasad: February 5, 2013

https://swarajyamag.com/insta/iim-calcutta-to-increase-seats-in-mba-programme from-2019-session-to-facilitate-rolling-out-of-ews-quota

Prerona Datta:Content Curator| January 18th, 2023

Press Trust of IndiaNovember 16, 2021

Phadnis A and Singh P (2006): Indian reservation policy - a study of its effects in IIMB

http://repository.iimb.ac.in/handle/123456789/4108

Special Correspondent (2019): The Telegraph, November19, New Delhi

Thakur M and Babu R (2017): IIMs and Reservations, EPW, April 1

The Mint (2008): Aniek Paul and Aparna Kalra: HC stays OBC quota IIM Calcutta, May 15

http://www.livemint.com/Search/link/Author/Aviek-Paul-And-Aparna-kalra

The Economic Times (2008): Admission process back to square one,

IIMs wait for MHRD Boss

The Economic Times (2007): No funds for quota rollout: IITs, IIMs,

Group (2008): Final Report of the Group for Management Institutions

http://nitigov.in/planning-comission/gov.in/docs/govrep/repeddu.pdf

The Financial Express (2008): The SC/ST IIM grads earn 15-22% less than general category:

September 13, http://www.finacialexpress.com/Archives

The Times of India (2019): IIM-Calcutta hikes seats to start EWS quota, May 1

https://www.opindia.com/2019/01/10-seat-in-educational-institutions-to-be- increased-to-accommodate-the-reservation-for-economically-weaker-section/

The Central Educational Institutions (Reservation in Admission) Act, 2006, May 20

http://in.rediff.com/money/2006/may/20iim.htm,

The Print: Kriritika Sharma:22 November, 2019 **New Delhi:**

The wire (2018): IIM Ahmadabad Rejects Gujarat High Court's Request for a Reservation in the PhD Program, Jan 17, The WIRE, New Delhi

Wagde Anil (2019): Widening the Catchment Areas Will Improve Results: In Defense of Reservation for Faculty in IIMs. November 30. (He was the main petitioner in a High Court Case against IIMA for failing to implement reservation in faculty and PhD position. He is an alumnus of IIMC and now based in Chicago.) www.news18.com/news/opinion/widening-the-cathment-areas-will-improve-results

Zee News (2004): IIMC resolution to abide by Calcutta HC decision, May 12

CHAPTER 2.3

IIMC Annual Report: 2013-2014

Lype George (2004): What will the fees at the IIMs now be? July 13

Ray Joydeep (2013): IIMA Moves Supreme Court Against Fee Cut, February 6.

Sastry Trilochan (2004): Fee Reduction Has Paralysed IIMs, February 11.

www//rediff.com/fee-reduction-has-paralysed-iims

Shrivastava V (2018): IIMs do not want government say in fee structure, Jun 21 https://www.shiksha.com/news/iims-do-not-want-government-say-in-fee-structure-

Thakore Dilip (2004): Outrage! Joshi's IIM-Grab Angers Middle Class India,

Education World, March

Zee news (2004): IIM Calcutta Moves SC Against Fee Cut, Kolkata, Apr 13

https://zeenews.india.com/news/nation/iim-calcutta-moves-sc-against-fee-cut_154166.html

Zee news (2004): IIMC resolution to abide by Calcutta HC decision, May 12

NOTES:

[1]Mr. Murthy is the chairman of the Infosys Technologies and also Chairman of IIMA

[2]Mr. Rao is the Chairman of MphasiS Ltd.

CHAPTER 2.4

Agha Eram (2020): IIM Calcutta Teachers Write to Govt. against Director, Seek Intervention to Help Arrest Decline, News18.com, December 9, new Delhi

Bhargava R (2011): Government as an owner of IIMs is not equipped to discharge, Sep. 04

Chopra Ritika (2021):At IIM Calcutta, its teachers versus Director over her powers,The Indian Express, New Delhi, January 26,

. http://theindianexpress.com/profle/author/ritika-chopra/

ChowdhurySubhankar (2021): IIM Calcutta issues code of conduct for teachers and officials, August 20, The Telegraph

Centre's Bid To Attain Greater Control,Dec 8.

https://thelogicalindian.com/trending/heads-of-iims-stand-against-centres-proposal-to-have-greater-control-over-institutions-25291

Deccan Herald (2021): IIM's code, a retrograde step, April 28

https://www.deccanherald.com/opinion/second-edit/iim-s-code-a- retrograde-step-979688.html

Kini R G (2015) Don't Do This To The IIMs, Jun 29

https://swarajyamag.com/politics/dont-do-this-to-the-iims

Madaik Devyani (2020): Attempt of Reversal Of Powers': Directors Of IIMs Criticise

NambiarPranav (2021): IIM Calcutta Experiences A Power Strife

https://edumate.tv/iim-calcutta-experiences-a-power-strife/5562/

Roy Suryagni (2021): Two days after sick leave, first woman director of IIMC resigns amid conflict with board, Kolkata, March 22

The Financial Express (2021):Academic Freedom Critical: IIM-C's Board Has Done a Disservice to the Institution, April 15.

https://www.financialexpress.com/opinion/academic-freedom-critical-iim-cs-board- has-done-a-disservice-to-the-institution/2233265/

The Indian Express (2021): IIM-Calcutta Faculty Face New Code of Conduct, April 12,

https://indianexpress.com/article/education/iim-calcutta-faculty-face-new-code-of-conduct-

Wikipedia: TheIndian Institute of Management Act, 2017

Yadav Ritu (2021): IIM-Calcutta Director Quits Year Before Her Term Ends Over

Conflict With Board, The Logical Indian Crew, Kolkata, March 22.

SECTION - III

CHAPTER 3.1

Uberoi Chanchal (2009): Down the Memory Lane, IISc Alumni Association

V. S. Chand and T V Rao (Edited) (2011): Nurturing Instructional Excellence, Indian Institutes of Management. New Delhi, Macmillan.

CHAPTER 3.2

Chattopadhayay Gouranga (2008): The Journey Continues (book)

http://WritersWorkshopIndia.com

Mukherjee Chandan and Others (2020): N Krishanji: An Excellent Teacher and Principled Intellectual, EPW, COMMENTARY, http://nkrishnaji.webnode.com

CHAPTER 3.4

Bagchi Amiya (2014): Obituary: Nirmal Chandra: www.insafbulletin.net/archive/2264>

Chandra Nirmal K (1988): The Retarded Economies; Foreign Commination and Class Relations in India and other Emerging Nations, Oxford University Press for Sameeksha Trust, 1988.

Chandra Nimal K (1979): Monopoly Capital, Private Corporate Sector and the Indian Economy, 1931-1976", EPW, Special Number, August.

D'Mello Bernard: ON NAXALBARI: A book dedicated to Nirmal Chandra

D'Mello Bernard (20014): In Shared Sorrow: Remembering 'Comrade' Nirmal da.: Analytical Monthly Review, Kharagpur, W.B. May

IIMC website: N K C Memorial Lecture, October 2020

Khanna Sushil and Mohanty Mritunjoy (2014): Obituary: Nirmal Chandra

www.insafbulletin.net/archive/2264>

Mitra Ashok (2014): The Complete Economist" *The Telegraph*, April 4.

Pattnaik Prabhat (2014): Nirmal Kumar Chandra, (An obituary).

www.networkideas.org>news>apr-2014>nirmal-kumar.pdf

CHAPTER 3.7

Barman K C (2020): BANGARH, Archaeological Sites of Dakshin Dinajpur District.

Palarch's Journal of Archaeology, Vol. – 17, No. 12

http://archives.palarch.ni/indo-php/JAC/article/wikis/6545/6367

LIST OF TABLES, EXHIBITS AND FIGURES

SECTION – I

Table 1.2.1: Enrollment of Total and Women Students in PGP by Years

Batches	Year	Total Students	Women Students	Batches	Year	Total Students	Women Students
1	1964	39	2	26	1989	105	9
2	1965	70	3	27	1990	105	10
3	1966	80	2	28	1991	105	10
4	1967	80	2	29	1992	148	15
5	1968	90	3	30	1993	150	12
6	1969	90	3	31	1994	150	15
7	1970	100	3	32	1995	150	14
8	1971	80	2	33	1996	148	15
9	1972	100	2	34	1997	263	20
10	1973	90	2	35	1998	260	20
11	1974	100	3	36	1999	270	20
12	1975	90	3	37	2000	272	20
13	1976	90	6	38	2001	265	20
14	1977	120	6	39	2002	256	25
15	1978	102	6	40	2003	256	25
16	1979	128	6	41	2004	261	20
17	1980	90	6	42	2005	259	25
18	1981	123	9	43	2006	322	30
19	1982	100	6	44	2007	280	25
20	1983	105	5	45	2008	278	25
21	1984	100	6	46	2009	383	35
22	1985	105	9	47	2010	362	43
23	1986	105	9	48	2011	350	33
24	1987	105	9	49	2012	404	51
25	1988	105	9	50	2013	462	107

Data are estimated till 24th batch while 25th batch onward are actual Annual Reports IIMC

Table 1.2.2: Year-wise Total Fees for Two Years in PGP

(In Rupees)

Batches	Year	Total Fees		Batches	Year	Total Fees
1	1964	1090		26	1989	5460
2	1965	1090		27	1990	5460
3	1966	1290		28	1991	5460
4	1967	1290		29	1992	25150
5	1968	1550		30	1993	35750
6	1969	1550		31	1994	51250
7	1970	1800		32	1995	82000
8	1971	1800		33	1996	92000
9	1972	2100		34	1997	103000
10	1973	2100		35	1998	156500
11	1974	2350		36	1999	167500
12	1975	2350		37	2000	207000
13	1976	2700		38	2001	225200
14	1977	2700		39	2002	254200
15	1978	3100		40	2003	254200
16	1979	3100		41	2004	254200
17	1980	3400		42	2005	302000
18	1981	3400		43	2006	351000
19	1982	3650		44	2007	400000
20	1983	3650		45	2008	610000
21	1984	3650		46	2009	906000
22	1985	3910		47	2010	1350000
23	1986	3910		48	2011	1350000
24	1987	3910		49	2012	1356000
25	1988	4910		50	2013	1356000

Data are estimated till 24th batch while 25th batch onward are actual Annual Reports IIMC

Table 1.2.3: Total and Women Fellowship Awardees by Years

Batches	Year	Total FP Awardees	Women FP Awardees		Batches	Year	Total FP Awardees	Women FP Awardees
1	1975	1	0		21	1995	1	0
2	1976	5	1		22	1996	3	0
3	1977	4	0		23	1997	1	0
4	1978	1	0		24	1998	4	0
5	1979	1	0		25	1999	3	0
6	1980	2	0		26	2000	3	2
7	1981	0	0		27	2001	3	0
8	1982	1	0		28	2002	6	2
9	1983	6	0		29	2003	4	0
10	1984	3	0		30	2004	3	2
11	1985	4	0		31	2005	5	1
12	1986	4	1		32	2006	10	1
13	1987	4	0		33	2007	10	1
14	1988	3	0		34	2008	10	2
15	1989	4	0		35	2009	7	3
16	1990	2	0		36	2010	7	0
17	1991	1	0		37	2011	5	0
18	1992	1	0		38	2012	10	3
19	1993	1	0		39	2013	9	2
20	1994	2	0		40	2014	7	1

Source: www.iimcal.ac.in/programme/doctorl/doctoral-dissertations

Table 1.7.1: Global Ranking of IIM Calcutta

Agencies	2012	2013	2014	2015	2017	2018	2019	2020	2021	2022
FT: MBA Global					95	78	49	42	44	56
FT: MM: Global		19	13	16	28	23	17	21		
FT: MM: Asian						3	2	2	2	
FT: MM: Indian						2	1	2	2	
QS: MBA Global						94			79	76
QS: MBA Asian								12	12	14
QS: WUR MBA.						94				76
QS: WUR: MIM					46					
CEMS:MIM Global	3	7	5	4						

QS: Quacquarelli Symonds based in London, MM: Master in Management,
CEMS: Global Alliance in Mgmt. Education MIM: Master in Intl. Mgmt.
WUR: World University Ranking

Table 1.7.2: Indian Ranking of IIM Calcutta

Agencies	2016	2017	2018	2019	2020	2021	2022
NIRF*	3	3	3	3	3	3	
Business Today		3		2	2	1	2
Outlook India					3	3	3
Jagran Josh					3		
India Today						1	
Shiksha						3	

*NIRF: National Institutional Framework Ranking by MHRD

Exhibit 1.8.A: Different Programs Introduced in the Institute (Chronologically)

Year	Serial No. and Name of the Program	Type	Duration	Intake
1961	1. Advanced Management Program (AMP)	NR	3 - 5 days	30 to 40*
1964	2. Post Graduate Program in Management (PGDM)	R	2 years	40@
	3. Executive Development Program (EDP)	NR	3 -5 days	30 to 40*
	4. In-Company Training	NR	10 -15 days	30 to 40@
	5. Consultancy	NR	10 -15 days	30 to 40@
1971	6. Fellowship Prograam in Management (FPM)	R	3 - 5 years	1 to 3@
1981	7. Certificate in General Management (CGM)	NR	2 years/ Evening	30 to 40*
1992	8. PGP in Computer Aided Management (PGDCM)	R	2 years	50@
1994	9. Post Graduate Diploma in Business Management (PGDBM) by replacing CGM (Serial No. 7)	NR	3 years/ Evening	40@
2007	10. Post Graduate Program for Executives (PGP-Ex)	R	One year	40 @
	11. Post Graduate Program for Executives in VisionaryLeadership in Management (PGPEX-VLM)	R	One year	40@
2008	12. Long Duration Program (LDP)	NR	1 year	20to 200@
2015	13. Post Graduate Diploma in Business Analytic(PGDBA) by replacing PGDCM (Serial No. 8)	R	2 years	50@

Note: R indicates residential while NR indicate non-residential
@ indicates intake per annum while * indicates intake per batch
The Programs that are not running were - the AMP, CGM and PGDCM.

Table 1.8.1: Year-wise Enrolment of Total, PGDM, PGDCM and Female Students

Batch	Years	Total	PGDM	PGDCM	Women (Nos.)	Women (%)
1	1964-66	39	39	0	2	5.13
2	1965-67	70	70	0	3	4.29
3	1966-68	80	80	0	2	2.50
4	1967-69	80	80	0	2	2.50
5	1968-70	90	90	0	3	3.33
6	1969-71	90	90	0	3	3.33
7	1970-72	100	100	0	3	3.00
8	1971-73	80	80	0	2	2.50
9	1972-74	100	100	0	2	2.00
10	1973-75	90	90	0	2	2.22
11	1974-76	100	100	0	3	3.00
12	1975-77	90	90	0	3	3.33
13	1976-78	90	90	0	6	6.67
14	1977-79	120	120	0	6	5.00
15	1978-80	102	102	0	6	5.88
16	1979-81	128	128	0	6	4.69
17	1980-82	90	90	0	6	6.67
18	1981-83	123	123	0	9	7.32
19	1982-84	100	100	0	6	6.00
20	1983-85	105	105	0	5	4.76
21	1984-86	100	100	0	6	6.00
22	1985-87	105	105	0	9	8.57
23	1986-88	105	105	0	9	8.57
24	1987-89	105	105	0	9	8.57
25	1988-90	105	105	0	9	8.57

Data are estimated till 24th batch while 25th batch onwards are actual as in Annual Reports IIMC

Continued ....

Table 1.8.1: Year-wise Enrolment of Total, PGDM, PGDCM and Female Students

Batch	Years	Total	PGDM	PGDCM	Women (Nos.)	Women (%)
26	1989-91	105	105	0	9	9.52
27	1990-92	105	105	0	10	9.52
28	1991-93	105	105	0	10	9.52
29	1992-94	148	105	43	15	10.14
30	1993-95	150	105	45	12	8.00
31	1994-96	150	100	50	15	10.00
32	1995-97	150	105	45	14	9.33
33	1996-98	148	105	43	15	10.14
34	1997-99	263	210	53	20	7.60
35	1998-00	260	210	50	20	7.69
36	1999-01	270	220	50	20	7.41
37	2000-02	272	220	52	20	7.35
38	2001-03	265	215	50	20	7.55
39	2002-04	256	206	50	25	9.77
40	2003-05	256	206	50	25	9.77
41	2004-06	261	210	51	20	7.66
42	2005-07	259	210	49	25	9.65
43	2006-08	322	270	52	30	9.32
44	2007-09	280	230	50	25	8.93
45	2008-10	278	226	52	25	8.99
46	2009-11	383	348	35	35	9.14
47	2010-12	362	309	53	43	11.86
48	2011-13	350	298	52	33	9.43
49	2012-14	404	353	51	51	12.62
50	2013-15	462	410	52	107	23.16

Note: PGDCM started in 1992 and discontinued in 2015

Data are estimated till 24th batch while 25th batch onwards are actual as in Annual Reports IIMC

Table 1.8.2: Enrollment of Total and Women Students in PGP by Decades

Period	Years	Duration (Years)	Total Student	Women Students	Women Students (%)	Growth# in Enrolment (%)
Decade 1	1964-1973	10	819	24	2.93	6.54
Decade 2	1974-1983	10	1048	56	5.34	1.28
Decade 3	1984-1993	10	1133	98	8.65	3.74
Decade 4	1994-2003	10	2290	194	8.47	7.29
Decade 5	2004-2013	10	3361	394	11.72	6.09
1st Half	1964-1988	25	2387	122	5.11	2.05
2nd Half	1989-2013	25	6264	644	10.28	5.69
Entire Period	1964-2013	50	8651	766	10.41	3.72

By fitting lognormal curve

Table 1.8.3: Total and Women Fellowship Awardees by Decades

Period	Years	Duration (Years)	Total FP Students	Women FP Students	Women FP (%)
Decade 1	1975-1984	10	24	1	4.17
Decade 2	1985-1994	10	26	1	3.85
Decade 3	1995-2004	10	31	6	19.35
Decade 4	2005-2014	10	80	14	17.50
First half	1975-1994	20	50	2	4.00
Second Half	1995-2014	20	111	20	18.02
Total Period	1975-2014	40	161	22	13.66

Source: www.iimcal.ac.in/programme/doctorl/doctoral-dissertations

Table 1.8.4: Fellowship Awardees by Groups in Different Decades

GROUPS	1975-1984	1985-1994	1995-2004	2005-2014	TOTAL
MIS	0	2	10	26	38
OPR+OPRSYS*	8	8+2	6+4	5+3	27+9
FIN & CON	7	5	2	11	25
OGBH	1	1	5	7	14
ECON	4	3	1	4	12
MKTG	3	2	1	4	10
STRATMG	0	0	0	8	8
RD	1	1	0	5	7
HRM	0	1	2	3	6
SOCIO& ORS	0	1	0	3+1	5
TOTAL	24	26	31	80	161

*OPRSYS is an allied group of OPR

Table 1.8.5: No. of Faculty Members by Groups in Different Decades

Groups	1974-75	1984-85	1995-96	2004-05	2014-15
OPR#	8	10	12	14	14
ECONOMICS	6	6	7	7	12
MIS	4	4	8	10	12
FIN & CONTROL	4	8	9	7	8
PPM*	3	6	8	7	9
BEHABIOURAL	3	9	6	5	8
MKTG	4	4	4	4	11
PMIR/HRM	6	3	4	4	5
STRATEGIC	0	0	2	1	8
ETHICS (MCHV)	0	0	0	1	5
Total	38	50	60	60	92

*PPM consist Sociology, Regn. Dev, Envir.etc. # OPR include Statistics & System Analysis

Table 1.8.6: Quinonal Faculty Members, Students and Student Teacher Ratios

Years	1964	1969	1974	1979	1984	1989	1994	1999	2004	2009	2013
Teachers	24	24	38	42	50	51	53	71	60	64	88
Students*	39	180	190	230	205	210	300	530	517	661	866
S/T Ratio	1.6	7.5	5.0	5.5	4.1	4.2	5.7	7.5	8.6	10.3	10.1

* Students of PGP I & II combined, but excludes PGPEX and PGPEX-VLM students

Table 1.8.7:Year-wise Total Fees at Current and Constant Prices

(In Rupees)

Batches	Year	Current Price	Constant Price		Batches	Year	Current Price	Constant Price
1	1964	1090	8059		26	1989	5460	6000
2	1965	1090	7398		27	1990	5460	5460
3	1966	1290	7818		28	1991	5460	4822
4	1967	1290	6904		29	1992	25150	19642
5	1968	1550	8296		30	1993	35750	26707
6	1969	1550	8065		31	1994	51250	34471
7	1970	1800	9016		32	1995	82000	49514
8	1971	1800	8821		33	1996	92000	51292
9	1972	2100	9542		34	1997	103000	54377
10	1973	2100	8053		35	1998	156500	71967
11	1974	2350	7037		36	1999	167500	74664
12	1975	2350	6755		37	2000	207000	87917
13	1976	2700	8468		38	2001	225200	91928
14	1977	2700	7740		39	2002	254200	99883
15	1978	3100	8753		40	2003	254200	95896
16	1979	3100	8178		41	2004	254200	92928
17	1980	3400	8038		42	2005	302000	106095
18	1981	3400	7085		43	2006	351000	115955
19	1982	3650	7113		44	2007	400000	124143
20	1983	3650	6285		45	2008	610000	174755
21	1984	3650	5813		46	2009	906000	231977
22	1985	3910	5922		47	2010	1350000	310706
23	1986	3910	5452		48	2011	1350000	286558
24	1987	3910	5031		49	2012	1356000	262036
25	1988	4910	5754		50	2013	1356000	236390

Source: Annual Reports, IIM Calcutta (Base 1990 =100)

Fees are estimated till 24th batch while 25th batch onwards are actual, Annual Reports IIMC

Table 1.8.8.A: Total Fees by Components (Upto 28th Batches)

(In Rupees)

Period	Batch	Admis	Tuition	Accom.	Cautio	Assoc	Cours	Comp	Total
1964-66*	1	100	200	240	100	50	400	0	1090
1965-67*	2	100	200	240	100	50	400	0	1090
1966-68*	3	100	300	240	100	50	500	0	1290
1967-69*	4	100	300	240	100	50	500	0	1290
1968-70*	5	100	400	300	100	50	600	0	1550
1969-71*	6	100	400	300	100	50	600	0	1550
1970-72*	7	100	400	400	100	100	700	0	1800
1971-73*	8	100	400	400	100	100	700	0	1800
1972-74*	9	100	400	600	100	100	800	0	2100
1973-75*	10	100	400	600	100	100	800	0	2100
1974-76*	11	100	400	800	150	100	800	0	2350
1975-77*	12	100	400	800	150	100	800	0	2350
1976-78*	13	100	600	900	200	100	800	0	2700
1977-79*	14	100	600	900	200	100	800	0	2700
1978-80*	15	100	800	1000	200	100	900	0	3100
1979-81*	16	100	800	1000	200	100	900	0	3100
1980-82*	17	100	1000	1000	200	100	1000	0	3400
1981-83*	18	100	1000	1000	200	100	1000	0	3400
1982-84*	19	100	1000	1000	250	100	1200	0	3650
1983-85*	20	100	1000	1000	250	100	1200	0	3650
1984-86*	21	100	1000	1000	250	100	1200	0	3650
1985-87*	22	100	1000	1200	250	160	1200	0	3910
1986-88*	23	100	1000	1200	250	160	1200	0	3910
1987-89*	24	100	1000	1200	250	160	1200	0	3910
1988-90	25	100	1000	1200	250	160	1200	1000	4910
1989-91	26	100	1000	1200	800	160	1200	1000	5460
1990-92	27	100	1000	1200	800	160	1200	1000	5460
1991-93	28	100	1000	1200	800	160	1200	1000	5460

Continued..........

Note: All fees are to be paid by two Annual Instalments till 28th batch.

Fees are estimated till 24th batch while 25th batch onwards are actual, Annual Reports: IIMC.

Admis.– Admission Fees Accomod. – Accommodation Charges,

Assoc.– Association Fees Course– Course Materials Charges

Comp.– Computer Charges Develop – Development Fees

Medical– Medical Insurance

Table 1.8.8.B: Total Fees by Components (29th Batches Onwards) (In Rupees)

Period	Batch	Admis	Tuition	Accom.	Caution	Assoc	Course	Comp.
1992-94	29	100	12000	1200	400	300	1200	2400
1993-95	30	500	15000	2400	400	300	2400	4800
1994-96	31	500	24000	4000	400	400	3000	9000
1995-97	32	1000	48000	10000	500	400	1200	10800
1996-98	33	1000	58000	10000	500	400	1200	10800
1997-99	34	2000	68000	10000	500	400	1200	10800
1998-00	35	8000	102000	12000	6000	1000	3000	14400
1999-01	36	0	120000	12000	6000	1000	3000	14400
2000-02	37	0	150000	12000	6000	500	7000	18000
2001-03	38	0	168000	12000	6000	500	7000	18000
2002-04	39	0	186000	12000	6000	500	18000	18000
2003-05	40	0	186000	12000	6000	500	18000	18000
2004-06	41	0	186000	12000	6000	500	18000	18000
2005-07	42	0	186000	18000	6000	600	24000	30000
2006-08	43	0	216000	18000	6000	600	30000	36000
2007-09	44	0	264000	18000	6000	600	30000	36000
2008-10	45	0	360000	24000	6000	600	72000	60000
2009-11	46	0	564000	27000	6000	1000	121500	81000
2010-12	47	0	852000	48000	6000	1000	204000	114000
2011-13	48	0	852000	48000	6000	1000	204000	114000
2012-14	49	0	852000	54000	0	1000	340000	0
2013-15	50	0	852000	54000	0	1000	340000	0

Period	Batch	Library	Alumni.	Medical	Develop	Total		
1992-94	29	7200	350	0	0	25150		
1993-95	30	9600	350	0	0	35750		
1994-96	31	9600	350	0	0	51250		
1995-97	32	9600	500	0	0	82000		
1996-98	33	9600	500	0	0	92000		
1997-99	34	9600	500	0	0	103000		
1998-00	35	9600	500	0	0	156500		
1999-01	36	9600	500	1000	0	167500		
2000-02	37	12000	500	1000	0	207000		
2001-03	38	12000	500	1200	0	225200		
2002-04	39	12000	500	1200	0	254200		
2003-05	40	12000	500	1200	0	254200		
2004-06	41	12000	500	1200	0	254200		
2005-07	42	30000	2200	1200	4000	302000		
2006-08	43	36000	2200	1200	5000	351000		
2007-09	44	36000	2200	1200	6000	400000		
2008-10	45	60000	800	1200	25400	610000		
2009-11	46	67500	800	1350	35850	906000		
2010-12	47	81000	1000	2000	47000	1356000		
2011-13	48	81000	1000	2000	47000	1356000		
2012-14	49	0	1000	2000	100000	1350000		
2013-15	50	0	1000	2000	100000	1350000		

Note: In 29th batch onwards, all fees are to be paid by six Instalments prior to each Semester.

Table 1.8.8.C: Share of Components in Total Fees (In Percent)

Period	Batch	Admis	Tuition	Accom.	Cautio	Assoc	Cours	Comp	Total
1964-66*	1	9.17	18.35	22.02	9.17	4.59	36.70		100.00
1965-67*	2	9.17	18.35	22.02	9.17	4.59	36.70		100.00
1966-68*	3	7.75	23.26	18.60	7.75	3.88	38.76		100.00
1967-69*	4	7.75	23.26	18.60	7.75	3.88	38.76		100.00
1968-70*	5	6.45	25.81	19.35	6.45	3.23	38.71		100.00
1969-71*	6	6.45	25.81	19.35	6.45	3.23	38.71		100.00
1970-72*	7	5.56	22.22	22.22	5.56	5.56	38.89		100.00
1971-73*	8	5.56	22.22	22.22	5.56	5.56	38.89		100.00
1972-74*	9	4.76	19.05	28.57	4.76	4.76	38.10		100.00
1973-75*	10	4.76	19.05	28.57	4.76	4.76	38.10		100.00
1974-76*	11	4.26	17.02	34.04	6.38	4.26	34.04		100.00
1975-77*	12	4.26	17.02	34.04	6.38	4.26	34.04		100.00
1976-78*	13	3.70	22.22	33.33	7.41	3.70	29.63		100.00
1977-79*	14	3.70	22.22	33.33	7.41	3.70	29.63		100.00
1978-80*	15	3.23	25.81	32.26	6.45	3.23	29.03		100.00
1979-81*	16	3.23	25.81	32.26	6.45	3.23	29.03		100.00
1980-82*	17	2.94	29.41	29.41	5.88	2.94	29.41		100.00
1981-83*	18	2.94	29.41	29.41	5.88	2.94	29.41		100.00
1982-84*	19	2.74	27.40	27.40	6.85	2.74	32.88		100.00
1983-85*	20	2.74	27.40	27.40	6.85	2.74	32.88		100.00
1984-86*	21	2.74	27.40	27.40	6.85	2.74	32.88		100.00
1985-87*	22	2.56	25.58	30.69	6.39	4.09	30.69		100.00
1986-88*	23	2.56	25.58	30.69	6.39	4.09	30.69		100.00
1987-89*	24	2.56	25.58	30.69	6.39	4.09	30.69		100.00
1988-90	25	2.04	20.37	24.44	5.09	3.26	24.44	20.37	100.00
1989-91	26	1.83	18.32	21.98	14.65	2.93	21.98	18.32	100.00
1990-92	27	1.83	18.32	21.98	14.65	2.93	21.98	18.32	100.00
1991-93	28	1.83	18.32	21.98	14.65	2.93	21.98	18.32	100.00

Based on Table- 1.8.8.A

Table 1.8.8.D: Share of Components in Total Fees(In Percent)

Period	Batch	Admis	Tuition	Accom.	Caution	Assoc	Course	Comp.
1992-94	29	0.40	47.71	4.77	1.59	1.19	4.77	9.54
1993-95	30	1.40	41.96	6.71	1.12	0.84	6.71	13.43
1994-96	31	0.98	46.83	7.80	0.78	0.78	5.85	17.56
1995-97	32	1.22	58.54	12.20	0.61	0.49	1.46	13.17
1996-98	33	1.09	63.04	10.87	0.54	0.43	1.30	11.74
1997-99	34	1.94	66.02	9.71	0.49	0.39	1.17	10.49
1998-00	35	5.11	65.18	7.67	3.83	0.64	1.92	9.20
1999-01	36	0.00	71.64	7.16	3.58	0.60	1.79	8.60
2000-02	37	0.00	72.46	5.80	2.90	0.24	3.38	8.70
2001-03	38	0.00	74.60	5.33	2.66	0.22	3.11	7.99
2002-04	39	0.00	73.17	4.72	2.36	0.20	7.08	7.08
2003-05	40	0.00	73.17	4.72	2.36	0.20	7.08	7.08
2004-06	41	0.00	73.17	4.72	2.36	0.20	7.08	7.08
2005-07	42	0.00	61.59	5.96	1.99	0.20	7.95	9.93
2006-08	43	0.00	61.54	5.13	1.71	0.17	8.55	10.26
2007-09	44	0.00	66.00	4.50	1.50	0.15	7.50	9.00
2008-10	45	0.00	59.02	3.93	0.98	0.10	11.80	9.84
2009-11	46	0.00	62.25	2.98	0.66	0.11	13.41	8.94
2010-12	47	0.00	62.83	3.54	0.44	0.07	15.04	8.41
2011-13	48	0.00	62.83	3.54	0.44	0.07	15.04	8.41
2012-14	49	0.00	63.11	4.00	0.00	0.07	25.19	0.00
2013-15	50	0.00	63.11	4.00	0.00	0.07	25.19	0.00

Period	Batch	Library	Alumni.	Develop	Medical	Total		
1992-94	29	28.63	1.39	0.00	0.00	100.00		
1993-95	30	26.85	0.98	0.00	0.00	100.00		
1994-96	31	18.73	0.68	0.00	0.00	100.00		
1995-97	32	11.71	0.61	0.00	0.00	100.00		
1996-98	33	10.43	0.54	0.00	0.00	100.00		
1997-99	34	9.32	0.49	0.00	0.00	100.00		
1998-00	35	6.13	0.32	0.00	0.00	100.00		
1999-01	36	5.73	0.30	0.00	0.60	100.00		
2000-02	37	5.80	0.24	0.00	0.48	100.00		
2001-03	38	5.33	0.22	0.00	0.53	100.00		
2002-04	39	4.72	0.20	0.00	0.47	100.00		
2003-05	40	4.72	0.20	0.00	0.47	100.00		
2004-06	41	4.72	0.20	0.00	0.47	100.00		
2005-07	42	9.93	0.73	1.32	0.40	100.00		
2006-08	43	10.26	0.63	1.42	0.34	100.00		
2007-09	44	9.00	0.55	1.50	0.30	100.00		
2008-10	45	9.84	0.13	4.16	0.20	100.00		
2009-11	46	7.45	0.09	3.96	0.15	100.00		
2010-12	47	5.97	0.07	3.47	0.15	100.00		
2011-13	48	5.97	0.07	3.47	0.15	100.00		
2012-14	49	0.00	0.07	7.41	0.15	100.00		
2013-15	50	0.00	0.07	7.41	0.15	100.00		

Based on Table- 1.8.8.B

Table 1.8.9: Decadal Growth in Total Fees at Current and Constant Prices

Years	Deca-des/	*Batches*	Ranges of Total Fess in Rupees		Annual Growth(%)	
			Current Price	Constant Price*	Cur.. Pr.	Con. Pr*
1964 - '73	1	*1 -10*	1,090– 2,100	8,059 – 8,053	8.30	1.93
1974 - '83	2	*11 - 20*	2,350– 3,650	7,037 – 6,285	5.54	- 0.91
1984 - '93	3	*21- 30*	3,650– 35,750	5,813- 26,707	24.64	14.12
1994 -' 03	4	*31 - 40*	51,250– 2,54,200	34,471 – 95,896	19.19	11.88
2004 - '13	5	*41 - 50*	2,54,200 – 13,56,000	92,928 - 2,36,390	24.65	14.46
1964 - '88	1st	*1 - 25*	1,090 -- 4,910	8,059 – 5,734		
1989 – '13	2nd	*26 - 50*	5,460-- 13,56,000	6,000 – 2,36,390		
1964-'13	Total	*1 - 50*	1,090 --13,56,000	8,059– 2,36,390	17.55	8.69

* Constant Price with the Base 1900=100, # Annual Growth by fitting Lognormal.

Table 1.8.10: Log-linear Trend of Total Fees at Current and Constant Prices

Batches	Period	Years	Constant (b)	Coefficient (m)	R -Square	t-Value	d. f..	Growth (%)
A: At Current Price								
1 to 10	1964 - 1973	10	6.891	0.0797	0.97	15.62	8	8.30
11 to 20	1974 - 1983	10	7.172	0.0539	0.95	12.42	8	5.54
21 to 30	1984 - 1993	10	3.178	0.2203	0.67	3.99	8	24.64
30 to 40	1994 - 2003	10	5.625	0.1756	0.94	11.36	8	19.19
40 to 50	2004 – 2013	10	3.397	0.2204	0.92	9.91	8	24.65
1 to 50	1964 – 2013	50	5.803	0.1600	0.92	23.11	48	17.35
B: At Constant Price								
1 to 10	1964 - 1973	10	8.902	0.0191	0.37	2.18	8	1.93
11 to 20	1974 - 1983	10	9.064	- 0.0091	0.07	- 0.75	8	- 0.91
21 to 30	1984 - 1993	10	5.533	0.1321	0.43	2.47	8	14.12
30 to 40	1994 - 2003	10	7.187	0.1122	0.92	9.76	8	11.88
40 to 50	2004 – 2013	10	5.942	0.1351	0.82	5.99	8	14.46
1 to 50	1964 – 2013	50	7.282	0.0834	0.75	12.07	48	8.69

Table 1.8.11: Average Annual Charges of Different Fees by Decades

(In Rupees)

Batches	Period	Total Fees		Tuition Fees	
		Current Price	Constant Price	Cur.Price	Cons. Price
1 to 10	1964 – 1973	1,566	8,197	340	1,780
11 to 20	1974 – 1983	3,040	7,545	760	1,844
21 to 30	1984 – 1993	9,757	9,060	3,500	3,052
31 to 40	1994 – 2003	1,59,285	71,191	1,11,000	48,930
41 to 50	2004 – 2013	8,23,520	1,94,154	5,18,400	1,22,428
1 to 50	1964 – 2013	1,99,434	58,030	1,26,800	35,607

Batches	Period	Course Materials Charges#		Accommodation Charges	
		Current Price	Constant Price	Cur. Price	Const. Price
1 to 10	1964 – 1973	600	3,135	356	1,830
11 to 20	1974 – 1983	940	2,327	940	2,368
21 to 30	1984 – 1993	4,120	3,707	1,300	1,434
31 to 40	1994 – 2003	31,040	14,325	10,600	4,969
41 to 50	2004 – 2013	2,27,600	53,363	32,100	7,712
1 to 50	1964 – 2013	52,860	15,371	9,059	3,662

Including Computer fees and Library fees

Table 1.8.12: Decadal Growth of Different Charges by Decades

(In Percent)

Batches	Period	Tuition Fees		Course Materials Charges#	
		Current Price	Constant Price	Curr. Price	Cons. Price
1 to 10	1964 – 1973	8.45	2.07	8.71	2.32
11 to 20	1974 – 1983	12.03	5.20	5.14	- 1.28
21 to 30	1984 – 1993	28.81	17.93	30.55	19.53
31 to 40	1994 – 2003	24.20	16.58	10.91	4.10
41 to 50	2004 – 2013	23.76	13.65	27.39	16.97
1 to 50	1964 – 2013	21.10	12.17	16.12	7.56
Batches	**Period**	**Accommodation Charges**		**Development Charges***	
		Current Price	Constant Price	Current Price	Const. Price
1 to 10	1964 – 1973	12.03	5.44	----	----
11 to 20	1974 – 1983	2.71	- 3.56		
21 to 30	1984 – 1993	4.89	- 3.96	----	----
31 to 40	1994 – 2003	7.95	1.32	----	----
41 to 50	2004 – 2013	19.35	9.60	50.79	37.86
1 to 50	1964 – 2013	11.80	3.56	----	----

Including Computer fees and Library fees, * Introduced in 2005.

Table 1.8.13: Growth of Different Charges in Entire Period:

At Current and Constant Prices

(In Percent)

Items of Fees	Current Price	Constant Price
1. Total Fees	17.35	8.69
a. Tuition Fees	21.10	12.17
b. Course Materials Fees	16.12	7.56
c. Accommodation Charges	11.80	3.56
d. Development Charges*	50.79	37.86

*Development Charges introduced in 2005 and rates are for last ten years.

Table 1.8.14: No. of Total Manpower in the Institute in Benchmark Years

Year	Faculty Members	Research Staff	Administrative Staff	Total	Changes (+/-)
1962-63*	3	0	10	13	......
1965-'66	24	2	40	66	(+)53
1970-'71	30	2	50	82	(+)16
1975-'76	38	2	60	100	(+)18
1980.-81	48	0	300	348	(+)248
1985-86	50	12	400	462	(+)114
1990-91	53	12	485	550	(+)88
1995-96@	55	12	404	471	(-)79
2000-'01	69	11	329	409	(-)72
2005-'06	60	10	287	357	(-)52
2010-'11	75	5	245	325	(-)32
2015-'16	87	2	159	249	(-)76
2018-19	90	0	99	189	(-)60

* Estimated for 1962 to 1985, @ Actual since 1995

SECTION - II

Table 2.1.1: Category-Wise Student Intake after PwD, OBC and EWS Quota

(Some Benchmark Years after 2006)

A: Number of Students by Category							
Category	OPEN	NC-OBC#	SC	ST	PwD@	EWS	TOTAL
2006	247	0	48	21	6	--	322
2009	229	74	53	15	12	--	383
2012	218	125	65	25	11	--	444
2015	219	126	69	35	14	--	463
2019	211	127	73	36	24	9	480
B: Percent of Students by Category							
Category (Quota)	OPEN (45.5)	NC-OBC (27%)	SC (15%)	ST (7.5%)	PWD (5%)	EWS (10%)	TOTAL (100%)
2006	76.71	0	14.91	6.52	1.86	--	100.00
2009	59.79	19.32	13.84	3.91	3.13	--	100.00
2012	47.40	27.06	14.95	7.57	3.03	--	100.00
2015	47.30	27.21	14.90	7.56	3.02	--	100.00
2019	43.96	26.46	15.20	7.50	5.00	1.88	100.00

@ PwD introduced in 2003 with 4 students. # NC-OBC introduced in 2007

* EWS introduced in 2019,

Table 2.1.2: Minimum CAT Percentile Required for Different Categories in 2009-10

CATEGORY	SECTION 1 (Out of 100)		SECTION 2 (Out of 96)		SECTION 3 (Out of 160)		Total (Out of 356)		Difference from Open Category
	Score	Percen Tile	Score	Percen tile	Score	Percen tile	Score	Percen tile	
OPEN	38	95.52	38	95.86	51	95.87	133	98.97	0
OBC	25	84.83	28	84.92	32	84.97	98	94.44	-4.53
SC	20	77.65	20	69.39	21	70.63	76	86.60	-12.37
ST	20	77.65	20	69.39	16	61.05	56	73.29	-25.68
PWD	20	77.65	20	69.39	16	61.05	56	73.29	-25.68

Source: Prepare Your Exam (2009): Selection Criteria for IIM Calcutta in 2009-10 http://www.prepareyourexam.com/selection-criteria-for-iim-calcutta

Table 2.1.3: Increasing Number of Women Students in Recent Time

(In Number)

Period	2010	2012	2014	2018
Women Students	43	51	115	115
Total Students	362	404	442	462
Women(%)	11.87	12.62	26.02	24.89

Table 2.2.1: Faculty Representative in IIMs by SC, ST and OBC Category (2018-19)

IIMs:	Sanctioned	General	OBC	SC	ST	Existing@
Ahmadabad	120	97	NA	NA	NA	97
Bangalore	120	106	2	1	0	109
Calcutta	126	91	2	0	0	93
Lucknow	103	80	2	1	0	83
Indore	150	104	NA	NA	NA	104
Kozhikode	80	67	4	1	0	72
Total (Six)@	699	545	10	3	0	558
Share (%)@	-----	97.67	1.79	0.54	0.0	100.00

@Computed Source: MHRD data.

Table 2.2.2: Social Status of Existing Faculty Members in IIMs on 2019

IIMs:	Existing	General	OBC	SC	ST
Ahmadabad	104	104	0	0	0
Bangalore	107	104	2	1	0
Calcutta	86	86	0	0	0
Kozhikode	25	22	2	1	0
Indore	104	104	0	0	0
Lucknow	87	84	2	1	0
Shilong	20	20	0	0	0
Total (Seven)	533	524	6	3	0
Share (%)	100.00	98.31	1.13	0.56	0.0

Source: Indian Express.

Table 2.2.3: Distribution of Faculty Members in IIMs by Census Category

IIMs:	SC	ST	OTHERS*	TOTAL
Calcutta	0	0	83	83
Ahmadabad	0	0	96	96
Bangalore	0	0	86	86
Lucknow	1	0	73	74
Indore	0	0	88	88
Kozhikode	1	0	65	66
Shilong	1	1	20	22
Rohtak	1	0	13	14
Raipur	0	0	14	14
Ranchi	0	0	15	15
Kashipour	0	0	33	33
Tiruchirapalli	0	0	19	19
Udaipur	0	0	32	32
Total (13)	4	1	637	642
Share (%)	0.62	0.16	99.22	100.00

*Note: *Out of 637 faculty members in the "Other" group, 17 belong to the OBC category (Among 99.22% of Others, 96.58% were General and 2.64% OBCs.*

Source: Right to Information applications to individual IIMs and MHRD.

Table 2.2.4: No. of Fellowship Scholars in Different IIMs

IIMs:	Dissertation Submitted@	Enrolled in Fellowship*	Total Doctoral Students
Ahmadabad	408	134	542
Calcutta	248	89	348
Bangalore	279	105	384
Lucknow	102	119	221
Indore	87	89	176
Kozhikode	41	83	124
Raipur	17	27	44
Ranchi	13	26	39
Total (8)	1195	663	1858

Source: @ IIM Libraries Consortium. *www.iimlibrariesconsortium.ac.in/thesis/iims,*
* IIMs websites.

Note: No students completed Doctoral Dissertations in five IIMs at Kashipur, Rohtak, Shilong, Tiruchirapalli and Udaipur till March 2022.

Table 2.3.1: Recipients of NBFA Students by Categoryof Students in 2011-13

Category	No. of Students			No. ofNBFA Recipients			Extent of NBFA (%)		
	1st Year	2nd Year	Total	1st Year	2nd Year	Total	1stYear	2nd Year	Total
OPEN	217	219	436	9	12	21	4.15	5.48	4.82
SC	61	69	130	8	13	21	13.11	18.84	16.15
ST	28	35	63	6	6	12	21.43	17.14	19.05
NC-OBC	120	125	245	25	47	72	20.83	37.60	29.39
DA	12	14	26	4	2	6	33.33	14.29	23.08
Total	438	462	900	52	80	132	11.87	17.32	14.67
Amount of Total NBFA (Rs. lakh)				14899	26019	40918			
NBFA per Recipient (Rs. lakh)				2.86	3.25	3.10			

Table 2.3.2: Number and Share of NBFA Receipents by Category of Students

Category	Total Students Nos.	NBFA Recipients Nos.	NBFA Recipients (%)	Total Students by Category	NBFA Recipients by Category
OPEN	436	21	4.82	48.44	15.91
SC	130	21	16.15	14.44	15.91
ST	63	12	19.05	7.00	9.09
NC-OBC	245	72	29.39	27.22	54.55
DA	26	6	23.08	2.90	4.55
Total	900	132	14.67	100.00	100.00

SECTION - III: LIST OF EXHIBITS

Exhibit 3.3.1: Significant Events of Academic and Professional Journey

Period/ Campus	Employment Status	Academic and Professional Achievements	Job Descriptions
1974 to 1977 (Emerald Bower)	Junior Project Assistant (Monthly todaily wage)	Passed a one year Certificate Course on Statistical Methods and Application from ISI.	Tabulation and Analysis of Villagesurvey data from Burdwan villages
1977 to 1987 (Joka)	Junior Project Assistant (Monthly contract basis)	a) Passed Programming and Applications of Computers (ISI) b) Published a dozen of Features in Bengali. c) Presented a Paper on Panchayat in a seminar at IIMC	a) Surveyed 18 villages in ten districts of West Bengal. b) Assisted Prof. Chandra in connection to his research papers in EPW and his Book
1987 to 1996 (Joka)	Permanent Cadre of Research Assistant	a)Attended a MDP on MCA Teachers' Training at IIMC. b) Passed BA (Spl.Hons) and M. A. in Economicsfrom Rabindra Bharati University a)Attended PGP classes in Economics with PGP Students and Appeared at Term exams. c) Published a Paper in our house Journal DECISION c) Presented Papers in Institute of Social Sciences in Calcutta.	a) Assisted Prof. Chandra in connection to his research papers in EPW. b) Assisted Dr. Ashok Mitra in a RBI sponsored Project a) Assisted Prof. Chandra in connection to his research papers in EPW. b) Assisted Dr. AshokMitra in connectionwith the Education Commission on PrimaryEducation in WB
1997 to 2010 (Joka)	Research Assistant	a) Presented Papers in the Seminars by NCERT at Bhubaneswar and New Delhi. b) Presented Paper inInternati - onal Seminar at Delhi Univ. c) Presented a Paper in the Seminar at Agri-Horticulture Society of India, Calcutta d) Presented Papers in Seminar at JadavpurUniversity e) Published articles in The Economic Times and The Statesman. f) Published more than a dozen of Working Papers	a) Assisted Profs. VNR and RC in the Project - Status of Primary Education, b) Assisted Profs. RC, SC, SB, US etc. in their Projects on Food Processing, c) Evaluation of SSA and post-TLC. d) Performed Invigilation duty in all PGP, PGPEX, PGPEX-VLM exams. e) Assisted CAO to prepare a Papers for Board Meeting.

Exhibit 3.3.2: My Academic Achievements after Joining the Institute

Courses Completed	Year	Duration	Institute
1. One Year Evening Course in Statistical Methods and Applications.	1975	1 Year	Indian Statistical Institute
2. Programming and Applications of Electronic Computers.	1981	6 Weeks	Indian Statistical Institute
3. MCA Teachers' Training	1987	10 Weeks	IIM Calcutta
4. B A (Special Honours) in Economics	1987	1 Year	Rabindra Bharati Univ.
5. M A (Economics)	1989	2 Years	Rabindra Bharati Univ.

Exhibit 3.3.3: List of Publications

1. Publications

i) Publication in the Journal

The article "Liberalisation, Biotechnology and Third World Agriculture" was published in IIMC House Journal 'DECESION', Volume – 22, No. 4, October - December, 1995.

ii) Publications in Seminar Proceedings

1. The article "The Common School System: Elitist Education for Privileged Class?" was Chapterised in the book, "Common School System: Retrospect and Prospect" Edited by Sharma A K and Arora G L,Published by the NCERT, New Delhi, 2000.
2. The article "Panchayat and Management of Rural Economic Growth"was Chapterised in the book "Research Gaps in Management". Eds. Prof. A.K. Chowdhuri, Prof. Binod Kumar, Prof. M S Misra and Dr. K K Chaudhury,Publications Division, IIM Calcutta,1980

iii) Publication in Newspapers (English)

1. Winds of Change: Agriculture Part I: *The Business Standard,* August 26, 1995, Calcutta.
2. Market Limits Reforms Success: Agriculture Part II: *The Business Standard,* August 27, 1995, Calcutta
3. A Fools Paradigm: Bengal's Primary Education: *The Economic Times,* March 21, 1997, Calcutta
4. End of Innocence: The State of Child Labour in West Bengal, *The Economic Times,* September 26, 1997, Calcutta
5. Primary Education: Role of Panchayat Leaders, *The Statesman,* May 26, 1998, Calcutta.
6. Role of Panchayat Members in Rural Development, PTI Features, May 13, 1983, Press Trust of India, Mumbai

7. Importance of Invalid Votes, Analysis of West Bengal Election, PTI Features, 26 July, 1982, Press Trust of India, Mumbai.

iv) Publications in Newspapers (Bengali)

a) In Bhumilaxmi, an Ananda Bazar Group of Publications

1. *Graammer Hatasha O Andhakar Dik* (Economic Miseries in Rural Life), 7 June, 1977
2. *Khet Majoor O Nunyatama Majoori* (Agricultural Labours and Minimum Wage), 4 November, 1977
3. *Krishi Arthanitite Kit Nashak Ousadh* (Pesticides in Agricultural Economy), 28 November, 1977
4. *Paschim Banglar Graam* (Villages in West Bengal by Population Size), 24 April, 1978
5. *Gramme Darridrya Bereche* (Increasing Trend of Poverty in Rural Area), 21 July, 1978
6. *Gramme Darridrya Bereche*Ki? (Is the Poverty in Rural Area Increasing), 4 Sept. 1978
7. *Paat Chaser Arthaniti* (Economics of Jute Cultivation), 15 September, 1978
8. *Grammer Satkara 54 Janer Langal Nei (*54% Rural Households Have no Plough), 2 June, 1980
9. *Kutcha Bari O Pucca Bari* (Mud Houses and Pucca Houses), 7 July, 1980

b) In CURTAIN, A Bengali Fortnightly Political Magazine from Hooghly

1. *Paschim Banglar Krishak: Bhumika* (Peasantry of West Bengal: Introduction), 16-31 June, 1981, Volume 4, Issue 30.
2. *Paschim Banglar Krishak: Krishak O Taar Jami* (Peasantry of West Bengal: Land Distribution), 1-15 July, 1981, Volume 5, Issue 1
3. *Paschim Banglar Krishak: Grihapalit Pashupakhi* (Peasantry of West Bengal: *Domestic Animals*), 16-31 July, 1981, Volume 5, Issue 2.

4. *Paschim Banglar Krishak*: Paribahan (Peasantry of West Bengal: Transportation), 16-30 August, 1981, Volume 5, Issue 4.

c) In Dainik Basumati, A Bengali Daily run by Government of West Bengal

1. Phasaler Daam O Chasir Swartha (Agricultural Price and Peasant's Interest), Dainik Basumati, 8 October, 1982
2. Gramer 50 Shatangsha Loker Aay Mot Ayer 14 Shatangsha (50% of Rural Population Earn 14% of Total Income), Dainik Basumati, 29 October, 1982
3. Gramer Loker Sangshar Kharach, Part – I (Consumer Expenditure of Rural People) Dainik Basumati, 21 December, 1982
4. Gramer Loker Sangshar Kharach, Part – II (Consumer Expenditure of Rural People) Dainik Basumati, 22 December, 1982
5. Gramer Loker Reen O Sanchay, (Indebtedness and Savings of Rural People), Dainik Basumati, 1 January, 1983

d) In Aajkaal, a Daily Newspaper

1. *Biswayan O Prathamik Shiksha* (Globalisation and Primary Education): Aajakaal, A Bengali Daily, May, 2001, Calcutta.

Exhibit 3.3.4: Papers Presented in the Seminars

Title of the Paper Organisations and Venues Year

Title of the Paper	Organisations and Venues	Year
1. Policy Level Constraints in Universalising Primary Education in West Bengal	South Asian Conference on Education, Central Institute of Education, Delhi University, Delhi	1999
2. ANANDA PATH in West Bengal: Innovation in Primary Education: A Resume	Regional Seminar on Researches in School Effectiveness at Primary Stage, Organised by NCERT New Delhi, Held at Regional Institute of Education, Bhubaneswar, Orissa.	1999
3. The Common School System, Elitist Education for Privileged Class?	National Seminar on Common School System, Organised by NCERT, New Delhi	1998
4. Floriculture and Rural Development : Impact of Biotechnology	Jadavpur University (EIABS), Calcutta	1997
5. Biotechnology in Indian Agriculture	Agri-Horticultural Society of India, (Calcutta Chapter)	1997
6. Globalisation and Its Impact on Indian Agriculture	Indian Institute of Social Science, Calcutta	1995
7. Management of Rural Credits Towards the Upliftment of Rural Poor	Comprehensive Area Development Corporation (CADC), Govt. of W.B.	1980
8. Panchayat and Rural Economic Growth	National Seminar on ResearchGaps in Management. IIM Calcutta	1980

Exhibit 3.3.5: Working Papers Published (Chronologically)

WP Number	Title of the Paper	Year
1. WPS-493/2004*	Engineering Education in Market Paradigm West Bengal Experiences,	2004
2. WPS-466/2003	Reforming the Engineering and Technical Education in Market Paradigm	2003
3. WPS-461/2002	Genesis and Growth of Engineering and Technical Education in West Bengal: Colonial Period to Market Paradigm	2002
4. WPS-414/2001	Schoollessness and Literacy: A Look into District Hooghly in West Bengal	2001
5. WPS-375/1999	Determinants of Non-Enrolment: Myths and Realities: At Primary Education in West Bengal	1999
6. WPS-374/1999	Policy Level Constraints in Universalizing Primary Education in West Bengal	1999
7. WPS-350/1999	ANANDA PATH (Joy in Learning) in West Bengal - A Resume	1999
8. WPS-344/1998	Management of Primary Schools by Community Participation	1998
9. WPS-332/1998	Economic Reforms and Education Through Common School System	1998
10. WPS-306/1997	Floriculture and Rural Development	1997
11. WPS-290/1997	Export Oriented Floriculture in India	1997
12. WPS-272/1996	Liberalistion, Bio-Technology and Third World Agriculture	1996
13. WPS-237/1995	Globalisation and Its Impact on Indian Agriculture	1995
14. WPS-220/1994	Structural Deterioration in Indian Agriculture	1994
15. WPS-205/1993	Agricultural Reforms in the New Economic Policy	1993
16 WPS-190/1993@	An Essay on Social Justice	1993
17 WPS-145/1990@	On to the Realm of Prosperity	1990

* This was printed as a Booklet and was printed by the Press. All the Working Papers were inA4 size bound volume of Xerox Copies. @ Jointly with Mr. Atul C Manna

LIST OF FIGURES

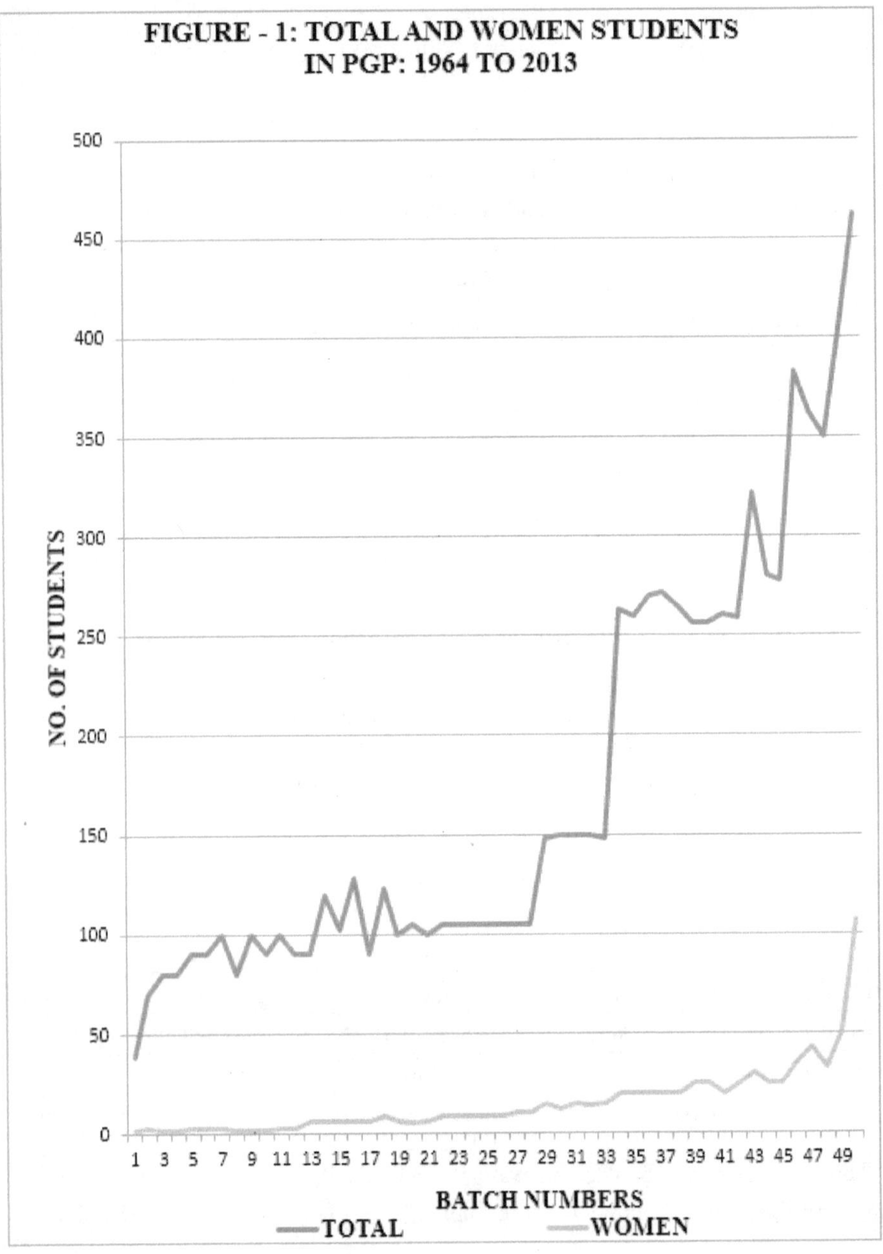

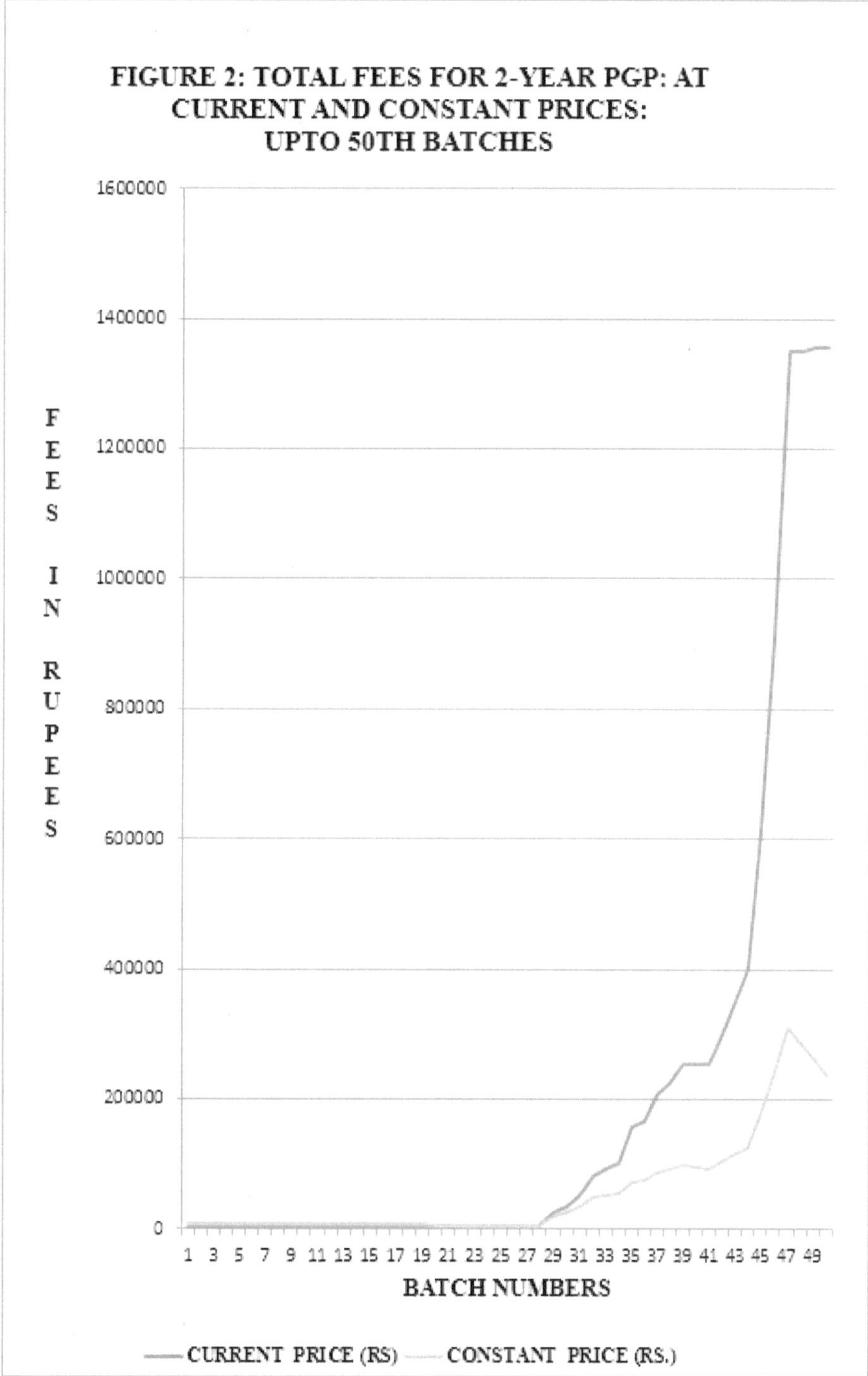

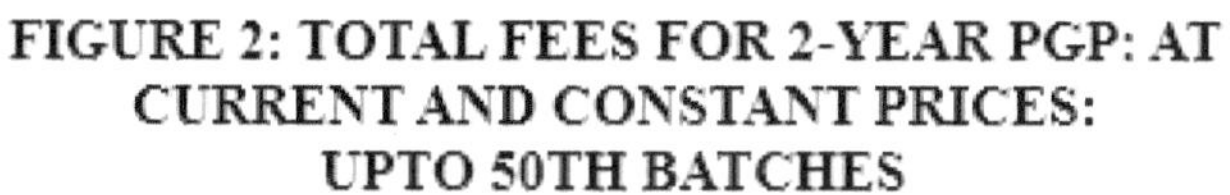

FIGURE 2: TOTAL FEES FOR 2-YEAR PGP: AT CURRENT AND CONSTANT PRICES: UPTO 50TH BATCHES
FEES IN RUPEES
1600000
1400000
1200000
1000000
800000
600000
400000
200000
0
1 3 5 7 9 11 13 15 17 19 21 23 25 27 29 31 33 35 37 39 41 43 45 47 49
BATCH NUMBERS
CURRENT PRICE (RS)
CONSTANT PRICE (RS.)

SUBJECT INDEX

NAME INDEX

www.ingramcontent.com/pod-product-compliance
Lightning Source LLC
LaVergne TN
LVHW091137150826
845672LV00005B/962
9798891337770